alias **Man Ray**

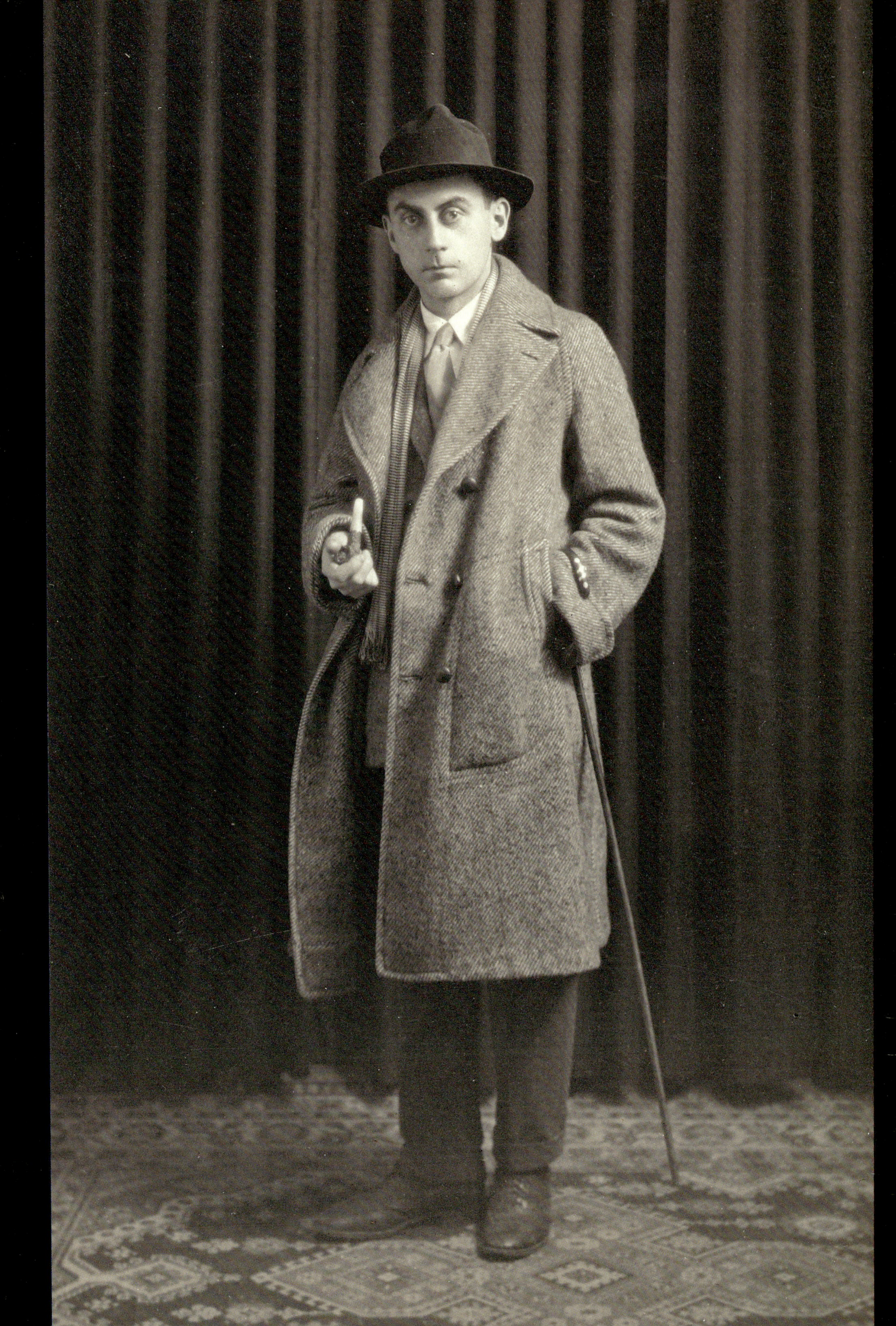

alias Man Ray

The Art of Reinvention

Mason Klein

With contributions by

George Baker

Lauren Schell Dickens

Merry A. Foresta

The Jewish Museum, New York
Under the auspices of the Jewish Theological Seminary of America

Yale University Press, New Haven and London

This book has been published in conjunction with the exhibition *Alias Man Ray: The Art of Reinvention*, organized by The Jewish Museum and presented from November 15, 2009, to March 14, 2010.

The Jewish Museum
Director of Publications: Michael Sittenfeld
Curatorial Publications Coordinator: Jenny Werbell
Text edited by Anna Jardine and Michael Sittenfeld

Yale University Press
Publisher, Art and Architecture: Patricia Fidler
Senior Editor, Art and Architecture: Michelle Komie
Manuscript Editor: Heidi Downey
Production Manager: Mary Mayer

Designed by Steven Schoenfelder
Set in Californian and Clarendon type
Printed in Singapore by CS Graphics

The Jewish Museum
1109 Fifth Avenue, New York, New York 10128
thejewishmuseum.org

Yale University Press
P.O. Box 209040, New Haven, Connecticut 06520-9040
yalebooks.com

Library of Congress Cataloging-in-Publication Data

Klein, Mason.
    Alias Man Ray : the art of reinvention / Mason Klein ; with contributions by George Baker, Lauren Schell Dickens, Merry A. Foresta.
       p. cm.
    "This book has been published in conjunction with the exhibition Alias Man Ray: The Art of Reinvention, organized by The Jewish Museum and presented from November 15, 2009, to March 14, 2010."
    Includes bibliographical references and index.
    ISBN 978-0-300-14683-7 (cloth : alk. paper)
1. Man Ray, 1890–1976—Exhibitions. 2. Man Ray, 1890–1976—Psychology. I. Man Ray, 1890–1976. II. Baker, George (George Thomas), 1970–. III. Foresta, Merry A. IV. Dickens, Lauren Schell. V. Jewish Museum (New York, N.Y.) VI. Title.
N6537.R3A4 2009
709.2—dc22   2009021634

A catalogue record for this book is available from the British Library. This paper meets the requirements of ANSI/NISO z39.48-1992 (Permanence of Paper).

10 9 8 7 6 5 4 3 2 1

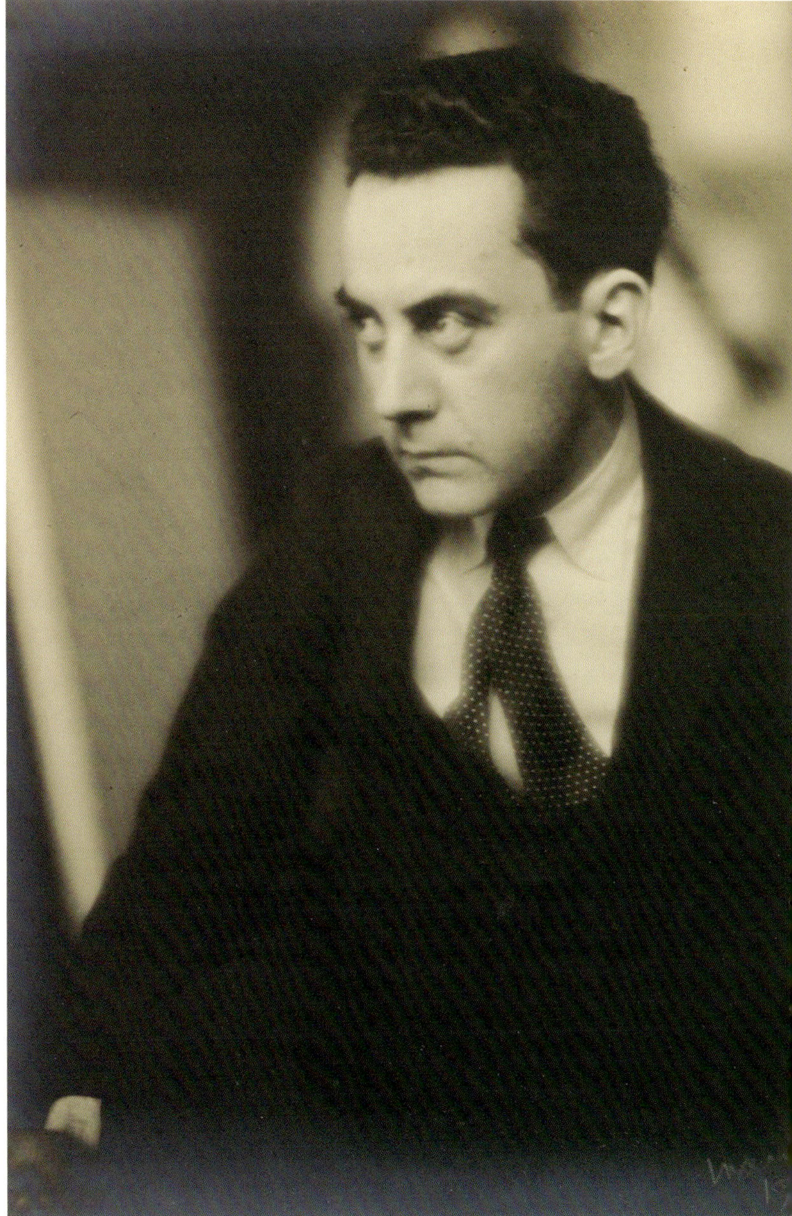

Cover illustrations: (front) *Indestructible Object (or Object to Be Destroyed)*, 1964 (replica of 1923 original). Metronome with cutout photograph of eye on pendulum, 8⅞ × 4⅜ × 4⅝ in. (22.5 × 11 × 11.6 cm). The Museum of Modern Art, New York, James Thrall Soby Fund; (back) *Self-Portrait* (detail), c. 1947. Lithograph on zinc plate, 8 × 6¹/₁₆ in. (20.3 × 15.7 cm). Courtesy of Timothy Baum, New York
Page ii: *Self-Portrait with Pipe, Paris*, 1921. Gelatin silver print, 5³/₁₆ × 3¼ in. (13.2 × 8.3 cm). The J. Paul Getty Museum, Los Angeles
Page iv: *Self-Portrait*, 1924. Vintage silver print, 8¹/₁₆ × 6⁵/₁₆ in. (20.5 × 16.0 cm). Collection of Timothy Baum, New York
Page vi: *Image à deux faces* (detail), 1959. Oil on canvas, 78¼ × 59 in. (200 × 149.9 cm). Collection of Mr. and Mrs. George L. Lindemann, Florida
Page x: *Self-Portrait in His Studio at 31 bis rue Campagne Première, Paris*, c. 1925. Gelatin silver print, 6⅛ × 4½ in. (15.6 × 11.4 cm). Private collection

Contents

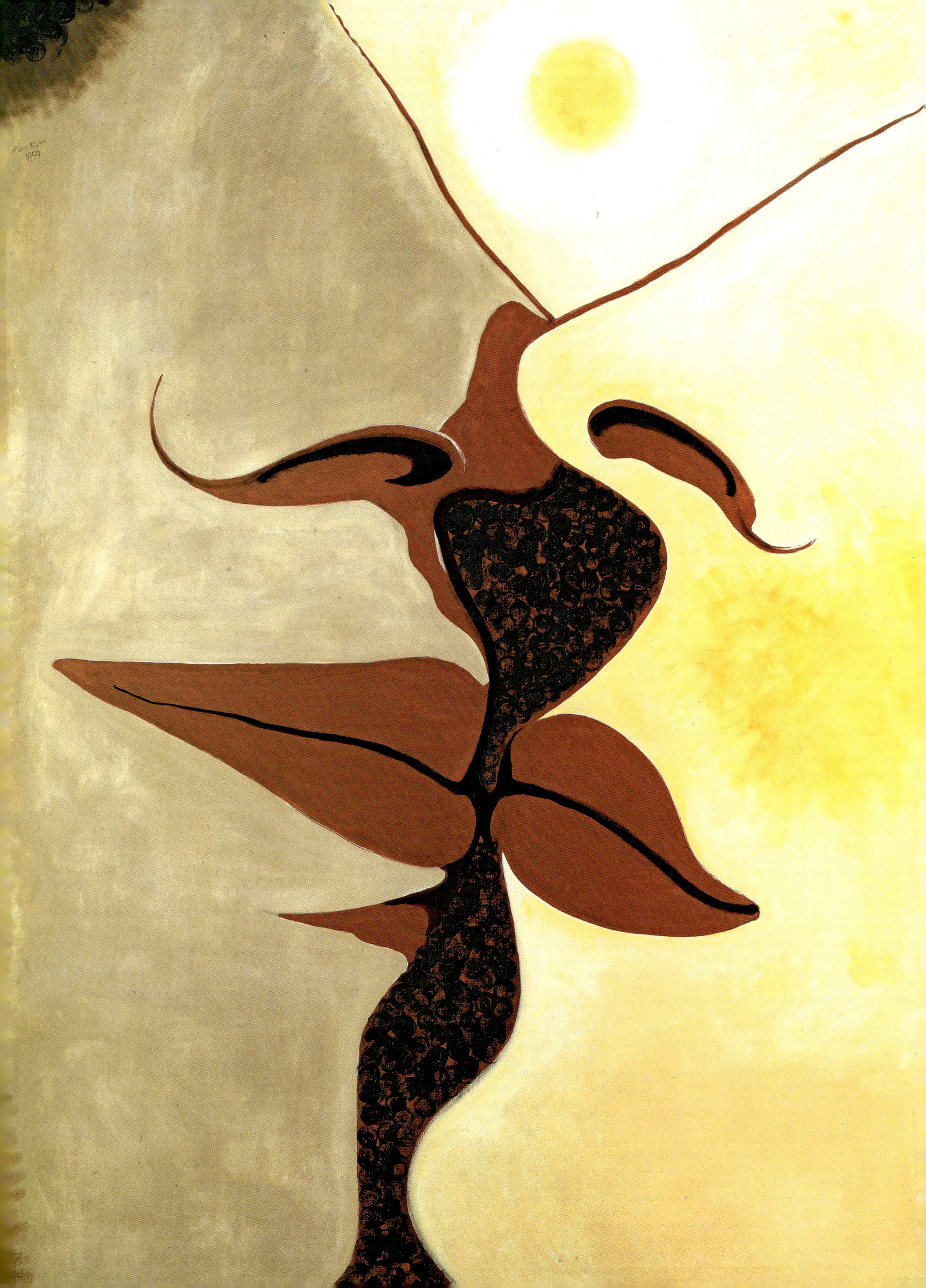

Man Ray
1959

Donors to the Exhibition

Alias Man Ray: The Art of Reinvention is supported by generous grants from S. Donald Sussman and the David Berg Foundation. Major funding was also provided by the Peter Jay Sharp Foundation, the National Endowment for the Arts, the Anna-Maria and Stephen Kellen Foundation, the Leon Levy Foundation, Ellen S. Flamm, and the Lisa and John Pritzker Family Fund. Additional support was provided by the Neubauer Family Foundation Exhibition Fund and other donors.

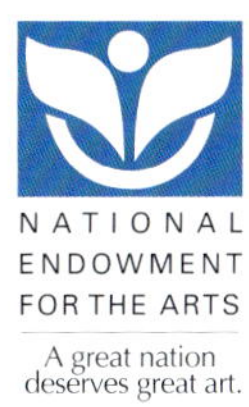

The exhibition is sponsored by the Jerome L. Greene Foundation.

The catalogue is funded through the Dorot Foundation publications endowment.

Lenders to the Exhibition

Public Lenders to the Exhibition

Albright-Knox Art Gallery, Buffalo

Allen Memorial Art Museum, Oberlin, Ohio

Fondazione Marguerite Arp, Locarno

The Baltimore Museum of Art

Bibliothèque littéraire Jacques Doucet, Paris

Bowdoin College Museum of Art, Brunswick, Maine

Columbus Museum of Art, Ohio

The J. Paul Getty Museum, Los Angeles

Solomon R. Guggenheim Museum, New York

Harvard Theatre Collection; Houghton Library;
  Widener Library, Harvard University, Cambridge,
  Massachusetts

Heckscher Museum of Art, Huntington, New York

Hirshhorn Museum and Sculpture Garden,
  Smithsonian Institution, Washington, D.C.

The Jewish Museum, New York

Kunsthalle Bielefeld, Germany

Kunsthaus Zürich

The Menil Collection, Houston

The Metropolitan Museum of Art, New York

Montclair Art Museum, New Jersey

Musée national d'art moderne, Centre Pompidou, Paris

Museum of Fine Arts, Houston

The Museum of Modern Art, New York

National Gallery of Art, Washington, D.C.

New Orleans Museum of Art

Rare Books Division and Spencer Collection,
  Humanities and Social Services Library,
  The New York Public Library

The Ohio State University Libraries

The Penrose Collection, England

Philadelphia Museum of Art

The Phillips Collection, Washington, D.C.

Museum of Art, Rhode Island School of Design

San Francisco Museum of Modern Art

Smithsonian American Art Museum,
  Washington, D.C.

Tokyo Fuji Art Museum

Rare Book and Manuscript Library,
  University of Pennsylvania

University of Wisconsin—Milwaukee Libraries,
  Archives Department

Whitney Museum of American Art, New York

Private Lenders and Galleries

Neil Baldwin

Collection of André Baum, New York

Collection of Karen Amiel Baum, New York

Collection of Timothy Baum, New York

The Bluff Collection LP

Isidore Ducasse Fine Arts

Daniel Filipacchi

Collection of Sandra and Gerald Fineberg

Joel and Paula Friedland

Mr. and Mrs. Edward A. Fuller

Collection Goldberg/d'Afflitto

Richard and Ronnie Grosbard Collection

Rosalind and Melvin Jacobs Collection

Joy of Giving Something, Inc.

The Kantor Collection, Beverly Hills, California

Mark Kelman, New York

Private collection of Thomas and
 Janine Koerfer-Weill

Collection of Gérard Lévy, Paris

Collection of Mr. and Mrs. George L. Lindemann,
 Florida

Private collection of Cornelia and Meredith Long

Loïc Malle, Paris

Collection of Marion Meyer

Betsy Wittenborn Miller, New York

Peter and Renate Nahum

Francis M. Naumann Fine Art, New York

Sylvio Perlstein Collection, Antwerp

Private collections

Collection of Joan and Michael Salke,
 Naples, Florida

Richard and Ellen Sandor Family Collection

Collection of Steven M. Sumberg

Morris Trichon

Scott and Beth Ullem

Constance and Albert Wang

Collection of Sarah and Gary Wolkowitz

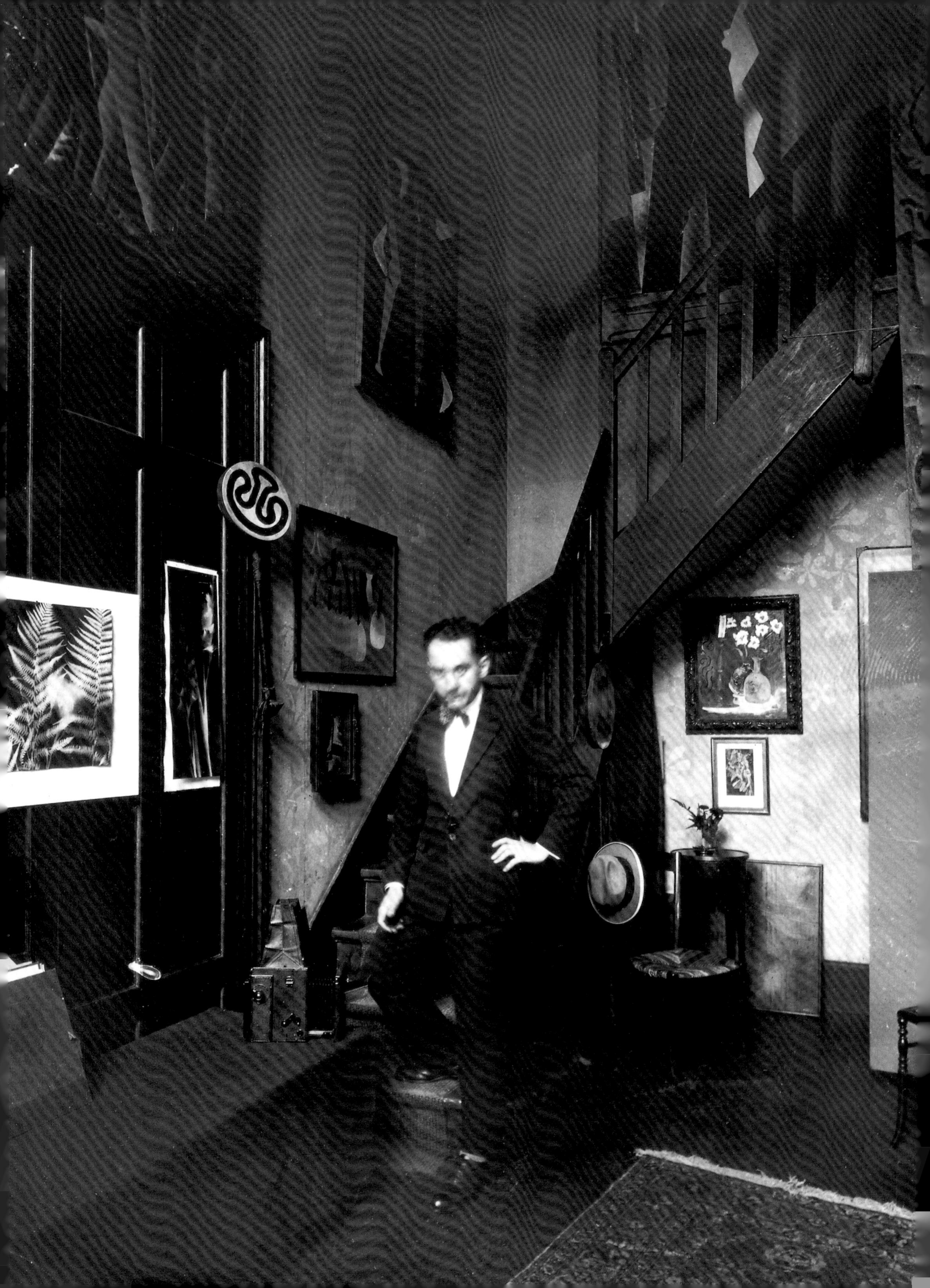

foreword

When speaking to colleagues, friends, and trustees about the possibility of mounting a Man Ray exhibition at The Jewish Museum, I encountered both surprise and delight—surprise at learning of the artist's identity as a Jew of Russian heritage, born Emmanuel Radnitzky, and delight that the Museum was dedicating a one-person show to an artist whose tremendously varied body of work is so greatly admired. We are very pleased to be able to present *Alias Man Ray: The Art of Reinvention*—the first multimedia retrospective in the United States of the artist's work in twenty years, and the first exhibition in a major museum in New York since 1974.

One goal of The Jewish Museum's exhibitions program is to present art of the highest quality simultaneously with a strong narrative. The tension between the two takes the form of an exploration of Jewish culture and Jewish identity through art. But what is the narrative in *Alias Man Ray*? It is, in a way, the obverse of one-person Jewish Museum exhibitions that have explored the absorption, referencing, and influence of Jewish identity for an artist. Here the narrative concerns an artist's resistance to revealing his identity, including his Jewishness. Yet, as curator Mason Klein points out, Man Ray's family history emerges time and again as a frame of reference, even as he continues to find ways to be free of it.

Alias Man Ray offers a contrast to recent exhibitions of his work that have focused on one medium (photography) or featured the artist as a participant in Dada and Surrealism. Instead, this exhibition explores the full breadth of Man Ray's life and work, and his ambivalence toward disclosing his familial roots. The organization of the show and the essays in this catalogue explore the ways Man Ray negotiated his identity as an assimilated Jew and as an artist in the context of an era—especially from the 1910s to the 1940s—of radical new ideas and ideological challenges to cultural and nationalist identity.

In titling the exhibition *Alias Man Ray*, Mason Klein not only states his premise about Man Ray's willful construction of a veiled identity but creates an opportunity for a new analysis of the work in light of the artist's personal history. Thus the viewer of the show and the reader of this fine catalogue are offered an extraordinarily revelatory journey as Klein deploys his skill as art historian and his astute understanding of the human psyche. The result is a captivating and moving investigation of an artist whose work so brilliantly embraced contradiction—inviting one to know and not know him, to be at once charmed and mystified, delighted and shocked.

My great thanks to Mason Klein for creating the concept for the exhibition, as well as contributing his insightful essay to this volume. Added thanks to Merry Foresta, founding director and senior curator of the Smithsonian Photography Initiative (and organizer of the 1988 Man Ray retrospective *Perpetual Motif*), for her fascinating discussion of the critical response to Man Ray's work, and George Baker, associate professor of art history at the University of California, Los Angeles, for his illuminating essay on Man Ray's working-class roots and their impact on his art. In these pages you will also find an extensive and engaging cultural timeline by Lauren Schell Dickens, Neubauer Family Foundation Curatorial Assistant at The Jewish Museum; we are grateful as well for her able assistance with all areas of the project. As always, I extend my tremendous appreciation to all staff members of the Museum, who are not only highly talented and expert in their work but also enthusiastic participants in the mission of the Museum.

The exhibition comprises more than two hundred works borrowed from private and public collections in the United States, Europe, and Japan. Many thanks to those lenders listed on pages viii–ix for their essential participation. It is indeed a privilege to have these important works in the galleries of The Jewish Museum.

The preparation and realization of *Alias Man Ray*, from research to exhibition design, was a multiyear project that required the involvement of many enthusiastic donors, including S. Donald Sussman, the David Berg Foundation, the Peter Jay Sharp Foundation, the National Endowment for the Arts, the Anna-Maria and Stephen Kellen Foundation, the Leon Levy Foundation, Ellen S. Flamm, the Lisa and John Pritzker Family Fund, and the Neubauer Family Foundation Exhibition Fund. My great thanks to all of them and to the exhibition sponsor, the Jerome L. Greene Foundation. Further thanks are due the Dorot Foundation for our publications endowment.

Finally, I thank the exceptionally loyal and committed Board of Trustees of The Jewish Museum, who encourage the exploration of the Jewish experience through remarkable art exhibitions. With their financial and moral support, along with the generosity of lenders and donors to the exhibition and the exemplary efforts of the staff, significant new light is shed on the art of Man Ray. This innovative presentation offers new knowledge of what impelled the conflict between concealment and liberation in May Ray's life and work, challenging our powers of interpretation and providing great pleasure in the process.

Joan Rosenbaum
Helen Goldsmith Menschel Director
The Jewish Museum

acknowledgments

Alias Man Ray is, surprisingly, the first exhibition of the artist's diverse body of work at a New York museum in decades. Man Ray was an artist who sought to free himself from fixed identity, and from his familial ties to the influx of immigrants in America at the beginning of the twentieth century. This makes him an ideal subject for an institution vested in the broadest critical reevaluation of art and cultural history. For The Jewish Museum, *Alias Man Ray* is a poignant homecoming for perhaps the first avant-garde Jewish artist of the twentieth century.

This project involved the assistance of many people, too numerous to name here. I wish to express my profound gratitude to them, as well as the institutions, lenders, and sponsors who have generously made *Alias Man Ray* possible.

This publication and exhibition could not have been realized without the cooperation of the Man Ray Trust and the sustaining support of those perennial figures within the *joie de Man Ray milieu*. For their generous assistance and contributions of time, counsel, and loans, I owe special thanks to Timothy Baum, Francis Naumann, and Andrew Strauss; and for their sundry acts of goodwill, Neil Baldwin, Eric Browner, Daniel Filapacchi, Marcel and David Fleiss, Merry Foresta, Wendy Grossman, Roz Jacobs, Mark Kelman, Frank Kolodny, Marion Meyer, Ishihara Teruo, and Virginia Zabriskie.

I wish to extend my appreciation to my many colleagues at The Jewish Museum: first and foremost, Joan Rosenbaum, Helen Goldsmith Menschel Director, whose encouragement, along with the attentive guidance of Ruth Beesch, deputy director of program, provides the bedrock support for any project at the museum. Norman Kleeblatt, Susan and Elihu Rose Chief Curator, has been a valued colleague and a stalwart advocate of this enterprise.

Lauren Schell Dickens, Neubauer Family Foundation Curatorial Assistant, had the daunting task of coordinating numerous aspects of the exhibition, which she accomplished with consummate grace. Her agile intelligence and organizational skills were tested often. I also thank interns Charles Gariepy and Laura Phipps for ably and energetically assisting us both.

For the vigor with which he embraced this project and intrepidly oversaw all aspects of the catalogue, I am indebted to Michael Sittenfeld, director of publications at The Jewish Museum.

His devoted and good-humored attention to all matters of the exhibition bolstered the project. For remaining unflustered by deadlines and to-do lists, I extend heartfelt thanks to Jenny Werbell, curatorial publications coordinator. It has been my privilege again to work with Anna Jardine, whose editorial skills and thoroughness of fact-checking humbled and made me forever grateful.

The exhibition designers, architects Tim Culbert and Celia Imrey, of Imrey Culbert, grasped the exhibition's thesis and conceived an elegant, imaginative way to present a disparate array of work. Artistically collaborating with them was graphic designer Steven Schoenfelder and lighting designer Sara Schrager, who further enhanced the overall installation vision.

Numerous curatorial colleagues at The Jewish Museum have been supportive and enthusiastic throughout the project: Daniel Belasco, Henry J. Leir Assistant Curator; Susan Braunstein, curator of archaeology and Judaica; Susan Tumarkin Goodman, senior curator; Andrew Ingall, assistant curator; Karen Levitov, associate curator; Vivian Mann, curator emeritus; Claudia Nahson, curator; and Aviva Weintraub, associate curator and director of the New York Jewish Film Festival. In addition, Lynn Thommen, deputy director for external affairs, and Sarah Himmelfarb, associate director of development, institutional giving, worked hard to fund the exhibition; Susan Wyatt, senior grants writer, shaped our successful proposal to the National Endowment for the Arts with imperturbable will; and other colleagues supported my efforts: Nelly Silagy Benedek, director of education; Niger Miles, audiovisual coordinator; Anne Scher, director of communications; and Alex Wittenberg, communications coordinator.

Jane Rubin, director of collections and exhibitions, and her colleagues, especially Amanda Thompson, assistant registrar, and Dolores Pukki, coordinator of exhibitions, were vital in managing logistics. Director of operations Al Lazarte fulfilled his role as the sage contractor, helping us realize the budgetary merits of pragmatism. To him and his staff, especially Mark Lesser, Valeriy Ognev, Nikolay Silenko, and Devon Simmonds, I express my gratitude.

Along with Joan Rosenbaum, I would like to offer my thanks to the private collectors and lending institutions listed on pages viii–ix. In addition, I also want to thank the following individuals and institutions for their support of the exhibition: Brian T. Allen, Mary Stripp, and R. Crosby Kemper at the Addison Gallery of American Art; Robert Berman; Arthur Brandt; Maura Kehoe Collins; Catherine Evans, chief curator, Columbus Museum of Art; Ira Drukier; Aaron and Rosa Esman; Marilyn and Larry Fields; Anne M. Lyden, associate curator of photographs, and Virginia Heckert, associate curator of photographs, J. Paul Getty Museum; Irene Lotspeich-Phillips, registrar, Getty Research Institute; Annemarie Sawkins, associate curator, Haggerty Museum of Art, Marquette University; Erik H. Neil, director, and Kenneth Wayne, chief curator of collections and exhibitions, Heckscher Museum of Art; Michael E. Shapiro, Nancy and Holcombe T. Green, Jr., Director, High Museum of Art; Gil and Joan Hofheimer; Geri E. Solomon, assistant dean of special collections/university archivist, Axinn Library, Hofstra University; Adina Kamien-Kazhdan, David Rockefeller Curator of Modern Art, Israel Museum; Tobia Bezzola, curator, Kunsthaus Zurich; Larry List; Carol Eliel, curator of modern art, Los Angeles County Museum of Art; Giorgio and Gio Marconi, Fondazione Marconi; Josef Helfenstein, director, Franklin Sirmons, curator of modern and contemporary art, and Kristin Schwartz-Lauster, Menil Collection; Malcolm Daniel, curator in charge of the Department of Photographs, Metropolitan Museum of Art; Gail Stavitsky, chief curator, Monclair Art Museum; Peter C. Marzio, director, Anne Wilkes Tucker,

Gus and Lyndall Wortham Curator of Photography, and Dell Zogg, Museum of Fine Arts, Houston; Anne Temkin, chief curator of painting and sculpture, John Elderfield, chief curator emeritus, Peter Galassi, chief curator of photography, Susan Kismaric, curator, Department of Photography, Cora Rosevear, associate curator, Department of Painting and Sculpture, Jodi Hauptman, associate curator, Department of Drawings, Feri Daftari, assistant curator, and Susan L. Palamara, exhibitions registrar, Museum of Modern Art; Patrick Elliot, senior curator, Scottish National Gallery of Modern Art; Martin E. Sullivan, director, National Portrait Gallery; Antony Penrose, director, and Ami Bouhassane, registrar and archivist, Lee Miller Archives, and curator, Penrose Collection; Michael R. Taylor, Muriel and Philip Berman Curator of Modern Art, and Innes Shoemaker, Audrey and William H. Helfand Senior Curator of Prints, Drawings, and Photographs, Philadelphia Museum of Art; Quentin Bajac, curator, Department of Photography, and Olga Makhroff, registrar, Musée national d'art moderne, Centre Pompidou; Thaddaeus Ropac; Steven Roth; Gabriel Catone, Andrew Ruth, and Michael Jerch, registrar, Ruth Catone; Sandra S. Phillips, senior curator of photography, San Francisco Museum of Modern Art; Lorie Savage; Alain Tarica; Maggie Trichon; Madeline Weinrib; Hermann Arnhold, director, and Erich Franz, curator, at the Westfälisches Landesmuseum für Kunst und Kulturgeschicte; Peter Williamson; Violet Hamilton, Wilson Centre for Photography; and Jock Reynolds, Henry J. Heinz II Director, and Jennifer Gross, Seymour H. Knox, Jr., Curator of Modern and Contemporary Art, Yale University Art Gallery.

I wish to thank the following individuals and auction houses who facilitated loans: Bill Acquavella at Acquavella Gallery; Jonathan Boos; Beverley Calté; Jeffrey Deitch at Deitch Projects; Jeffrey Fraenkel at Fraenkel Gallery; Howard Greenberg, Karen Marks, Ali Price, and Margit Erb at Howard Greenberg Gallery; Edwynn Houk Gallery; Phillips de Pury & Company; Hollis Taggart Galleries; Margo Schab; Michael Senft; Bruce Silverstein at Silverstein Photography; Sotheby's, New York and Paris; Adam Boxer at Ubu Gallery; and the Zabriskie Gallery.

I am grateful to everyone who contributed to this volume: Merry Foresta and George Baker, for their thoughtful and illuminating texts; Lauren Schell Dickens, for her considered and well-researched cultural timeline; Steven Schoenfelder, who produced an exquisite design; and Richard Goodbody, for photographing many of the works reproduced in these pages. I want to thank the staff of our copublisher, Yale University Press, particularly Patricia Fidler, Michelle Komie, Heidi Downey, and Mary Mayer.

To all who have so liberally given of their time, and helped in incalculable ways, I wish to express my deepest appreciation. For their understanding and love, witness and support, I am particularly grateful to Alice Attie and Royce Howes, Maurice Berger and Marvin Heiferman, Anouk Cézilly and Marc Sillam, Rebecca Dreyfus, John and Helga Klein, Amy Schewel, Jill Silverman Van Coenegrachts, Sandy Starkman, and Edouard Vaval and Eve Zatt.

And, finally, I feel blessed in thanking my wife, Elizabeth Sacre, not simply for her wise psychoanalytic and editorial input, but for always stunning me with her inexhaustible kindness.

Mason Klein
Curator of Fine Arts
The Jewish Museum

You see,
I try to walk the
tightrope of accomplishment
between the chasms of notoriety and oblivion;
were I not a product of my time,
I should never be conscious of
anything but my accomplishments.
Hence the desire to become
a tree en espalier!

— MAN RAY

alias **Man Ray**

Mason Klein

In mid-career, Man Ray had a life mask made, a bronze cast of which, adorned with a pair of his glasses, he placed in a plain wooden box amply cushioned with newsprint. He titled the assemblage *Auto Portrait* (1933; fig. 1). The original plaster bust itself was to be photographed for the cover of what would be the first comprehensive publication of his work, *Photographs by Man Ray 1920 Paris 1934* (fig. 2). After nearly a decade and a half in Paris, Man Ray felt moored, socially and artistically. Yet the stoic countenance of *Auto Portrait* belies a wariness toward artistic summation, as if he were anticipating what would be an ongoing dilemma: If his work was acclaimed, it would be only for his photographs, not for his painting. To be confined in any way was insufferable to Man Ray. Why else would he depict himself defensively, boxed in, uncannily "entombed" by the criticism of others, mocking a death mask?

When the album appeared, its cover startling in color, the initial bust overlooking a complex still life of Surrealist objects that enigmatically defined Man Ray's world, it was acclaimed in Paris and panned in the United States. But it was the American audience whose redemption he sought, and whom he may well have addressed in the introductory essay, "The Age of Light," in which he speaks of himself as one who "so deforms the subject as almost to hide the identity of the original, and creates a new form." Perhaps this added component, the mutability of subject and of the medium itself, able to change its character and resist categorical definition, was too much for the American positivist sensibility. His sheer inventiveness and the multiplicity of the album's subjects were seen as "trickery," and

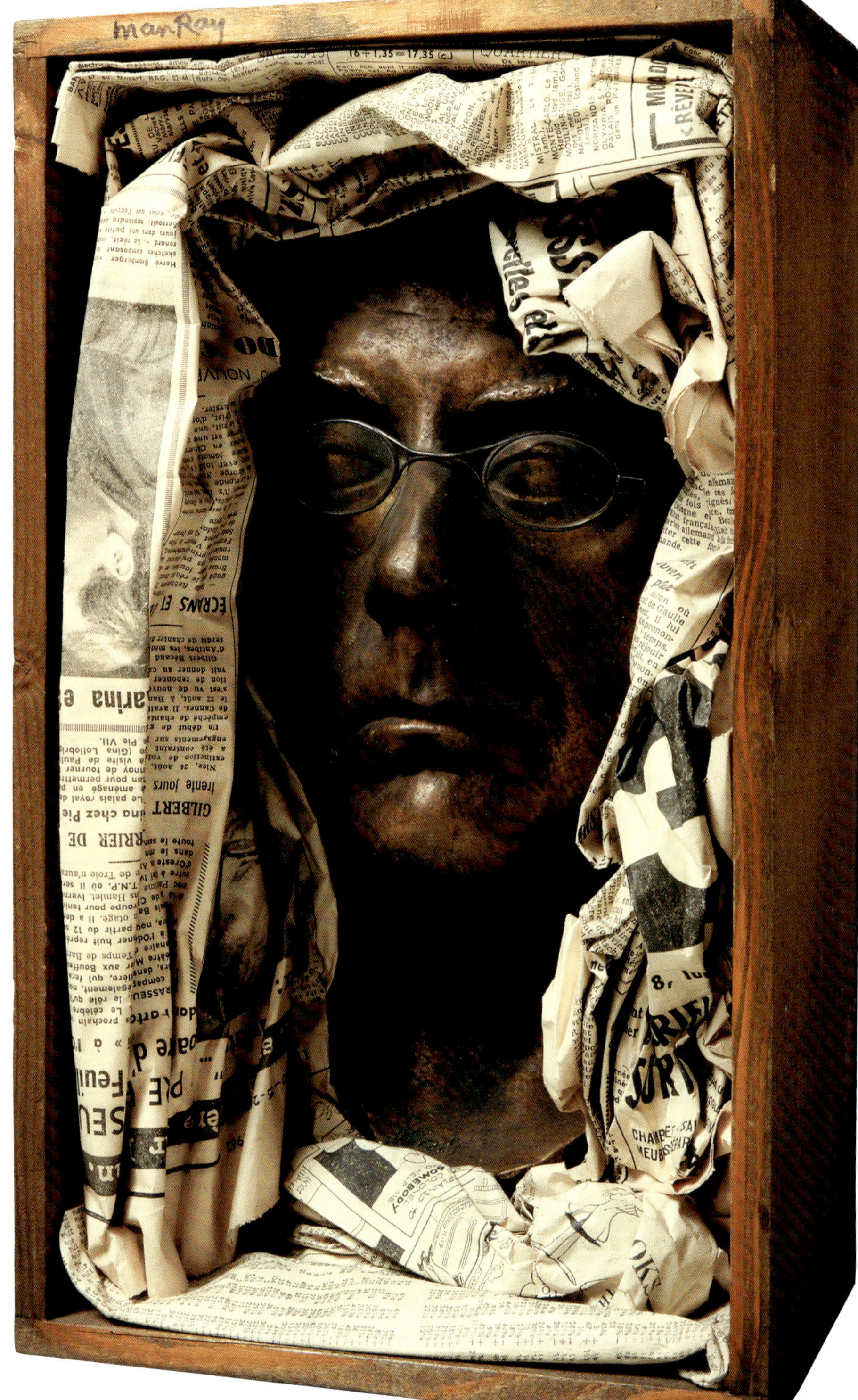

Fig. 1. *Auto Portrait*, 1933. Mixed media: bronze, glass, wood, and newsprint, 14 × 8¼ × 5⅛ in. (35.6 × 21.1 × 13.7 cm). Smithsonian American Art Museum, Washington, D.C., Gift of Juliet Man Ray

his manipulation of the medium as retrogressive.[1] With
unerring intuition, Man Ray had anticipated in *Auto Portrait* the American critics' inability
to accept his brand of ambiguity and multiplicity, his refusal to conform to expectation,
and his redefinition of photography as something as slippery and uncontainable in its various guises as the artist himself. In France, the very notion of identity was less restricted

and more abstract—even one's citizenship was undifferentiated and mysterious; loyalty to the Republic was all that mattered. But in America, origins mattered; they were not to be tampered with. Identity had to be pure and defined, worn on one's sleeve.

the Wayward knight

It has become a commonplace to regard Man Ray as the paradigmatic modernist, recasting the concept of artistic identity in terms of his protean practice as painter, photographer, sculptor, object maker, filmmaker, printmaker, poet, essayist, and philosopher. While such artistic diversity ought to broaden our understanding of an artist, in Man Ray's case it has served mostly to refract our sense of who the artist was and what his work was about.

When Neil Baldwin's biography of Man Ray appeared in 1988, its author was one of the first to spell out the connection between Man Ray's decision to change his family name and his desire to avoid discrimination for being Jewish.[2] But only within the last decade or so could the question of "Jewish identity" even be approached within the discipline of art history, as both the sense of "otherness" and the unique character of self-determination within Judaism came to be understood as formative factors in the development of twentieth-century cultural Jewish identity.[3]

The question of his ethnicity has yet to be adequately considered in terms of Man Ray and his work.[4] His need both to conceal and to reveal himself, often at the same time, is a phenomenon that cannot be divorced from the historical period in which he lived, an era that witnessed not only the rise of nation-state identity and xenophobia but also unprecedented waves of immigration, class-consciousness, and anti-Semitism.[5] In light of the virtual absence of "Jewish" artists, at least in avant-garde Western European art, the question of their emergence has been largely ignored as long as assimilation has been excluded from the dominant critical discourse. As far as Man Ray is concerned, however, the dialectics of assimilation are a pervasive component of the artist and his work.

In this essay I will examine how the complex veiling of identity (given the unavoidable persecution mania that being Jewish meant in the first half of the twentieth century, especially for an avant-garde modernist) manifests itself as an ongoing process of subterfuge and self-assertion. The artist's identity complex cannot be reduced to or explained by assimilation alone, which, while an inherent aspect of twentieth-century Jewry, is one that, in the

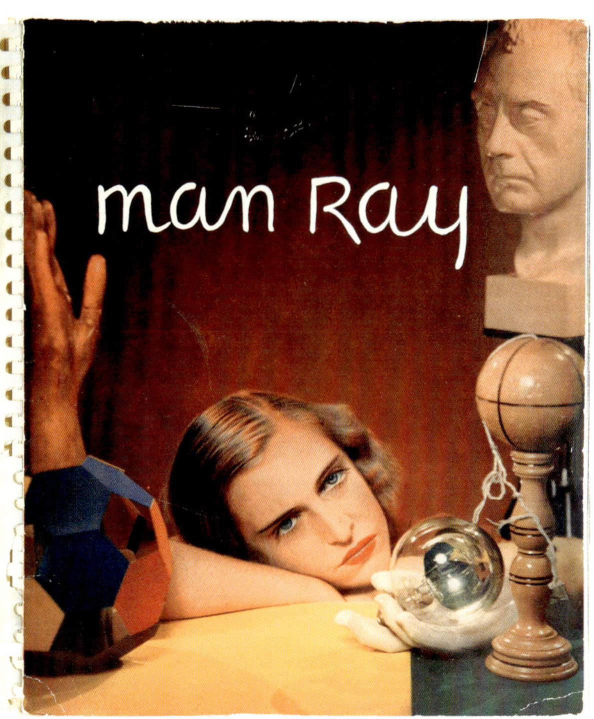

Fig. 2. Cover of *Photographs by Man Ray 1920 Paris 1934* (1934). Rosalind and Melvin Jacobs Collection

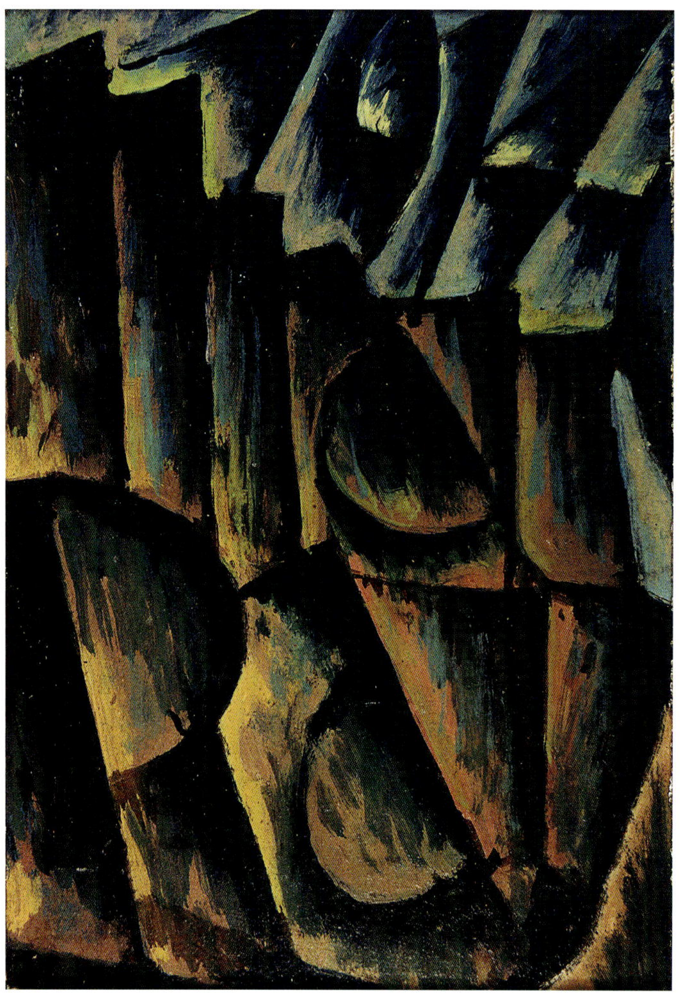

Fig. 3. *Man Ray 1914*, 1914. Oil on canvas, 6¹³⁄₁₆ × 5 in. (17.3 × 12.7 cm). The Penrose Collection, on loan to the National Galleries of Scotland

words of the scholar Barbara Kirshenblatt-Gimblett, "explains too much and too little." She provides another way of understanding the phenomenon, offering the idea of "distinction without difference."[6] Yet even this does not apply to Man Ray, who needed to be anonymous yet not blend in with the crowd.

Such a conundrum becomes a critical part of his work, enhanced by the revelation of its internal logic: Man Ray was able to use his art to reconcile his alienated situation, to be at once assimilated and an outcast. It is precisely in the way he carves out a literal "signature" identity, the most obvious example of which is his tellingly small but powerful painting *Man Ray 1914* (fig. 3), that his nominal artistic persona erupts with the force of

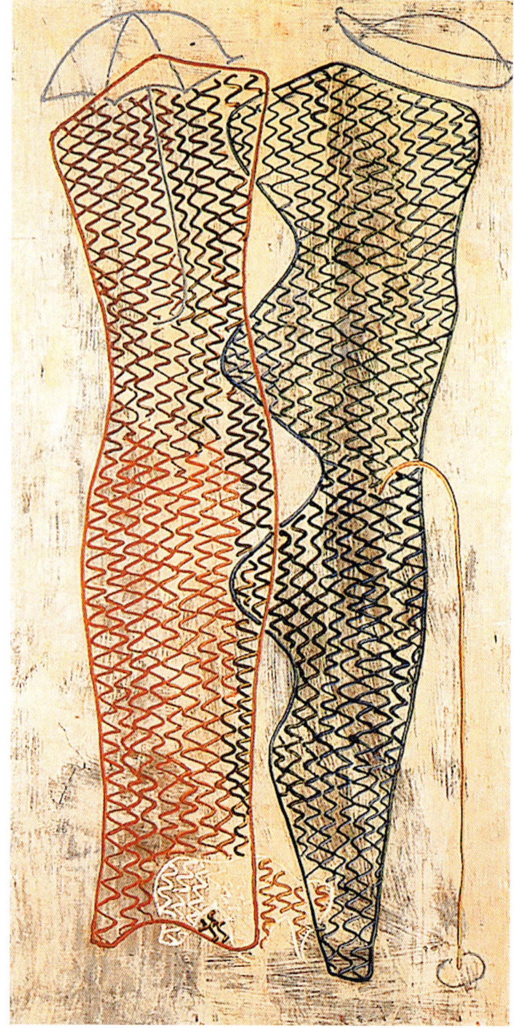

Fig. 4. *Gens du monde*, 1929. Oil on silver leaf and copper, 78¾ × 39⅜ in. (200 × 100 cm). Collection of Marion Meyer, Paris

World War I. Or it is inscribed in the far
more encrypted but still self-referential
squiggle paintings (such as *Gens du monde*,
1929; fig. 4), remnants of the wire dress
forms he was familiar with as the son of a
tailor, resurrected here as surrogate manikins composed of nothing but the artist's
endless initials, whose simple transparency belies his need to remain opaque (fig.
5). Such work reflects the tension within
Man Ray's conflicted drives toward exposure and concealment, which developed
from an entrenched alienation stemming
from his childhood, the root of his intense
separation from and passive aggression
toward what his family represented, and
the source of his identity formation.[7]

In his 1977 study of Man Ray,
Arturo Schwarz avoids the subject of
ethnicity entirely, obviously deferring to
Man Ray's insistent silence on the subject. Instead, Schwarz defines Man Ray
art-historically, citing Dada and Surrealism as "instrumental in liberating him
from established artistic and technical
categories." For Man Ray, "freedom did

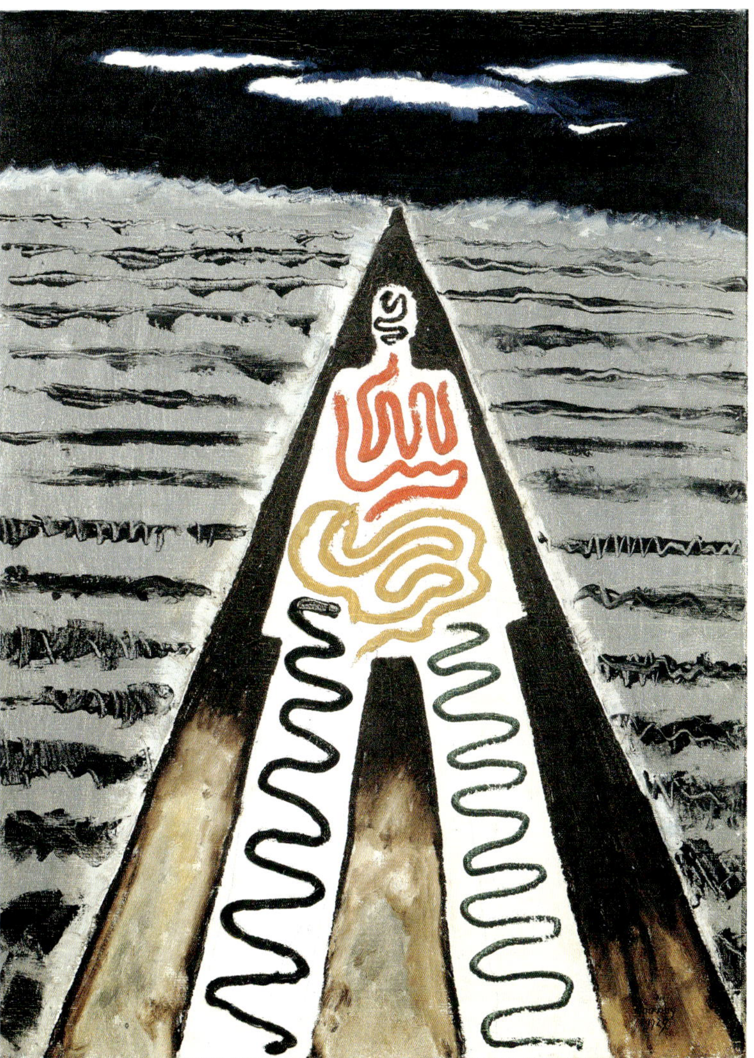

Fig. 5. *Une nuit à Saint-Jean-de-Luz*, 1929. Oil on canvas, 28¼ × 21¼ in.
(73 × 54 cm). Musée national d'art moderne, Centre Pompidou, Paris

not have to be conquered, it was part of his nature, as natural as breathing." As the artist
himself wrote, "I simply try to be as free as possible. In my working; in the choice of my subject. No one can dictate to me or guide me. They may criticize me afterwards, but it is too
late. The work is done. I have tasted freedom."[8]

Such freedom hardly came naturally. Emancipation from the repressive narrow-
mindedness of the Old World had to be fought for, in order to engender the almost hermetic
space—geographical, physical, psychological—within which he could create. This lifelong
effort, in all its forms, provides the context for a revisionist study of his work, bound, to
quote again the artist's metaphor, to the character of a "tree en espalier." To cast the artist's
suppression of his past and obfuscation of his identity as simply an anarchistic need to
assert a particular individualism is understandable but inadequate.

There has been an unreserved acceptance of Man Ray's elevation of the notion of
"freedom" to the level of the abstract, the imaginative, the transcendent, and of his libera-

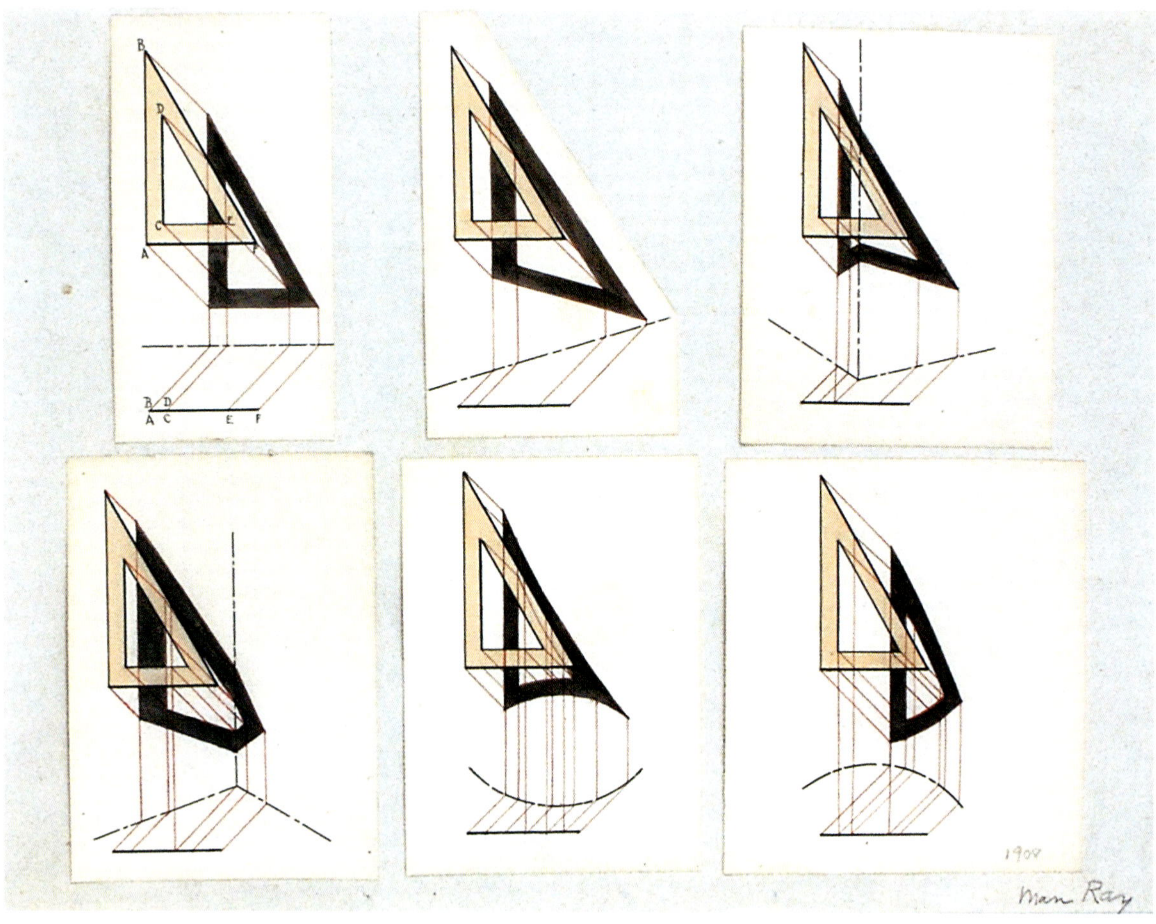

Fig. 6. *Triangles*, 1908. Pencil, ink, and watercolor on paper, 10¼ × 13¾ in. (26 × 34.9 cm). Francis M. Naumann Fine Art, New York

tion from established categories: "Perhaps the final goal desired by the artist is a confusion or merging of all the arts, as things merge in real life."[9] Yet his notion of the "final goal" for the artist—to confuse or merge the arts, creating an ultimate mayhem of categorical distinction just as "things merge in real life"—is an apt metaphor for assimilation. The question remains, then, how to address Man Ray's "anonymity," within the context of historical assimilation, so that it can help explain the nature of his varied oeuvre and its numerous techniques and aesthetic strategies. How can one doubt that his unceasing sense of alienation has its roots in his immigrant, Jewish upbringing, or that his unrelenting assumption of an outsider's position, his refusal to be codified or tempted to settle into a comfortable position—in effect, his desire to *not* fully assimilate—defines his "otherness," his irrevocable status as an outsider?

In this essay I examine Man Ray's life and work as a deliberate, ongoing attempt to reinvent himself and his art, and to reconcile his need to obscure but still declare himself. A psychological reading allows for an understanding of the seeming contradiction between Man Ray's achronological methodology and the fact that he not only kept extensive notes on the whereabouts of his works but could recall the "virtual month, day, and year of their creation."[10] On the occasion of his first retrospective, in 1944 at the Pasadena

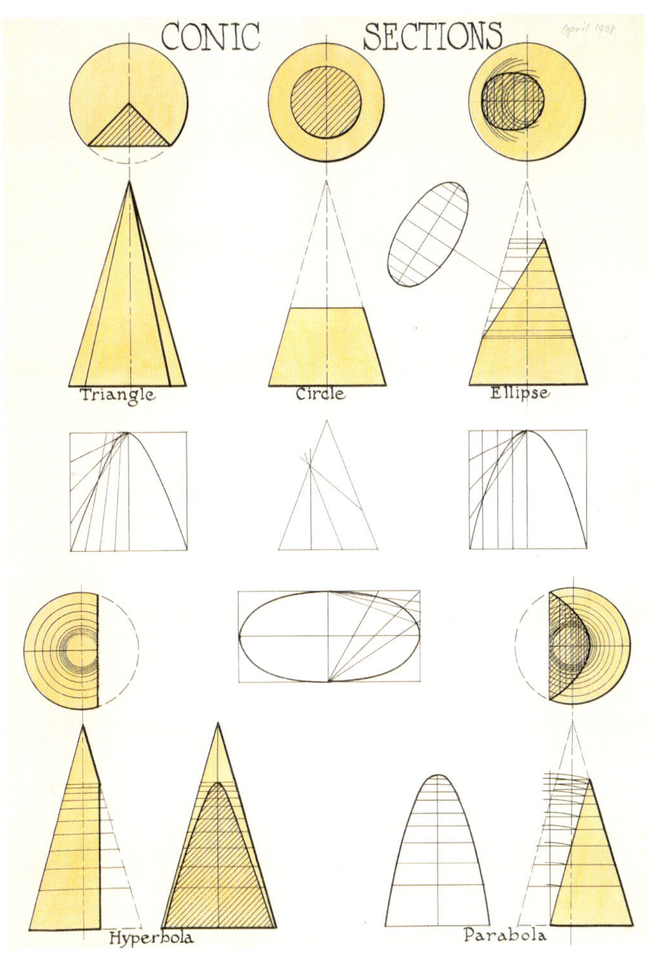

Fig. 7. *Conic Sections*, 1908. India ink and watercolor on paper, 13¼ × 9¹¹/₁₆ in. (35 × 24.6 cm). Musée national d'art moderne, Centre Pompidou, Paris

Art Institute, for example, Man Ray made it clear that an artist's career should not be bound to linear, developmental logic: "The chronological list of paintings does not imply any fancied progress. I do not believe in progress in art."[11] This patent disregard for progressive development accorded with his rejection of the rules of the game that more often than not confounded those who sought to situate him critically, or assess his work in terms of its quality, coherence, or purpose.

It could be argued that, in terms of artistic practice, Man Ray anticipated postmodernist theory in his efforts to dismantle belief systems based on such ideas as unity and hierarchy. As an artist and a subject, Man Ray remains a paradigm of multiplicity, his art fiercely challenging traditional interpretation. Even in his earliest work, which he kept and cherished his whole life—high school mechanical drawings that deal with geometry and perspective (figs. 6–8)—the young artist, in his fascination with duality, concealment, and shadows, is already, perhaps unconsciously, confronting the authority of a binding identity. His constant reversion to and revision of earlier works kept him on the defensive. His desire was to confound, to subvert expectation, by recycling his work in seeming variation, thus playing with the concept of a copy, challenging the very notion of a vintage "original," even publishing an essay titled "I Have Never Painted a Recent Picture."[12] As underscored in his

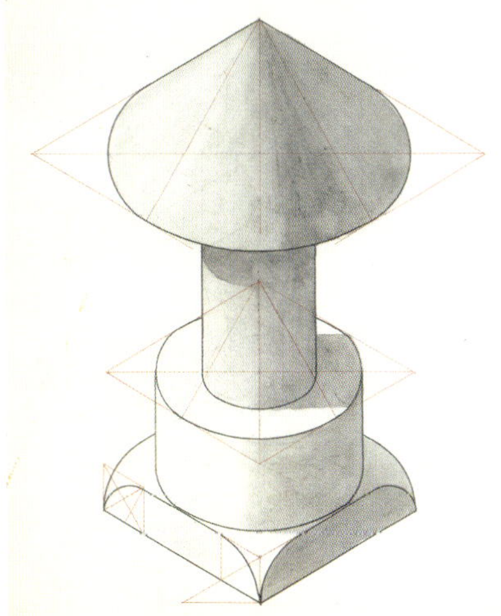

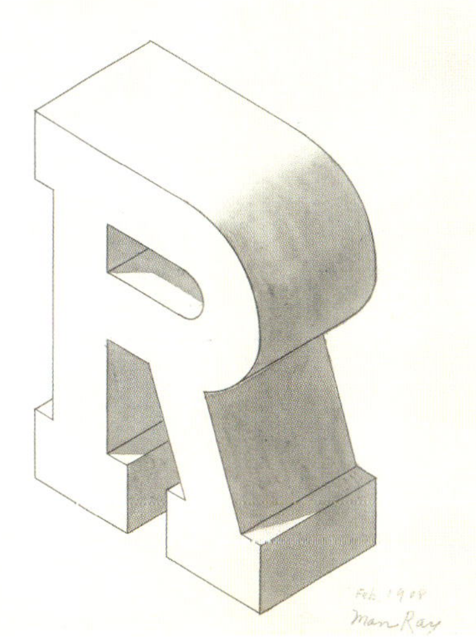

Fig. 8. *Letter "R,"* 1908. Pencil and ink on paper, 7¹/₁₆ × 12⅞ in. (17.9 × 32.8 cm). Musée national d'art moderne, Centre Pompidou, Paris

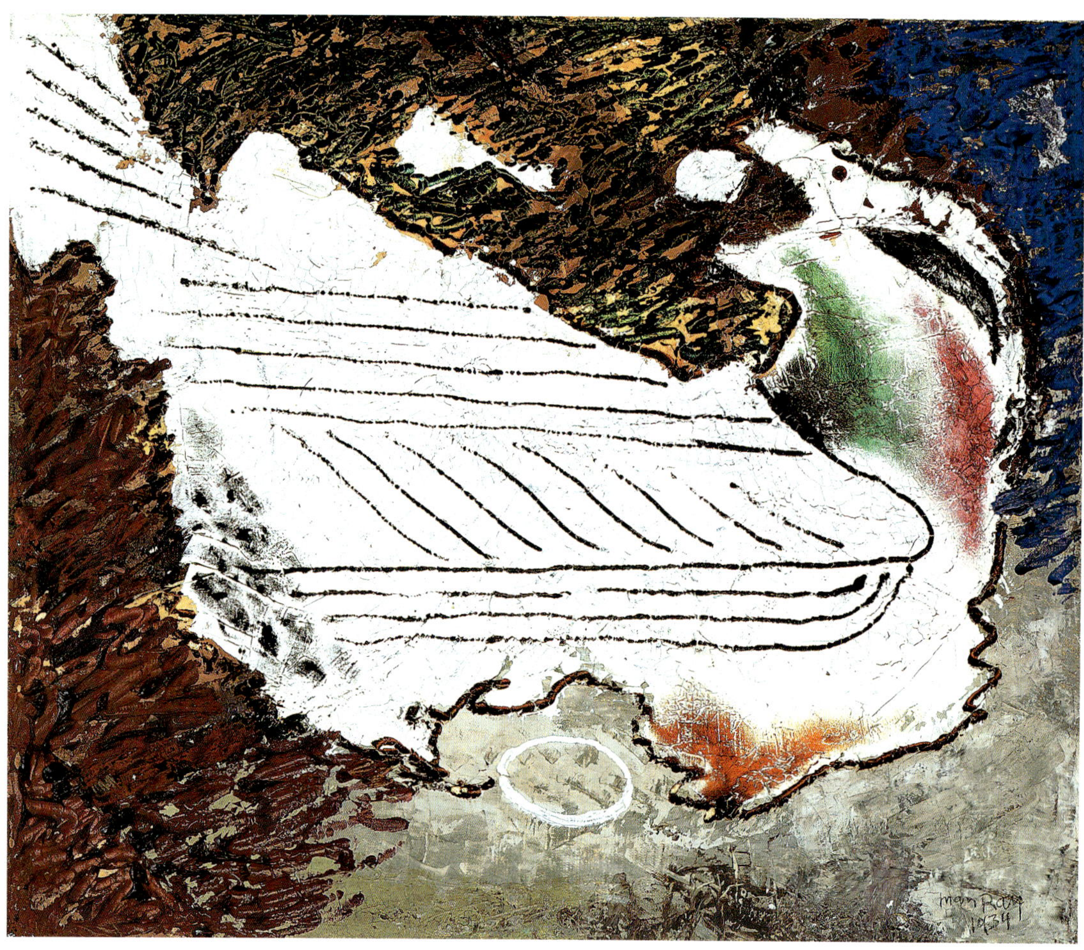

painting *Bird from Nowhere* (1934; fig. 9), Man Ray incorporates the critique of the original within the mythology of his own origins, summoning an ancient ouroboros-like creature that consumes itself, invoking ideas of cyclicality and infinity, of no beginning and no end.

When he was asked whether a work was an original, Man Ray's favorite response was, "To create is divine, to reproduce is human."[13] In his own humble way he managed to evade the distinction. And deservedly so, for he was rarely to be found not doing both—creating something new and renewing something old. Likening his process to that of book publishing, the artist diminished the value of the original, seeming rather to savor and indulge in the far more estimable copyright. Reproducibility, in fact, came naturally to him, even before he started making paintings or photographs, or his beloved objects. In high school art and mechanical drawing courses he acquired the proficiency to render a subject repeatedly, or to conceive of an object as infinitely alterable, as in his drawing *Triangles* (1908), comprising six draftsman's triangles and the shadows they cast, each of which varies with the curve or angle of the wall in front of which it is suspended.

Similarly, in his first important series of collages, *The Revolving Doors* (1916–17; fig. 10), Man Ray continues to meditate on the multiple ways a delimited subject can be observed or represented, here within the two-dimensional coordinates of the picture

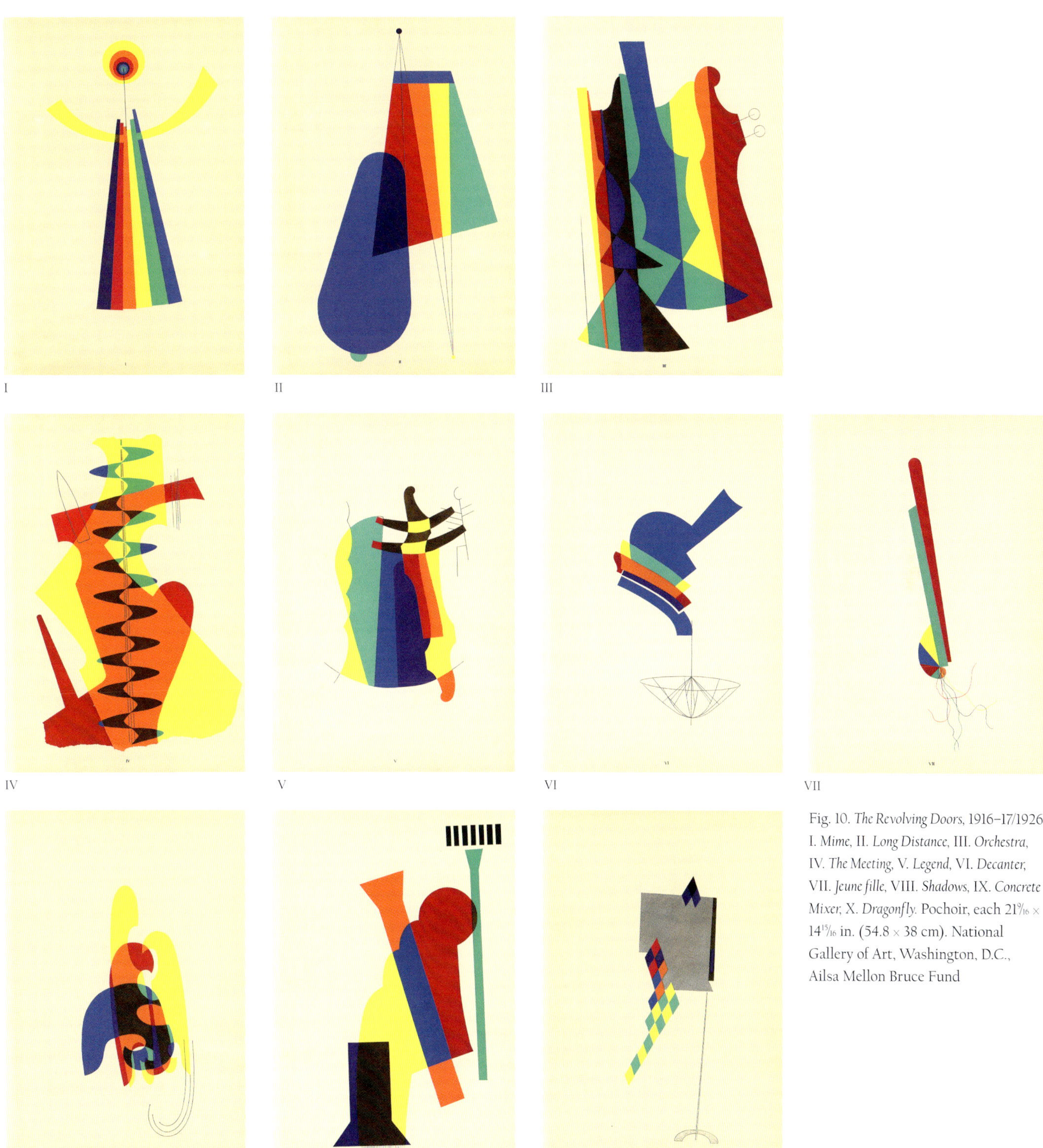

Fig. 10. *The Revolving Doors*, 1916–17/1926.
I. *Mime*, II. *Long Distance*, III. *Orchestra*,
IV. *The Meeting*, V. *Legend*, VI. *Decanter*,
VII. *Jeune fille*, VIII. *Shadows*, IX. *Concrete
Mixer*, X. *Dragonfly*. Pochoir, each 21⁹⁄₁₆ ×
14¹⁵⁄₁₆ in. (54.8 × 38 cm). National
Gallery of Art, Washington, D.C.,
Ailsa Mellon Bruce Fund

plane. Along with *Triangles*, other early studies, such as *Parallel Perspective* (1907), demonstrate his concern and mastery of a drawing's single vanishing point. *Untitled* (1908; fig. 11), in which a device drives an endless loop of film, can be seen as a generative, even revelatory, work, suggesting the conceptual as well as the formal seeds of certain fixations that resonate throughout Man Ray's more than six decades of work.[14]

Complementing the incipient blend of exactness and permutation of his early investigations was the relevant visual experience that he absorbed at home as the child of a vest maker, surrounded by a multitude of fabrics that invigorated the standard pattern of a waistcoat. Such exposure, enhanced by the skills of the industrial arts learned and refined at school, would serve him well. Mining his environment, adapting whatever he could find to some creative end, was a habit he never stopped indulging. As much as he was a dreamer, he was also a pragmatist who would use the material at hand, just as he took advantage of the vocational experiences acquired as a young man working as an engraver, doing layout work in an advertising office, and serving as a draftsman for a cartography company.

One must return to *Triangles*, though, as the artist would himself toward the end of his life—reverting to making shadow drawings as a final refrain to his career, as in *Unconcerned But Not Indifferent* (c. 1970; fig. 12)—to appreciate how organic Man Ray's artistic evolution was as he proceeded toward methods of multiplicity, reproducibility, the making of copies, homonymic wordplay, or the three-dimensional punning objects he never seemed to stop producing. One can connect *Triangles'* assumption of a single vanishing point to the metaphorical significance such a concept held for Man Ray throughout his life—in terms of both his rejection of the idea of a single point of origin and his conflicted wish for part of his reality to vanish.

While Man Ray's view of his art as nondevelopmental is a concept related to his subversion of the notion of an "original" bound to a past, it also relates to his refusal, in a way, to grow up. This fundamental flight from the past radically determines his need to consistently affirm his self-determination, through a

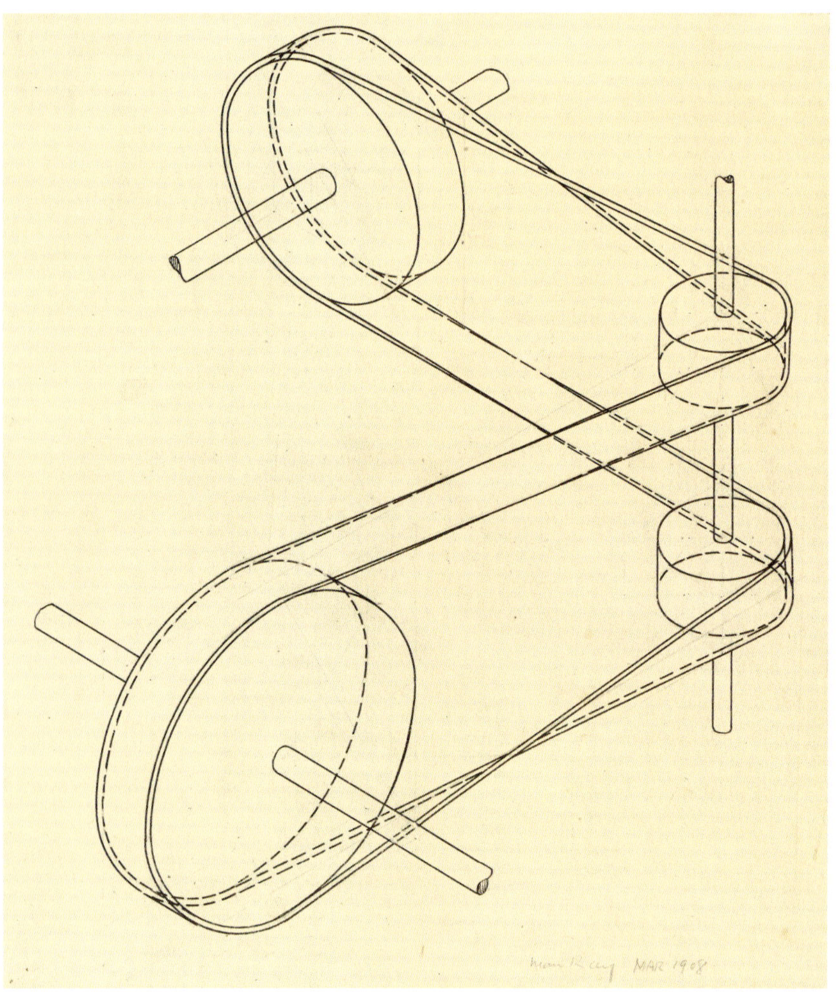

Fig. 11. *Untitled*, 1908. Ink and pencil on paper, 8¾ × 7⅛ in. (22 × 19.3 cm). The Museum of Modern Art, New York, Gift of Mrs. Sylvia Pizitz

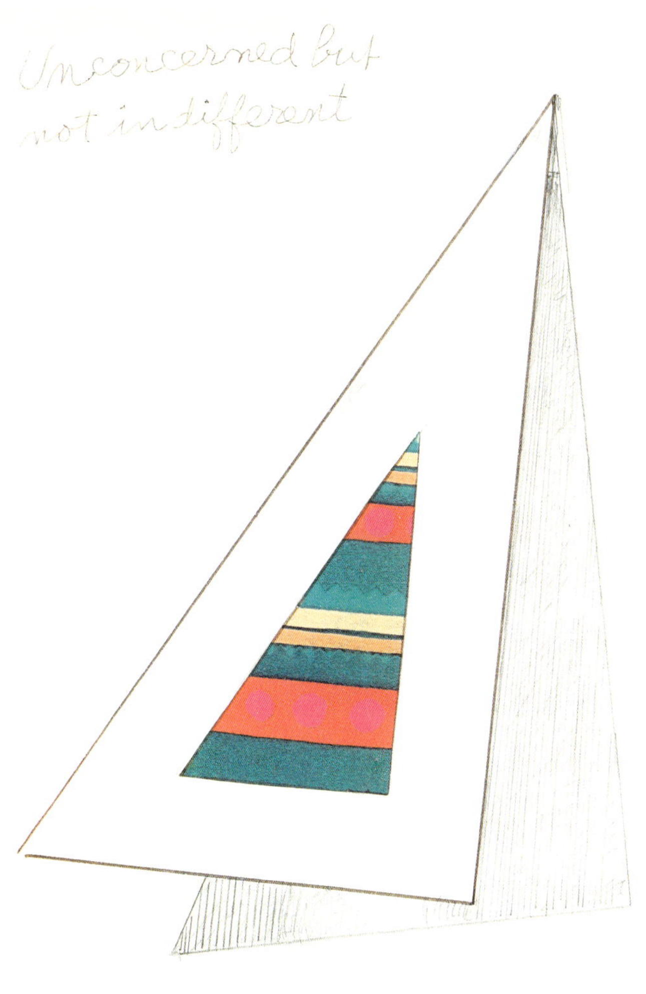

Fig. 12. *Unconcerned But Not Indifferent*, c. 1970. Black felt-tip pen, pencil, and paper on collage, 13⅛ × 10¼ in. (33.4 × 26 cm). Collection of Scott and Beth Ullem

continuous chronicling of his life in innumerable self-portraits (figs. 13 and 14), as if losing a particular hold on the present would force him to face the past and those who stood in the way of his fulfilling his acute need to create his own world, in which he could reside with a childlike "omnipotent autonomy."[15]

Man Ray's emergence as an artist involved a struggle with his identity. His "self-assertion," or individuation as a mature artist, coincidentally occurred on the cusp of an unprecedented zeitgeist, the transnationalism of Dadaism, whose anarchistic core resisted any authoritative effort to reduce, define, or codify its identity. As part of the anarchistic movement in New York before World War I, Man Ray held on to his Dadaist predilection throughout his life. Yet the view of Man Ray as a lifelong Dadaist, whose constancy lay in his obdurate refusal to be typed, or to compromise his antisocial Whitmanesque individualism founded on an unconstrained independence, can no longer suffice to explain his idiosyncracies, which surface as contradictory tendencies toward both freedom and suppression. It is undeniable, however, that if Man Ray remained true to anything in his stylistic itinerancy, it was to this willfulness of the imagination and celebration of the self and its unrestrained, nonhierarchical expression through art; but in Man Ray's case, it was

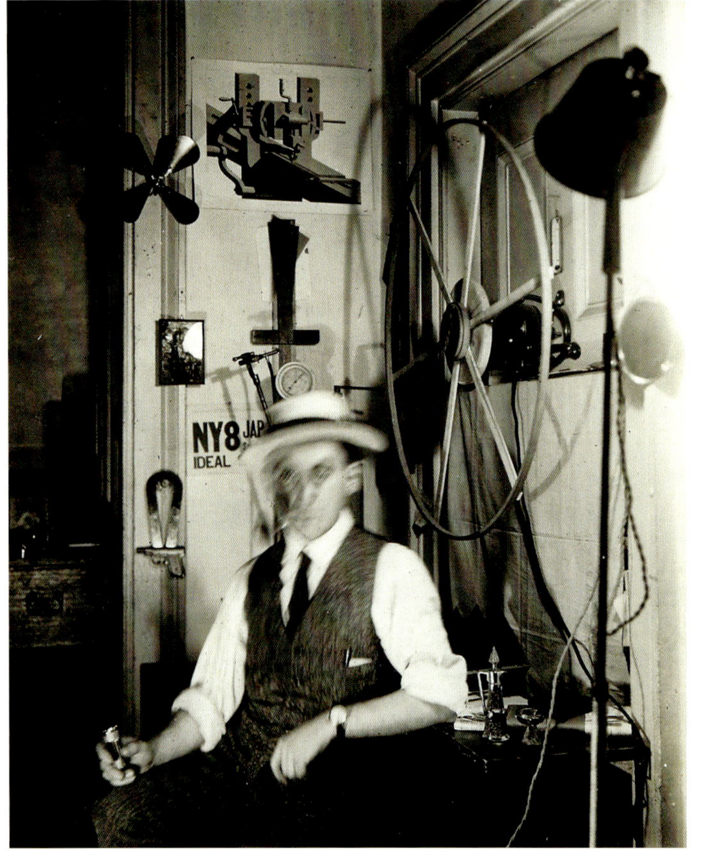

Fig. 13. *Man Ray dans son atelier*, 1920. Gelatin silver print, 4¾ × 3¾ in. (12 × 9.5 cm). Chancellerie des universités de Paris—Bibliothèque littéraire Jacques Doucet, Paris

Fig. 14. *Untitled (Self-Portrait with Camera)*, 1930, printed 1935/36. Solarized gelatin silver print, 4¾ × 3½ in. (12.1 × 8.9 cm). The Jewish Museum, New York, Purchase: Photography Acquisitions Committee Fund, Horace W. Goldsmith Fund, and funds provided by Judith and Jack Stern

to a universal, anonymous self, one whose compromised individualism was mitigated, at the same time, through an obsessive and incessant mode of self-inscription.[16]

As an egocentric, anarchistic phenomenon, the eruption of Dadaism was the perfect movement for Man Ray, with its spontaneous and defiant forms, which lacked specificity and programmatic direction, and its self-mocking manifestos that required no alignment. In seeking to provide an international refuge from a world grown foul with the "senilities of grown-ups," Hugo Ball specified the purpose of founding (with his wife, Emily Hennings) the Cabaret Voltaire: "It is necessary to define the activity of this cabaret; its aim is to remind the world that there are independent men —beyond war and nationalism—who live for other ideals."[17] With its rejection of nationalist chauvinism and its effort to replace hierarchical thinking with a simple understanding of the notion of the multiplicity of meaning, Dadaism more than facilitated Man Ray's need to escape the insularity of his ethnicity. It also provided him an unlimited opportunity to relate his diverse agenda within a social paradigm that suited his need for acceptance and independence. Indeed,

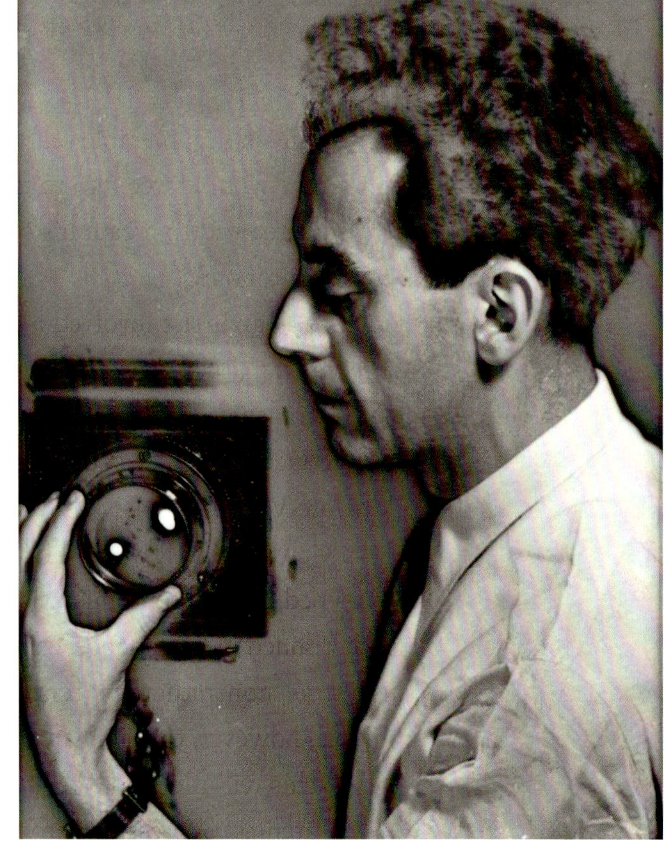

the group dynamic does not even really apply to Dadaism, which arose in a crescendo of iconoclastic individualism in response to the anti-individual, collective experience of World War I.

These sociopolitical realities would begin to mesh with Man Ray's aesthetics in the social and intellectual environment of the art classes he took at the Ferrer Center, where, in 1912, he began studying with the painter Robert Henri and the critic John Weichsel. There he would be encouraged to consider tradition critically, in order to understand the irrelevance of the past, and cultivate the freedom necessary to find oneself in the present. Everything he was learning at the Ferrer Center was in some way integrated within this process—to filter out the past while engaging the artistic and sociopolitical realities of the present, principally the international zeitgeist of anarchism.[18]

Man Ray's movement toward an art of defiance and critique of a priori systems of belief, of biases based on notions of origins and fixed identity, positioned him perfectly to join, three years later, Marcel Duchamp's revolt against an exhausted "retinal" tradition of aesthetics. Together they would help initiate New York Dada, a branch of the international movement that abhorred the rise of cultural chauvinism and xenophobia throughout Europe during the Great War.

But as he expressed in a letter to Tristan Tzara in June 1921, since "dada cannot live in New York," Man Ray had to move to where Dada's heart was beating stronger (fig. 15). In so doing, far from suffering an "eradication of character," he simply found an audience that did not care where his family came from, or notice his "Brooklyn" dialect, but that cherished his "American" difference, his unfixed character, and his willingness to join in fighting Europe's stale and festering pretense of taste and culture. In Europe, Man Ray found himself able to disdain and combat the very inflexibility of Old World values that he felt his Russian Jewish family represented. It was never the movement that compelled him, though; what drove him to Europe was a collection of motives with a common purpose— his need to defeat a hierarchical thinking in favor of an egalitarianism that he would embrace throughout his life.

One must ultimately look beyond art-historical rubrics, which have almost everywhere served as the background for understanding Man Ray, especially the early work, in order to ascertain signs of who he was and why he might have created work of such variety and contradiction. It is Man Ray's underlying tendencies—to rapidly digest a maximum of artistic styles, to synthesize a theory of commonality within all the arts, to obliquely identify or inscribe himself within his work, and to remain an independent figure within the artistic milieus he navigated—that one must examine to comprehend the link between his conduct and the work he produced. As one who subscribed to artistic openness yet maintained extreme personal secrecy regarding his past, negotiating the concept of identity problematically his entire life, Man Ray cannot be divorced from his sense of tainted origins, a sense that permeates his oeuvre. The need for privacy inflects his work in countless ways, and his insistence on maintaining mystery became a self-obsession, to the point of narcissism.

Aside from his being the sole American within the Parisian avant-garde, Man Ray's marginal status, or need to remain isolated, has been noted by others, but mostly in the context of his anarchistic individualism rather than as a component of his complex psychological makeup. As Neil Baldwin has described: "It was more comfortable for Man Ray to deny

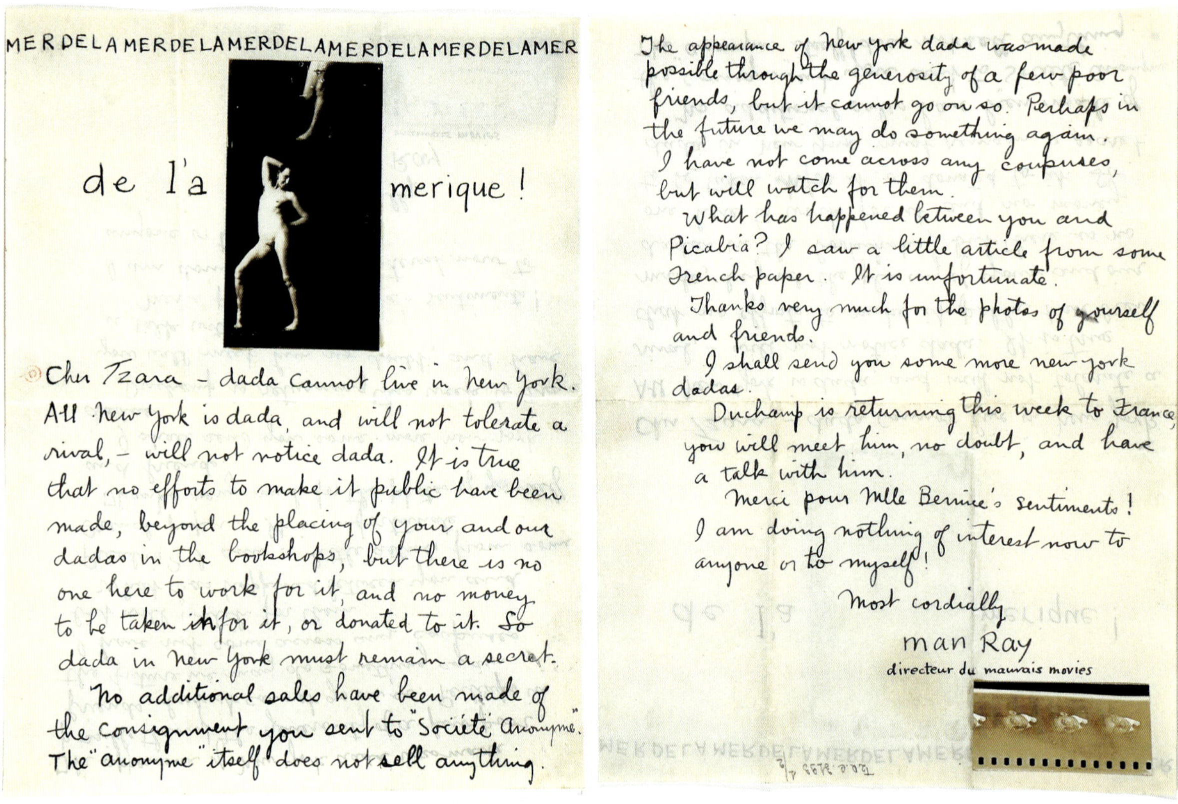

MER DE LA MER DE LA MER DE LA MER DE LA MER DE LA MER

de l'a merique !

Cher Tzara – dada cannot live in New York. All New York is dada, and will not tolerate a rival, – will not notice dada. It is true that no efforts to make it public have been made, beyond the placing of your and our dadas in the bookshops, but there is no one here to work for it, and no money to be taken in for it, or donated to it. So dada in New York must remain a secret.

No additional sales have been made of the consignment you sent to "Société Anonyme". The "anonyme" itself does not sell anything.

The appearance of New York dada was made possible through the generosity of a few poor friends, but it cannot go on so. Perhaps in the future we may do something again.

I have not come across any coupures, but will watch for them.

What has happened between you and Picabia? I saw a little article from some French paper. It is unfortunate.

Thanks very much for the photos of yourself and friends.

I shall send you some more New York dadas.

Duchamp is returning this week to France you will meet him, no doubt, and have a talk with him.

Merci pour Mlle Bernice's sentiments! I am doing nothing of interest now to anyone or to myself!

Most cordially

man Ray
directeur du mauvais movies

Fig. 15. Letter from Man Ray to Tristan Tzara, New York, June 18, 1921. Chancellerie des universités de Paris—Bibliothèque littéraire Jacques Doucet, Paris

the existence of the Dada movement [in New York] than to admit that he preferred to maintain a stance outside it." Others have similarly expressed this aspect of Man Ray's character—remaining marginalized—most notably Francis Picabia, whose ink drawing *Dada Movement* (1919) charts a particular strain of antiformalist self-negation within modernism, beginning with Jean-Augusto-Dominique Ingres and Camille Corot, including more than thirty-five people, and leading to Picabia's own Dada magazine, *391*, but omits Man Ray's name. Another figure who noted the artist's proclivity to remain in the wings was the collector and art patron Katherine Dreier; she might have been encouraged to think of the artist this way at a meeting she convened at her home in New York to discuss the inception of the city's first "museum of modern art" with Duchamp.[19] At the meeting, Man Ray suggested the name Société Anonyme, unaware that the expression did not refer to an anonymous society but was the French designation for a corporation.

A serious lack of critical contextualization was certainly evident in October 1966 when Philip Leider reviewed for the *New York Times* the first multimedia retrospective of Man Ray's work, held at the Los Angeles County Museum of Art.[20] Leider first commends the museum's "kaleidoscopic" exhibition schedule, which included, in addition to Man Ray, a show of lithographs by Josef Albers and a comprehensive survey of graphics by Pablo Picasso, two European artists of extraordinary focus and signature style. In contrast, Man Ray's career was seen as demonstrating a lack of coherent artistic identity, a judgment implied by the critic's choice of title for his review: "Man Ray, Wandering Knight." Leider's critique, however, hinges on his perception of the artist as having virtually forfeited his American identity through a "complete submission" to the European avant-garde, a Faustian transaction that Leider summarily relates:

> Man Ray was not the only American artist forced to come to grips with the revelation of the advanced state of European art displayed at the Armory Show in 1913, but he is certainly the only one who responded to the problem by simply converting himself into a European artist. In this sense, the large retrospective reveals him as biographically, but not artistically unique. The only American artist to *succeed in assimilating* himself completely into the European-based avant-garde of Dada and Surrealism, Man Ray was already a European artist long before his first trip there in 1921. . . . Indeed it is not so much the success of Man Ray's *complete absorption* into the currents of European art that surprises, singular though that success was, but its thoroughness. One searches . . . in vain for some *trace* of the American grain beneath the Parisian polish, some irrepressible, unruly native element beneath the European chic. That it is *not to be found* explains perhaps, in part, why the story of the exhibition is that of a problematic artist whose work never attained the depth and conviction to be found in, say, Stuart Davis, who took from Europe what his *native sensibility* needed, without suffering the eradication of character that comes with complete submission. [italics added]

As a result of this fatal attraction to the European avant-garde, Man Ray, in Leider's view, lost himself in his total obeisance to European culture, his "native" identity worn away without a trace. At best, the erstwhile American becomes a penumbra, a shadowy quotient of the true inventive brilliance of Duchamp, in whose thrall the younger artist had fallen a half-century before, spellbound, "frittering away a creative lifetime." As a mere cipher, whose "inveterate eclecticism would seize in passing upon elements of Magritte, Picabia, and de Chirico . . . Man [Ray] was never to become his own man."

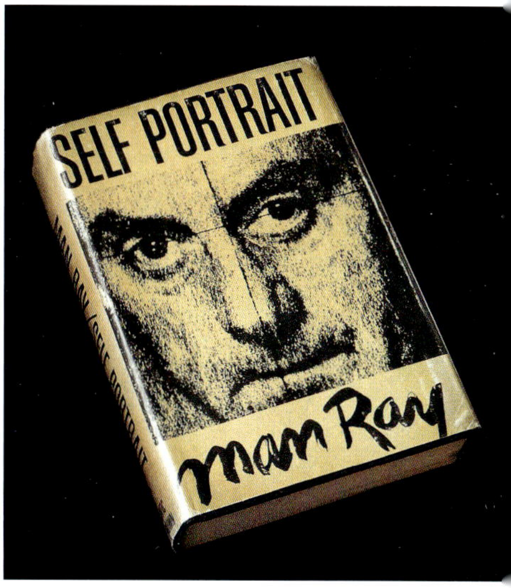

The implications of such a judgment, that the artist lacked a substantive identity, are never addressed beyond his lack of stylistic coherence. In fact, the subject of his background is considered as fleetingly by the artist himself in his "autobiography," *Self Portrait*, published in 1963 (fig. 16). Deracinated, subsumed by Parisian "polish" and European "chic," Man Ray lacks "depth and conviction." Leider questions the efforts of the exhibition curator, Jules Langsner, "to find out what is 'seminal' in Man Ray" rather than to "isolate, if possible,

Fig. 16. Cover of *Self Portrait* (1963)

what complex of factors it was that prevented Man Ray from emerging as a major artist." The critic's myopic view reduces the artist to being a "Europeanized" American, thus precluding his seeing Man Ray as an individual, much less as an American whose very "native" qualities had endeared him to Europeans in the first place. Leider illustrates the extent to which Man Ray was lost, by citing "perhaps the saddest works in the exhibition . . . the found objects created during the forties and fifties, tied to the withered roots of an exhausted Dada, while, ironically, all around him, the roots [of Abstract Expressionism] from which he had cut himself at so costly a price, had begun to sprout." These "roots" of an American art represent precisely the kind of elevated formalism that the artist had not only practiced but also largely rejected decades before. The artist had transcended the nationalist cultural interests, the new American art, and retained his Dadaist sensibility while collaborating in every medium with artists of various nationalities for more than half a century.[21]

While neither Leider nor the curator refers to Man Ray's origins or his name change, the question remains as to what extent such biographical information makes his work more evocative or intelligible. Had his Jewish identity been known, would all the indicators of his life and work, invoked critically—his "inveterate eclecticism," "complete absorption," "assimilating himself completely"—have been inflected with new meaning? Would the idiosyncratic diversity of Man Ray's work, his habituated behavior, obsessions, and aesthetic strategies have suggested the possibility of an alienation so profound that it dictated a life's work? Or would the title "Wandering Knight"—after an inscription the artist wrote beside a chessboard, "The knight wanders all over the board," an encrypted reference to his rootlessness—have implied the theme of the outcast Wandering Jew? Speculative as a viewer's perception may be, it is clear that Leider saw the proverbial writing on the wall and could not read it. But Man Ray's gambit of obscurity, his knowing exactly what he was doing when he typically—yet obliquely—inscribed himself in his work, was just like the movement of the knight, the only chess piece that can move sideways as well as jump over other pieces, enabling it to escape confinement and closed positions. It is hardly surprising that it was both his and Duchamp's favorite piece.[22]

When the artist died in 1976, his identity and critical status were, at the very least, unresolved. Apart from Man Ray's photography, the panoply of his

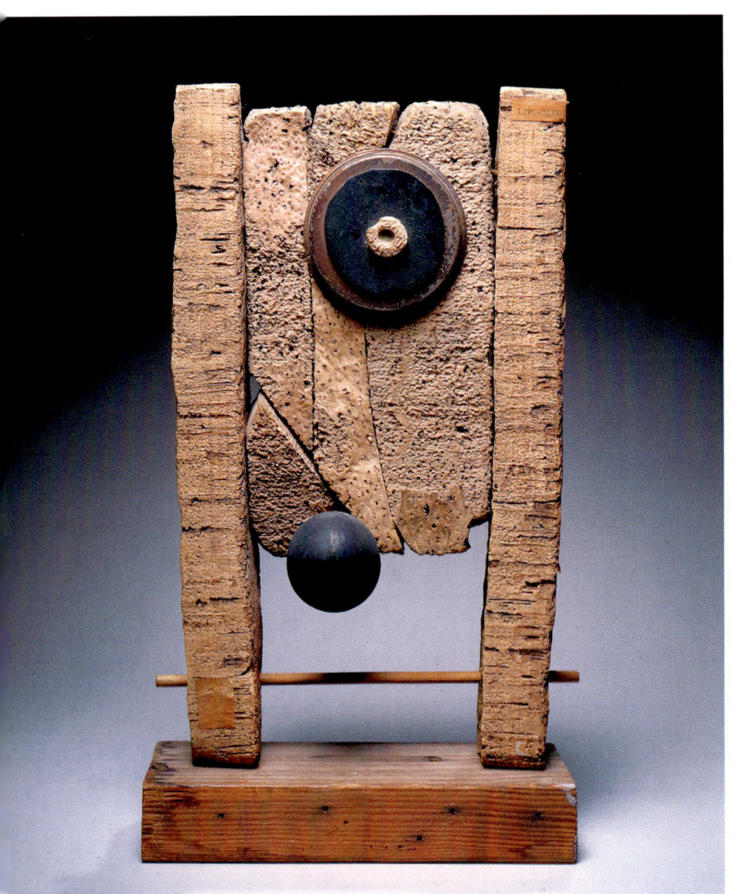

Fig. 17. *Life Saver*, 1944. Cork, wood, metal, rubber, and candy, 15 × 9 × 3½ in. (38.1 × 22.9 × 8.9 cm). High Museum of Art, Atlanta, Purchase with Fay and Barrett Howell Fund

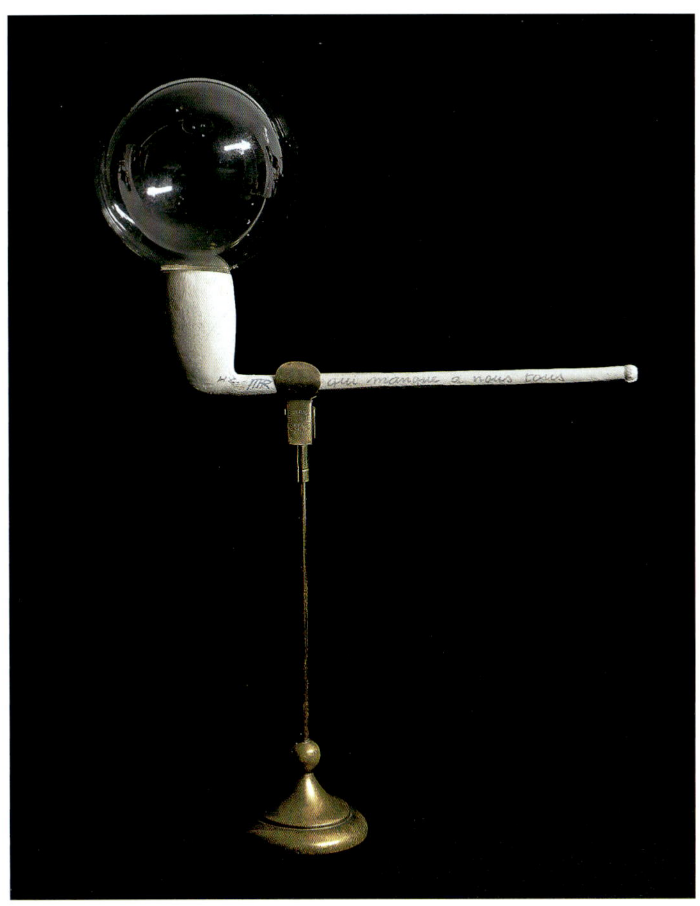

Fig. 18. *What We All Lack*, 1971–72. Clay pipe
with glass bubble, 12 × 7 × 3 in. (30.5 × 17.8 ×
7.6 cm). Private collection, courtesy of
Timothy Baum, New York

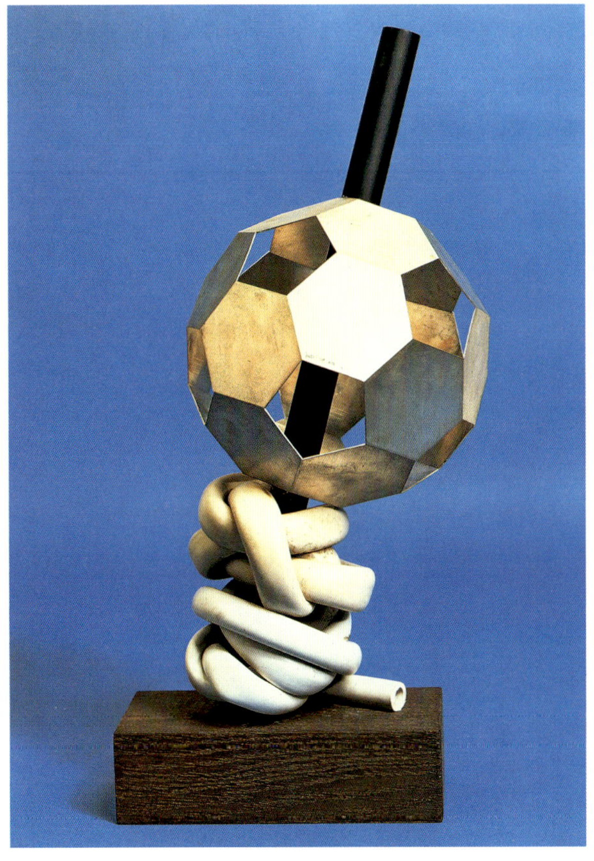

Fig. 19. *Non-Euclidian Object I*, 1932 (1973 edition). Aluminum, steel, and plastic tubing on wooden base, 19 × 7 × 7
in. (48.3 × 17.8 × 17.8 cm). Collection of Timothy Baum,
New York

painting styles, the unevenness of aesthetic finish, and the spew of three-
dimensional puns—"objects of my
affection"—vigorously released, especially in editions, toward the end of his
life, rendered the judgment of his
work problematic for many critics
(figs. 17–19). This was alleviated neither by his embrace of contradiction
nor by his defiant demeanor—both
parts of his consummate artistic persona. Man Ray had come to resemble
his beloved "objects of affection," in
their capacity "to amuse, annoy, bewil-
der, mystify, inspire reflection, but not

to arouse admiration for any technical excellence."[23] Thus on some level it should not have surprised him, at the age of seventy-nine, when, in 1970, an exhibition of his paintings in New York prompted yet another critic to write that "things didn't really add up," concluding that "Man Ray [would] undoubtedly go down in history as a clever, mildly outrageous artist who never quite found himself."[24]

Such a judgment, a refrain of Leider's review, was proffered as well by others, who recognized Man Ray's gifts as a photographer and the importance of his early work, but questioned the contrivance of his other unrestrained pursuits, or whose analytical readings of artists hinged on a perceived crystallization of their development.[25] The irony of reducing the artist to one who "never quite found himself" rests on the fact that Man Ray's continuous stylistic ambling and experimental, creative renewal were based, despite his desire for critical recognition, on an underlying paradoxical desire *not* to be found. His conflicted need for "anonymity," when it came to his past, and his wish for critical acknowledgment and exposure were problems not to be resolved in his lifetime. That the artist's agenda of identity suppression has been largely overlooked is understandable, given how few people today even know that the artist was Jewish, or that he was once called Emmanuel (Manny) Radnitzky.[26]

His change of name, his subsequent rejection of family, and his expatriation to Paris in 1921 secured him not just a comfortable distance from his roots but also a new status as the American odd man out.[27] This erasure of "origins" precipitated his cultivation, even fetishization, of his artistic persona—all integral to his formative methodology and aesthetic strategies to subvert authority and deny the relationship between name and self. In changing his name from the colloquial "Manny" to the nameless "Man," Man Ray lost and found himself in anonymity.

the Writing On the wall

For Man Ray, the difficulty of being freely in the world in the 1910s was not significantly different from that of facing anti-Semitism in Hollywood and the rest of the United States in the 1940s, when he wrote the words quoted in the epigraph. While acknowledging his "checkmate" position, his desire to become "a tree en espalier," to enjoin the social throng in some veiled manner, he was simply admitting what he had always felt. The tightrope that he tries to walk, in the 1940s and throughout his forced return to the United States, balancing "notoriety" and "oblivion," is no different from the one he managed skillfully to negotiate decades earlier in his perhaps most significantly revealing painting, *The Rope Dancer Accompanies Herself with Her Shadows* (1915–16; fig. 20). This key narrative work underlines the complex manner in which he would at once inscribe himself in his work and gloss over his past, to be in the spotlight and yet refuse the simple legitimacy of social inclusion. It was vital to him to maintain the anonymity and freedom upon which he insisted his artistic career depended.

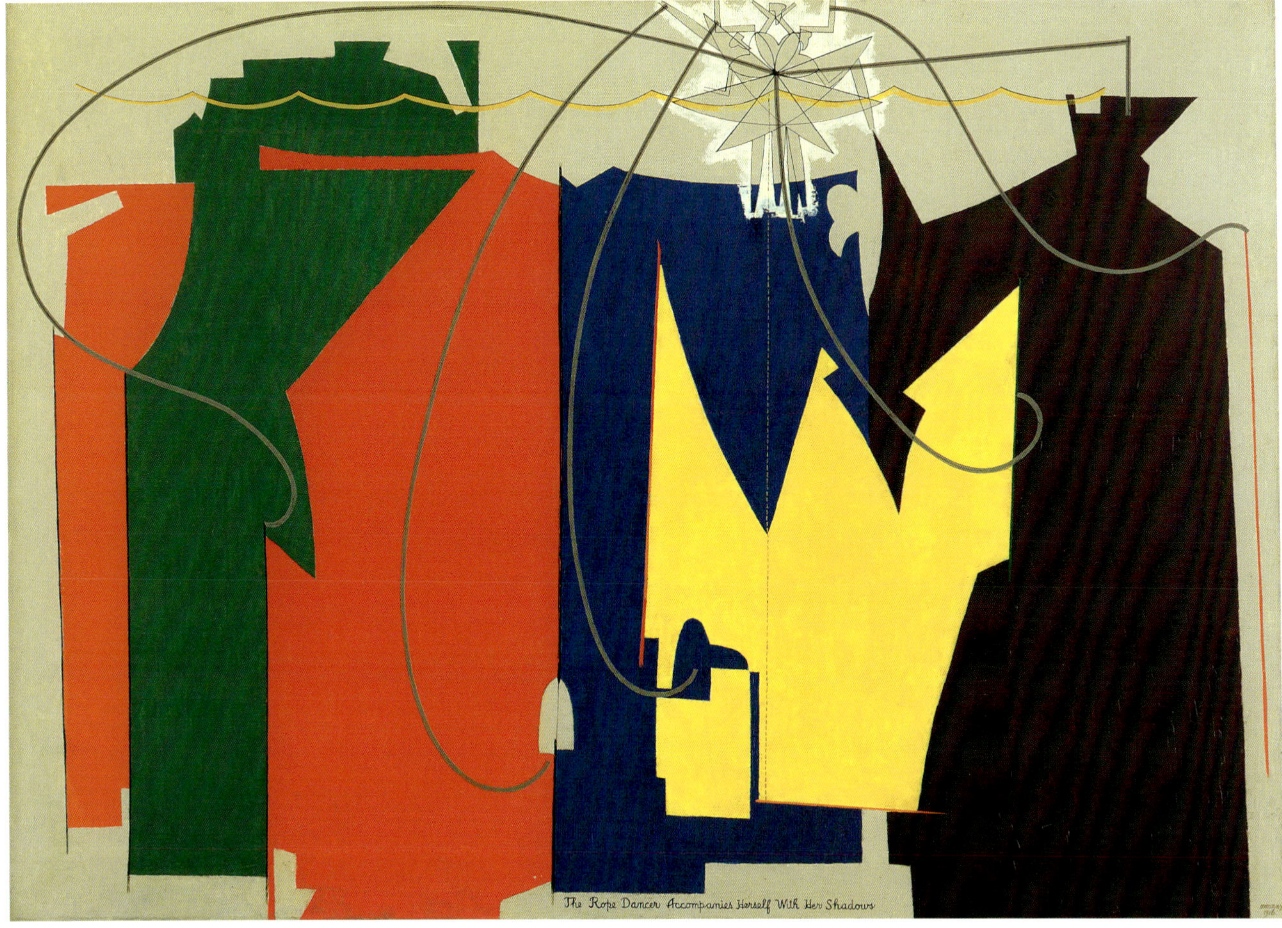

Fig. 20. *The Rope Dancer Accompanies Herself with Her Shadows*, 1915–16. Oil on canvas, 52 × 73⅛ in. (132.1 × 186.4 cm). The Museum of Modern Art, Gift of G. David Thompson, 1954

The painting, begun toward the end of the year that he met Duchamp, possesses, as various scholars have observed, formal iconographic affinities with Duchamp's *The Large Glass (The Bride Stripped Bare by Her Bachelors, Even)* (which, while conceived in 1913, was assembled starting in 1915 and not physically completed until 1923).[28] While one could easily continue to speculate on the influence exerted by the elder Frenchman, this essay is concerned with the specificity of Man Ray's agenda. Beyond any superficial similarities, *The Rope Dancer* distinguishes itself in its defining departure from the dominant two-dimensionality that preoccupied him while he lived at an artists' colony in Ridgefield, New Jersey (he was there for more than two years, beginning in the spring of 1913), and also as the first significant post-Ridgefield work, an unquestionably personal statement, painted upon his reentry into the fray of the New York art world.

Once he returned to New York, in December 1915, Man Ray was honing a sense of his artistic identity, which had been coalescing during his experimental and introspective period in Ridgefield. He was now fortified with an optimism derived principally from a successful one-person show at the Daniel Gallery in New York, and bolstered by an article by John Weichsel, "New Art and Man Ray," published in the journal *East and West*.[29] With a resurgence of confidence, he appropriately chose—at this important professional juncture—the metaphor of the tightrope walker, an early modernist archetype of man's effort to realize both an equilibrium and a higher goal. That his new work's original title was *The Theatre of the Soul* (after a play by the Russian director and playwright Nikolai Evreinof) hints that the painting was initially moored to content considerably weightier than acrobatics.[30] Yet the work has never been regarded from such a vantage. It has been viewed literally, as an illustration of a tightrope walker the artist had seen at a vaudeville performance, which he described in *Self Portrait* almost a half-century later, in recalling the painting's evolution:

> The subject was a rope dancer I had seen in a vaudeville show. I began by making sketches of various positions of the acrobatic forms, each on a different sheet of spectrum-colored paper, with the idea of suggesting movement not only in the drawing but by a transition from one color to another. I cut these out and arranged the forms into sequences before I began the final painting. After several changes in my composition I was less and less satisfied. It looked too decorative and might have served as a curtain for the theater. Then my eyes turned to the pieces of colored paper that had fallen to the floor. They made an abstract pattern that might have been the shadows of the dancer or an architectural subject, according to the trend of one's imagination if he were looking for a representative motive. I played with these, then saw the painting as it should be carried out. Scrapping the original forms of the dancer, I set to work on the canvas, laying in large areas of pure color in the form of the spaces that had been left outside the original drawings of the dancer. No attempt was made to establish a color harmony; it was red against blue, purple against yellow, green versus orange, with an effect of maximum contrast. The color was laid on with precision, yet lavishly—in fact, the stock of colors was entirely depleted. When finished, I wrote the legend along the bottom of the canvas: *The Rope Dancer Accompanies Herself with Her Shadows.*[31]

In an earlier recollection, in response to a Museum of Modern Art questionnaire, Man Ray omits any reference to having alighted on chance effects, but does suggest a more distanced technique, eschewing brushes in favor of painting "the whole [work] with specially shaped palette knives."[32] While the inventive manner of abstracting the painting's narrative, the distancing of the artist's presence in the work, and the relative compositional dependency on chance effects have been noted, a reading of the painting's symbolism has been effectively ignored.[33]

Yet as the work that could be said to represent his return to public exposure, *The Rope Dancer* assumes special significance. It is the quintessential enactment of the dilemma the artist faced throughout his life in registering his public versus his private identity, just as the rope dancer dematerializes in assuming the color of its background, a figure virtually eclipsed by its shadows with only its vestigial white aura defining its visibility. Reduced thus to a veiled presence, almost exclusively represented by the six primary and secondary colors of the spectrum, Man Ray, the private figure, now subject to public scrutiny, withdraws, hidden safely behind his surrogate artistic projections.

This private concealment is further inscribed, or encrypted, in the painting's various references to his past—the ubiquitous tailor's patterns, the two irons in the lower center of the painting, and the range of colors—the last, especially, relating to his childhood,
to the red shirt he wore at his high school graduation and the full spectrum of crayons and
pencils he pilfered from a local store as an adolescent. The boldness of the primary colors
all but shields the "artistic" dancer and her virtuoso movements, while paradoxically
broadcasting the artist's invisibility, no less than the written portrait he presents decades
later. In his memoir Man Ray comments on *The Rope Dancer*'s visual effects, and recalls meeting Stieglitz standing in front of it. "He thought it very significant—it vibrated," Man Ray
remembers, "in fact, it was almost *blinding*" (emphasis added).[34]

As an illustration of the "fateful" walk, or individuation process, which I contend
was complex for Man Ray, *The Rope Dancer* also represents the apotheosis of his early efforts
to reconcile the poles of his conflicted identity or to veil it. His continuing preoccupation
with such a process is evidenced in a range of works, most notably in one of his earliest
aerographs, *Suicide* (1917; fig. 21),
originally named *The Theatre of the
Soul.* In this curious painting, which
prefigures both Alexander Calder's
mobiles and Alberto Giacometti's
Surrealist kinetic structures, Man
Ray depicts two ovoid shapes that
are strung like marionettes, one
appearing to be in irritable contact
with a sharply pointed comblike
object. The composition, not unlike
that of *The Rope Dancer,* suggests a
more symbolically personal content
than a mere illustration of the dramatic narrative of Evreinof's play.
For the two identical ovoid shapes
clearly resemble blank faces—a possible reference to the artist's sense of
dual identity—whose relationship
is defined by their relative mobility,
unsettling suspension, and the
proximity of one anonymous face, in
particular, to the dangerous, prickly
article that occupies the center of
the space.

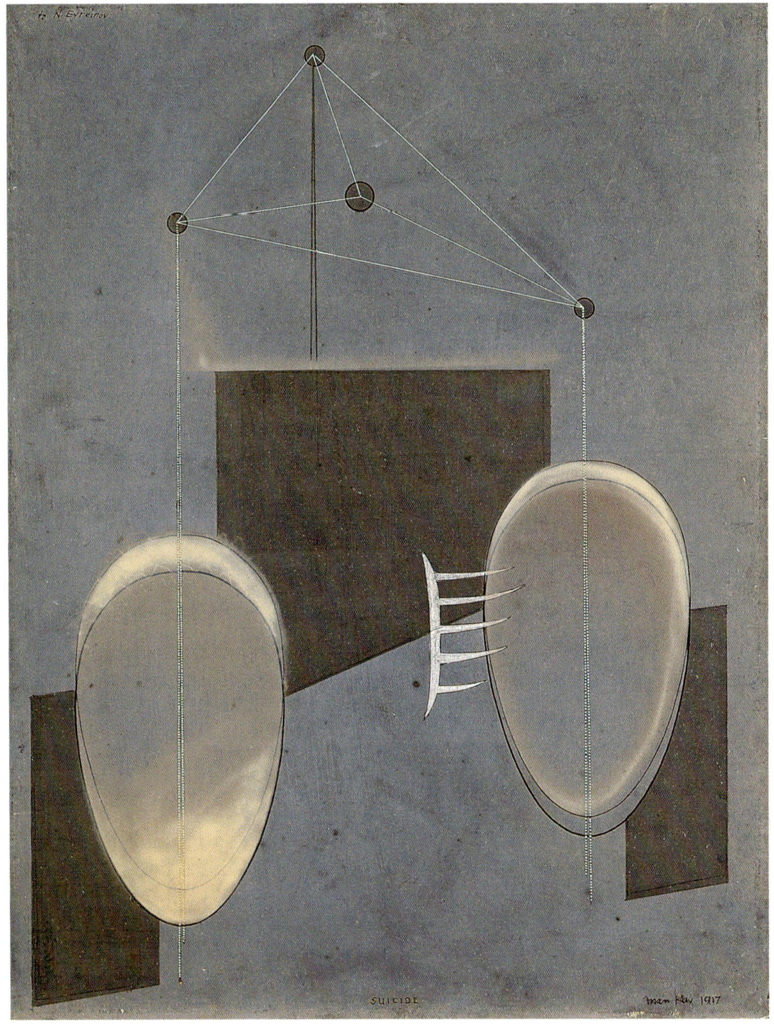

Fig. 21. *Suicide*, 1917. Gouache with pencil, India ink, white ink, varnish, and
incised lines on paperboard, 24¹/₁₆ × 18¹⁵/₁₆ in. (61.1 × 48.1 cm). The Menil Collection, Houston

diminutive **Boldface**

The personal narrative of *The Rope Dancer* was initiated by a complementary work, which Man Ray painted before returning to New York from Ridgefield. A year earlier, he had begun to confront directly the integral contradiction that characterized his relationship to the world, through the opposed attributes of revelation and concealment. As a marker of his adoptive artistic persona, *Man Ray 1914* (see fig. 3) favors the former but represents a dynamic melding of these two attributes. One would be hard pressed to find a more symbolic visual personification of the artist's unique brand of assimilation than the metaphoric fusion of genres that this merging of landscape and self-portraiture offers. In constructing a Cubist landscape out of the letters of his newly adopted name (upending the prescribed alignment of the mechanical style of lettering that he had perfected in high school), the barely five-foot-tall Man Ray was broadcasting his public identity while privately remaining hidden, assimilated, through an act of mimicry or camouflage. He had, literally and figuratively, become one with both his art and environment.[35]

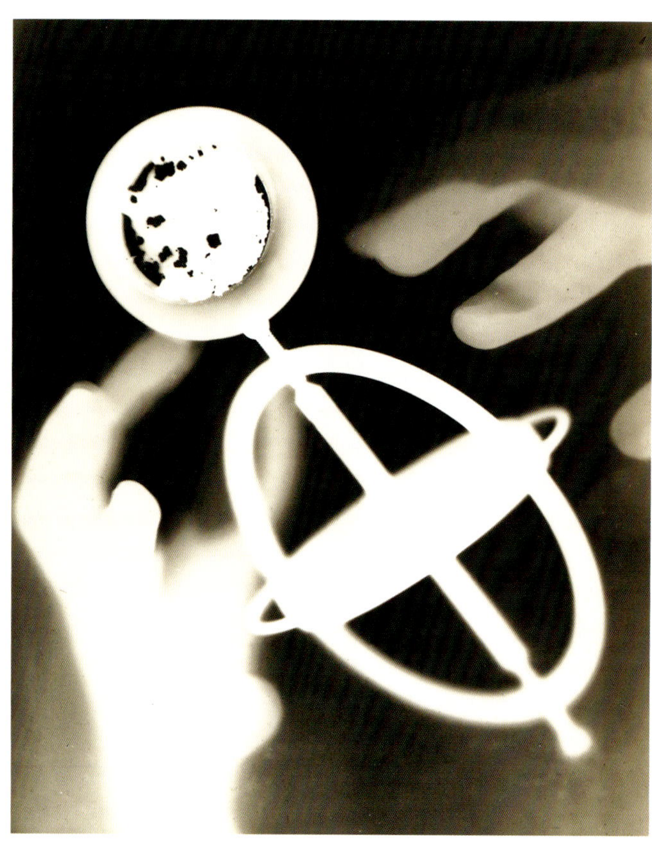

Fig. 22. Plate 4 from *Les champs délicieux (Fields of Delight)*, 1922. Gelatin silver print from rayograph, 8½ × 6¹¹⁄₁₆ in. (21.7 × 17 cm). The Ohio State University Libraries

Despite its diminutive size, barely seven by five inches, *Man Ray 1914* spells out the artist's name and the painting's date in the Cubist manner, with ragged, boldly dark, outsize but constrained letters, bound by the limited space of the canvas. This wry conflation of self-portraiture with the self-referentiality of Cubism—a style that names itself through the undressing of its own painterly means of illusionism—was indeed ironic. For in spelling out his name through the vocabulary of Cubism, Man Ray was mimicking Cubism's self-referential language in order to project his own identity, exclusively within the artistic terms of his persona. Fascinated by a depiction of reality that required the elimination of a fixed vanishing point and with it the illusion of perspective, Man Ray instantly conveys a sense of the whole through the language of Cubism's encoded "surface," preferring over the specificity or identifiability of an individual object in the world its generic or "nominal" qualities. Such nonspecificity would characterize many of his later rayographs, or cameraless photographs, which seemed to proffer an X-ray-like appearance

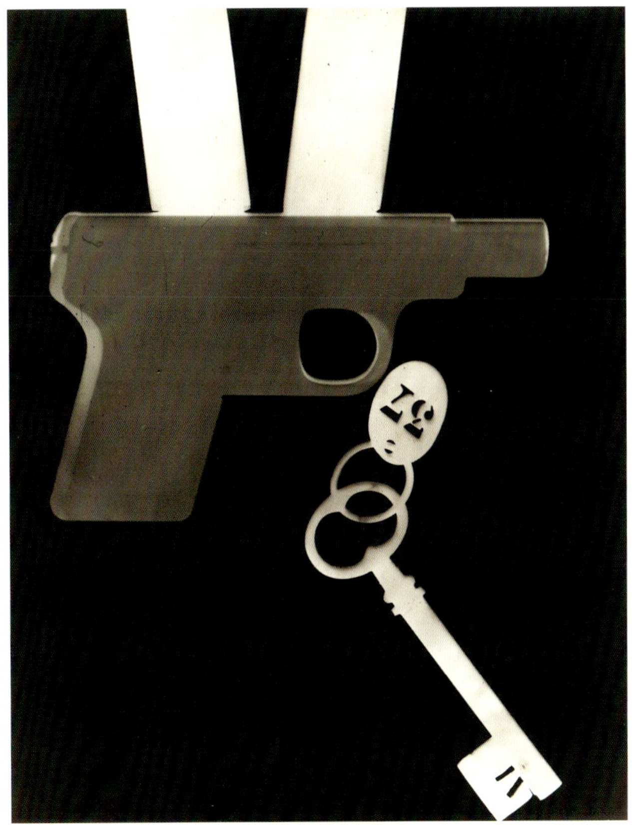

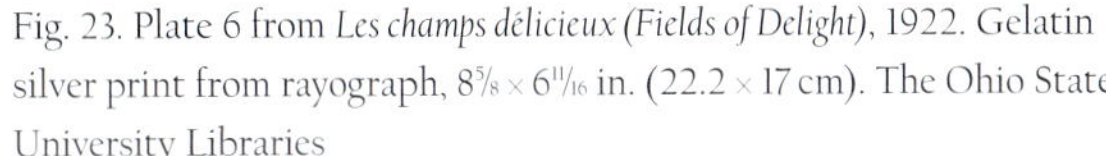

Fig. 23. Plate 6 from *Les champs délicieux (Fields of Delight)*, 1922. Gelatin silver print from rayograph, 8⅝ × 6¹¹⁄₁₆ in. (22.2 × 17 cm). The Ohio State University Libraries

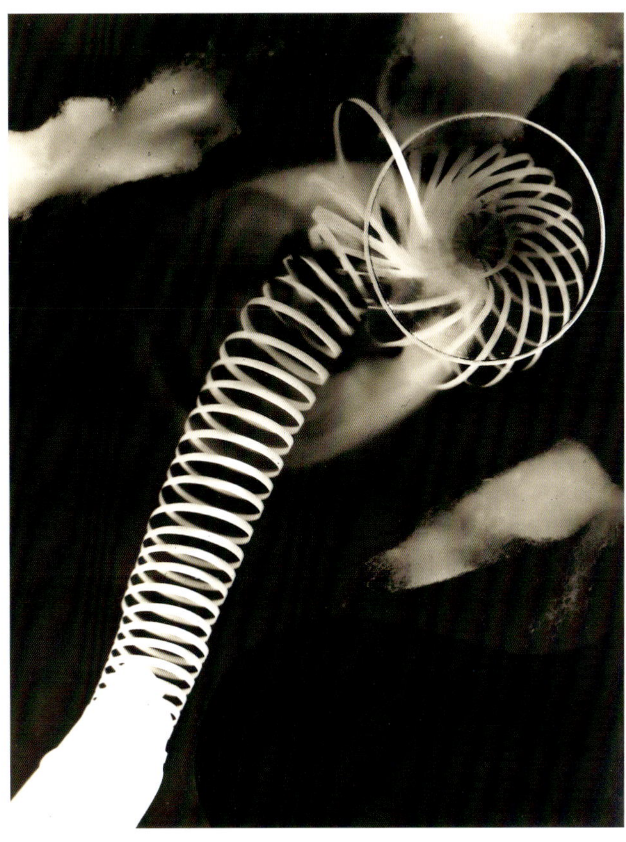

Fig. 24. Plate 8 from *Les champs délicieux (Fields of Delight)*, 1922. Gelatin silver print from rayograph, 8⅝ × 6¹¹⁄₁₆ in. (22.2 × 17 cm). The Ohio State University Libraries

but rendered only a trace of their subjects' forms (figs. 22–25). Moreover, with *Man Ray 1914*'s specific typography referring to his dual artistic concerns, as well as Cubism's vernacular use of language—which he had seen at the Armory Show months before, in Georges Braque's 1912 *L'affiche de Kubelick (Le violon)*—Man Ray was dramatically, albeit modestly, "making his mark on cubism."[36]

In projecting his name and date from the promontory of the Palisades in New Jersey, from the cliffs that face New York, it was as if the artist were proclaiming as defiantly as possible his new artistic persona from deep within the bedrock of his environment, the predominantly literary artists' colony in Ridgefield. In its humble dimensions, *Man Ray 1914* (see fig. 3) is a powerful expression of equivalence between the uncertainty and violence of a world suddenly engaged in war and the disquieting, if not cataclysmic, experience of individuation that the young Man Ray was experiencing. It signaled his freedom from a

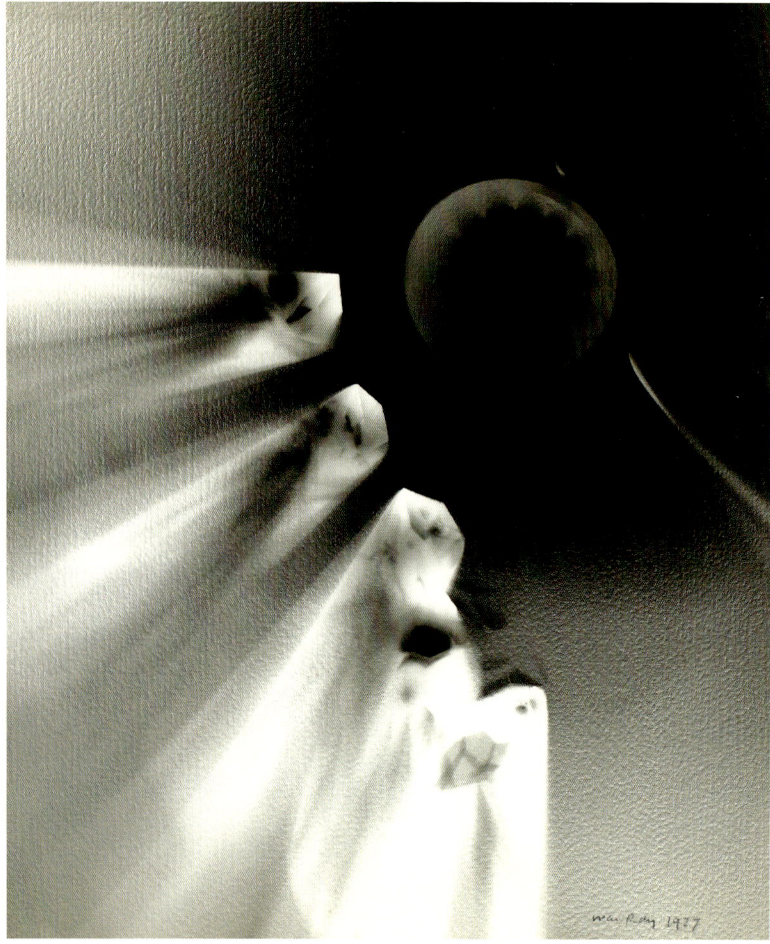

Fig. 25. *Rayograph*, 1927. Gelatin silver print, 11¹⁵⁄₁₆ × 9¹⁵⁄₁₆ in. (30.3 × 25.2 cm). Museum of Fine Arts, Houston, Museum purchase with funds provided by the Caroline Wiess Law Accessions Endowment Fund, Manfred Heiting Collection

prescribed past and a proscribed future (his family's unhappiness with his chosen career), through his nominal emergent artist persona, and within a little more than a year of leaving his family home and marrying the Belgian poet Adon Lacroix.[37]

The emotional impact of his new coalescing life—as an artist, now with his own "family"—resonates in this modest canvas, as Man Ray underscores his need to break with the past, betraying his late-adolescent rebellion in rejecting his family and its Old World culture, and replaces it with his own separate, insular reality. The painting's dramatic upheaval of ground conveys not only the indeterminate future of the world but the timorous tremors that plagued the artist, who was on the verge of exposing himself to criticism, the psychological drama he would soon allegorize in *The Rope Dancer*. Therefore, inasmuch as *Man Ray 1914* serves as a defiant statement of youthful idealism and hope, the deceptive grandiosity of its signature masks the artist's personal insecurity as he sets out on a path that he seems to intuit will be difficult.

It is this convergence of the private and the public that is given eloquent expression in *Man Ray 1914*, whose incisive typographical letters and mottled shadowing define both the towering cliffs of New Jersey and Man Ray's incipient presence in the world as bona fide artist and writer. His new, unsteady "signature" identity nevertheless bellows cataclysmically during wartime, its fortitude outweighing its stature, barely contained within its tight confines.

the long **e**xposure

While Man Ray was a restless individual, always on the move, incessantly hunting for things, jotting down ideas, fiddling about, drawing, it is less a fidgety restlessness than a furtive presence that certain portraits of him evoke.[38] One of the earliest known of these, an extremely rare image of the young artist, is a photograph presumed to have been taken by Alfred Stieglitz (fig. 26).[39] The work foreshadows Man Ray's later series of self-portraits that serve to idiosyncratically document him—an elusive presence—in the world at large. While the date of this photograph has been variously estimated, it presents, according to the artist's memoir, the young Manny Radnitzky in about 1912, the year that he and his brother, Sam, both still living at home, decided together that their Russian name was a particular encumbrance as they sought employment, and so decided to shorten it to Ray.[40]

For Man Ray, it was the beginning of a period of momentous transition; frustrated by the various limitations his family posed as he sought to develop and become an artist, he was deeply aware of his need to get away. In Stieglitz's photograph, he is caught leaning slightly to his right, just enough to be partially outside the picture frame. This tilt and breach of boundary produce an ambiguous

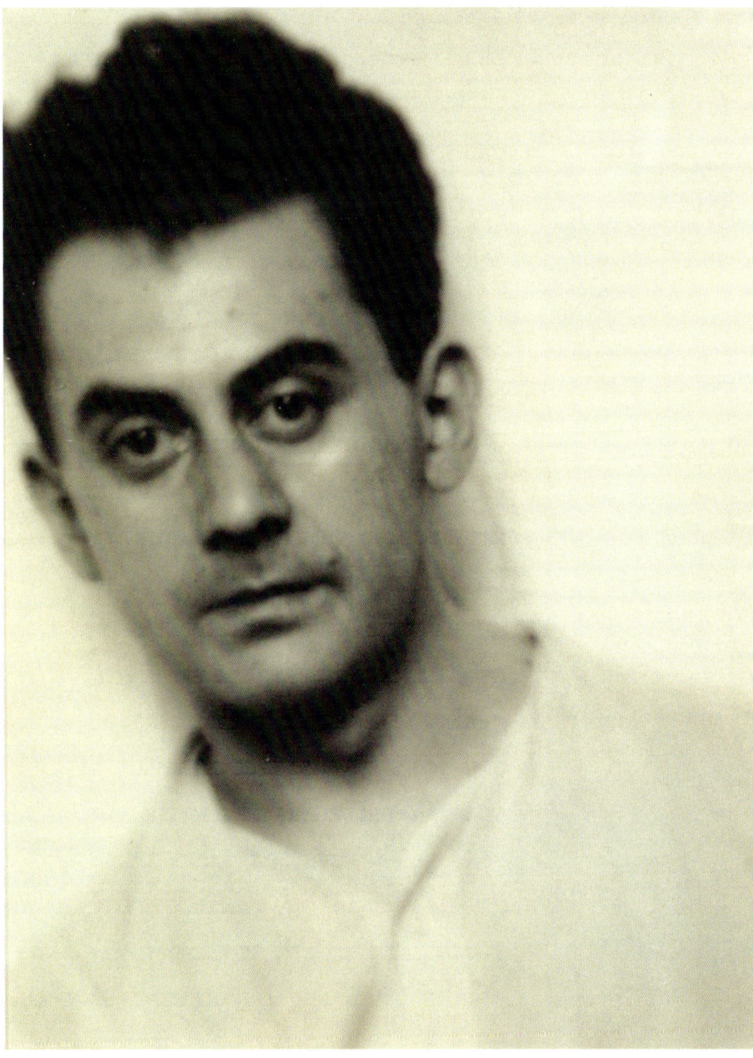

Fig. 26. Attributed to Alfred Stieglitz (American, 1864–1946). *Portrait of Man Ray*, c. 1915. Gelatin silver print, 11 × 8 in. (27.9 × 20.3 cm). Tokyo Fuji Art Museum

effect that can be read as either impatience, a result perhaps of the long exposure that Stieglitz needed, or a response to the camera's "mystery and source of intimidation," which the artist said he felt "before he took up photography."[41] It was surely one of his earliest serious encounters with the camera, certainly with portraiture, and with an esteemed older artist whose worldly mentorship we know impressed him. Indubitably, it is the episode that he recalls in *Self Portrait*, when on one of his lunch-hour visits to the stretch of galleries on Fifth Avenue, he stopped in at his favorite, Stieglitz's little gallery, 291, named after its numerical address on the avenue. Man Ray's description signals the importance of the episode:

> When no one else was in the gallery, he [Stieglitz] set up his old camera on its rickety tripod, asking me to stand in front against the wall. The gallery was small, but quite light with its neutral walls and muslin-screened skylight. He told me the exposure would be rather long, but to keep looking at the camera; I might blink my eyes, it wouldn't matter nor show. He produced a hoop stretched with cheesecloth, uncapped his lens, and began waving the hoop over my head, moving about like a dancer, watching me closely. It lasted about ten seconds. I have since seen photographers with more modern instruments shooting at one hundredth of a second, perform similar gymnastics, but before making the exposure. With Stieglitz, it was simultaneous and synchronized.[42]

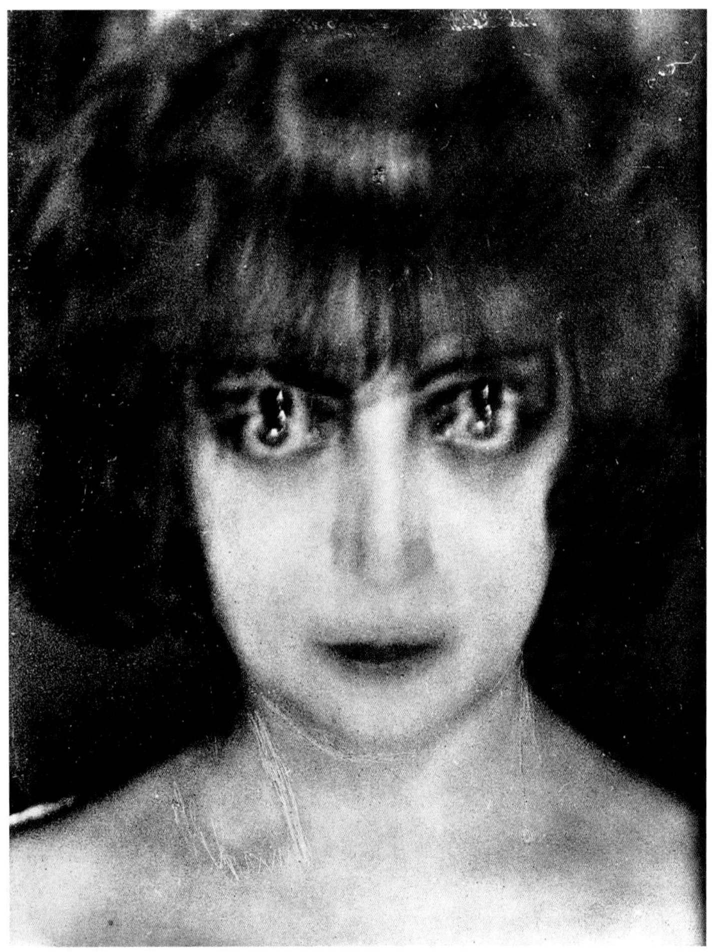

In his recollection, Man Ray is fascinated by the performance aspect of Stieglitz's technique. He did not adopt it as a portraitist himself, being, on the contrary, particularly unobtrusive and fluid in his manner, but the residue of the social interaction of such practice remained (figs. 27–29). Lasting, too, was Stieglitz's precedent of putting photography on a par with painting (although Man Ray would downgrade photography's mechanical aspect), of elevating the standard for the medium through experimentation, and of course simply the fact of having his portrait taken. For this need to chronicle himself, as he evolved from the "timid, unsocial, and bewildered young man, groping in the dark" to the dapper cosmopolitan disclosing his entrée within the fashion world, would be displayed in the innumerable self-portraits he produced.[43]

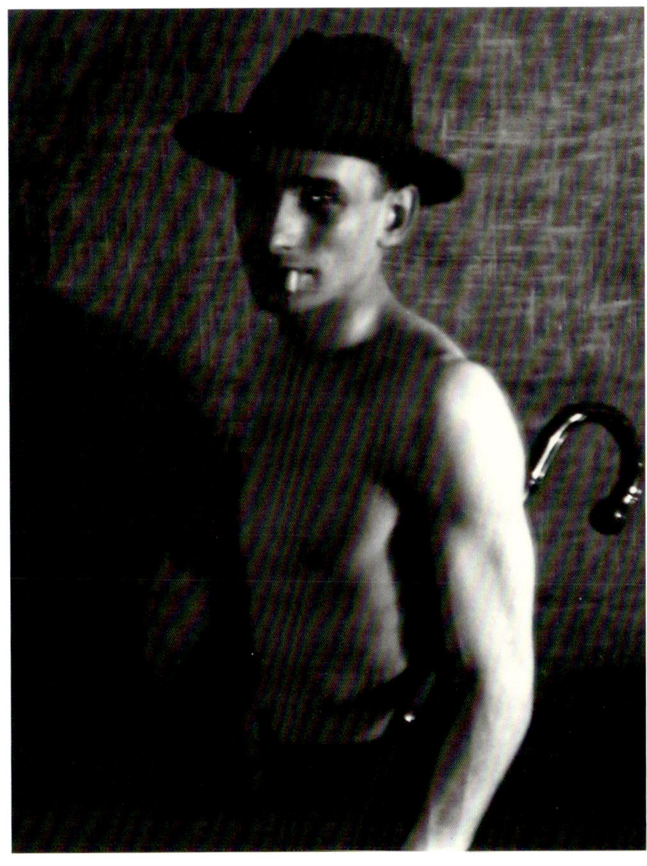

What Stieglitz's photograph finally reveals, in catching the young artist faintly ill at ease, inclined outside the picture frame, and slightly out of focus—the blur softening the youthful inquisitiveness of his face—is Man Ray's timidity and insecurity. This latter aspect hints at his guarded nature, as someone who soon would perform his own kind of gymnastics, constructing an artistic persona and allegorically staging his own constitution of identity, as he began to differentiate the private from the public. It was to such circumscription that Man Ray refused to submit. And it is just this subtle sense of privacy, bordering on a desire not to be seen, that Stieglitz's photograph tellingly captures.

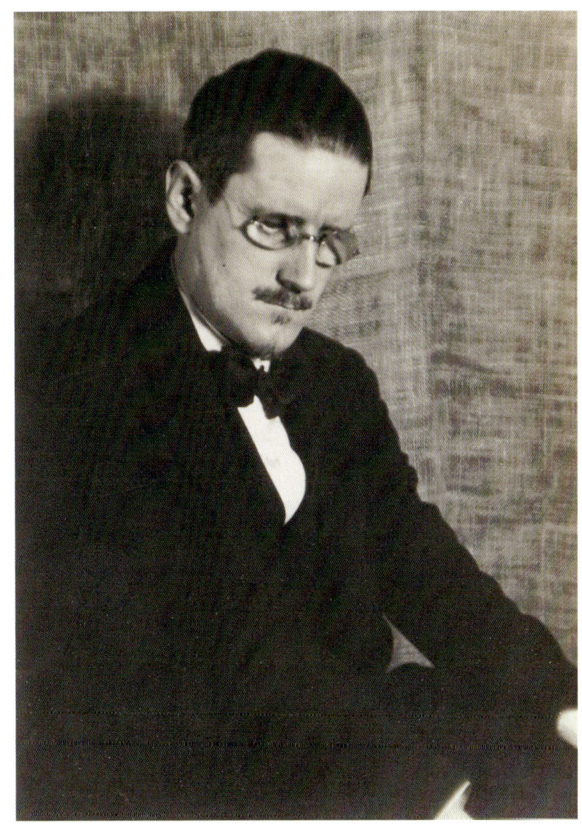

One sees an even more explicit depiction of the artist's veiled identity in another portrait, made some two decades later. A 1934 ink drawing by Picasso convincingly shows that Man Ray did not outgrow this inward aspect (fig. 30). Man Ray met Picasso in Paris in the early 1920s, when, for lack of any other source of income, he photographed other artists' works. He documented a number of Picasso's pre-Cubist canvases and subsequently maintained a cordial relationship with him. Picasso was one of Man Ray's idols; the Spaniard's work had awed him since he had first seen it at 291, and Picasso inspired the fantasy of a different kind of existence in the world. Man Ray identified with Picasso's single-mindedness about art, but he saw him, too, as so many others have, as "a man who was aware of all that was going on about him and in the world in general . . . who reacted violently to all impacts, but had only one outlet to express his feelings: painting."[44] Although one could say that both artists never stopped chronicling their lives, their manner of being and of registering their experience could not have been more antithetical. Picasso's sovereign confidence and autonomy permitted him to be emotionally open and physically present in a way that the cautious, defended Man Ray could never be. Picasso unconsciously engaged the world, voraciously recording each moment as he phenomenologically experienced it; upon seeing a photograph he would realistically reproduce it, and then repaint it in any manner of style. The philosophical Man Ray was, by contrast, analytical, self-conscious, one who mulled over his art; he was personally invested in it, one might say, in an entirely different light.

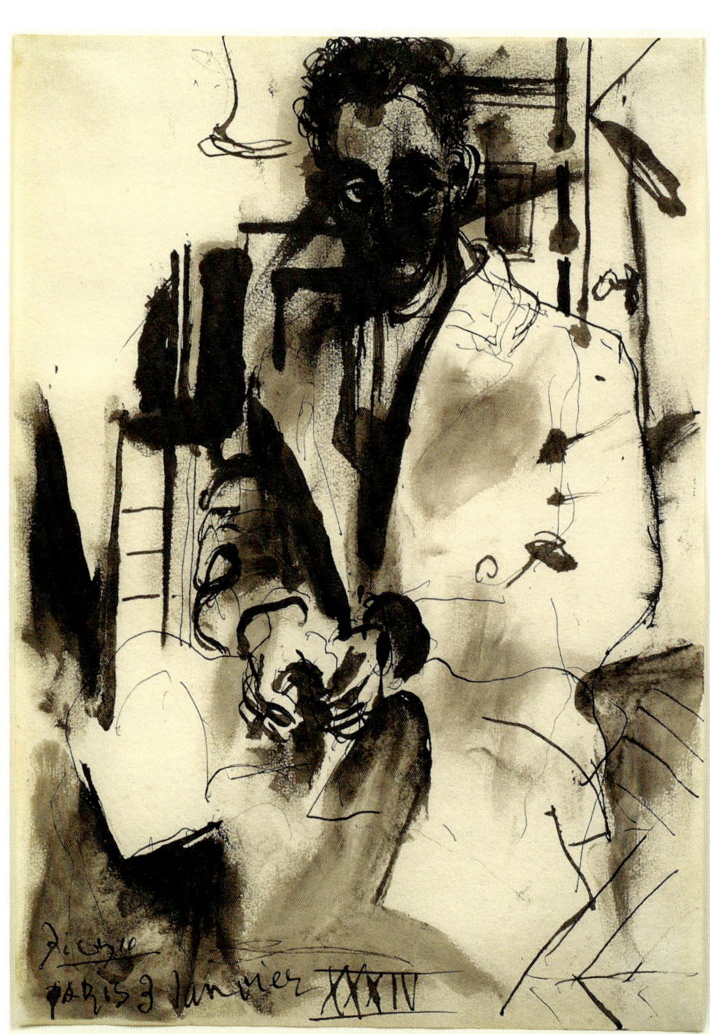

Fig. 30. Pablo Picasso (Spanish, 1881–1973). *Portrait of Man Ray*, 1934. India ink on paper, 13⅝ × 9¾ in. (34.5 × 24.8 cm). The Kantor Collection, Beverly Hills, California

Picasso, who, according to Man Ray, "never forgot anything" and always reciprocated a favor, offered to make a drawing of him for his forthcoming *Photographs by Man Ray 1920 Paris 1934*, a book that would be "as close to a straight autobiographical résumé as he had ever come."[45] The resulting pen-and-ink work presented the American artist as hidden, seen through a pall of blotted ink. In *Self Portrait*, the observant Man Ray, whose own memory would selectively lapse with frequency, recalls the incident in detail, and touches on the uncanny truthfulness of the portrait: "I liked the idea that [Picasso] had struggled with this one—besides, it had much of me in it, standing there in my overcoat—a good deal of me—any unpracticed eye could see that, especially an unpracticed eye could see it."[46]

Reading Man Ray's wry response to this portrait, one wonders what a *practiced* eye might have seen. But the question of not being "seen" had always been the point, as both an unwanted and a desirable thing. Here, despite the obscuration that Picasso had intuitively sensed was a part of Man Ray's psyche, smudging the drawing almost to the point of enshrouding his subject, Man Ray ignores the possibility that this was intentional, jokingly commenting that even—and especially—an "unpracticed" eye, unused to the linear clarity that Picasso could exercise brilliantly with ease, might still discern that the subject was Man Ray. For this was the central paradox of Man Ray's work: Just as smoothly as he could conceal the truth from others, some- times the truth could elude him. One can only suspect the significance the portrait had for him, given the requited ink drawing Man Ray made of Picasso in 1955, more than twenty years after the fact, replete with splotched face.

The question of opacity or a ten- dency to withdraw or withhold, and not fulfill the viewer's expectations, was one that Man Ray had addressed in numerous works in New York before leaving for Paris, most notably in what has been called the "first proto-Dada assemblage," a work that also intro- duced his audacious wit. *Self-Portrait* (1916), Man Ray's first publicly exhib- ited assemblage, now lost, was fortu- nately reproduced in a photograph after it appeared in his second show at the Daniel Gallery, in January 1917 (fig. 31). One of the earliest "assemblages," *Self- Portrait* marked a departure for the artist, not only in its fusion of found object and painting, but also in its man- ner of defiance of artistic expectation. "*Self-Portrait* was the butt of much jok- ing," the artist later recalled. "On a background of black and aluminum

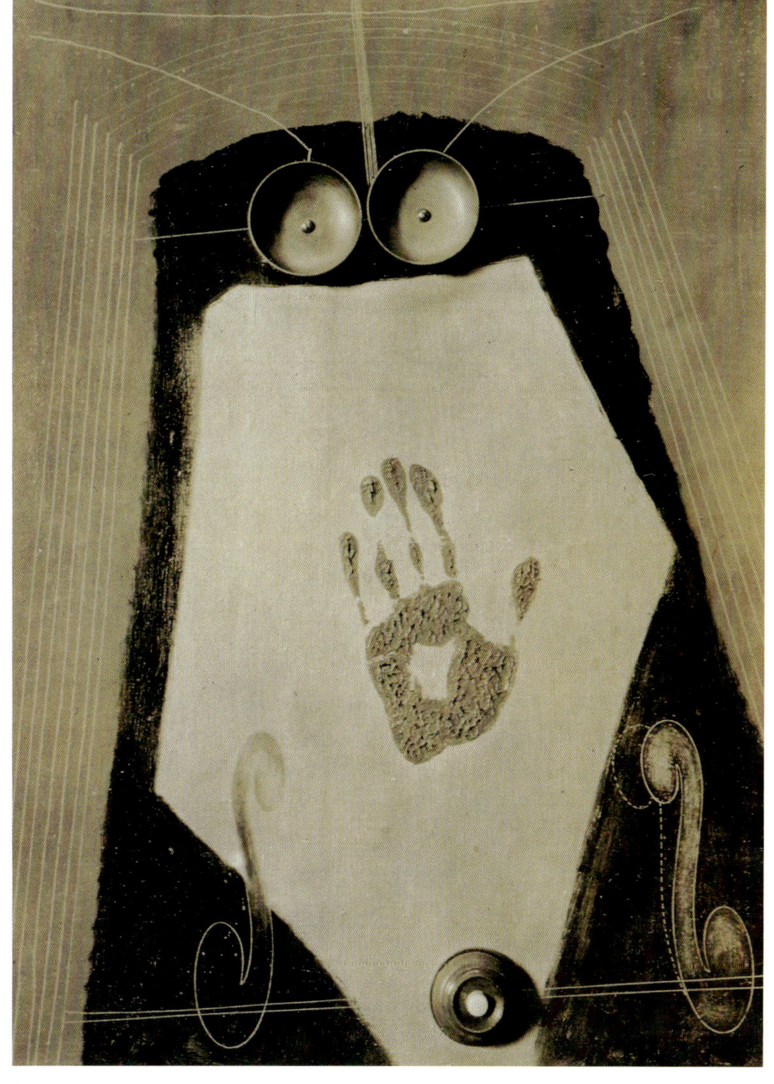

Fig. 31. *Self-Portrait,* 1916. Gelatin silver print, 3¾ × 2¾ in. (9.5 × 7 cm). J. Paul Getty Museum, Los Angeles

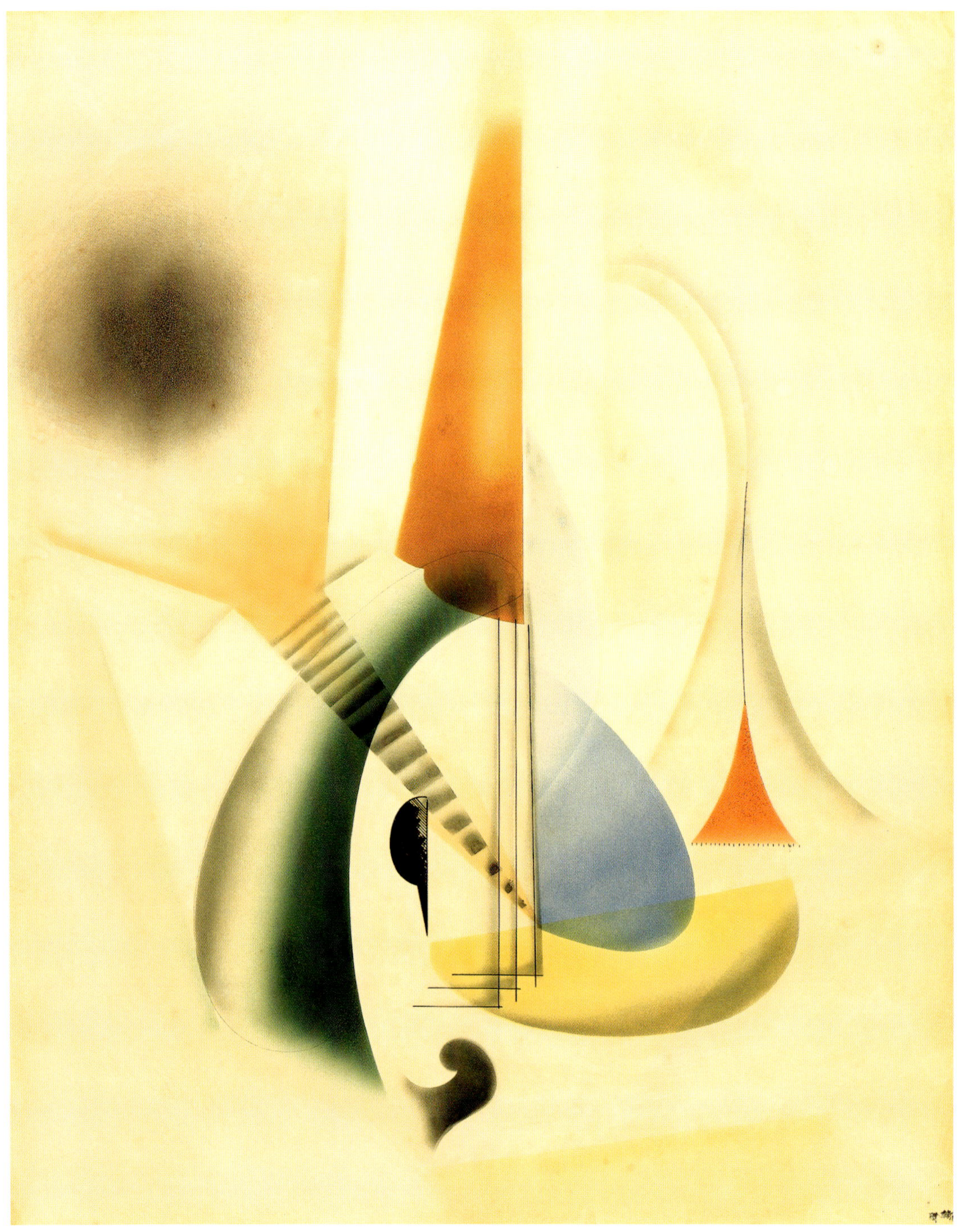

paint I had attached two electric bells and a real push
button. In the middle, I had simply put my hand on the
palette and transferred the paint imprint as a signa-
ture. Everyone who pushed the button was disappointed that the bell did not ring."[47]

Beyond this proto-Dada engagement of the spectator, it is the insignia of the individual, an imprint of the artist's hand at the doorway and threshold of the work, denying
any illusory passage beyond that point, that provides the significant meaning. This pregnant "gesture" ostensibly confirms Man Ray's ongoing concern with the "flat plane on

which the elements [of painting] are brought to play, linking these absolute qualities directly to his wit, imagination and experience, without the go-between of a 'subject.'" But it also suggests, along with another work from this period, *Painting with Hand Imprint*, that the go-between might be the artist himself. This is particularly true in the case of the self-portrait, where Man Ray's resolve to withdraw further, and more important, to do so through the surrogate signature of his artistic persona—equating the French word for "hand," or *main*, phonetically, with his own name, "Man"—assumes an emblematic resonance.[48]

The silent bell and the hand are symbolic of a resistance that would prove far more adamant than the mere refusal to yield to an illusionistic space. The failure of the painting to satisfy, to deliver the goods, rang a new, albeit conceptual, bell, signaling a reversed set of terms: in ambiguously representing a handprint, emblematic of the individual, the artist was in fact withholding it, distancing the hand and thus privileging idea over craft, as well as anonymity over identification. And by calling such a work a self-portrait, Man Ray was proclaiming just how difficult, yet important, such an enterprise was for him.

What Man Ray was distancing himself from was a direct and transparent presence in the act of painting, a process of detachment that would intensify with the use of an airbrush in his aerographs (figs. 32 and 33). These have been viewed in terms of his progression toward a Dada-oriented sensibility, Duchamp's influence becoming evident in the shift toward a more mechanical approach to art, deemphasizing the retinal in favor of the conceptual, promoting the idea as the foundation of his art. The combination of found objects and painting in the 1916 *Self-Portrait* may have created confusion, but moreover, it encouraged certain expectations on the part of viewers, and then failed to deliver.

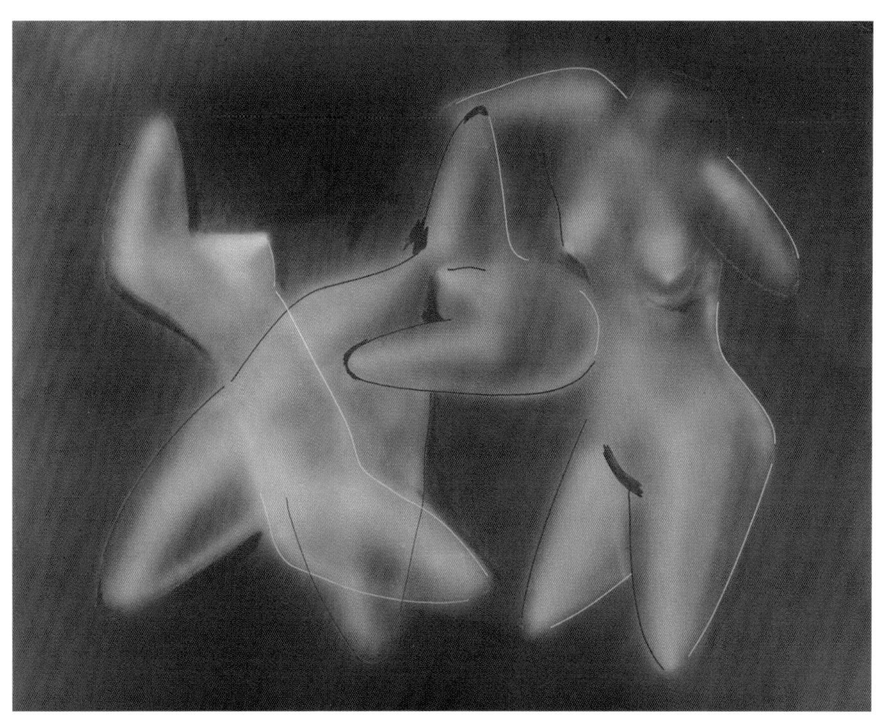

Fig. 33. *Preconception of Violetta*, or *Nudes* (lost airbrush painting), 1919. Gelatin silver print, 8¹¹/₁₆ × 10¹³/₁₆ in. (22.4 × 27.5 cm). Private collection, France

While exhibiting all of Man Ray's concerns at the time with the confinement of two-dimensionality, *Self-Portrait* was also probably the first serious articulation of his overarching narrative of privacy.

But two-dimensionality was also a theoretical preoccupation. In a rather ambitious effort, the artist privately published his formalist principles in a pamphlet he hand-printed

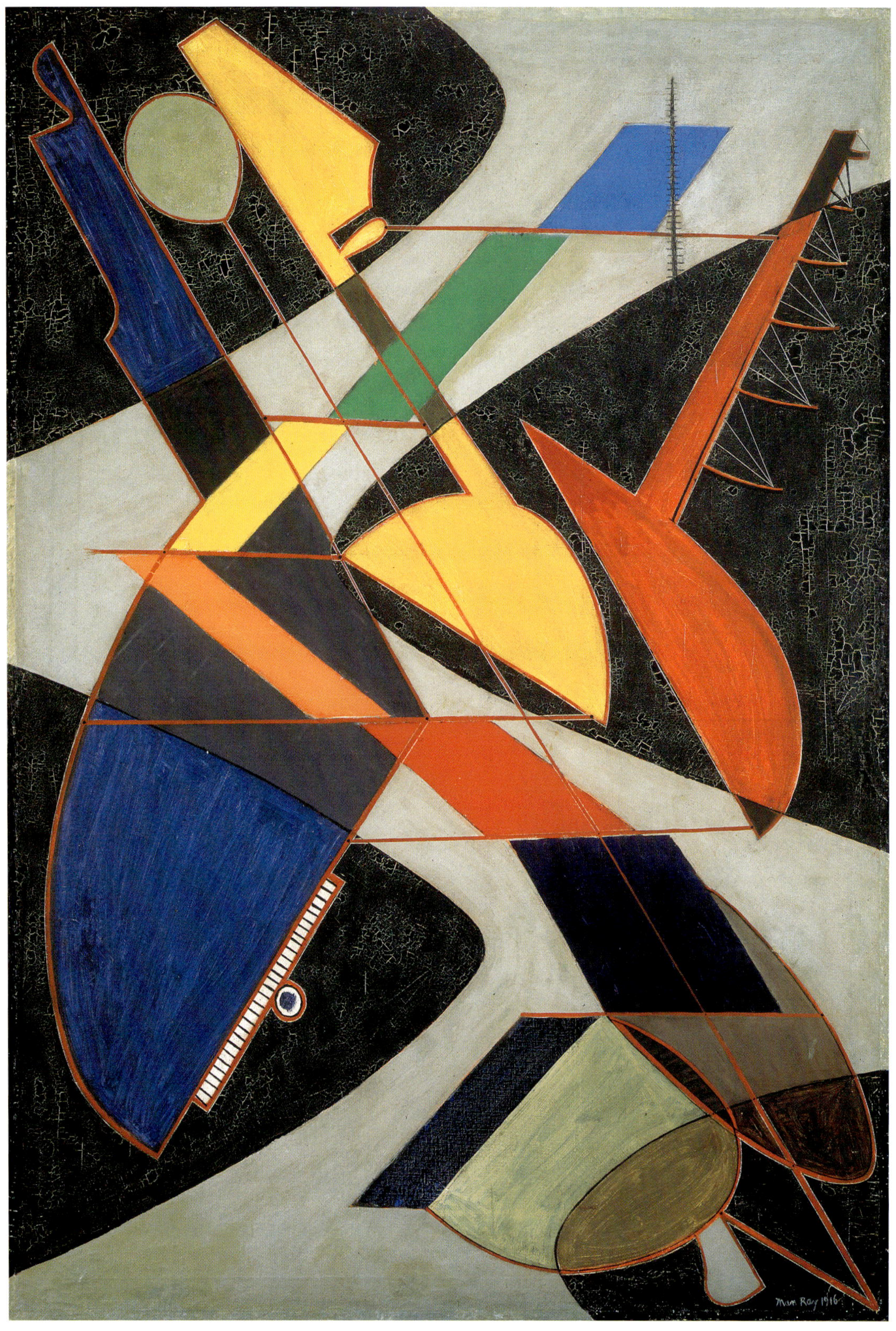

Fig. 34. *Symphony Orchestra*, 1916. Oil on canvas, 52 × 36 in. (132.1 × 91.4 cm). Albright-Knox Art Gallery, Buffalo, George B. and Jenny R. Mathews Fund, 1970

in 1916, *A Primer of the New Art of Two Dimensions.* According to the *Primer,* all the arts—the "static" (painting, sculpture, architecture) and the "dynamic" (music, dance, literature)— could be related and understood in terms of their adaptability to two dimensions. Without contemplating Man Ray's efforts to define in formalist terms an equivalency within the arts, it is clear that he was seeking to structurally align them. And this synthesizing impulse and its manner of implementation are relevant here, for the idealistic notions that propelled his formalist inquisition, and his efforts to interrelate the arts—as in *Symphony Orchestra* (1916; fig. 34) or *Dance* (1915)—were rooted in his desire, at a time of extraordinary political and social upheaval, for global rapport through the arts. Such fervent idealism was described in a later interview, in which he reminisced about feeling how "wonderful [it would be] to do paintings like music, that are abstract, that would be immediately accepted, understood by all nations."[49]

These ideas scarcely originated from home.[50] But one of his first artistic statements, a patchwork quilt titled *Tapestry,* clearly did (1911; fig. 35). Man Ray would increasingly, albeit indirectly, refer to his childhood environment, and *Tapestry,* made just before he left his family home in Brooklyn, is perhaps the initial generative work in this regard, emerging as it did from the random scraps of textiles culled from his father's cutting-room floor. This patchwork quilt cum abstract painting, composed of 110 sample swatches of fabric— "readymade" designs, from tattersall to pinstripe to plaid, arranged in checkerboard squares and measuring more than fifteen square feet—represents not just the beginning of an unending resourcefulness of using materials at hand, but a symbolic rejection of the utilitarian in favor of the artistic. As such, the work assumes a definite significance, intimating Man Ray's serious painterly aspirations: he pinned his quilt to a sheet of canvas and signed it "Man Ray, 1911," as if to consecrate his first foray into abstraction and the subtle and shifting transitions of color from dark to light.[51] Within this integral shading one can discern the kind of abstracted figurative form, with arms raised, that would soon turn up in paintings, such as *Dance* or *Black Widow* (1915), that directly engage the ambiguous function of the shadow. This early and abstracted kernel of a two-dimensional figure, whose mirrored, or symmetrical, component anticipates the ulterior presence of other figures or of shadows (soon to be a signature preoccupation), suggests the symbolic weight that the latter accrue in Man Ray's work. Here, however, on the brink of his artistic emergence, Man Ray's mirrored reversal of the shading of the central figurative form suggests his quest for liberation as an artist. Indeed, the idealism embodied in *Tapestry* prefigures the idealism conveyed by *Dance* and other paintings of the 1910s. But despite the symbolism of that painting's title and Man Ray's then-hopeful wish for universal understanding of such forms, the registration and integration of the central figure and its shadow are far more complicated.

As notably engaged as Man Ray was at this time with exploring a theoretical program that would integrate the arts according to his *Primer,* his interest in their merging was likewise more complicated. The complexity would gradually manifest itself in his princi-

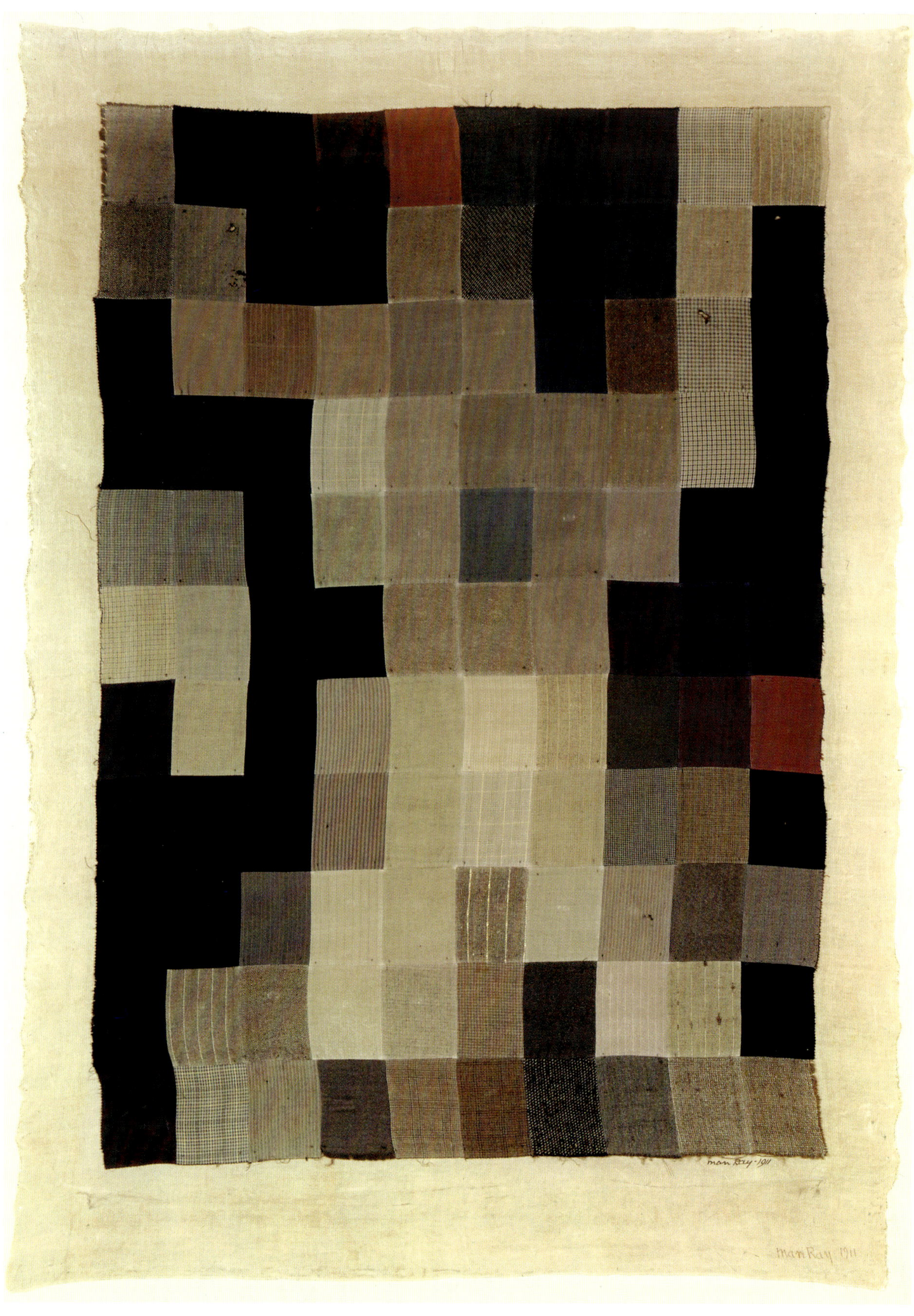

Fig. 35. *Tapestry*, 1911. Patchwork sewn on canvas, 82⅝ × 59¾ in. (210 × 151.8 cm). Musée national d'art moderne, Centre Pompidou, Paris

pal focus, on writing and art. The accomplished union of the two, achieved with his literary muse and wife, Adon Lacroix, is apparent in several of their collaborations. Man Ray's wish to evolve a literary/artistic form, "to confuse the arts," reflects his own need to defy categorical distinction, to constantly de-differentiate, to merge.

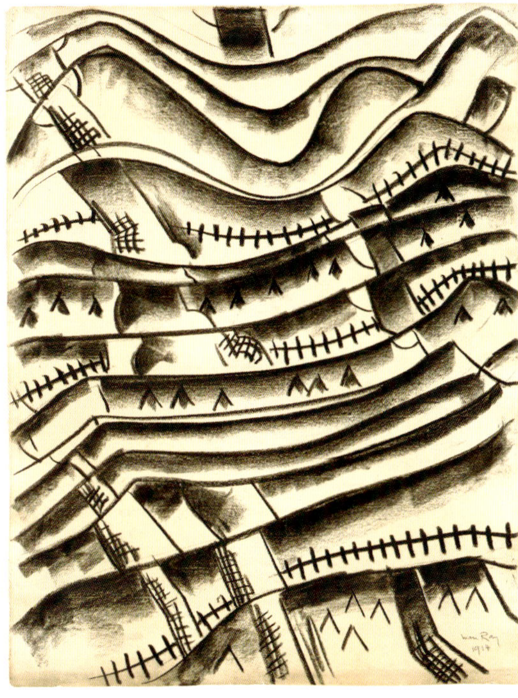

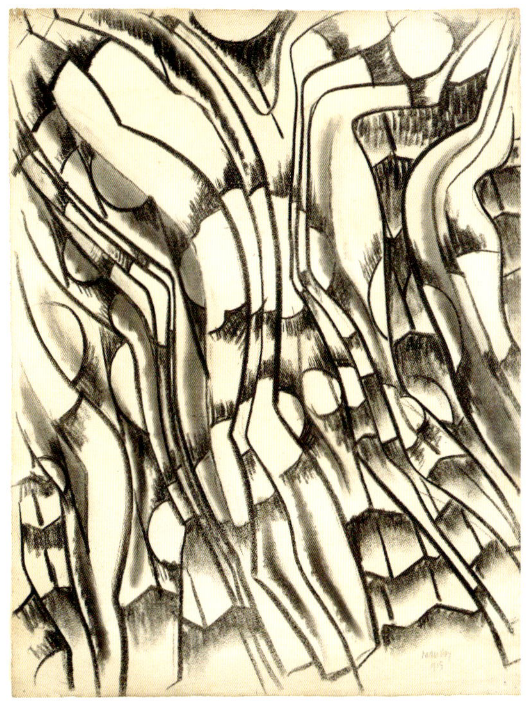

Fig. 36. *Ridgefield Landscape*, 1914. Charcoal on paper, 24¼ × 18¼ in. (61.8 × 47.8 cm). The Museum of Modern Art, New York, The Riklis Collection of McCrory Corporation

Fig. 37. *Untitled*, 1915. Charcoal on paper, 24⅛ × 18¼ in. (62 × 47.6 cm). The Museum of Modern Art, New York, Mr. and Mrs. Donald B. Straus Fund

Camouflage

Man Ray's withdrawal, or disappearance, within his work can be traced through various phases and iterations. The phenomenon of psychic and physical absorption in his art is enacted in numerous paintings from his Ridgefield period that contain a degree of dissolution of the body. As the artist would admit years later, in another Museum of Modern Art questionnaire, his earlier figurative studies had become absorbed within his landscapes, as can be seen in the drawings *Ridgefield Landscape* (1914; fig. 36) and *Untitled* (1915; fig. 37). This assimilation or loss of the body within its environs occurs in various ways. The psychic dimension, the artist's tendency to lose himself in his relationships, is nowhere more evident than in his conflation of himself and Lacroix, in *Dual Portrait* (1913; fig. 38), now lost, where Man Ray conflates his face with hers, and furthermore depicts their union within what appears to be her womb. Or the body is gradually absorbed within the environment, subtly at first, as in *Woman Asleep* (1913; fig. 39), in which Lacroix's silhouette assumes a terrainlike contour, her shoulder a steep outcropping, her hair a pond. In *Ramapo Hills* (1914; fig. 40), one sees a more obvious figurative disassembly, with a solitary, roughly hewn boulder, resembling a face, placed in front of a low range with a loosely figurative form, arm out-

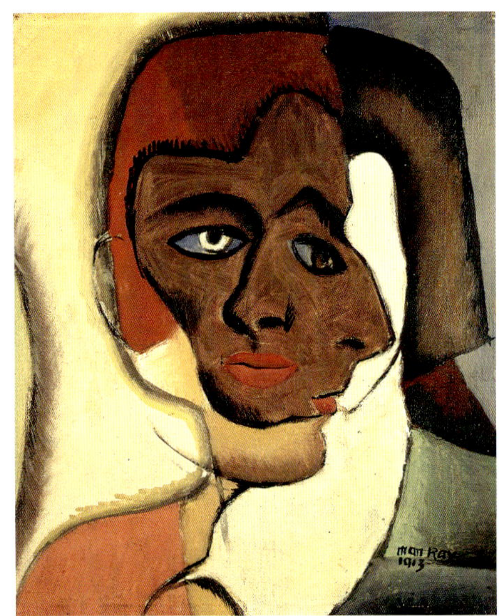

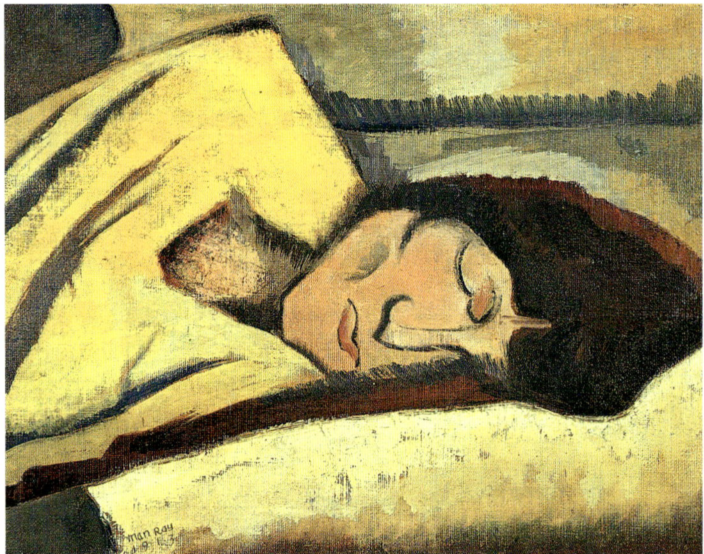

Fig. 38. *Dual Portrait*, 1913.
Oil on canvas, 11¹⁵/₁₆ × 9¹³/₁₆ in.
(30 × 24.9 cm). Present
whereabouts unknown.
Photograph courtesy of
Francis M. Naumann

Fig. 39. *Woman Asleep*, 1913.
Oil on canvas, 12 × 16 in.
(30.5 × 40.6 cm). Whitney
Museum of American Art,
New York, Purchase

Fig. 40. *Ramapo Hills*, 1914.
Oil on canvas, 20 × 19 in.
(50.8 × 48.3 cm). Private
collection, New Jersey

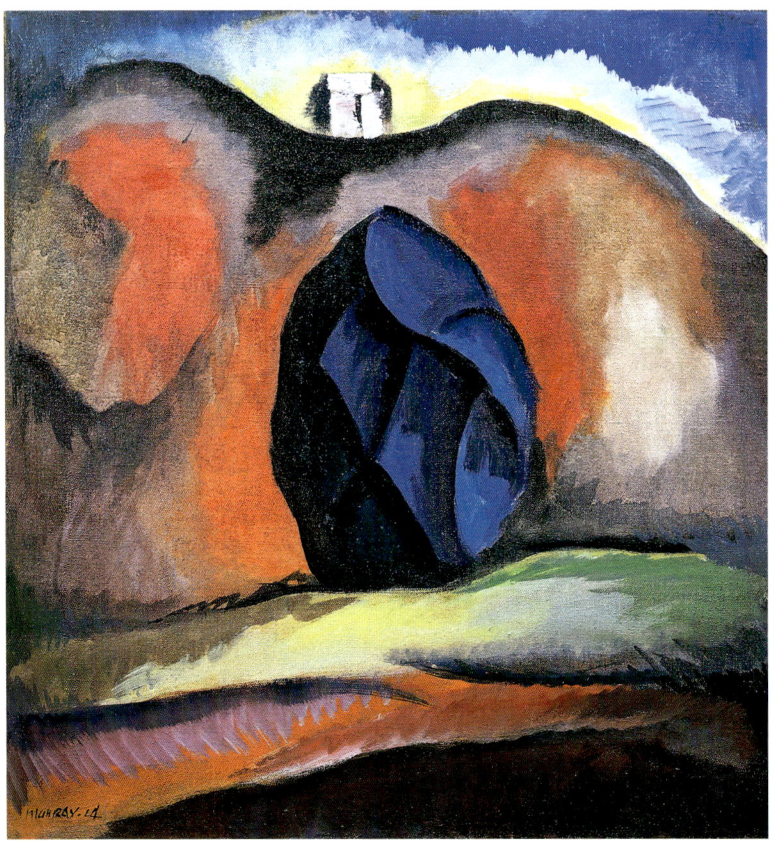

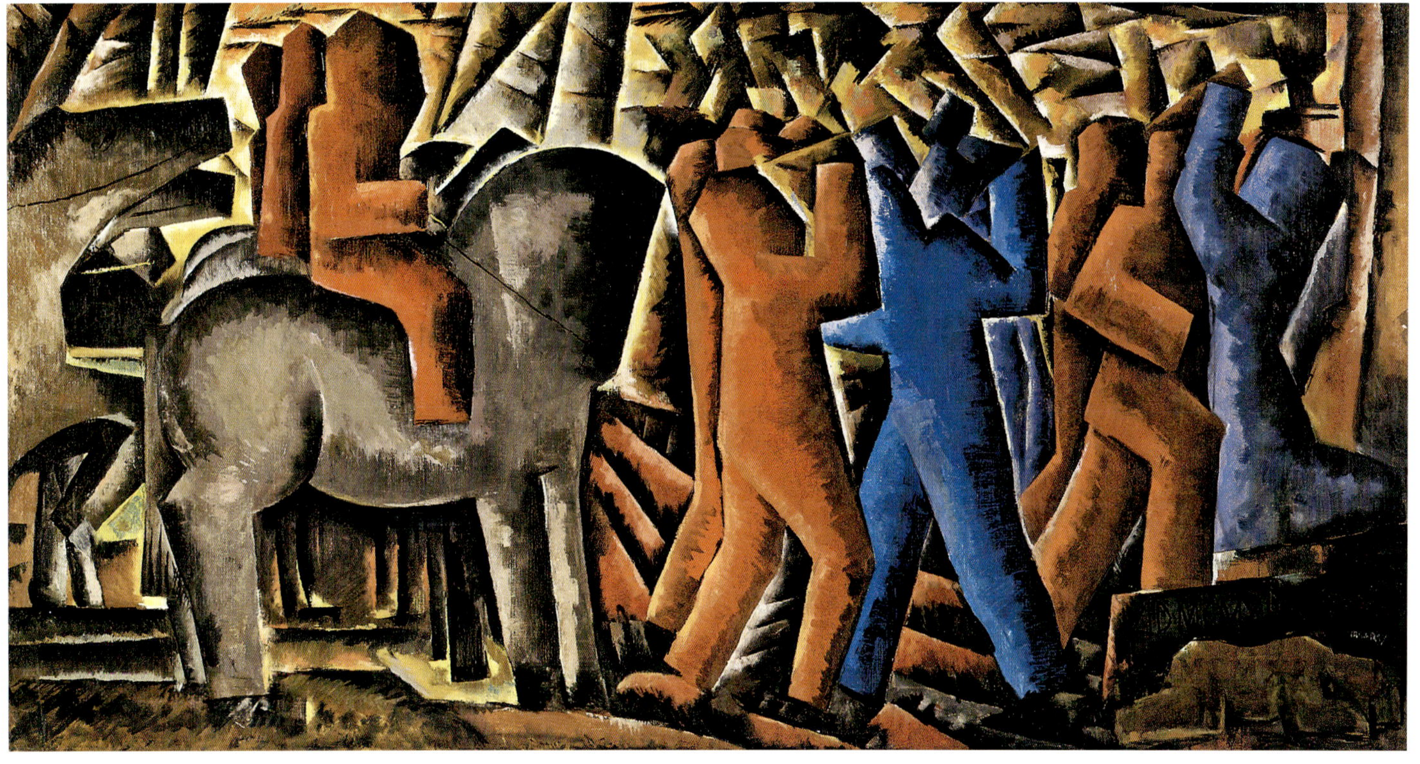

Fig. 41. *War (A.D. MCMXIV)*, 1914. Oil on canvas, 37 × 69½ in. (94 × 175.3 cm). Philadelphia Museum of Art, A. E. Gallatin Collection, 1944

stretched, beyond which a totemic head (similar to the one assuming monumental form in *Totem*, from 1914) peeks out. And in the more Cubist-derived landscapes, such as *The Rug* (1914), the fragmented body is assimilated in a far more random uniting of figuration and landscape.

Throughout the artist's early period, then, one can discern a trajectory that begins with a search for artistic identity and ends with a resolved anonymity: a path whose increasing withdrawal of self initially involves a merging of self with environment, as described above; then becomes a gradual exploration of the art of two dimensions, accompanied by a joining of the visual and the linguistic; and finally proceeds to mimicry and camouflage, forms of defense found throughout nature, and to assimilation (as in Man Ray's various stylistic adoptions of the European avant-garde).[52] This last modality develops suddenly into a much subtler adaption of figuration to landscape, in which the self becomes "other," not just merging with nature but also breaking down in a bodily repetition or disintegration within nature, as in *War (A.D. MCMXIV)* (1914; fig. 41) or *The Rug*. Here one can perceive a tug-of-war between figure and ground, as if the sanctity of each had to be equally recognized.

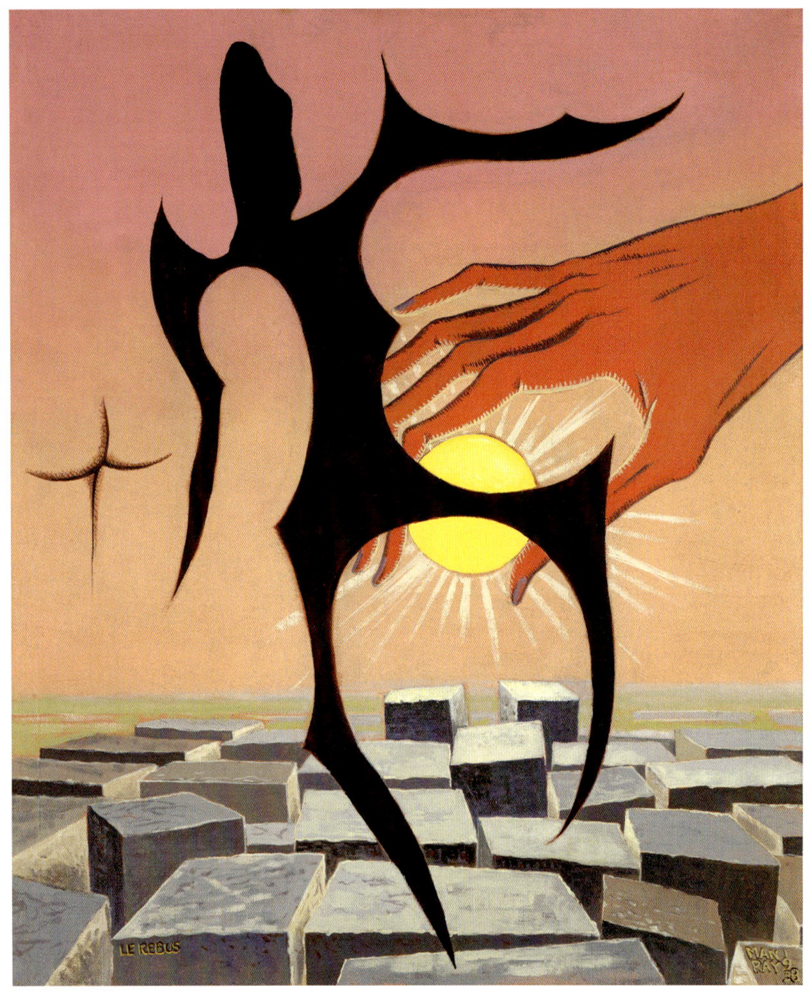

Fig. 42. *Le rebus*, 1938. Oil on canvas, 21⅝ × 18⅛ in. (55 × 46 cm). Musée national d'art moderne, Centre Pompidou, Paris

An altogether different kind of anatomical dispersion would surface in the late 1930s, as Europe headed toward a second war and the artist began to feel closed in, fearing the inevitable exposure of his identity. Such persecutory horror is doubly registered through the figure's literal constitution as negative space, as in the painting *Le rebus* (1938; fig. 42), a nightmarish reversal of reality that dramatizes Man Ray's acute sense of excruciating subjection to external forces, represented by the eroticized anatomical forms that impinge on him.

While Man Ray would continue to use the idea of camouflage, begun with the fusion of landscape and figuration in Ridgefield, he would increasingly include in other works of relative obfuscation or invisibility some form of self-inscription, whose presence within the work suggests his wish for singularity and his refusal of the legitimacy conferred by social inclusion. By adding such an element, if only through his elusive initials, he repeatedly and symbolically marks his identity in a particular way, one that simultaneously frames his artistic paradox: to be someone specific yet unnameable, to parry anonymity with individuality.

of Divers Identities

In one of Man Ray's earliest self-portraits, a 1914 ink drawing he included as the final illustration in *A Book of Divers Writings*, as a pendant to the portrait he rendered of his wife and coauthor, the artist appears reflective but still decisive (figs. 43–45). This emotion clearly differs from the book's opening leaf, an unequivocally anxious rendering of Lacroix, whose dark, frozen eyes convey her anxiety over the war and the status of her family, from whom she had not heard in six months. The book, while a true collaboration, bound to both its creators' pursuits, appears in large measure to have been driven by Man Ray, who generously foregrounded his wife's literary work as if acknowledging her tutelage. For it was through this brief, passionate marriage that Man Ray became a Francophile: Lacroix introduced him to the language and literature of the French avant-garde, reading to him Baudelaire, Mallarmé, Rimbaud, and Apollinaire, whose figurative imagery and melding of image

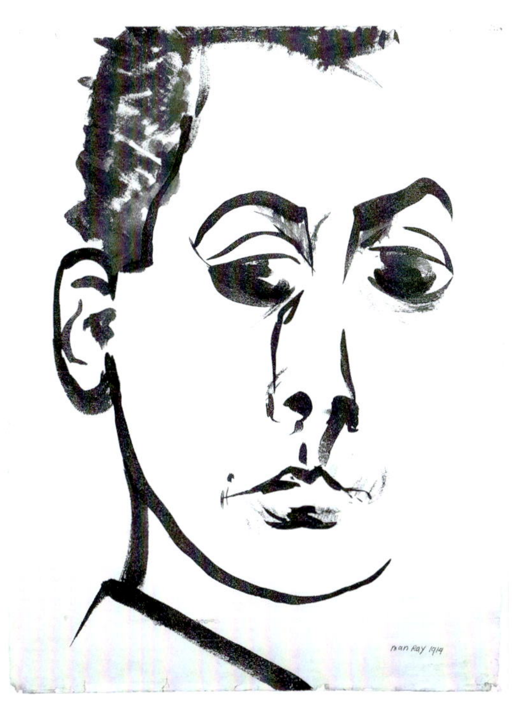

Fig. 43. Title page of *A Book of Divers Writings* (1915) by Adon Lacroix, designed and published by Man Ray. Book, each sheet 18¹¹⁄₁₆ × 12¼ in. (47.5 × 31.1 cm). Philadelphia Museum of Art, Louise and Walter Arensberg Collection

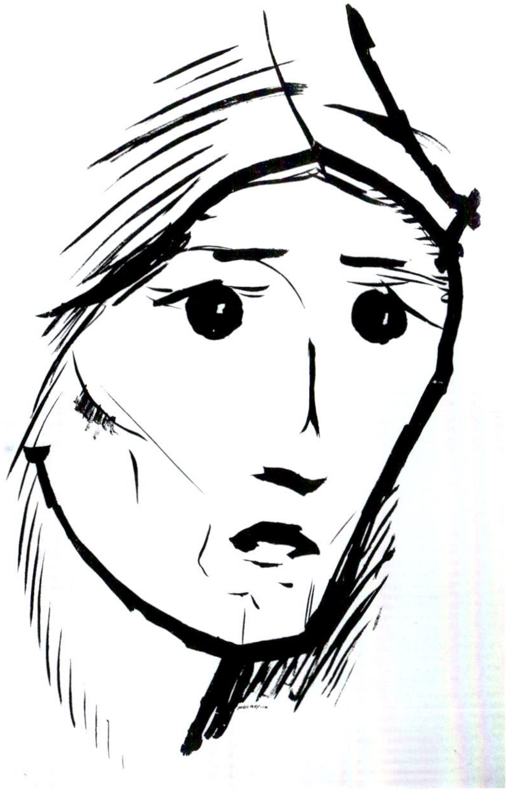

Fig. 44. *Self-Portrait*, 1914. Ink on paper, 24 × 17¾ in. (61 × 45.1 cm). Courtesy of Betsy Wittenborn Miller, New York

Fig. 45. Portrait of Adon Lacroix by Man Ray, from *A Book of Divers Writings* (1915). Book, each sheet 18¹¹⁄₁₆ × 12¼ in. (47.5 × 31.1 cm). Philadelphia Museum of Art, Louise and Walter Arensberg Collection

and word were of particular interest to Man Ray during his sojourn in Ridgefield, where he mingled within a literary milieu. Their ardent collaboration culminated in a carefully produced folio-size publication, featuring Lacroix's prose and poetry and Man Ray's design and illustrations, which he calligraphed and hand-printed.[53] The couple, who would be the subject of an article by their friend and colleague Alfred Kreymborg for the New York *Morning Telegraph* (subtitled "They Live on Twenty-Five Dollars a Month and Enjoy It"), indulged extravagantly in the production of their book, using the finest imported English Whatman paper. *A Book of Divers Writings* represented, in addition to their enraptured union, the synthesis of their work together and the realization of the ideals of the artists' colony in which they lived. They commented expressly on this symbolic uniting of poetry, art, and nature in a letter that they enclosed with a copy of the volume and sent to Kreymborg, seeking his assistance in publicizing their collaboration. Stating in a poetic addendum how the book "concreted the epitome of their work together," they described how it was composed of "elements from the animal, vegetable, and mineral kingdoms—leather, paper, and paint. Its spiritual elements are equivalents for fire, earth, and water. They are in terms of love, life, and art."[54] This symbolist expression of spiritual and physical elements functions also as topological thinking, mapping out various orders that could be combined in any manner. In its articulation, this private collaboration only hinted at Man Ray's seminal process of aesthetic synthesis.

The couple's experiential symbiosis of nature, art, and life manifested itself in an alchemical and organic integration of the book's material composition. On an elementary level, Man Ray's designs and illustrations accommodate Lacroix's writing. In a drawing that accompanies her poem "Trees," for example, he encapsulates their alliance as well as his own preoccupation with the relation between figure and ground that is the subject of many of his Ridgefield paintings (fig. 46). In a simple series of vertical elements of varying density, Man Ray illustrates the subject of the poem; the drawing also spells out its title, TREES—a subtle textual figuration of the poem's opening lines: "Wild black gracefully shaped trees / standing upright and rising toward the sky."

Under Man Ray's supervision, the collaborative fruition embodied in these soaring arboreal letters is his testament to his growth as a result of Lacroix's influence. Yet what he had earlier indicated, in the inextricably bound *Dual Portrait*, was more than the depth of their intellectual and emotional bond. *A Book of Divers Writings* embodies a good part of the couple's life, their youthful idyll and retreat to nature, as in a prose piece likening a robin's song to a love call, bordered by a brush-and-ink illustration of a bird above and a reclining pair of lovers below, and a poem titled, and reviling, "War," accompanied by an engraving of Man Ray's painting of the subject from the previous year. It is, however, the starkly different emotional states of their two portraits that bear most on reality, no less contrasting than the book's otherwise determined polarity between love and war, which in fact portends the couple's undoing.

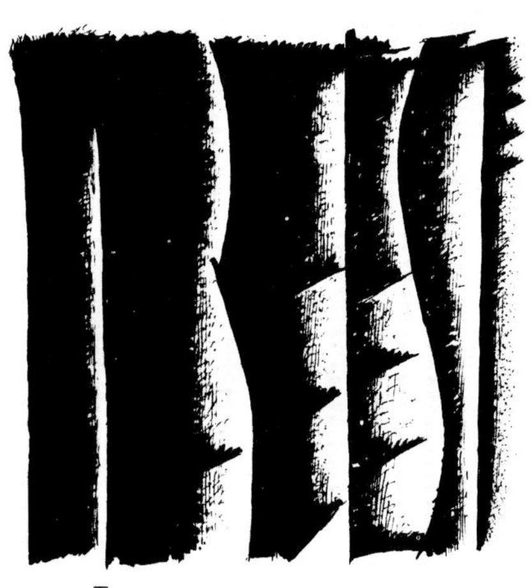

Fig. 46. "Trees" by Adon Lacroix, illustrated by Man Ray, from *A Book of Divers Writings* (1915). Book, each sheet 18¹¹⁄₁₆ × 12¼ in. (47.5 × 31.1 cm). Philadelphia Museum of Art, Louise and Walter Arensberg Collection

Man Ray, as he depicts himself, is a paradoxical mix of cool detachment and observant control who could not cope with his wife's insistent independence and sexual freedom; as she is gripped by worry about her family in Belgium and the war, both beyond her control, it is his contrasting expression, as he stares in her direction, that alludes to his need to control her. In his continuing demonstration of his metamorphic bent as an artist, Man Ray's proclivity to blur the distinctions between genre and media would not abate; his preoccupation with a blending of persons, himself with the object of his desire, is further evidence of his assimilative drive, his need to merge identities in a way that reflects an intolerance of boundaries and limits.

hybrid breeding

In the drawing *The Cosmic Urge*, Man Ray furtively inscribes his name with the limbs and camouflage of a dozen appendages belonging to a whimsical pair of copulating grasshoppers. The drawing graced the cover of the *Ridgefield Gazook*, possibly the first American proto-Dada periodical, whose only issue, number 0, appeared on March 31, 1915, entirely written, edited, and executed by Man Ray (fig. 47).[55] Composed of a single sheet folded to form four pages, its cover and contents exude the anarchistic and absurdist humor that would soon serve him well within Dadaist and Surrealist ranks: "Published unnecessarily whenever the spirits move us. Subscription free to whomever we please or displease. Contributions received in liquid form only. This issue limited to local contributors."[56] Along with its maker's otherwise concealed name, the cover drawing is explicitly signed "by Man Ray," accompanied by the phrase "with ape-ologies to PIcASSo"—a droll reflection on the animalistic drives he was indulging in his "primitive" immersion in rural Ridgefield.

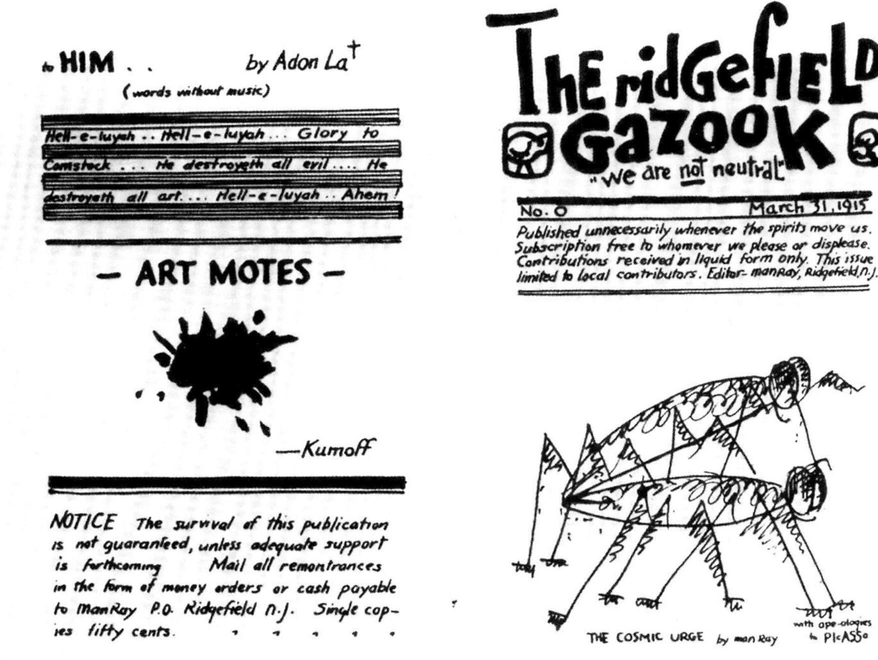

Fig. 47.
The Ridgefield Gazook, March 31, 1915, conceived and illustrated by Man Ray

As he became a more public, scrutinized figure, Man Ray's self-inscription took both covert and explicit form. In *The Cosmic Urge*, these two modes of expression are in equilibrium; "by Man Ray" exists alongside the artist's encoded identification of his private relationship with Lacroix (the letters L and A, and a † for Croix, French for "cross"), one clearly visible, the other encrypted. But his "ape-ologies to PIcASSo" refers to more than just the aforementioned animal urge. At this early stage, though, in doubling his signature, the emerging artist was referring to both his public and his private life—acknowledging his public identity as an artist, with questionably humble apologies to Picasso, and his private one, in terms of his personal status, a concept that must be seen alongside the "spatial" concerns, of an "interior" or "private" self, then being explored in radically different terms within the new poetry.

Aping or impersonating was what Man Ray had been doing for some time, in absorbing not only the foreign avant-gardes but also the people among whom he was living, his colleagues at the artists' colony at Ridgefield. For Man Ray, this form of imitation functions as a type of mimicry, often in concert with the sublation of his own difference (as in some of his Ridgefield paintings of himself and Lacroix)—as the kind of defense mechanism generally observed in nature—allowing him, so masked, to identify more freely with whatever he wished. In addition to having a keen sense of observation, and an awareness of himself in the world, Man Ray was exquisitely attuned to the various personalities surrounding him.[57] But in his parodies of his colleagues that comprise both "GRAFTSMANSHIP" and "SOSHALL SCIENCE," which appear on one page of the periodical, he demonstrates again a heightened interest in mimicry. Masking his own identifiable personage, the artist identifies himself through the personalities of his colleagues: Adolf Wolff ("Adolf Lupo"), Adon Lacroix ("Adon La†"), Hippolyte Havel ("Hipp O'Havel"), Manuel Komroff ("Kumoff"), and Alfred Kreymborg ("A. Kreambug"). This spoof of his friends and colleagues in the *Ridgefield Gazook* reflects Man Ray's readiness to challenge the sanctity of artistic identity. Moreover, his use of "graftmanship" suggests a hybrid breeding, in the grafting of the visual to the poetic and the propagating of a new, idealized art form with his wife. This ulterior agenda, the additional social topography, pervades Man Ray's consciousness and is related to the period's radical investigation of gender and sexuality as determinants within the field of modernism.

Even in "What Is 291?" the special number of *Camera Work* dedicated to Stieglitz's gallery, Man Ray's entry, an homage to the photographer, reflects his own inclination to differentiate the array of artistic personages with whom the photographer, mentor, and gallerist was associated. "The gray walls of the little gallery are always pregnant. A new development greets me at each visit, I am never disappointed," he wrote, identifying some of the more famous figures: "Cézanne the naturalist; Picasso the mystic realist; Matisse of large charms and Chinese refinement; Brancusi the divine machinist; Rodin the illusionist; Picabia surveyor of emotions; [Marsden] Hartley the revolutionist; [Abraham] Walkowitz the multiplier; [John] Marin the lyrist; [Marius] de Zayas insinuating; [Frank] Burty the intimate; the children, elemental." Man Ray introjects himself, in a form of honorific displacement, when he writes of Stieglitz (capitalizing, purposefully, the M of "Man"): "A Man, the lover of all through himself stands in his little gray room. His eyes have no sparks—they burn within. The words he utters come from everywhere and their meaning lies in the future. The Man is inevitable. Everyone moves him and no one moves him. The Man through all expresses himself."[58]

Like Stieglitz, Man Ray had rapaciously filtered and appropriated virtually the whole cast of European modernism. Stunned by the freedom and "absence of anatomy" of the Rodin drawings he had seen at 291 in 1908, he was even more galvanized by the artistic liberties of the Cubists at the Armory Show in 1913, demonstrating a passionate need to identify and grasp others' stylistic differences.[59] He quickly absorbed the divergent stylistic range of the avant-garde: from his Cubist-inspired portrait of Stieglitz to his emulation of Duchamp's *Nude Descending a Staircase* in *War (A.D.MCMXIV)*. Yet what distinguishes Man Ray's willingness to address and emulate the multiplicity of the avant-garde was his ability to absorb a plurality of styles—so thoroughly as if to appear to lose himself in the very experimental nature of the process.

In the many works that he would produce in 1915 at the height of his literary and social immersion in Ridgefield (for example, *Dance* and *Black Widow*, originally titled *Invention-Nativity*), it is not simply the headless figures that are symptomatic of this aversion to transparent and fixed identity, but also their overlapping and interpenetration. In the large painting *Promenade* (1916; fig. 48), whose central figure now appears whole, we can discern a more explicit self-identification. While the manikinlike head is easily identifiable, with the figure's obvious dummy form and armless upper torso, the bifurcated head anticipates the pairing of similarly ovoid figural heads in intense proximity in the aerograph *Suicide*, from the following year. In *Promenade*, kaleidoscopic forms revolve around the central figure, whose white navel-like nucleus is the hinge at the center of the painting. And, as an oblique hint of the work's symbolism, Man Ray includes a keyhole in the lower right, next to a form resembling a boomerang, implying that the dynamic between concealed past and revelatory present would constitute the means to unlocking his complex identity.

within **and** without

In addition to fostering her Francophile husband's interests in nineteenth-century avant-garde French literature, Lacroix encouraged his already pronounced interest in writing. In their idealized partnership, the subject of Kreymborg's journalistic piece, they engaged questions of gender, often employing the formalist devices of metaphor and metonymy, as some critics have noted in contrasting the two poems Lacroix and Man Ray published in the Summer 1915 issue of Kreymborg's little magazine *Others*, titled, respectively, "Intimacy" and "Three Dimensions." Through the conventional evocations of the feminine in figures of speech that suggest a state of interiority, or through such other spatial references that inti-

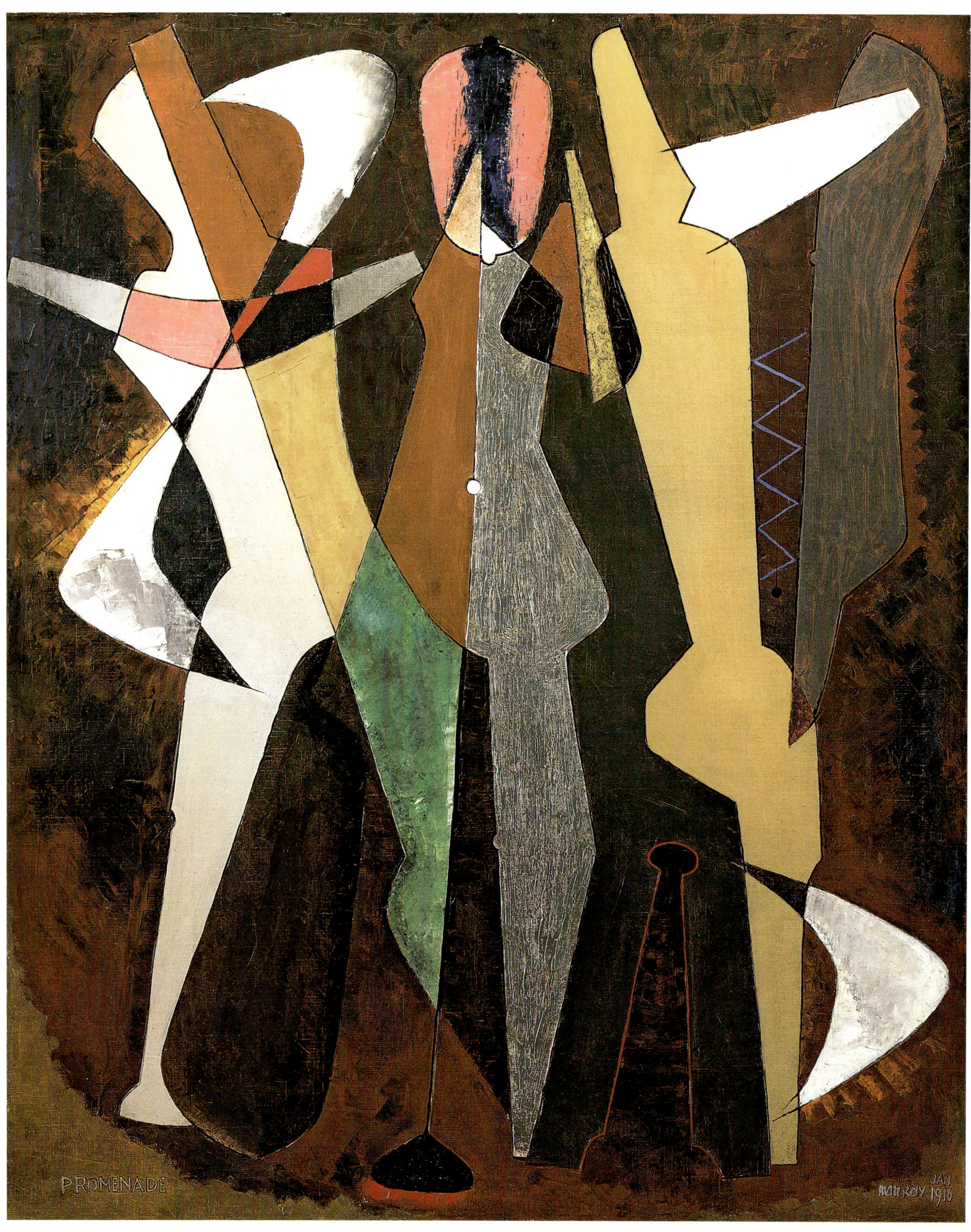

Fig. 48. *Promenade*, 1916.
Oil on canvas, 42 × 34 in.
(106.7 × 86.4 cm). Private
collection

mate proximity and inter-connection, Lacroix con-structs an interior that contrasts with Man Ray's concern with the mascu-line. "Three Dimensions" invokes terms of "exteri-ority, distance, and differ-entiation."[60] While such devices were intrinsic to the free-verse movement in poetry, one might con-sider the "gendered" as-pects of Man Ray's use of such categorical ideas within a narrower, more personal context.

In the intellectu-ally fertile environment of Ridgefield, Man Ray ad-dressed his particular sen-sitivity to the symbolic question of privacy, and began to conceptualize perhaps more con-sciously the formalist concerns with which he had been engaged for nearly two years—the conflation of three-dimensional space into the two-dimensional pictorial field. The problem of a psychologically charged yet insular space has, curiously, not been discussed in the literature. Most, if not all, of Man Ray's writ-ings and visual work from this period betray a preoccupation with boundaries and inte-rior/exterior spaces, beginning with his booklet of poems from 1914, *Adonism* (fig. 49), in praise of Lacroix. In several pieces in this hand-printed work, such as "Hieroglyphics," the artist ruminates on a figurative writing: "The snow has fallen— / A great white page lies open— / Naked black trees rise out of the white— / Words written in black on white— / A dead language."[61] In another poem, "Intrusion," he more clearly equates with awe his expe-rience of nature, especially the grandeur of a winter landscape, intruded upon by a figure, "as if an ink blot had fallen on this page and marred it."

But it is especially in 1915 that Man Ray reveals his specific psychological preoccu-pation with boundaries. In that year, together with Lacroix, he produced *A Book of Divers Writings*; wrote and designed the one issue of the *Ridgefield Gazook*; and published the explicit poem "Three Dimensions" in Kreymborg's journal:

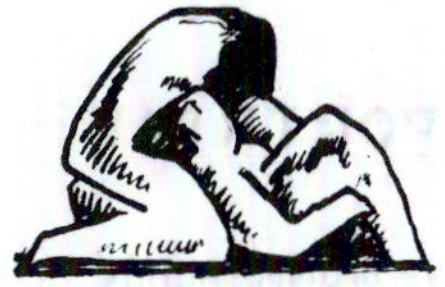

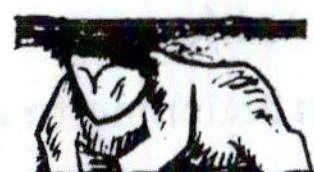

Fig. 49. "Spring" from *Adonism* (1914). Beinecke Rare Book and Manuscript Library, Yale University

Several small houses
Discreetly separated by foliage
And the night—
Maintaining their several identities
By light

Which fills the inside of each—
Not as masses they stand
But as walls
Enclosing and excluding
Like shawls

About little old women—
What mystery hides within
What curiosity lurks without
One the other
Knows nothing about.[62]

Notwithstanding his acknowledged commitment to the plastic possibilities of painting, Man Ray flourished in an environment populated more by writers than by artists; he focused on both canvas and word. Much of the literature has chosen to segregate the idea of space as an exclusively plastic, or formal, concern.[63] I would argue, however, that within Man Ray's formalist investigation of the plastic nature of two dimensions is an ulterior personal agenda, intimated poignantly in his poem dedicated to "three dimensions." The artist was approaching the modernist, Cubist-inspired resolution of the two-dimensional flatness of the pictorial support in terms of a space charged with contemporary social and psychological concerns.

That Man Ray's poem appeared in the auspicious little magazine *Others: A Magazine of New Verse* is noteworthy. The extreme unconventionality of its free verse was obvious; what was less so was its fostering of a political, artistic, and social cross-pollination in early-twentieth-century experimental literary and visual circles. This radical magazine promoted the broadest amalgamation of the avant-garde, uniting feminists, anarchists, socialists, communists, each voice registering with equal force.[64] As the magazine's title suggests—it sprang from the saying "The old expressions are with us always, and there are always others"—its socially inclusive intent was to represent those outside the mainstream, figures whose aesthetic or sexual identities refused to follow conventions.

This crucible of radicalism within which Man Ray found himself allowed him to rapidly assimilate a more conceptual understanding of an ambiguously gendered reading of art, which surely contributed to his natural alignment with Duchamp, whom he was to meet that fall. The movement was gender-liberating, providing women with a voice often more startling in its bold experimentation than that of men, who took for granted their

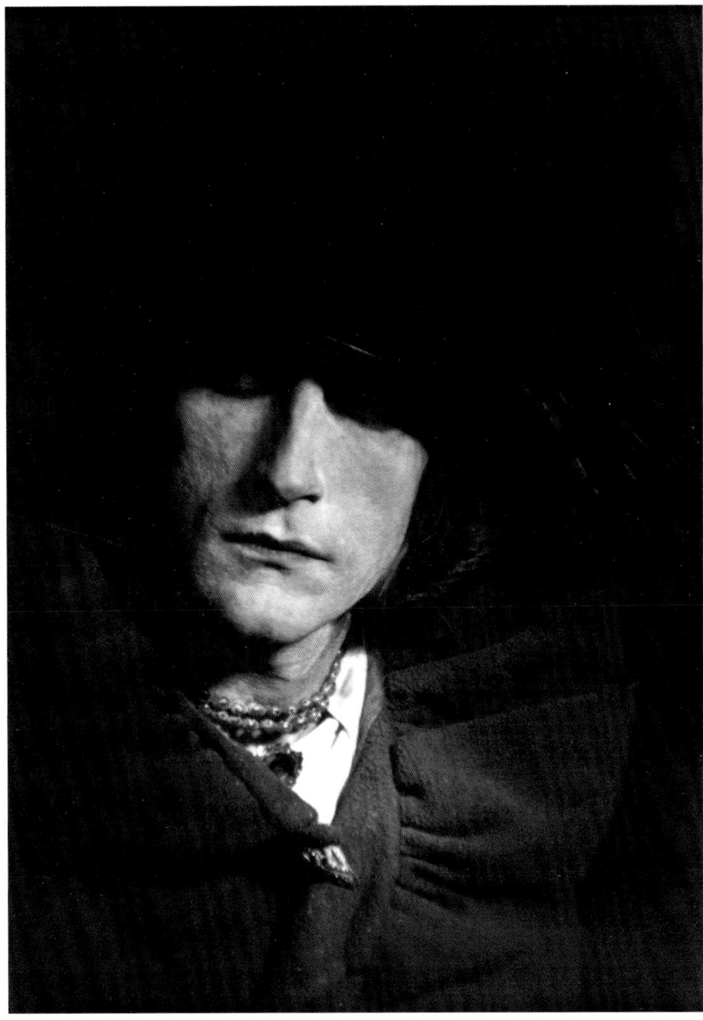

Fig. 50. *Portrait of Rrose Sélavy*, 1921. Gelatin silver print, 4½ × 3½ in. (11.4 × 8.9 cm). San Francisco Museum of Modern Art, Fractional and promised gift of Carla Emil and Rich Silverstein

freedom to enter the public domain in a more private manner. As a Jew and as an artist, Man Ray—along with Duchamp, who considered adopting a Jewish alter ego before choosing the more topical gender construction of Rrose Sélavy (fig. 50)—came of age at the beginning of the twentieth century, when questions of identity and culture were surfacing in remarkable ways, shifting through massive cultural migrations and, as nation-state identities aggressively asserted themselves throughout Europe, fueling a modern xenophobia.[65]

TENNIS, anyone?

Sometime in the 1950s, Man Ray photographed his old friend Marcel Duchamp wearing a necklace of Turkish coins around his head. Duchamp appears at once the grim sage and, with his familiar straight face and pursed lips about to break into a smile, the self-deprecating humorist. The photograph is a fitting portrait of a figure who had become a guru of irony—an artist who, for Man Ray, represented a refined balance between the lofty and the laughable. Perhaps more than any other artist, Man Ray understood the extent to which Duchamp had orchestrated his artistic life as an extension of his everyday being. Duchamp was continually constructing tedious machines and projects in his "usual meticulous manner," Man Ray observed, often having to repair them, "with the patience and obstinacy of a spider reweaving its web."[66] The artistic and intellectual encounter between these two

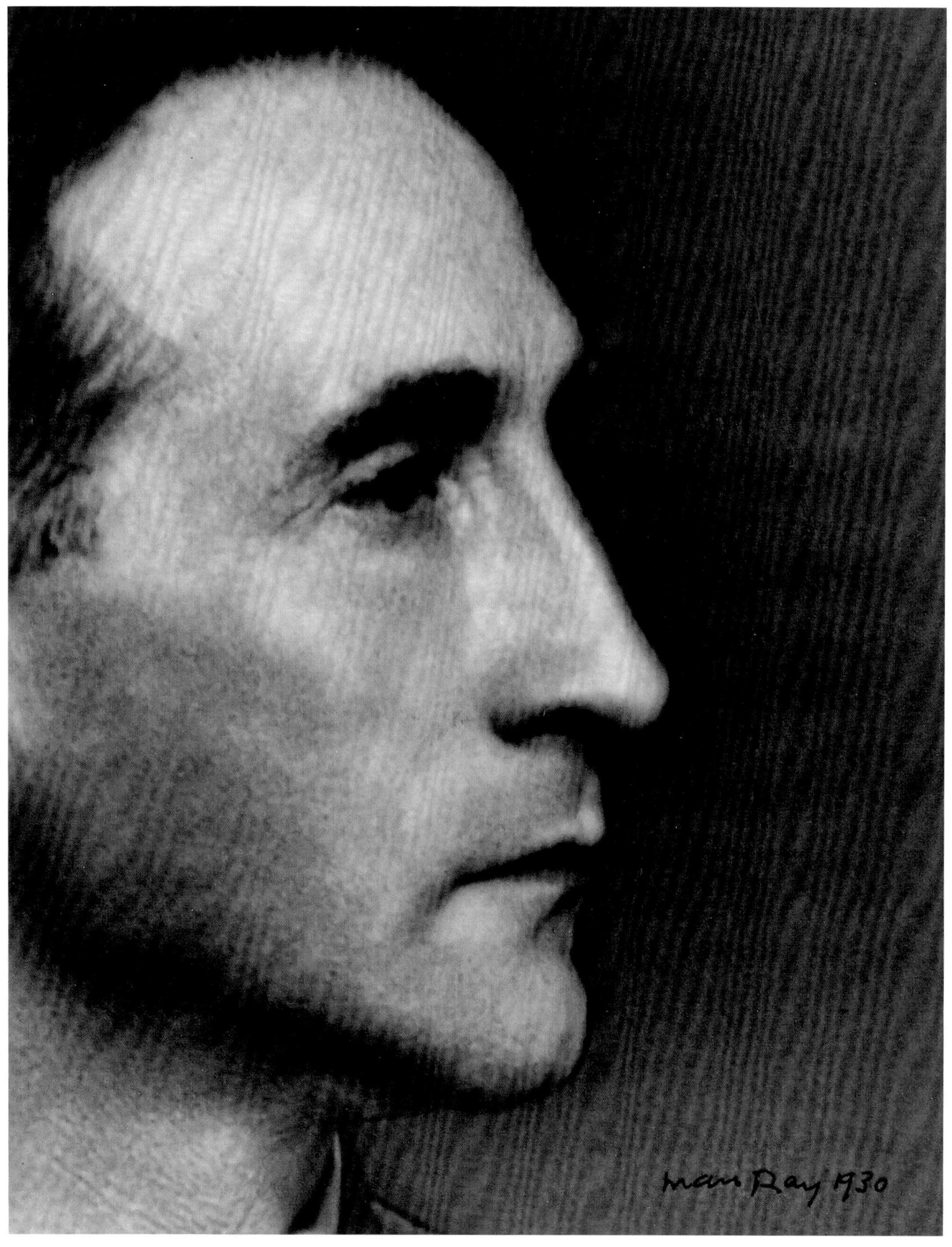

unlikely colleagues—strikingly different in physical appearance, cultural background, and personality— was remarkable in many ways.

Fig. 51. *Marcel Duchamp, Solarized Portrait*, 1930. Gelatin silver print, 11½ × 9 in. (29.2 × 22.9 cm). Collection of Sarah and Gary Wolkowitz

Man Ray met Duchamp on a fall day in 1915, when he was living in Ridgefield. Though neither spoke the other's language, this proved nothing more than a minor hindrance. It seems that from the day they met, Duchamp and Man Ray relished each other's company (fig. 51). The simplicity and pragmatism that would mark their long, easy collab-

oration and mutual affection was instantly apparent as they established a playful cama-
raderie. Each would soon discover their shared *bricoleur*'s love of invention and problem
solving, and they immediately alighted on an outdoor activity in which both could participate. According to Man Ray, they decided to mime a tennis match without net or court: "I
called the strokes to make conversation: fifteen, thirty, forty, love, to which [Duchamp]
replied each time with the same word: yes."[67] This exchange was the beginning of an artistic accordance that would resonate throughout their lives.

Such a lighthearted diversion was not simply a clever way to communicate; it also
signaled, at a critical juncture in early-twentieth-century modernism, a type of representation that reflects the way Duchamp and, to a great extent, Man Ray had already begun to
think. In mimicking a game of tennis they had seized upon an activity whose very sequen-
tial nature serves as a metaphor for the back-and-forth artistic volleying that would characterize much of their future relationship. In this game of "love," each serve, volley, or lob
was "returned" in a constant exchange, which took many forms.

The attachment of both artists to chess is well known. Duchamp went so far as to
"retire" from art to pursue the game more seriously; and for decades Man Ray would play,
design, or oversee the production of various chess sets. The aesthetics of the game, too, per-
vaded the work of both artists from early on. Consider their shared enchantment with
spoonerisms, which developed into interactive works, gadgets that had to be turned on or
actively engaged; into collaborations such as *Anémic Cinéma;* into Duchamp's *Rotoreliefs,* optical games to be played with the viewer; and into series such as his *Boîte-en-valise* (*Box in a
Suitcase*), a portable miniature monograph produced in various editions, and Man Ray's editions of "objects of my affection."

Unaware on their first meeting of the parallel nature of their interests and sentiments—from anarchism to engineering to the erotic—Man Ray and Duchamp enacted a
shadow dance, an innocent method of communication based on a conceptual commonality
and a need to posit their ambiguous identities. They shared an attitude, a philosophical
bent, an urge for mischief; and perhaps most important, neither took himself too seriously.

the enigma of id

In 1920, the year before he departed for Paris, Man Ray assembled an object, covered with
an army blanket and rope, that he titled *The Riddle,* or *The Enigma of Isidore Ducasse* (figs.
52–54). As would become typical, he promptly photographed the object and discarded it.
Until he re-created the work toward the end of his life, the photographic image served as
an homage to the nineteenth-century French writer Isidore Ducasse, better known by his
literary pseudonym, Comte de Lautréamont, to whose works Adon Lacroix had introduced
Man Ray five or six years before.

It was, however, Philippe Soupault and André Breton's rediscovery of this author
that rekindled his incendiary inspiration for the avant-garde, which had dimmed since the

Fig. 52. *The Riddle*, or *The Enigma of Isidore Ducasse*, 1920. Gelatin silver print, 12 × 16 in. (30.5 × 40.6 cm). Tokyo Fuji Art Museum

Fig. 53. *L'enigme d'Isidore Ducasse (The Enigma of Isidore Ducasse)*, 1920/71 (original maquette). Assemblage: sewing machine, blanket, strings, and wooden base, 16⅞ × 22½ × 8⅝ in. (43 × 57 × 22 cm). Israel Museum, Jerusalem, the Vera, Sylvia, and Arturo Schwarz Collection of Dada and Surrealist Art

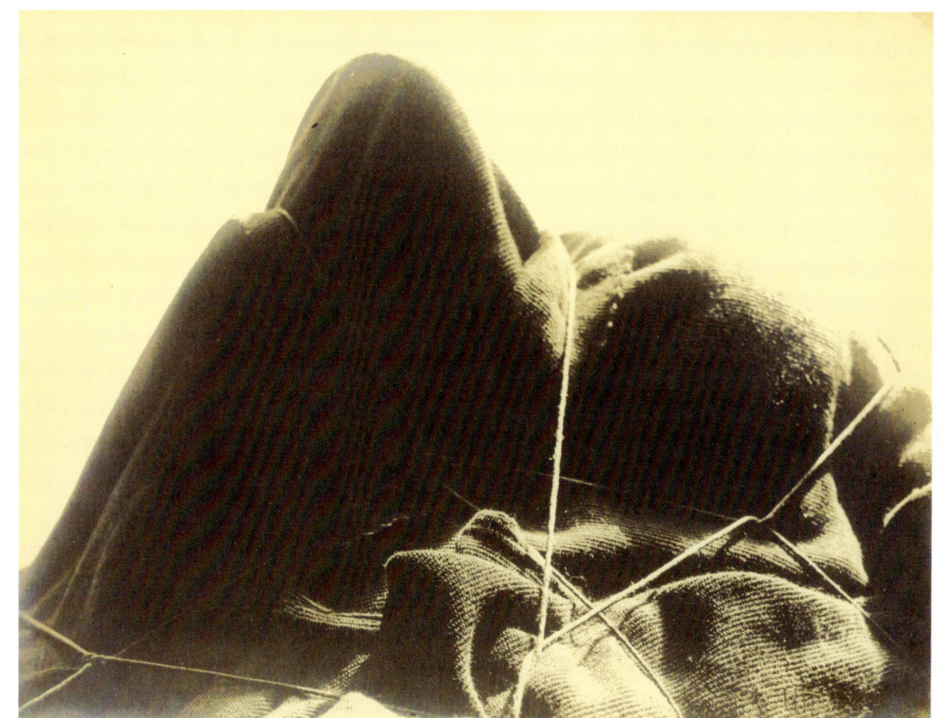

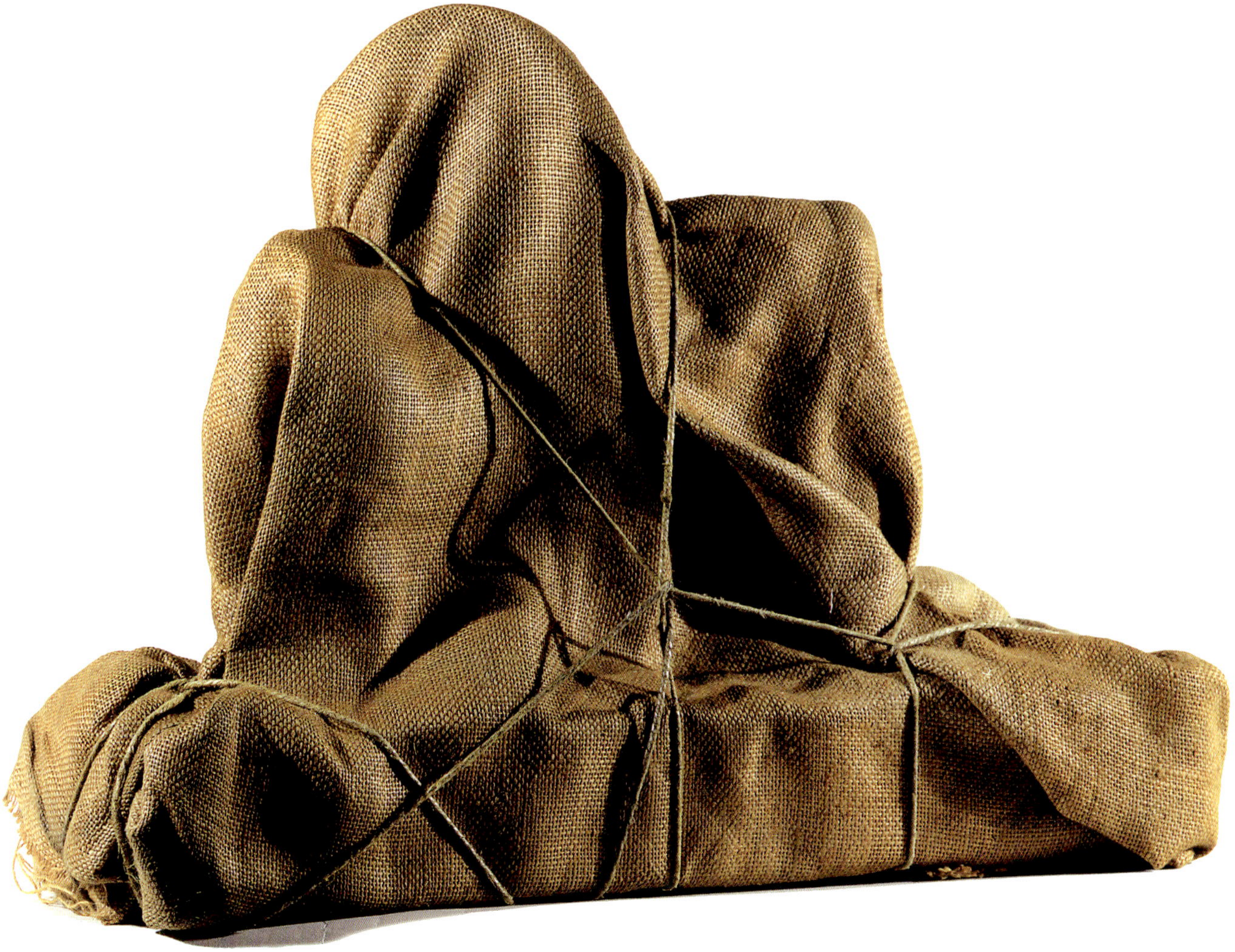

1890s, when such figures as Alfred Jarry and Remy de Gourmont had glorified him. Breton situated the Comte de Lautréamont as a precursor of Dadaism and Surrealism, and reprinted his "Poésies" in the journal *Littérature* in 1919. This, presumably, reawakened Man Ray's connection with Lautréamont.[68] Without doubt, the artist felt a profound affinity with this mysterious writer, who in his "Poésies" announced: "I will leave no memoirs." The life story of the Comte de Lautréamont, author of *Les chants de Maldoror* (the best known of his works), in fact remained a major riddle for years; hence the initial title of Man Ray's work.

But beyond that riddle lay another, one that becomes obvious only in terms of Man Ray's biography. When he first encountered *Les chants*, reading it in French with his wife's assistance during their time in Ridgefield, Man Ray may well have identified with it on a personal level. While the obvious connections and appeal that it would have for him are vast—its defiance of aesthetic, philosophical, religious, and moral conventions—his identification with Ducasse could easily have come from his own process of individuation and familial rejection. Baldwin insightfully stresses this connection, relating the relevance of the work to "Man Ray's own situation at the time he first read it," given the theme of "the child's obsessive struggle to separate from his parents, to achieve freedom through

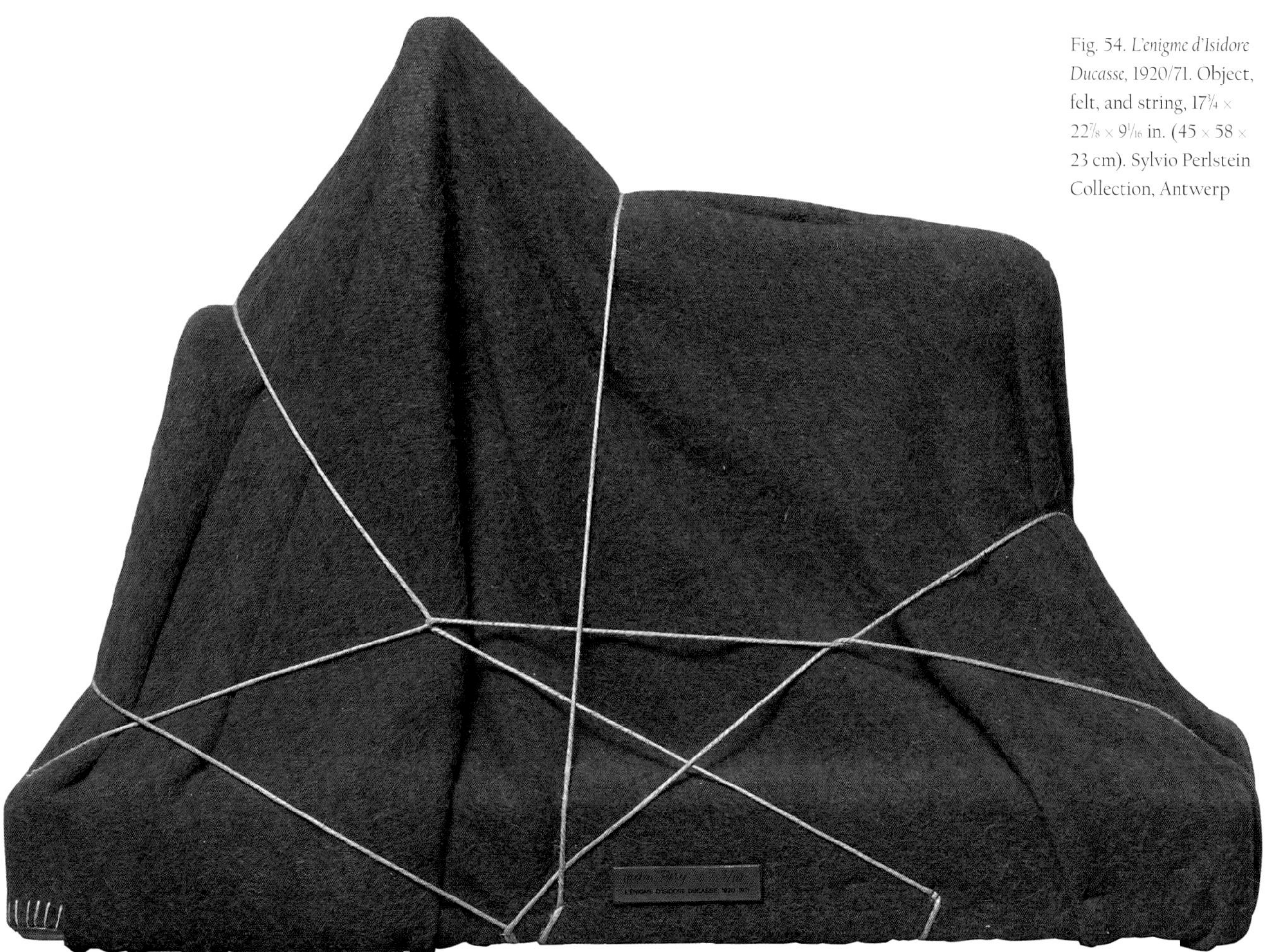

Fig. 54. *L'enigme d'Isidore Ducasse*, 1920/71. Object, felt, and string, 17¾ × 22⅞ × 9⅛ in. (45 × 58 × 23 cm). Sylvio Perlstein Collection, Antwerp

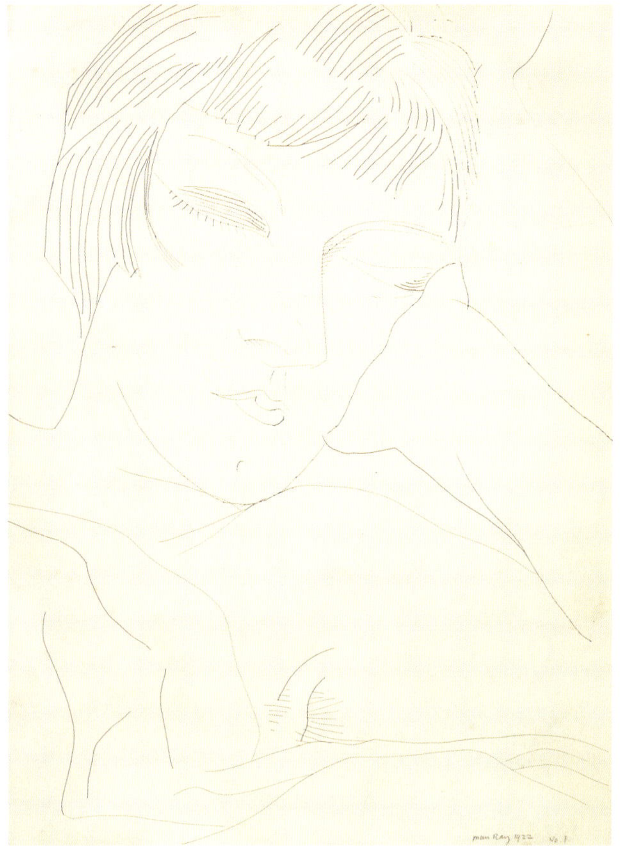

Fig. 55. *Kiki*, 1922. Cliché-verre, 9¼ × 6⅞ in. (23.5 × 17.5 cm). Collection of Timothy Baum, New York

escape."[69] Separation from parents—specifically, "acting out against a maternal entity"—is but one of the numerous themes that pervade *Les chants*, which is rife with the idea of needing to transcend, in some metamorphic or violent way, symbolic and corporal boundaries.

The emergence of the hermaphrodite in *Les chants*, for instance, as that symbol whose neutrality, or gender perfection, excludes it from the tainted "code of language" (as one scholar of the work has written), is especially relevant.[70] Man Ray synthesized a way to align the arts, adapting them to a two-dimensional matrix in his *Primer*, or to merge them, as in the aerograph's precise, mechanically photographic or printed appearance, and as in the cliché-verre technique with which the artist drew directly on an emulsion-coated plate and then exposed the plate to photographic-sensitive paper to produce both a monotype and a photograph (fig. 55). Here lies the symbolic value of his employment of the hermaphroditic form, as in the aerograph *Hermaphrodite* (1919), whose shape recalls the female figure in the 1914 painting *The Rug;* both works were created during periods in which Man Ray was intensely mixing and synthesizing media. The fact that *The Enigma of Isidore Ducasse* is invariably cast in a proto-Surrealist framework, because of its professed visualization of the famously quoted line from *Les chants*, "La rencontre fortuite sur une table de dissection d'une machine à coudre et d'un parapluie" ("The fortuitous meeting on a dissecting table of a sewing machine and an umbrella"), should not preclude a fuller interpretation of the work as self-reflective. What is striking about Man Ray's entire period of artistic activity leading up to and including his self-imposed exile to Europe is its egocentricity through some mode of self-inscription. This could be construed by turns as nostalgic or hostile, or both, as in the case of *The Enigma* or, for that matter, *Cadeau* (1921; see Foresta essay, fig. 6), the artist's first Dada work made in Paris, made hours before his gallery opening at Librairie Six. Both works allude to the complexity of self-identification in affirming and nullifying the past: *The Enigma*'s sewing machine refers to his sweatshop childhood, while the umbrella is a device of concealment; likewise, *Cadeau*, the celebrated iron, which he hurriedly purchased along with tacks and glue—the latter with the help of Erik Satie—and then altered by affixing the tacks to the iron's surface, is a double reference, to the garment trade and to New York's Flatiron Building.

The Enigma is generally seen as illustrating the line from *Les chants* quoted above, whose practical distillation into a fundamental Surrealist equation Man Ray later repeatedly identified with; he acknowledged that since first reading Lautréamont, he had been "fascinated by the juxtaposition of unusual objects and words." It was, of course, in the juxtaposition, rather than in the uniquely found and singularly christened readymade, that Man Ray's interest lay. But his use of the found object or the readymade was considerably different from that of his sometime conspirator: "My attitude toward the object is different from Duchamp's for whom retitling an object sufficed. I need more than one factor, at least two. Two factors that are not related in any way. The creative act for me rests in the coupling of these two different factors in order to produce something new, which might be called a plastic poem."[71] The contemplative pleasure provided by a found object's adequate aesthetic was all that Duchamp needed, as in *Fountain* (1917; see page 176). But for Man Ray, the singular, indivisible object was less appealing. Such plasticity was another way of altering the character and identity of a given object—the transformation necessary in order for something to become different or, better, ambiguous; hence the object is invariably contextualized, as in *The Enigma*; or combined with another object, for a double entendre, as in *Pain peint (Blue Bred)* (1958), or a play on words, as in *Table for Two* (1944; fig. 56).[72]

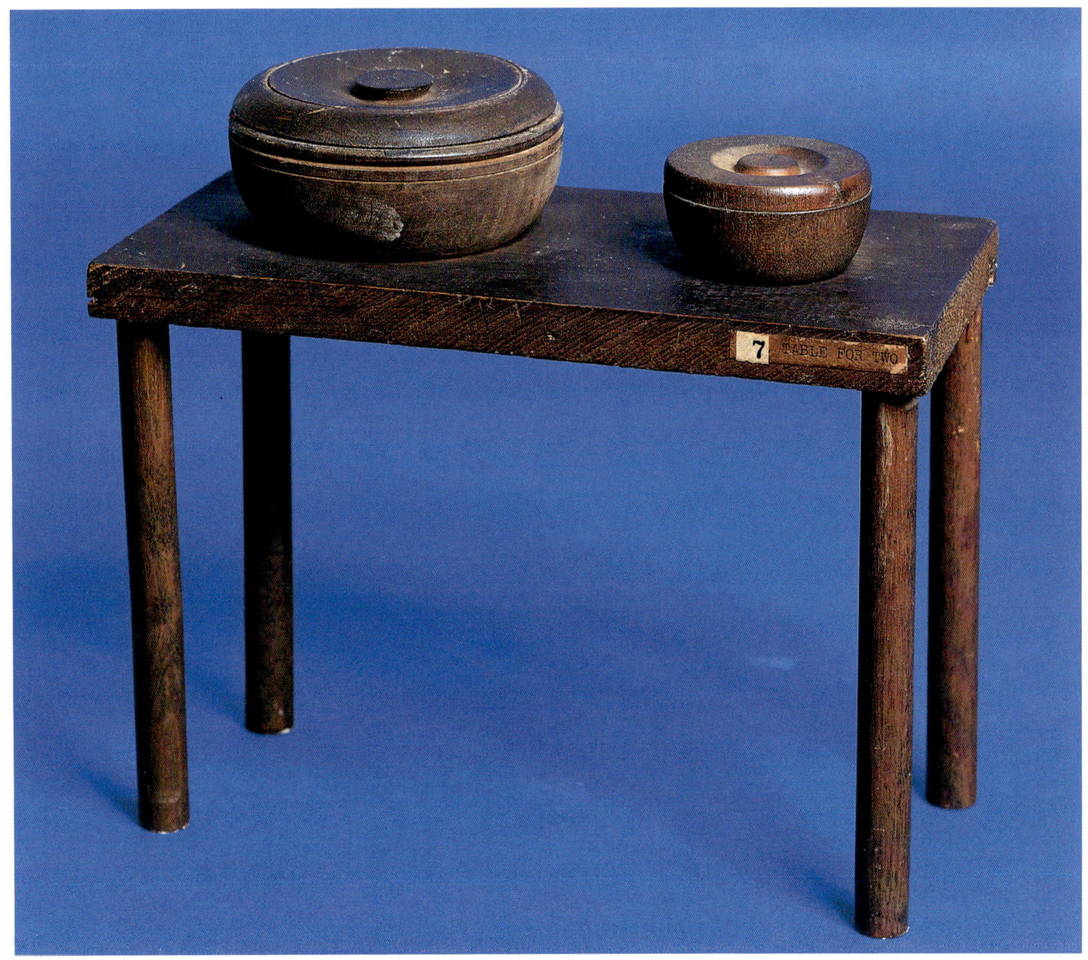

Fig. 56. *Table for Two*, 1944. Wood, 8⅝ × 9⅝ × 4¾ in. (22 × 24.5 × 12.1 cm). Collection of Timothy Baum, New York

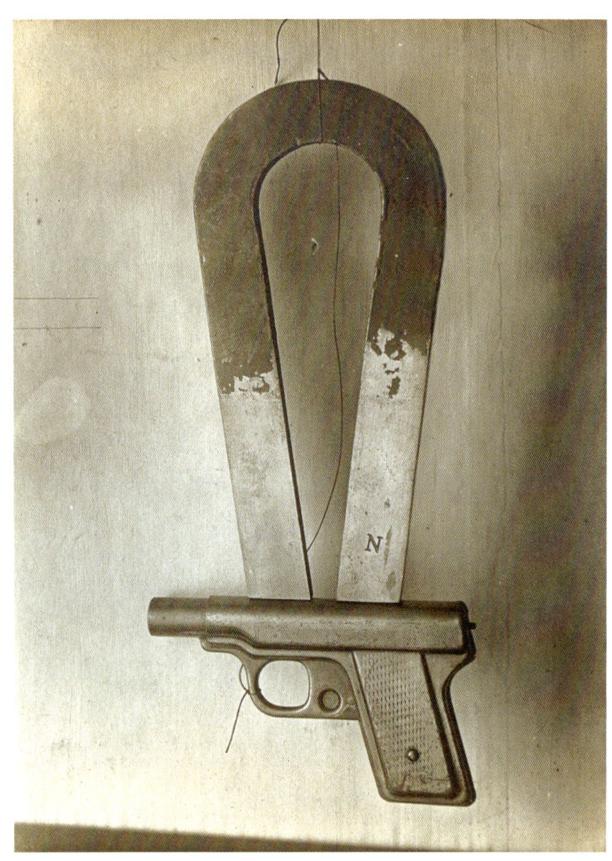

Fig. 57. *Compass*, 1920. Gelatin silver print, 4⅝ × 3⅜ in. (11.7 × 8.6 cm). Metropolitan Museum of Art, New York, Ford Motor Company Collection, Gift of Ford Motor Company and John C. Waddell, 1987

With works like *Compass* (1920; fig. 57), in which a handgun appears to be in the submissive grip of magnetic force, it is the power of the imagination that is pitted against the authority and certainty of science.[73] By calling the piece *Compass*, Man Ray demonstrates more than a quirky sense of humor. Exploiting the magnet's ambiguous engraved N, suggestive of a compass reading, the artist questions the fate of one's direction, implying perhaps as well, given the pistol's contravening orientation, the danger of going against convention.

Self-referential meaning, like the significant hidden iconography of *The Enigma*, remains to be deciphered; this and other works are unconcerned with satisfying the needs of the viewer, not unlike *Self-Portrait*, with its "doorbell" that failed to ring when pressed. Man Ray would, however, reveal the contents of *The Enigma* in the collage *Encounter Between a Sewing Machine and an Umbrella on a Vivisection Table (Lautréamont)* (c. 1932–33; fig. 58), but not before placing them on a vivisection table that dramatizes the work's "extenuating circumstances," the leitmotif of

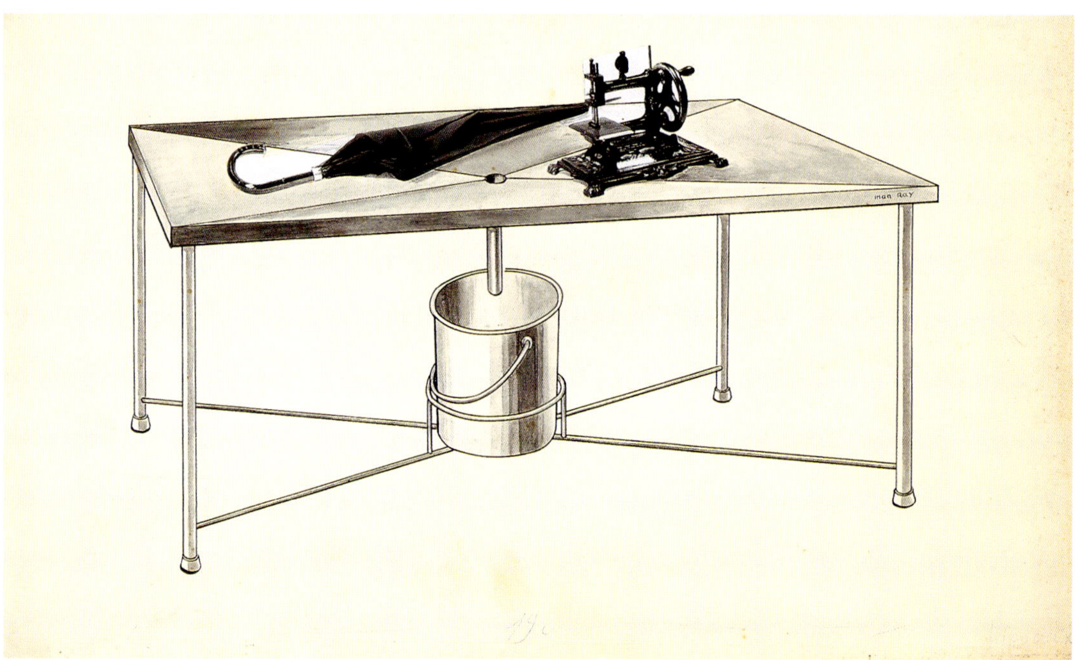

Fig. 58. *Encounter Between a Sewing Machine and an Umbrella on a Vivisection Table (Lautréamont)*, c. 1932–33. Collage, 10⅝ × 18½ in. (27.4 × 47.5 cm). Isidore Ducasse Fine Arts

clandestine identity. The subject's intrigue became even more acutely framed when the collage was published in the journal *Minotaure*, under the title *Enquête* (*Inquest*). Man Ray variously improvised the original assemblage, with several late maquettes and an edition of ten. In one version, the maquette for the 1971 edition (fig. 53), now in the Israel Museum, the artist's self-identification became more transparent than ever and even more anthropomorphic than the original.[74] Throughout *The Enigma*'s more than five decades of reiteration, Man Ray ostensibly pays homage to a literary figure whose excesses fiercely challenged the notion of boundaries and limits. In conjoining and then wrapping a sewing machine and an umbrella, Man Ray produces a pictorial equivalent of the riddle of the imagination, a perfect "cover-up" if ever there was one.

A Celebrated arrival

It was apparent to those who included him in their brigade of iconoclasts in Paris that Man Ray, the New York Dadaist for whom New York was not yet ready, was just right for their incendiary mix. Waiting for him at the Gare Saint-Lazare, when he stepped off the train that day in July 1921, was his friend and foreign overseer Marcel Duchamp, the unofficial savant of the avant-garde, whose collaborations in New York had served as endorsement enough. Within hours of Man Ray's arrival, Duchamp followed the American to Café Certa, a Dadaist haunt, where the essentially literary crowd of Breton, Soupault, Louis Aragon, Paul Éluard, and Jacques Rigaut was waiting in welcome, and where that evening Soupault came up with the idea of a Man Ray exhibition for the fall at his bookstore-gallery, Librairie Six.

The chemistry had been developing for some time, and in a letter to his American patron, Ferdinand Howald, Man Ray attributed his warm reception to the fact that the French "crave America." Beyond this unexpected interest in American culture and Duchamp's magic nod of approval, Man Ray's work had already been seen in Paris: his photographed object *Lampshade* (c. 1921; fig. 59) had been reproduced in Francis Picabia's magazine *391* the previous July. Man Ray's unpredictability and lack of pretense had appealed to Picabia, whose magazine had been named satirically after 291, the New York gallery of the forward-thinking Alfred Stieglitz. Furthermore, there had been the exchange with Tristan Tzara, whose letter "authorizing" a transatlantic Dada outpost Man Ray had published that April in *New York Dada*, which he coedited with Duchamp; it was the sole New York publication to define and affiliate itself with the short-lived European movement. The mock letter had been written in response to Man Ray and Duchamp's own tongue-in-cheek request for permission from Tzara to employ the word "Dada" in their title. In sanctioning its use and advo-

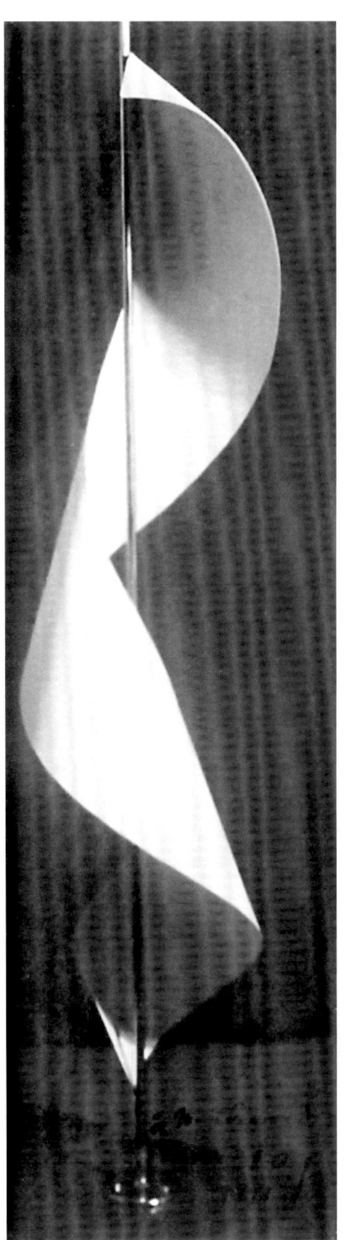

Fig. 59. *Lampshade*, c. 1921. Vintage photograph, 9⅜ × 2¹¹⁄₁₆ in. (23.9 × 6.8 cm). Private collection, New York

cating his proposed international *Dadaglobe* anthology, Tzara said, "Dada belongs to everybody . . . like the idea of God or the toothbrush."[75]

New York Dada's modest appearance in New York, followed by its creators' abandonment, underscored the tenuous, ephemeral, and self-destructively fraught nature of the movement itself. And Man Ray's personal letter to Tzara further foreshadowed the movement's problematic existence: "Dada cannot live in New York. All New York is dada, and will not tolerate a rival, will not notice dada. It is true that no efforts to make it public have been made . . . but there is no one here to work for it. . . . So dada in New York must remain a secret."[76]

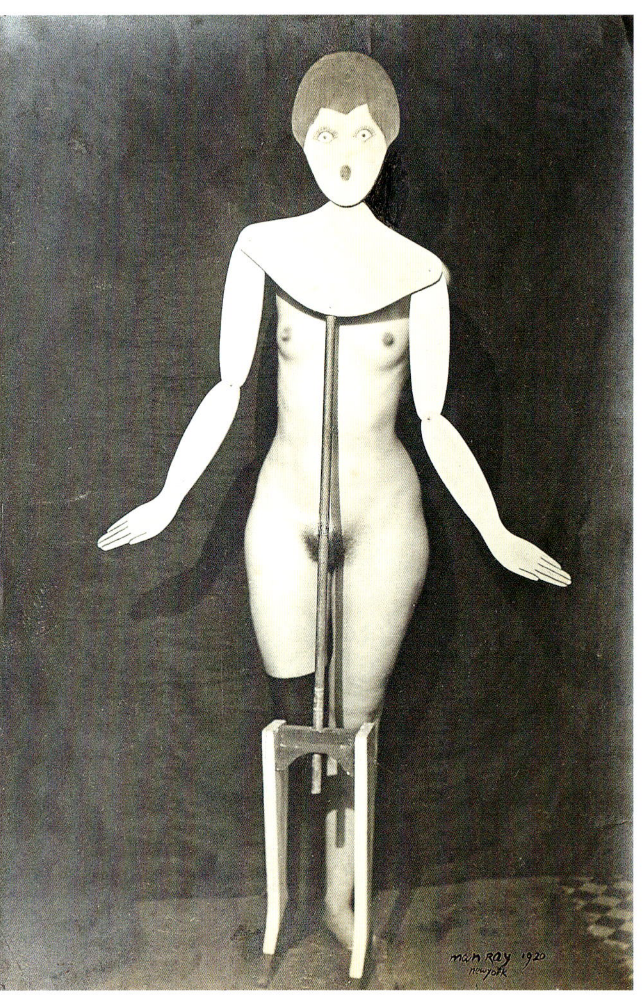

Fig. 60. *Dadaphoto (Coat Stand)*, 1920. Gelatin silver print, 16⅛ × 10⅞ in. (41 × 27 cm). Fondazione Marguerite Arp, Locarno

Man Ray had, therefore, become a celebrity even before he arrived in Paris, having garnered the favor of writers and artists of the avant-garde well before the summer of 1921. His work was known to them in all its uncategorizable glory; he was an American precedent, a cipher for the new who could sieve and process seemingly anything with the correct dose of serious humor, as his *Dadaphoto* (fig. 60), published in *New York Dada* that April, suggests. Representing Man Ray's hybrid talents as photographer, painter, and poet, *Dadaphoto* introduced him thoroughly and succinctly as an unlimited artist whose identity was no less concealed than that of the manikin (which introduced again his double phonetic surrogate, the French/English *main*/man) (figs. 61 and 62). The work—which included a graphic warning to "Keep Smiling" (appearing upside down on the page, beneath the photo) and a photographed assemblage of a human coat stand (later fittingly titled *Portemanteau*), whose composite identity was part nude, part manikin—underscored Man Ray's avant-garde status, his endearing affiliation with America spelled out in his credit line: "Trademark Reg."[77] With the figure's identity hidden behind the mask of a manikin, and its creator cited as anonymous, Man Ray had encoded a message of fabricated identity and ulterior symbolic meaning that suited the French perfectly.

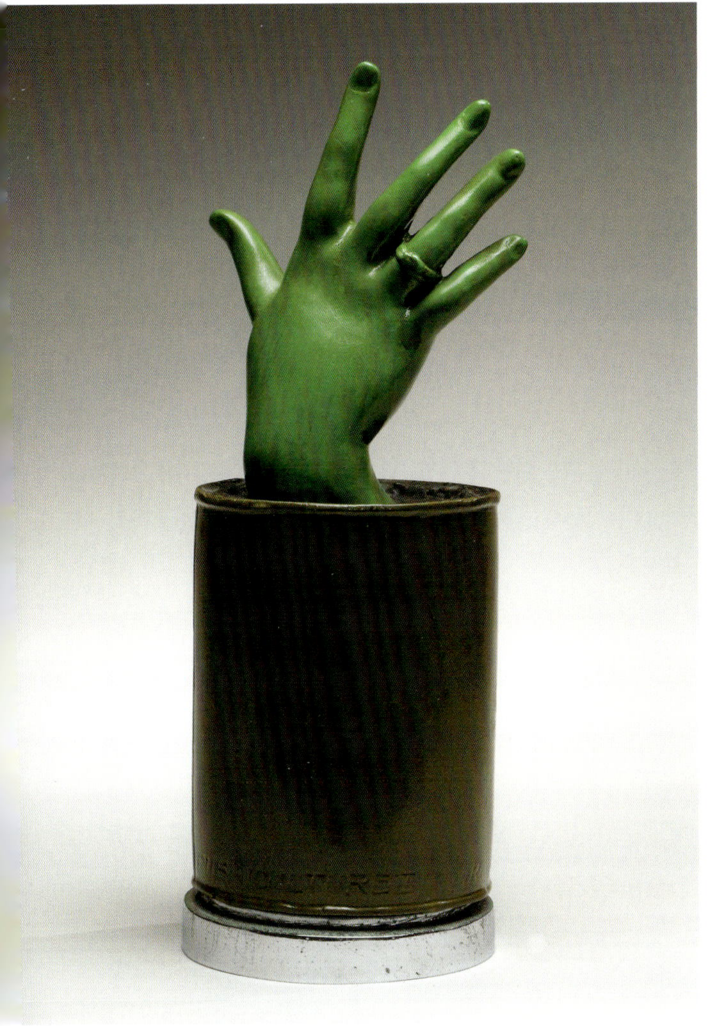
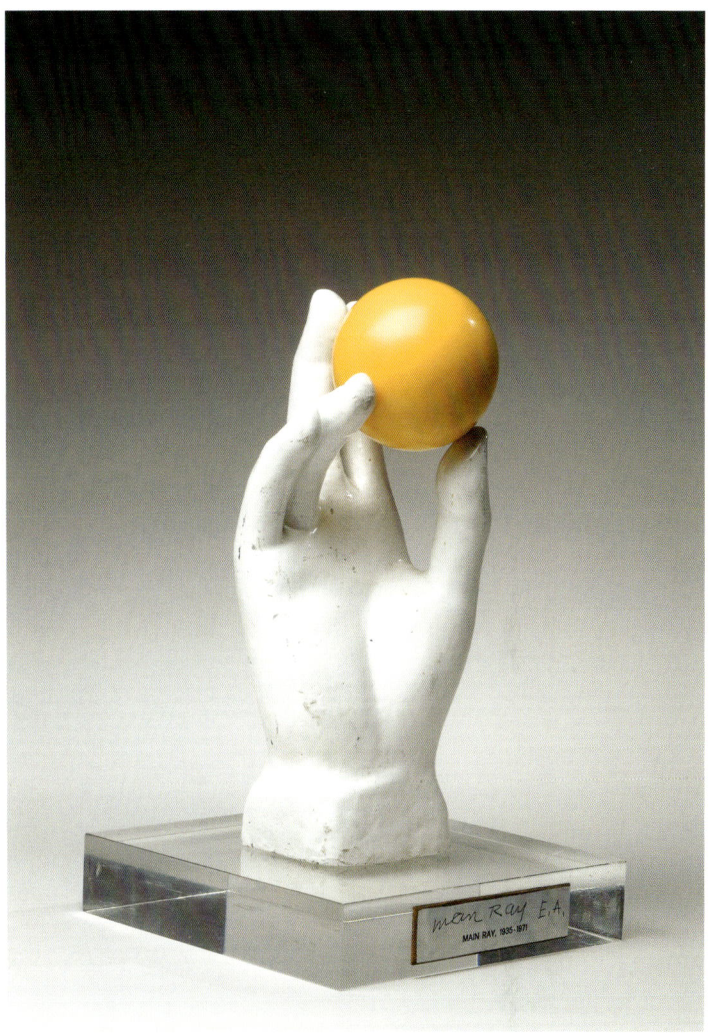

As the photograph bore Duchamp and Man Ray's dual imprimatur, literally with the *New York Dada* imprint, and that of American culture, *Dadaphoto* is clearly fraught with meaning or, at the very least, with the appropriate multiple entendre one would expect from an anointed Duchamp protégé. It refers to Man Ray, through its use of a manikin, which, one could say, was becoming his "registered trademark," having appeared in two paintings of his New York studio—*Interior,* or *Still Life + Room* (1918; fig. 63), and *La volière* (1919). Both these works are related to the dissolution of the artist's marriage to Lacroix. The titles of the 1918 painting support this reading, "interior" referring to the introspection that he had experienced in his marriage, and "still life," and the vase of three blooms, to the family he, Lacroix, and her daughter had been. The painting may also present a contrast between the purity represented by his 1914 *Madonna* (which appears on the rear wall; see page 170) and Lacroix's promiscuity, which led to the end of the marriage, signified by an empty chair paired with a dress dummy. A similar iconographic reading may be mined

Fig. 61. *Puericulture II,* 1964. Painted bronze, 11½ × 4 in. (29.2 × 10.2 cm). Courtesy of Timothy Baum, New York

Fig. 62. *Main Ray,* 1971. Marble and painted bronze, 9⅛ × 5¼ × 5¼ in. (23.2 × 13.3 × 13.3 cm). Collection of Karen Amiel Baum, New York

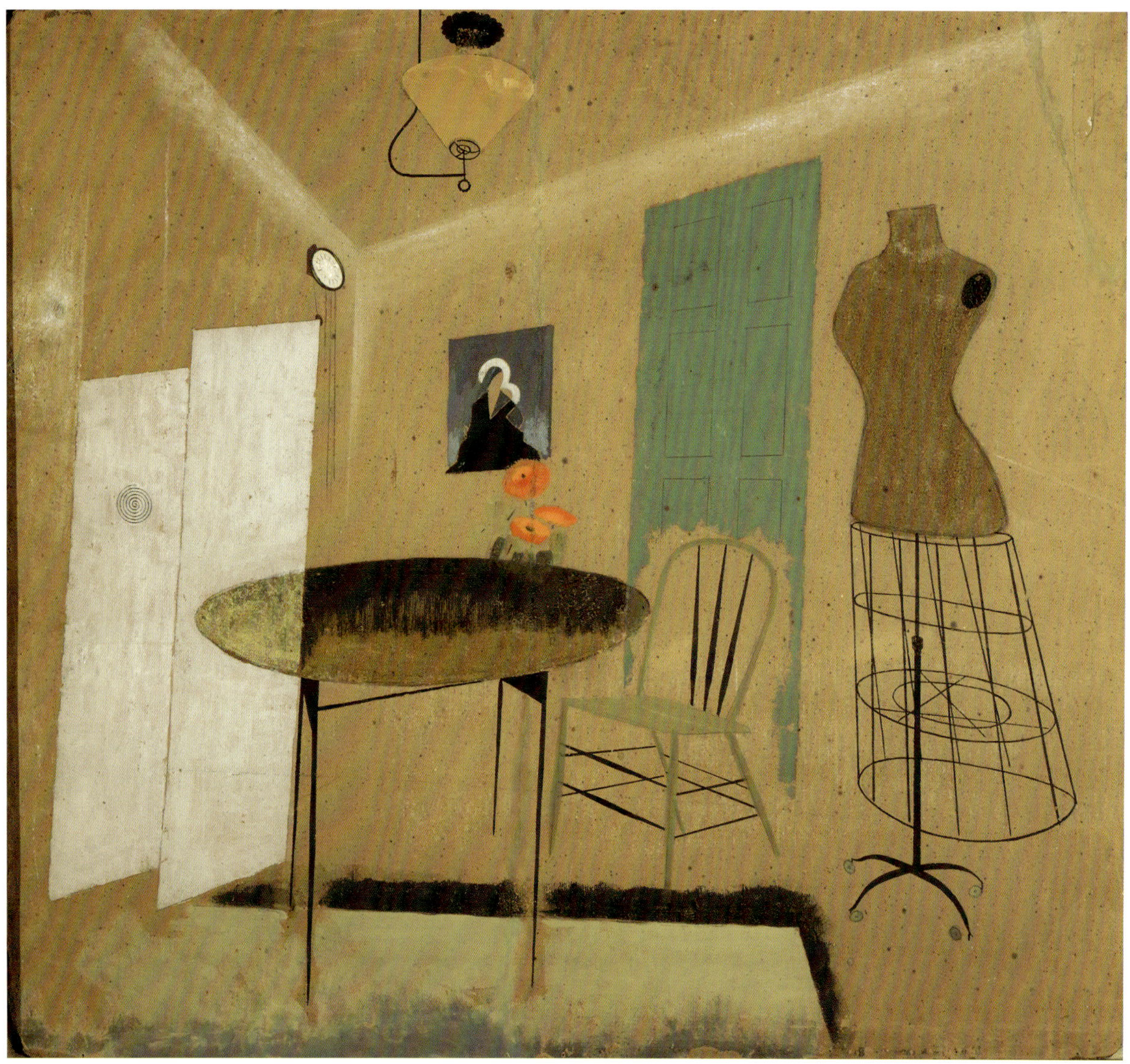

in *La volière*, whose title also suggests a reference to the artist's estranged wife (its original title, *Aviary*, yielded to the French translation in 1921), given its allusion to "flight" and the sexual freedom that Lacroix was known to have sought.

Both paintings show a manikin in the artist's studio, returning us again to Man Ray. Its use, albeit as a coat stand, in *Dadaphoto*, along with the naive optimism of "Keep Smiling," announces the artist as resiliently American, humorous and self-effacing. The coat stand and nude define the work as twofold and transitional—cryptically evoking the artist's past while broadcasting his artistic persona and future, and perhaps invoking Mark Twain's tailor's counsel: "Clothes make the man." Twain, whose considerable fame as a philosophical humorist and quintessential American had extended to the Continent, appended to this line the observation that "naked people have little or no influence on society," which might serve as a sardonic commentary on the fate of Dada in New York.[78]

Fig. 63. *Interior,* or *Still Life + Room,* 1918. Collage, paint, and airbrush on cement board covered with paper, 31¼ × 36 in. (80.7 × 91.4 cm). Tokyo Fuji Art Museum

Certainly by 1921, Man Ray had had ample exposure to Duchamp's punning skills and cultural commentary—not that he possessed, or would ever aspire to, anything approaching the Frenchman's linguistic subtlety. But he may well have wanted to demonstrate, at this moment, his own panache to this literate, Parisian crew.[79] It is also tempting to speculate that *Dadaphoto* functions as his "gestural" response to Tzara's welcome, his endorsement of Dada's brief reach to the other Atlantic shore. Such an intention might account for the pose of the manikin's arms, as if about to curtsy. Beyond this droll mode of self-introduction Man Ray might also have wanted to signal the kinship he already felt (manikin = man/*main*/kin) toward the French branch of the Dada family, which was to replace the family he had left behind. With this work appearing in the one and only issue of *New York Dada*, Man Ray succeeded in extending his own eloquent overture to the French avant-garde.

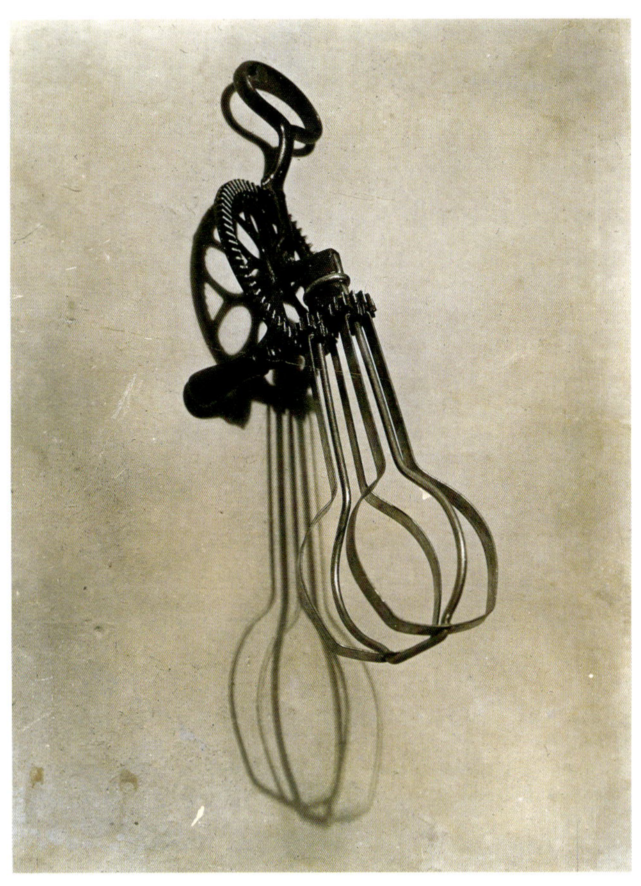

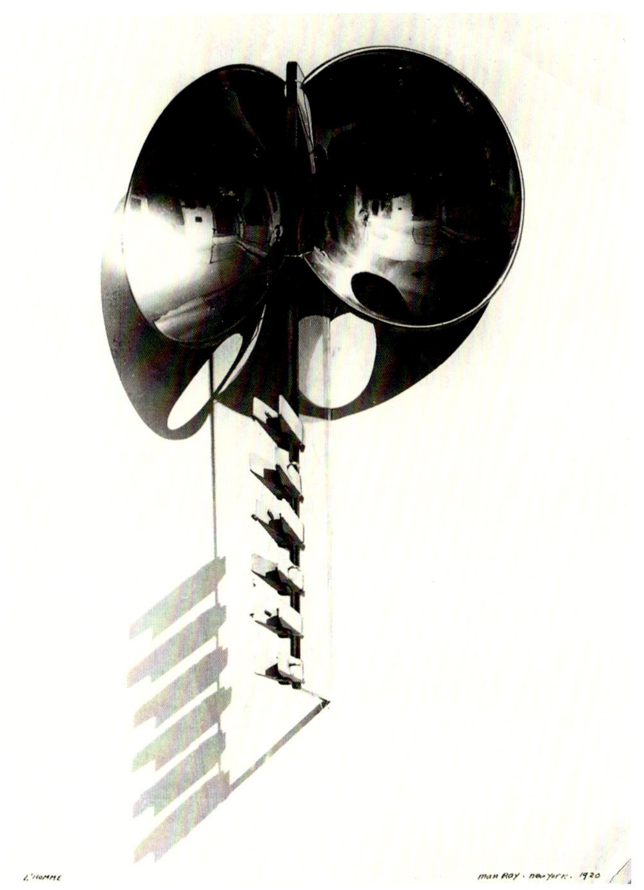

During Man Ray's correspondence with Tzara, the American had sent the Romanian two photographs: one of an eggbeater called *Man* (1918; fig. 64); the other of two metal light reflectors and six clothespins, called *Woman*, or *Integration of Shadows* (1918; fig. 65). Both were shown at *Salon Dada: Exposition Internationale* that spring, before Man Ray arrived in Paris. Rather than simply follow Duchamp's model, Man Ray was finding his own manner of dealing with the readymade. Were *Man* and *Woman* to be regarded as documentations of readymades (which the artist had already begun making, of Duchamp's work and his

Fig. 64. *L'Homme (Man)*, 1918. Gelatin silver print, 19 × 14½ in. (48.3 × 36.8 cm). Private collection, New York

Fig. 65. *L'Homme (Man)*, 1920. Gelatin silver print, 15⅜ × 11⅜ in. (39.1 × 28.9 cm). Fondazione Marguerite Arp, Locarno. This particular variant of this work, originally titled *Woman*, was renamed *Man* when it was exhibited at *Salon Dada* in 1921.

own), or as photographs in their own right? After his synthesis of genres (figurative/landscape; visual/verbal) at Ridgefield, and his mastery of the mechanical airbrush, which provided an industrial, even photographic, finish to his aerographs, Man Ray was on his way toward another amalgamation: the photographic animation of the readymade, exemplified by his photograph of laundry blowing on a clothesline, christened *Moving Sculpture* (1920). The work would be retitled *La France* when it was published on the cover of *La révolution surréaliste*, in 1926.

The names of *Man* and *Woman* were soon reversed, presumably by Tzara when he showed them at *Salon Dada*, an occurrence that must have delighted Man Ray. Such revision further undermined the status of the "original," already called into question by the fact that Man Ray would often dispose of or disassemble his objects after photographing them. In employing the very tools of his trade—reflectors for lighting and clothespins for drying prints—the artist's image of *Woman* was, to quote Rosalind Krauss, a "picture of its process of making [that] acknowledges a certain usurpation of the object by its photographic record." But such an image was clearly meant to become a trace of something absent, "a copy . . . that exists *without an original*."[80]

With little or no concern for any intrinsic aesthetic value to his pieces, Man Ray, unlike Duchamp, discarded them for the utilitarian objects they were, but only after capturing and recording their transformative moment and that, too, of photography. For in combining the objecthood of the readymade with the visual delectation of the immaterial, in the play of light and shadow, Man Ray produced another hybrid, new, mysterious, and not readily identifiable as the subject. This exceeded even Breton's characterization of the readymade as a "change of roles," and prefigured Louis Aragon's definition of the "marvelous" as that which intervenes as the contradiction of reality. In producing such work, whose categorical status was deliberately unclear, Man Ray was anticipating, by years, Breton's principle of "convulsive beauty."[81] Even in these works Man Ray continued to investigate what always fascinated him: shadows. In his two variants of *Woman*, one shows the line of clothespins casting its "indexical" trace, as any three-dimensional object does; but in the other version, titled *Integration of Shadows*, the shadow is an autonomous element, almost independent of its source.

It was quite clear to his French colleagues that their new, nondescript, and thus ideal "American" member would be the perfect exile, one on whom they could project their American craving, one whose unquestioned allegiance was to his new family and home. Yet the separation from his homeland was formidable, and one of the first works Man Ray created in Paris expresses how palpable a dislocation it was for him.

passage

If *Man Ray 1914* represents the artist's psychological and geographic breach with the past, the passage itself is the subject of an important work that Man Ray completed soon after arriving in Paris. It was as if he were acknowledging, however cryptically, not exactly a refusal to grow up but a need to start again, freed from a burdensome past, and in the city that he had dreamt of since adolescence.

The critic Philip Leider was not wrong in claiming that Man Ray had become Europeanized even before he left for Europe. Unlike those artists who made their obligatory pilgrimage to Paris, Man Ray knew he was leaving for good. The relocation is figuratively depicted in his collage *Trans atlantique* (1921; fig. 66), whose title comes from the popular term for ocean liner, the means of transport at the time, and is spelled out in the middle of the collage, connecting his points of embarkation and destination. The two locations are represented, respectively, by his photograph *New York 1920*, which shows the detritus of the past—mashed cigarette butts and ashes, used matchsticks—and by a partial map of Paris, a schematic rendering of the city he did not yet know. Man Ray flanked his transposition with a checkerboard, hinting that art, like chess, could be played on either side of the Atlantic. But it is the significant and hitherto unnoticed element that circumscribes this relocation—a giant tooth, whose linear contours are

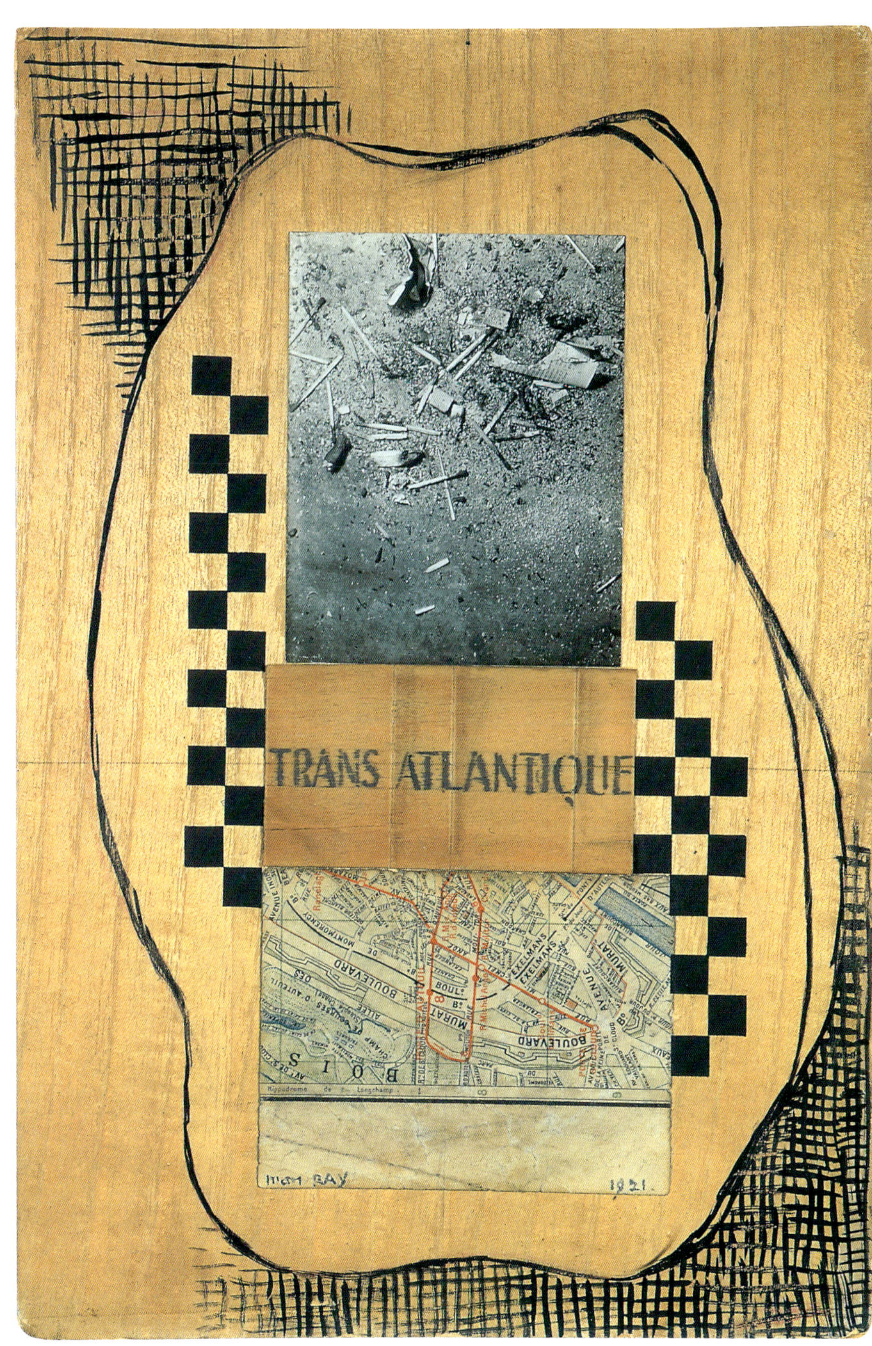

Fig. 66. *Trans atlantique*, 1921. Collage, 11½ × 9⁹⁄₁₆ in. (29.3 × 23.7 cm). Private collection, New York

buttressed by crosshatching (he is "crossing" the ocean, "hatching" a new life)—that encodes the work with an additional narrative: the depth and permanence of this extraction from his roots. The loss of a tooth also suggests the state of a child, and Man Ray does more than once refer to himself during this period in Paris as a "new-born baby."[82]

Change Of Roles

Man Ray's initial burst of activity upon his arrival in Paris was capped by the show of his paintings that opened on December 3, 1921, at Librairie Six, not even six months after he arrived in Paris. After the show failed to sell a single work, however, a nearly penniless but resourceful Man Ray took stock. Obliged to inform Ferdinand Howald of the outcome of the exhibition, he was philosophical in playing down the situation. It had, he wrote his patron, "placed [him] sort of apart from the huge mass of daubing that goes on here. Even the few recognized or 'arrived' painters regard me either in a spirit of conciliation or quiet fury." He further rationalized: "You have no idea of the jealousy and intrigue that goes on here in the art world. But that is merely a sign of its vitality."[83]

Perhaps he was hoping that Howald would infer that his need to generate income would necessitate a shift in aesthetic priorities. Rather than wait for recognition as a painter, Man Ray determined to become a professional photographer. When *Vanity Fair* started to publish some of his photographic portraits and his new "paintings with light," as Jean Cocteau referred to his rayographs, Man Ray had arrived. Purely intuitively, he had rekindled his youthful fantasy of being accepted as part of the haute monde. But such a career decision was hardly just felicitous. He presciently understood the incipient incorporation of photography in publishing, especially with respect to fashion, and realized the intersection of art and fashion represented by someone like the couturier Paul Poiret, who was also the first art collector to buy his rayographs.[84]

The purchase of four rayographs for the November 1922 issue of *Vanity Fair* by its editor, Frank Crowninshield, marked precisely the type of crossover reception that the artist desired, to various degrees, throughout his career. Within his first year in Paris he had exceeded the fantasies he had had as a student—standing, dreamily entranced, before John Singer Sargent's shimmering paintings—of being a "society portraitist." Now he was the one being sought by the arrivistes for whom a portrait by Man Ray practically guaranteed social status. In another and more modern medium than Sargent's, one that would produce an increasingly popular and commodifiable image, Man Ray was becoming a celebrity himself. The first retrospective publication of his photographs, *Photographs by Man Ray 1920 Paris 1934*, which included a short essay by Duchamp, "Men Before the Mirror," appeared as Europe was feeling the incipient spasms of fascism.

Among the various commissions Man Ray received during his first years in Paris, as he moved from painting to photography, was one from Jean Cocteau. The poet, who was among the first to applaud Man Ray's rayographs publicly for their radical use of light and space, and who claimed that they would "set painting free again," was at the time championing another young American, the Texas-born music hall performer, female impersonator, and trapeze artist Vander Clyde, who went by the stage name and persona Barbette. Cocteau had become enamored of Barbette since seeing him in his first performances in Europe in 1923, and he remained fixated on this apparition of gender. He engaged Man Ray to produce a series of portraits of the performer, whose extraordinary theatrical illusion of gender had captivated not just Cocteau, but also, it seemed, most of the rest of Paris, where he had become a cultural icon.

Man Ray had made Paris his home when France was dealing with the traumatic aftermath of the Great War, a conflict that had killed or maimed the bodies of men and upended the very foundations of gender. It had produced the modern woman, emboldened by her novel exposure through film and radio. During the decade that followed the war, every social convention was open to public challenge and, as a result, to transformation, as the boundaries that defined the sexes were no longer assumed to be naturally determined. Cultural determinants were questioned, and the very images and ideas that defined notions of gender identity underwent a vast, messy reconstruction: heroism was no longer an exclusively male domain, as the single woman assumed greater autonomy and as vanity, newly shrugged off by women, became a self-consciously male attribute. This was the context in which Man Ray photographed Barbette backstage preparing for an evening's performance (fig. 67); the image would illustrate Cocteau's equally famous and influential essay on the performer, published in the July 1926 issue of *Nouvelle revue française*, "Le numéro Barbette." Man Ray's photograph shows Barbette attaching her stockings to her specially outfitted girdle, which hides her anatomy and disguises her gender. Seeing her leg raised on a chair, a pose carefully chosen to fully expose and highlight the locus of supposed clarity, the confused viewer is forced to scrutinize the body for clues. The wig, makeup, and general posture are obviously feminine, challenging the implications of the muscular torso: the ambiguity crystallizes the slippery sexuality so brilliantly embodied by this chameleon of gender. It is just such momentary perplexity—of identity performed— that Man Ray intentionally frames.[85]

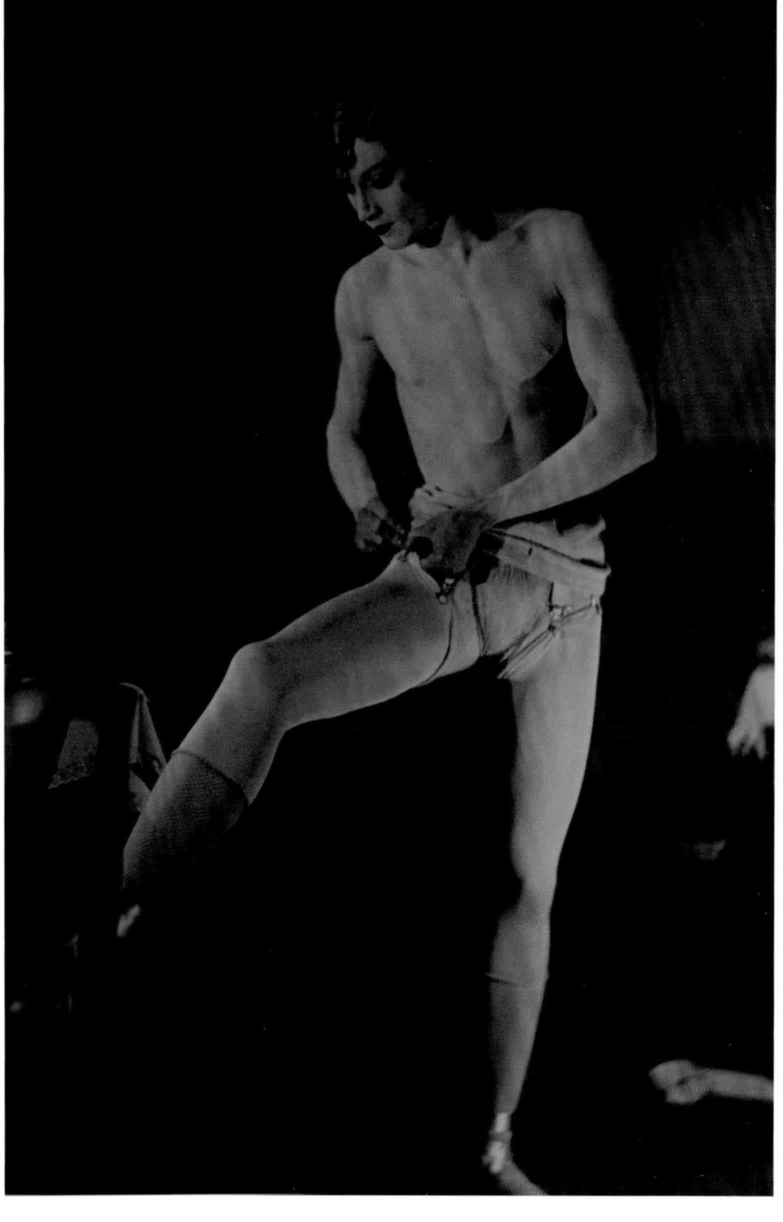

Fig. 67. *Barbette*, 1927. Gelatin silver print, 11¼ × 7⅛ in. (28.6 × 18.7 cm). The Museum of Modern Art, New York, Gift of James Thrall Soby

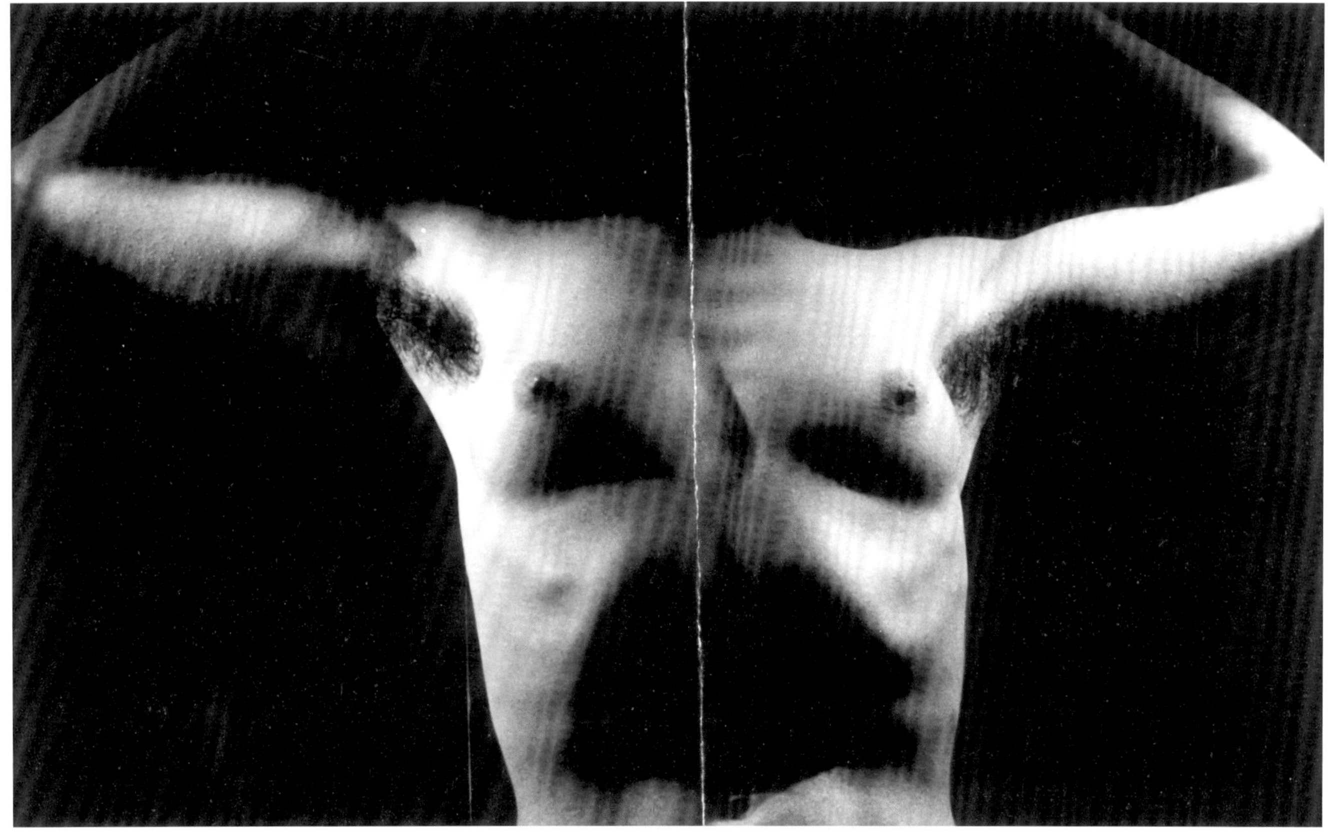

The fact that Man Ray's most metamorphic work begins soon upon his arrival in Paris is due partially to his being accepted among the avant-garde there and to his new sense of "fitting in," as the attention accorded him and his work mirrored more closely than ever the artistic persona he had contrived. Man Ray elevates his inventiveness with his Surrealist photographs—classic examples of the uncanny, in which the otherwise benign flow of reality is disrupted and the arrested present, in the form of the familiar or the normal, is allowed to transform itself into something quite different, as in *Minotaur* (1933; fig. 68), in which the mythic human and beast conjoin in the deftly manipulated shadows of a woman's torso that produce the head of the beast. The fascination with metamorphosis echoes this chapter in Man Ray's own narrative, his abandonment of New York reality for the embrace of the convulsively beautiful surreality of Paris.

First Man

The pressure that Man Ray exerted on his family and friends not to divulge anything about his past; the utter contrast between the trenchant severance with his past and the close, abiding custody he kept over his earliest drawings and paintings, even thematically revisiting his mechanical drawings and perspectival studies (fig. 69) late in life with a nostalgic significance normally accorded the dearest of loved ones; and the innumerable encrypted allusions to his roots throughout his art—these are just some of the idiosyncratic aspects of behavior that characterize Man Ray's unique identity complex.

His autobiographical *Self Portrait* begins with the statement: "My mother told me I made my first man on paper when I was three." It is as though, for the reader, this hasty announcement of Man Ray's artistic birth, the birth of his future public persona, is meant to eclipse his biological one, whose status is in fact further diminished by his declaration that "I myself just missed being born." It turns out that his mother, "horrified by the advances of my would-be father," balked at the prospect of staying with him, and they separated, only to meet up by chance a year later, when they "agreed to join their lives and possibly bring me into the world." Thus ends his parents' story, over almost before it began, with an ephemeral promise to bring him into the world.

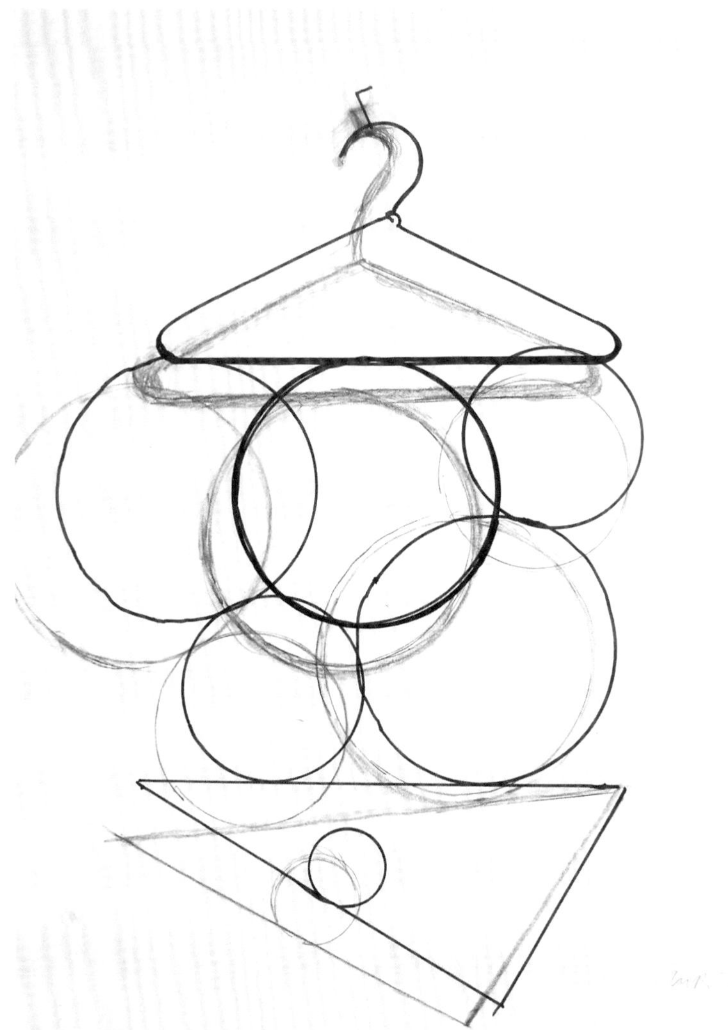

Fig. 69. *Shadows,* 1971. Ink on paper, 25½ × 19½ in. (64.8 × 49.5 cm). Francis M. Naumann Fine Art, New York

What is striking here is not just the brevity, alteration, or simple omission of facts concerning his parents and their early, stalled life together.[86] The strange locution of Man Ray's statement, that he "just missed being born," makes one wonder, momentarily, whether he would rather not have been. This framing of happenstance betrays indifference not to his own near nonexistence, but to that of his parents' marriage—a point cunningly made by the book's initial illustration, which the author placed opposite the opening text.

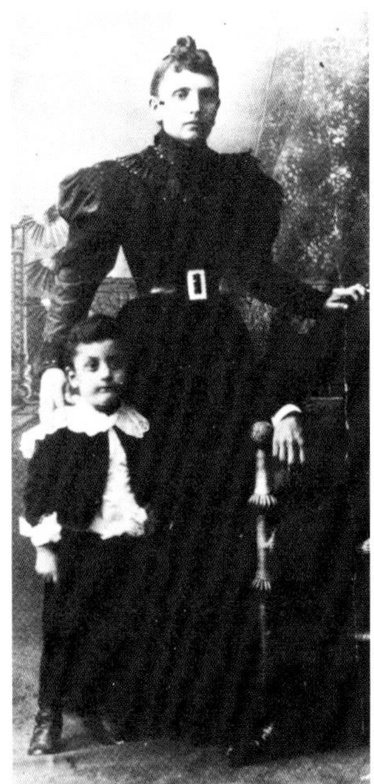

Fig. 70. Man Ray with his mother, 1896, as reproduced in the artist's book *Self Portrait* (1963)

Fig. 71. Man Ray with his mother, father, and sister Dora, 1896. Collection of Neil Baldwin

At first glance, the photograph of Man Ray with his mother, taken in Philadelphia in 1896, appears to be a typical period portrait (fig. 70). But one discerns that the seemingly mundane caption—"Man Ray with his mother"—is misleading because of the odd presence of an additional hand near the right edge. The image, actually half of a studio portrait the family had made in Philadelphia around 1896, when Man Ray was five years old, has been converted into a "nonfamily" portrait showing only the future artist standing beside his mother; the rest of the photograph, including his father and his sister Dora, has been cropped or torn away, surely a depiction of wished-for oedipal victory (fig. 71). All that remains of Melach (Max) Radnitzky is a disembodied hand—a fetishized body fragment (one of the many

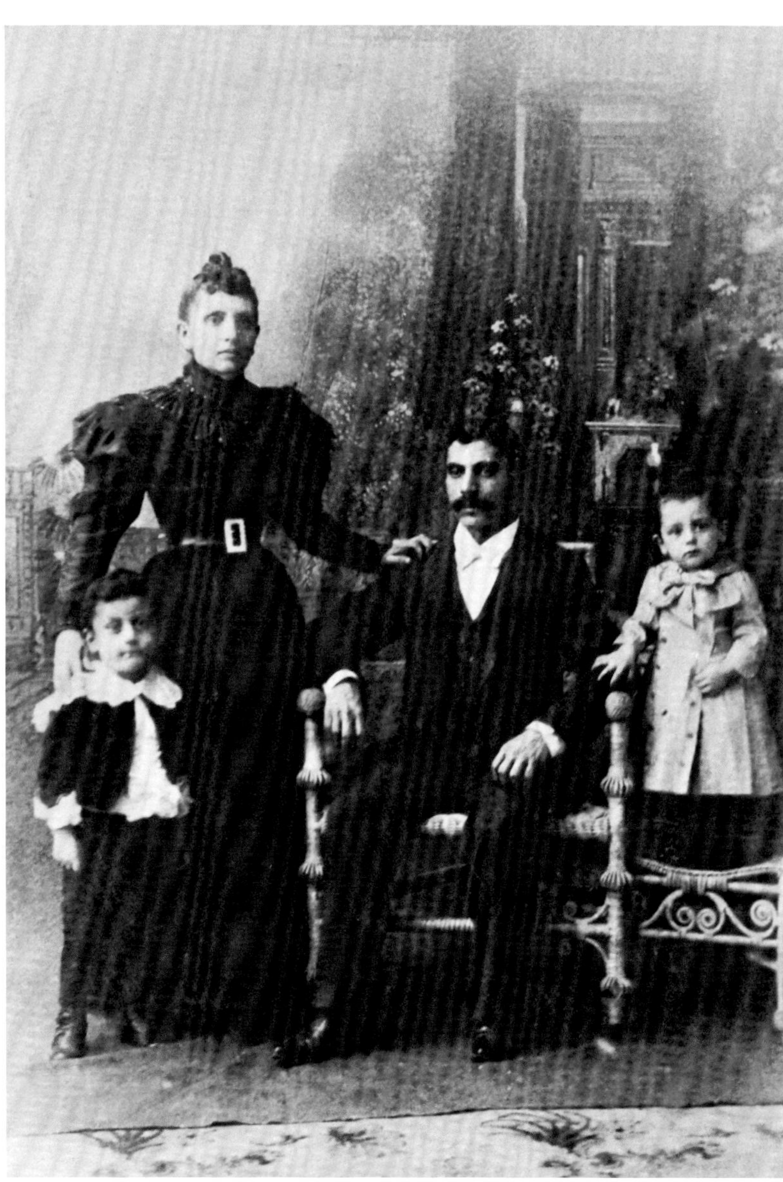

that recur in Man Ray's oeuvre), which functions here as a surrogate for the artist.[87] This interpretation could elucidate Man Ray's frequent inscription of himself within his work, as a symbolic "nominal" replacement of father by son. Man Ray may also have wished to leave an overt though encoded sign—a reference to his identity as an artist, whose freedom required a continual effacement of his origins.

This visual transposition with his father complements his autobiography's textual eradication of his family, a subject about which Man Ray refused to comment publicly. Combining techniques he employed throughout his career, fragmenting the body and cropping the image, he underscores what he specifically did not want to elaborate in the text, for the subject of the rupture between him and his family, particularly his parents, became increasingly rueful and sensitive later in life. As a stunningly blunt alteration of the book's solitary shred of evidence of his family's first seven years in Philadelphia, this act of documentary suppression is ironically revealing. Through a subtle mode of disclosure—a process at once destructive and re-creative—the artist cuts the family in half, leaving the unattached hand as a provocative self-portrait. Both in name and through the symbolic destruction of his lineage, Man Ray brackets more than just his need not to recognize his family; it is as if his existence depended on the obliteration of his Russian Jewish origins and the world in which he grew up, while he constitutes himself exclusively in the nonfilial terms of his artistic persona, the only, albeit amorphous, identity he will ever legitimize.

As such, this document of the family's life in Philadelphia becomes an appendage to, rather than an illustration of, the text, for it represents, in its silently manipulated form, that which could not be spoken. Again, Man Ray insists on having it both ways, displaying a picture whose worth is at least a thousand words, while providing a text that has nothing to do with the picture; characteristically, the artist both proves and disproves the "Chinese" proverb. Man Ray's autobiography becomes a creation myth, one in which a father is curiously absent. How can one not interpret such explicit behavior in a classic Freudian way?

But as Freud would have it, an oedipal victory is inevitably a Pyrrhic one, since the "triumphant" son cannot, of course, meet the task of satisfying the mother. To achieve safe passage through oedipal waters in a way that promotes development toward adulthood— the hallmarks of which include the capacity for whole relationships over part relationships, and for mutuality and empathy, and a respect for boundaries and limits—the boy must surrender rivalrous feelings toward the father and, instead, identify with and look up to him. It is exactly this that Man Ray defiantly refuses to do. By figuratively killing off the father, refusing his father's name, eliding him from the family portrait, even at the age of seventy-two, he effectively stunts his own psychological growth, retreating—and here we must shift to more recent schools of psychoanalytic thought—into a pre-oedipal, narcissistic world where boundaries are permeable; the capacity for guilt and empathy remains unachieved; merging is the predominant mode of relating; distinctions between generations are disregarded; other people are deemed mere mirrors of, or appendages to, the self, exist-

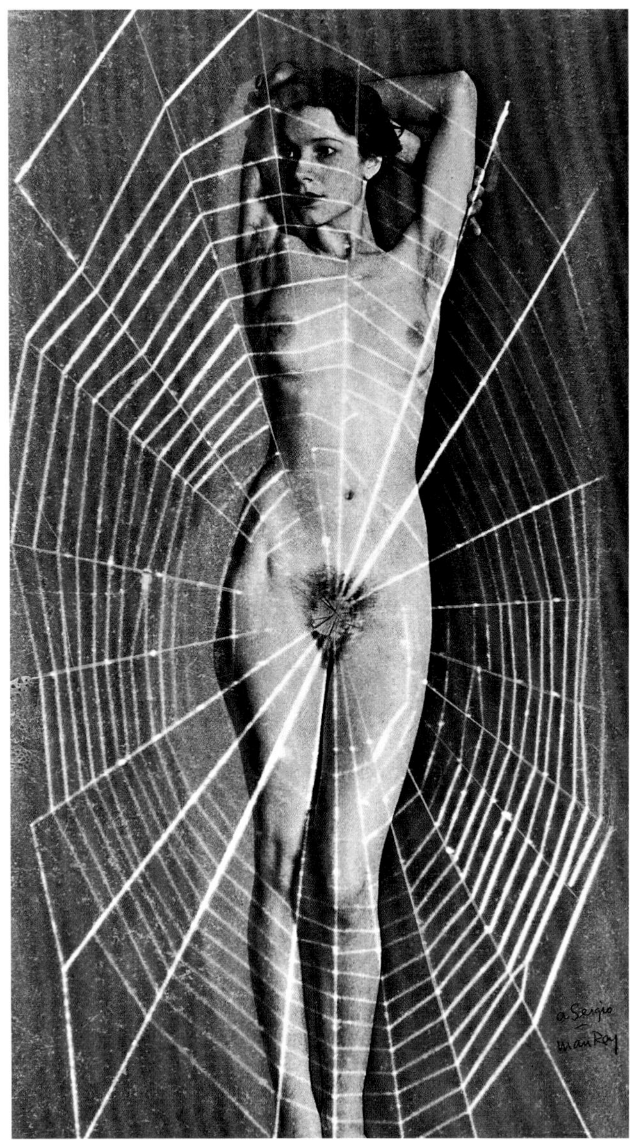

Fig. 72. *Spider Woman*, c. 1950.
Original silver print on white
card, 25 × 14½ in. (63.5 × 36.8 cm).
Collection of Karen Amiel Baum,
New York

ing only to meet the demands of that self, and if such imperious needs are not met, the response is rage.[88]

I would argue that Man Ray inhabited this shadowy world between boyhood and manhood, an attenuated adolescence, throughout his life. He preferred his (pregenital) version of creation, in which the child stages his own birth and confers upon himself the status of "Man," to the conventional one, in which the father plays the seminal role. It would follow for Man Ray that it was not a contradiction to exclude his parents from this self-constructed world, as he had his father from the family portrait, yet guiltlessly seek material support from them (and by extension practical support from his all-too-willing sister Elsie and later Naomi, her daughter). Certainly his ongoing economic dependence on his family was but one of several ways that he exercised regression, fulfilling the ideology of his chosen persona to exist unconstrained, through an unremitting insistence on freedom or, indeed, extreme nonconformity if not contrariness: the "part-objects" he both fetishizes and destroys; the aspect of "play" in his art; or conversely, when he was rejected and emotionally distressed, his reversion to an almost preverbal, dysfunctional, depressive state.

As Man Ray, he ruled over a princedom of his own making, his subjects the women he mentored, loved, and sought to control, and a brood of carefully tended, painstakingly documented works (fig. 72).

the sublimation of rage

This narcissistic side to Man Ray's personality countervails the self-effacing side, the tension between them expressing itself variously in the extreme mood swings for which he was known and in his curious embrace of contradiction, not the least examples of which were the concurrent needs to exert and relinquish control. A more complex view of his personality explains the extent to which the notion of cathexis functions in his life and work, in the particular quality of his emotional and erotic attachments to people and objects. And it explains the increasing range of symbolic inclusion of things associated with his youth, as in the sundry appearance of needles and thread, irons and sewing patterns (figs. 73 and

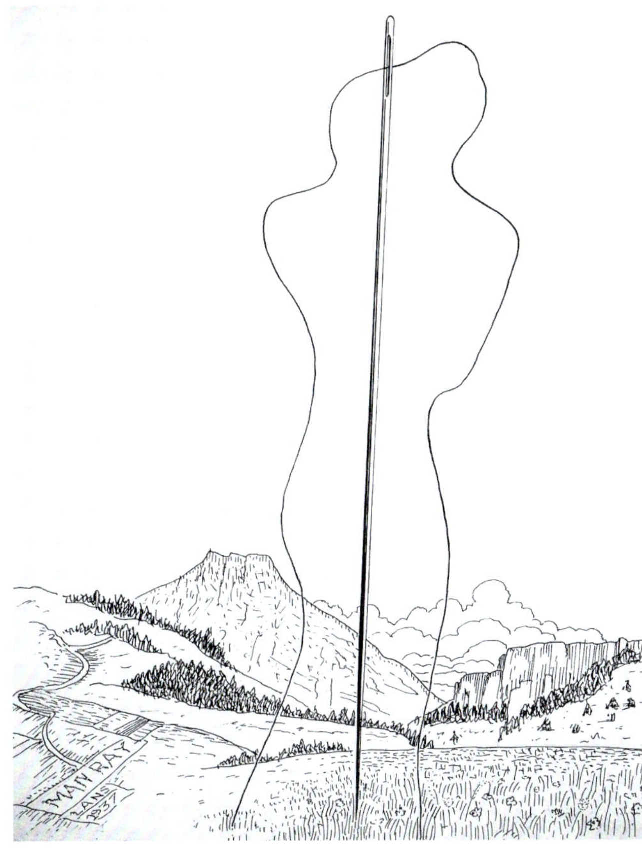

Fig. 73. *Fil et aiguille (Needle and Thread)*, 1937. Ink on paper, 13¼ × 9⅝ in. (36.2 × 24.5 cm). The Menil Collection, Houston

Fig. 74. *Lingerie*, from the portfolio *Electricité*, 1931. Photogravure from rayograph, 10⅛ × 8 in. (25.7 × 20.3 cm). Heckscher Museum of Art, Huntington, New York, Museum purchase with funds provided by Andrea B. and Peter D. Klein

74), as well as the preciously retained works from that period, specifically his mechanical drawings, all symptomatic of an underlying reparative need: he had to compensate for the sense of emptiness typically experienced by those suffering from narcissistic disorders, an emptiness compounded afresh by each successive registration of rejection or loss. While his sense of alienation, shame, or self-erasure found sublimated expression in more passive, defensive modalities, such as mimicry and displays of stylistic invention defying hierarchy or coherence, the internalization of loss and rejection that Man Ray associated, consciously or not, with his family reached an apotheosis in mid-career.

The most famous manifestation of his narcissism was his emotional/artistic response to his breakup with Lee Miller, the American who dallied in fashion as a model before determining that she wanted to meet Man Ray and be his protégée,

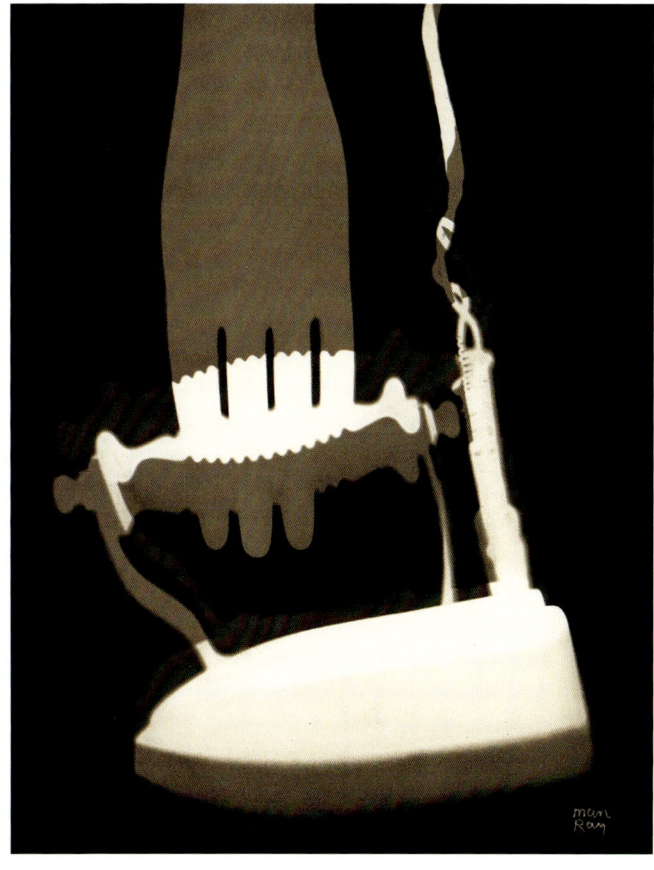

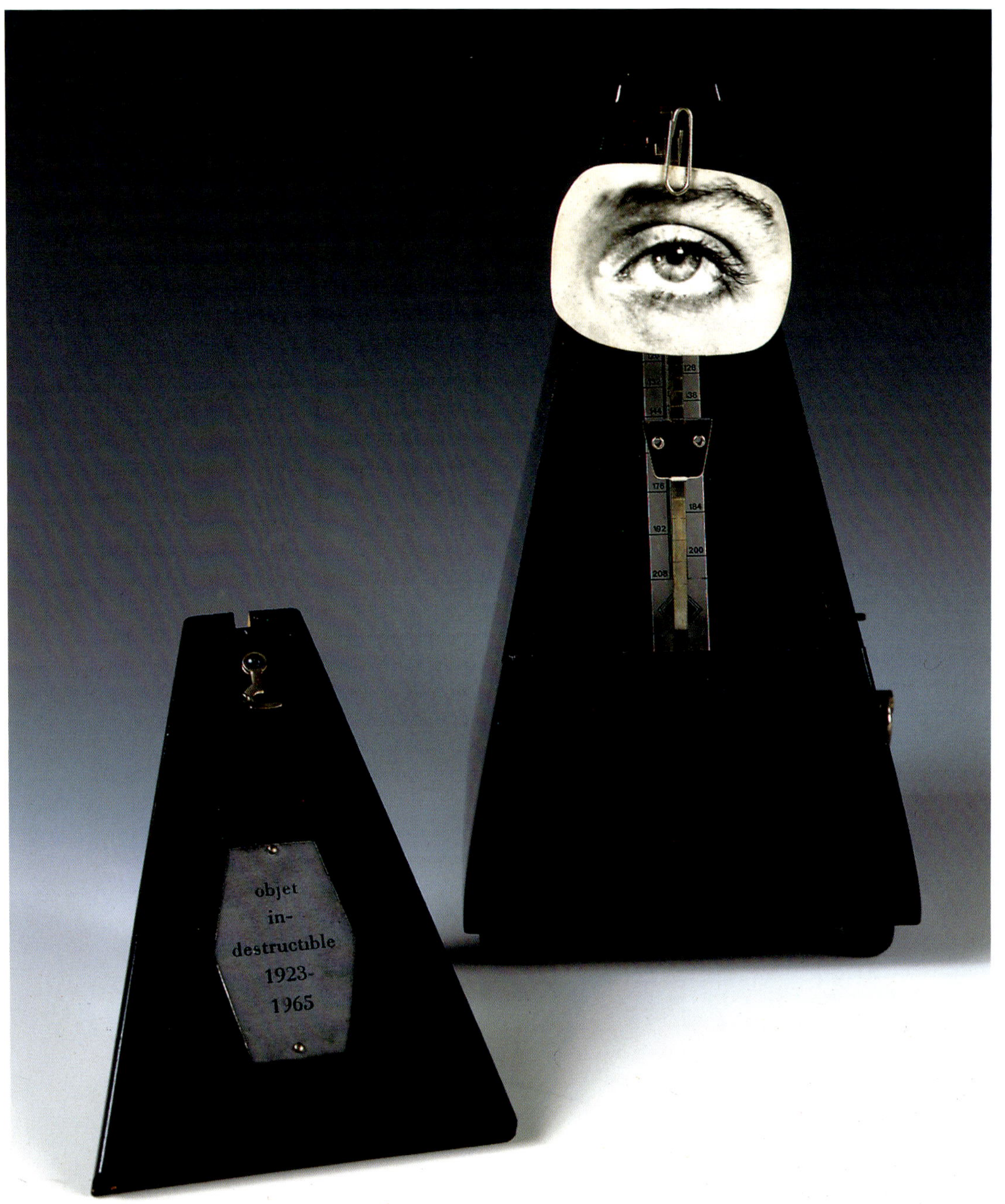

Fig. 75. *Indestructible Object*, 1923/65. Wood, fiber, metal, and paper on cardboard, 8½ × 4½ × 4½ in. (21.6 × 11.4 × 11.4 cm). Montclair Art Museum, New Jersey, Museum Purchase: Acquisition Fund

as straightaway she did, introducing herself to her chosen Pygmalion in 1929 and promptly becoming his Galatea, a role she played for nearly three years. She entered the scene at a time when the artist was struggling, bored with his "occupation" as a photographer, yet insecure and not fully acknowledged as a painter. He was inordinately vulnerable to her gradual challenge to and eventual competition with him in his own domain. Neil Baldwin captures his relationship with Miller, writing that Man Ray "[assumed] that her strong will, sense of direction and headstrong nature existed only insofar as they were handed down from him."[89] Her strong sense of autonomy,

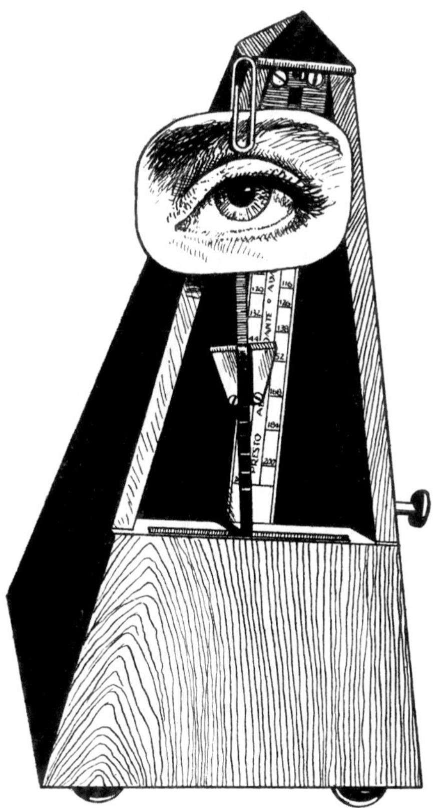

Fig. 76. *Object of Destruction (Drawing by Man Ray)*, 1932

Fig. 77. *Lee Miller's Eye*, 1932. Vintage photograph, with inscription on reverse, $3\frac{1}{8} \times 4\frac{1}{8}$ in. (7.9 × 10.5 cm). The Penrose Collection, England

even entitlement, her increasing independence from and ultimate rebuke of him, pushed him into a state of helpless rage, which he expressed in the form of murderous threats and obsessive defacements of her image. He sublimated that rage in one of his most famous works, *Object of Destruction*, first published in 1932 as a drawing of a metronome onto which was clipped a cut-out photograph of Miller's eye (figs. 75–77).[90] The accompanying caption to the drawing chillingly conveyed the artist's state of mind: "Cut out the eye from a photograph of one who has been loved but is seen no more. Attach the eye to the pendulum of a metronome and regulate the weight to suit the tempo desired. Keep going to the limit of endurance. With a hammer well-aimed, try to destroy the whole at a single blow."

From her perch as muse, Miller was evoked in numerous photographs

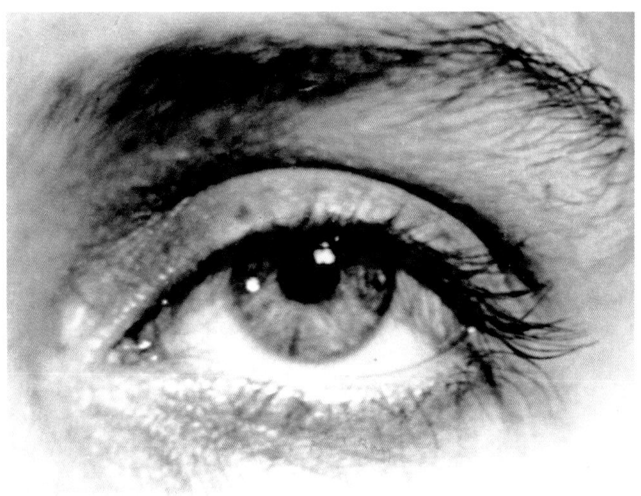

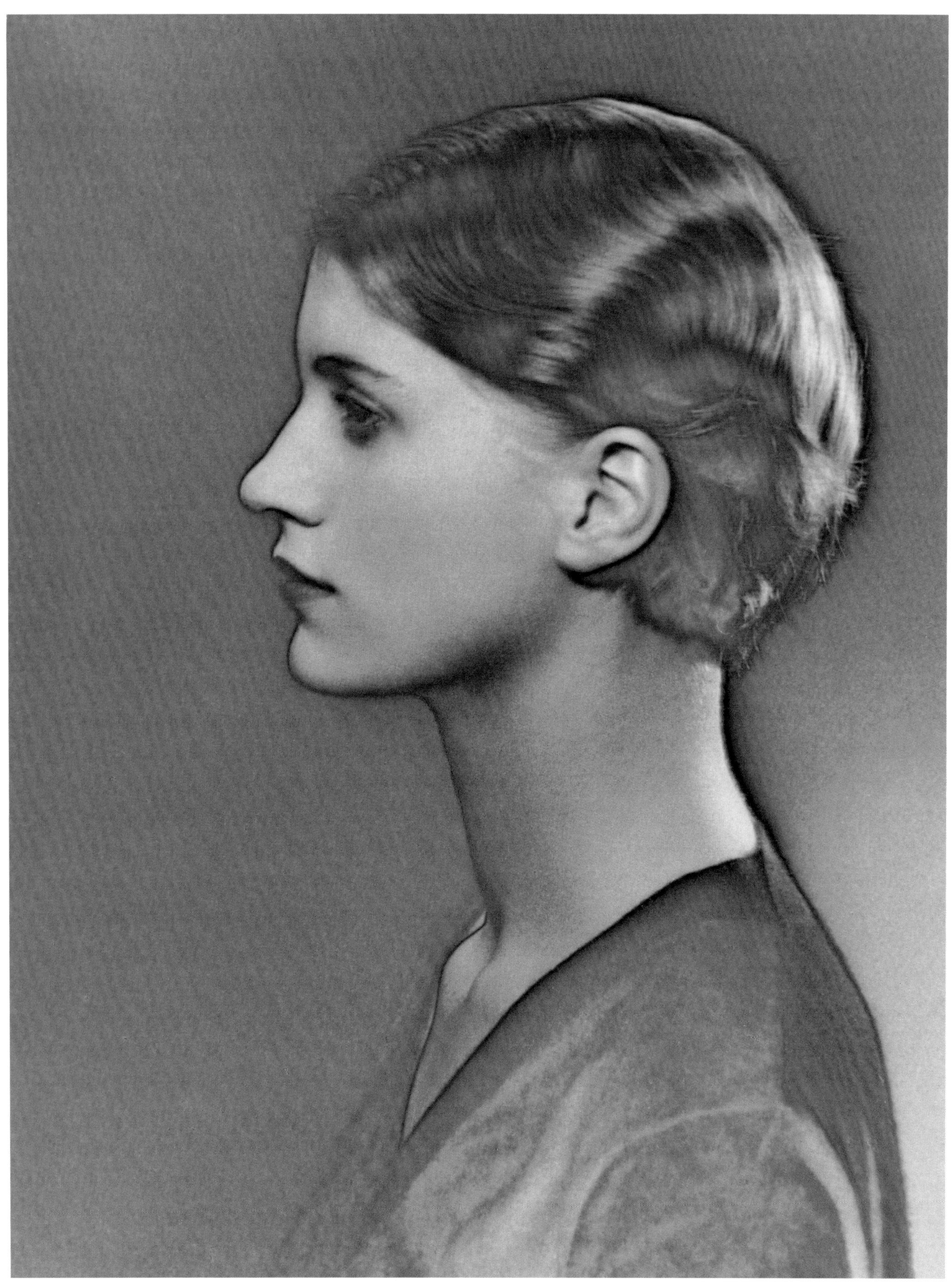

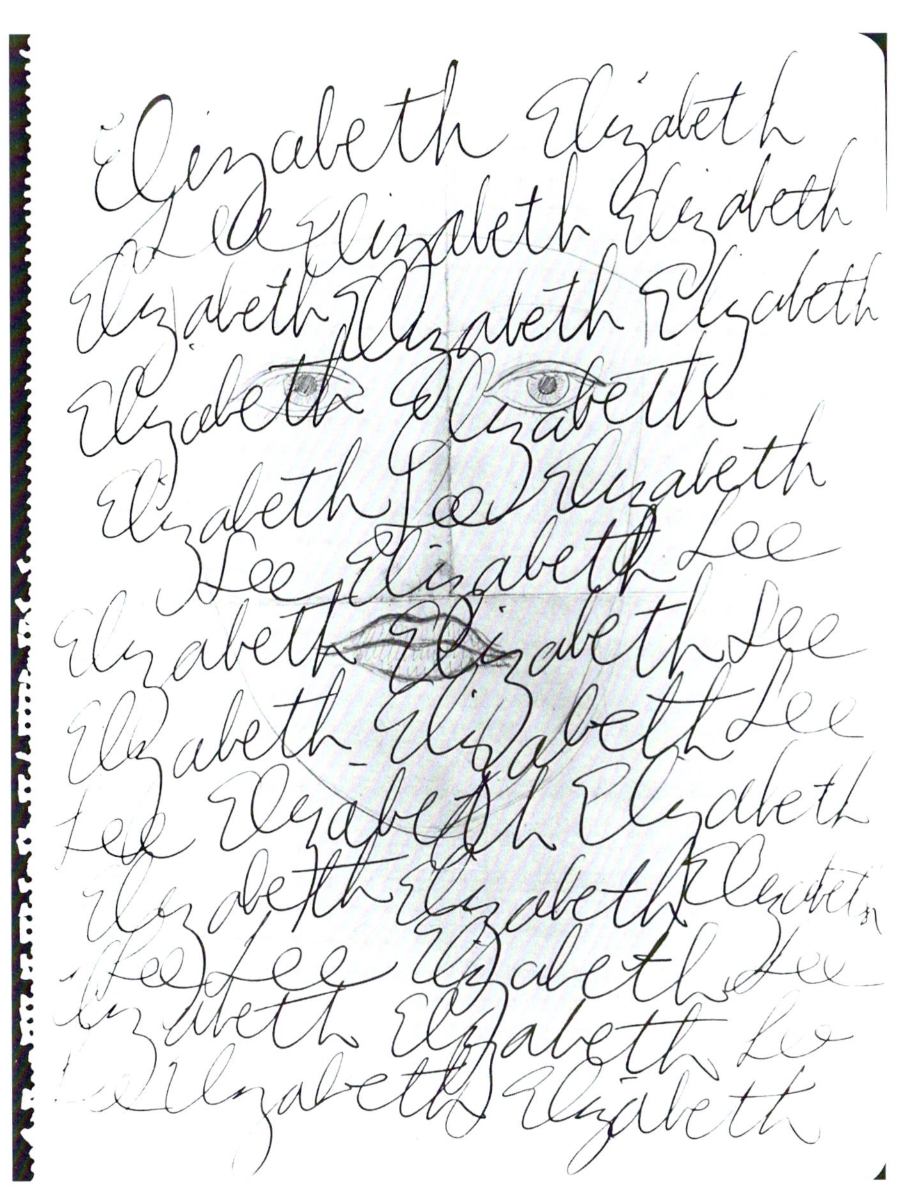

Fig. 79. *Elizabeth, Elizabeth, Lee…*, 1932. Page of notebook inscribed by Man Ray, 10⅝ × 8³⁄₁₆ in. (27 ×
20.8 cm). The Penrose Collection, England

that teem with obsessive objectification. Man Ray had progressively fragmented her
anatomy, as if she were a marionette—yet he knew on some level that he was the one whose
strings were being pulled (figs. 78 and 79). His reduction of Miller to anatomical fragments
devolves into a kind of violence. The artist's aggression also finds expression in the form of
self-assertion evident in the singularity and repetition of his artistic voice: his need to con-

tinuously inscribe and re-create himself, for instance in repainting works that he feared lost, or simply desiring to vary them ("I have never painted a recent picture"); and to surround himself with his art and "objects of affection," the virtual offspring that carefully define his self-contained universe.[91]

remember the *Maine*

Throughout his career, Man Ray made certain that his identity as an artist would supersede his biography. In the catalogue that accompanied his first show at Librairie Six, he provided an apocryphal history that would further secure the secrecy he cherished.[92] This brief fictitious profile contained the kernel of his future *Self Portrait*, an amusing mixture of candor and factual elision. His need to guard his privacy was respected and affirmed by his Surrealist colleagues. Embedded within that movement was a distaste for dredging up the past, especially the powerless period of childhood; the mandate of Surrealism, as it had been for Dada, was to overthrow authority. Personal history, furthermore, was considered extraneous to the imagination, which required immersion in the present. Thus, family, as Alain Jouffroy has noted, was "nothing more than an immense pile of dead leaves." But Man Ray was not only intent on disowning the past; he set out to inflect history, to control it as much as possible. While writing his memoir, the aging artist felt himself "in the thick of a critical struggle with posterity," and wished desperately to have a say in how he was understood and would be remembered. Even he had to concede that the whole story would be told someday: "You cannot shut the door in the face of history," he acknowledged, "because history will kick it in violently."[93] Yet for as long as he lived he kept the door shut, in much the same way as did his 1916 *Self-Portrait*, whose doorbell was never meant to function.

If his history had to be told, he wanted to sustain the myth of the artist by providing "inspiration, not information"; this, as he explained to Seymour Lawrence, his editor and then director of Atlantic–Little, Brown in Boston, was what he considered the "general purpose of the book." His insistence on walling off his artistic self from any extraneous material was a nonnegotiable matter, as he had made quite clear when he submitted his manuscript. Lawrence, a Man Ray enthusiast who commissioned the book, was puzzled by the lack of dates and details, and the omission of background material, and favored a more open approach. His considerable efforts to persuade the artist to be more forthcoming with information and reminiscences, pleading for "some [more] tangible detail," were stonewalled. Man Ray remonstrated that he was "allergic" to numbers and dates, and that the "whole book is meant to be ambiguous for the average reader." This, he said, "is my way, as in my painting."[94] And it seemed his attitude toward filmmaking as well, where he reflected his ambivalent relationship to reality. "I don't like films that show what happens in life," he commented in 1965. "I call films which persist in reproducing life 'keyhole' films." He even wrote *Self Portrait*, he said, "so as not to have to recount my past any more, and so that I could start living in the present."[95] The past would be suppressed in the service of a higher goal: the need to mythologize himself. In preparing the manuscript for publication he exerted complete editorial control, from the typeface to the choice of photographs and the exact way they would be laid out and captioned. His recollections, despite his noted flawless memory, would remain highly selective.

In perpetuating an elusive identity, Man Ray silenced any voice but his autonomous artistic one, just as he had been able, as an American, to remain detached from the extreme politics that factionalized the Surrealist ranks. This abiding facility to remain independent was evident from his initial engagement with the Dadaists in Paris, soon to be riven by Breton's call for ideological solidification of the Surrealist position in his First Manifesto of 1924. Moreover, Man Ray's self-imposed exile to Paris placed him in a group within which his American status functioned positively to differentiate him. One might say that it neutralized his Jewish "otherness," too (this clearly did not apply to those immigrant artists corralled under the name the School of Paris). In *Self Portrait*, he glosses over his parents' actual physical introduction and marriage, which in fact occurred on the same day, as something almost ephemeral, and immediately moves on to his earliest encounters with paint, which signal his real birth, as an artist.

The first encounter, in a prank when the artist was five, was a performative incident brash enough to rank as perhaps his first proto-Dada happening. Orchestrated by the mischievous maestro himself, it involved, in chronological order: a group of playmates, freshly painted house shutters, roving hands, smeared faces and clothing, and finally a parental "cold-blooded whipping." It is not until he turns seven that Man Ray becomes a more directed, inspired, and even experimental artist, when, right after being given a box of crayons as a birthday gift from his cousin, he uses them to color a detailed drawing he had copied from a newspaper picture of the USS *Maine*, sunk in Havana harbor. It is noteworthy that the artist refers to the sinking of the American battleship as "recent," when it in fact had occurred six months before, suggesting the lengths to which Man Ray was willing to go to include this one historical incident, which he chose for its significance. There were mixed reviews of his drawing of the *Maine* among family members, its faithful details of "turrets and guns" admired far more than the "arbitrary manner" in which he had employed the "full spectrum" of bright-colored crayons. Recalling this budding artistic experience in his memoir, Man Ray wrote that while he was unable to "refute the criticisms," he had felt entirely justified in his use of bright colors. "Since the original pictures were in black, I was perfectly free to use my imagination; besides, it was my way of expressing my patriotism."[96] Sixty-five years later, Man Ray was still defending his penchant for bright colors, and also linking such possible intemperance to his fidelity to his native land.

His patriotism had remained a sensitive matter, fraught with conflicting sentiments. The conflict had begun with his early critical treatment in New York and progressed with his achievement of fame as an expatriate whose success was founded in part on the perception of many Europeans of his indelible Americanness, his sense of which became only more complex as time passed. It was especially difficult for him during World War II, when he was forced to flee Paris and became a quasi-refugee and an exile in his own country.

Is it merely coincidental, then, that the artist chooses at the outset of his memoir the historical incident of the bombing of the *Maine*, a precedent of yellow journalism and jingoistic fervor, to introduce the charged personal topics of artistic license and patriotism? Given Man Ray's agenda of obscurantism—his very autobiography was subjected to extreme editorial manipulation in order to prop up the artist's creation myth—how could this precedent of media-driven and commodified history not resonate for the artist and assume greater than face value in the telling?

The black-and-white medium of newspaper illustration, which Man Ray felt entitled to embolden with his spectrum of colored crayons, was the same one through which William Randolph Hearst, the publisher of the morning *New York Journal*, had pressed his staff to conjure tales of Spanish conspiracy against American interests, and stories of brutal Spanish colonialist injustices against the Cuban people. Touting the Cuban rebels as freedom fighters, Hearst invoked America's own story: "Their proceedings have been animated by the same fearless spirit that inspired the patriot fathers who sat in Philadelphia on the 4th of July, 1776."[97] The publisher reportedly—but more than likely apocryphally—said, "You furnish the pictures and I'll furnish the war."

If the young artist enthusiastically imposed his colors on a carefully copied drawing, made after the stark record of a tragic, distant, commercially exploited event, here in *Self Portrait*, Man Ray was again coloring, if only figuratively, the black-and-white text that constituted the reconstruction of his youthful annals. On both occasions, as in the case of such reportage, the emphasis was on the bombastic rendering rather than on the factual occurrence, privileging the artist and the imagination in order to foster and shape a prescribed perception. In other words, in the very first pages of his autobiography, whose extreme editorialization at times renders truth as unrealistically as does a child's subjective use of color, Man Ray manages to allude to key personal, critical, and artistic matters. He was imposing his colors on a black-and-white world, with no more concern for authenticity than Hearst had had; Man Ray was remaking history in his own image, just as he would his art.

The choice of the *Maine* as both subject and object, as both foregrounded inspiration of his own aesthetic and ideological passions (color and liberty) and neutral, background reminiscence (a contrast oddly configured in *The Rope Dancer*), suggests an ancillary, but promiscuous, journalistic offshoot. Man Ray's own mythic self-aggrandizing poses the question of the *Maine*'s direct relationship to yellow journalism, and by extension, to the titular source of that medium: the Yellow Kid, a character from the extremely popular comic strip *Hogan's Alley*, one of the first to introduce color to newsprint and one that excelled in parodying social stereotypes and mocking classist behavior. Man Ray does not tell us how much shame he may have suffered for any discrimination sustained as a child, but we do know that he came of age when this popular comic strip had already emerged and that it addressed the inner-city immigrant world, with its ethnic tensions and mischievous gangs of kids.[98] Man Ray does give pride of place, in his cautious autobiographical selections, to his status as leader among the neighborhood boys but makes little mention of the beatings he occasionally took because, according to his sister Dora, of his slight stature. Such elision, like the omission from *Self Portrait* of his near-fatal attraction to Lee Miller, is, paradoxically, telling.

From the very first line of *Self Portrait*, Man Ray merges with his childhood artistic incarnation, wanting us to believe that whoever he was at any stage or place in his life was never any different from the person he was today. His identity could be known only through the fluid, ever-changing art that he produced, and kept reproducing. "It is permitted to repeat oneself as much as possible," he stated. "Nothing is more legitimate and more satisfactory. So long as you do not repeat others. Work until you have developed one single manner that is you, and no one else."[99]

the **E**arliest **O**bject of my affection

After warding off his critics, at age seven, and keeping his version of the USS *Maine* afloat, the artist's assumption of his creative destiny is virtually broadcast as he reflects with engrossed wonder on his youthful inventiveness, likening the diversity of his interests beyond painting to those of Leonardo da Vinci—ballistics, human anatomy, and all things mechanical. Such aggrandizement would not brook interference or repression, and Man Ray cites perhaps the most telling example of his enterprising and inventive young self, laying out further cause for his eventual need to leave home and seek distance from his family.

This incident is as telling of his own passionate will as it is of his scolding, overprotective mother's. After learning about a soapbox wagon her son had gone to considerable lengths to build, unfortunately with wheels stolen from another child's toy, she demolished it with an ax. Though she insisted she was prompted by fear for her son's safety, this excuse does not explain the extreme violence of her act. For this was no ordinary wagon; it was a locomotive he had made to distinguish himself in the neighborhood, "to outdo all the others" with his ingenuity. It was festooned with a barrel and a black-painted stovepipe, from which belched wads of cotton smoke, and he was as proud of his homemade vehicle as he was outraged to discover it reduced to a pile of splinters. Neither tears nor contrition aroused his mother's remorse or understanding of how significant this loss was to her son. "It took me a long time to forget," the artist recalled, adding ruefully, "I believe I never forgave her."

Despite this wounding estrangement, Man Ray interjects a rare sympathetic view. As if to compensate for the finality of the previous statement, he concedes his mother's "respect" for him in "matters of art and taste."[100] Man Ray cites not just her solicitation of his opinion at the milliner's, or when a new piece of furniture was to be acquired or a wallpaper chosen, but the fact that she accepted his offer to make a new lampshade for one that

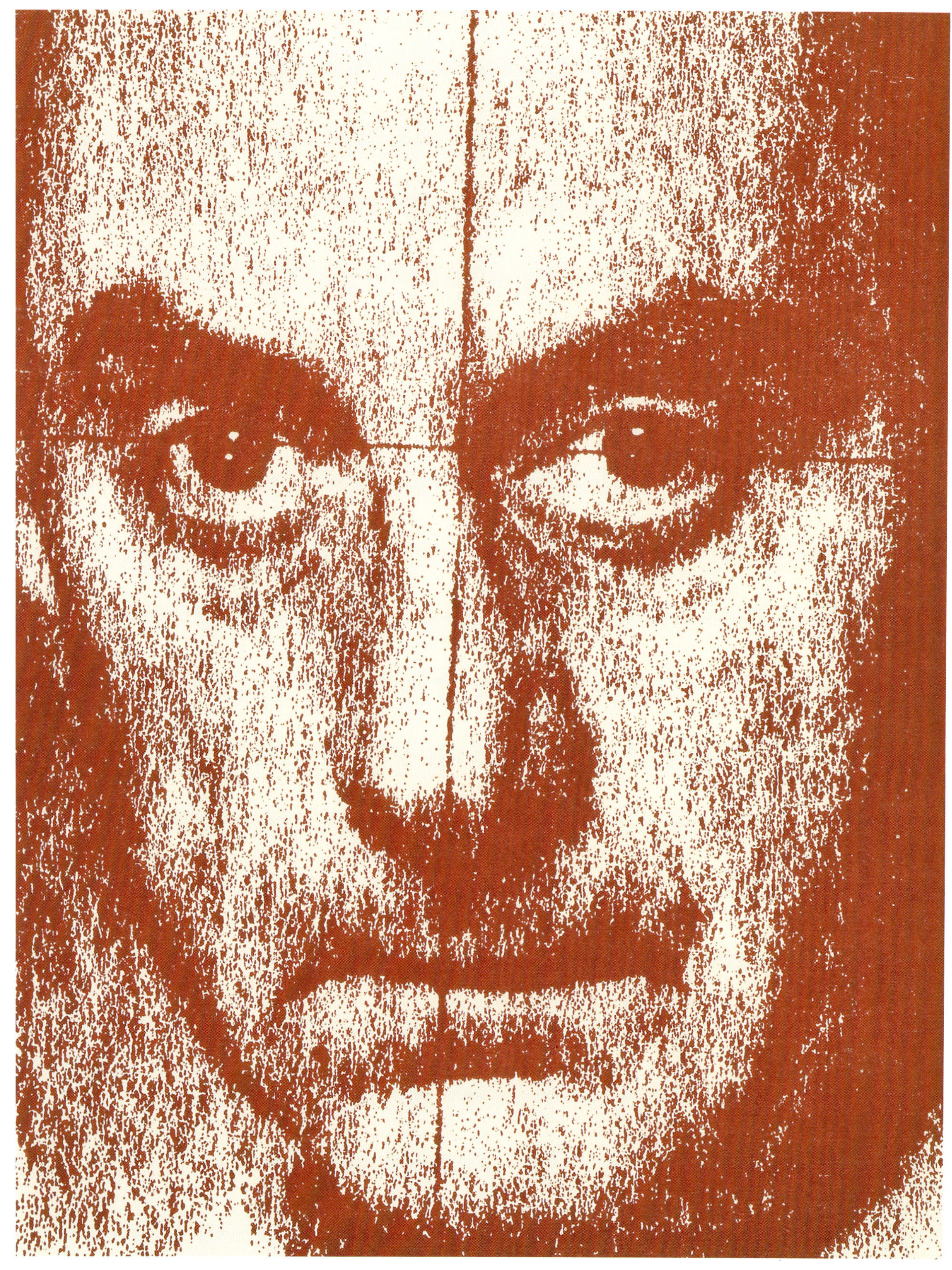

Fig. 80. *Self-Portrait*, c. 1947. Lithograph
on zinc plate, 8 × 6⅛ in. (20.3 × 15.7 cm).
Courtesy of Timothy Baum, New York

had fallen apart, and admired it greatly. Beyond this momentary rapprochement, there is an almost palpable urgency to snip any cloying tendrils of nostalgia wherever they might appear, lest they threaten to tug him back. The division between his life as an artist and his working-class family's resistance to it had been irrevocably determined. With his mind increasingly fixed on becoming a painter, he would take his paintbox along on "the elevated train to the end of the line, to the outskirts of Brooklyn—open country, barns, horses and cows grazing in the fields," where, "in solitude, he thought of himself as a Thoreau breaking free of all ties and duties to society." But this fantasy was not realized until, not yet twenty-three and fairly champing at the bit, he decided to move out of the family home in Brooklyn, to find real solitude and a space where he could work more seriously, unimpeded by the ceaseless chatter and commercial pressures of the city. The rusticity of Ridgefield, New Jersey, as he would recall in his memoir, provided him with the distance and inspiration he needed: "Cold clear water came from a well nearby. This, and the ten-minute walk through the woods, were to me the symbols of my escape from the sordidness in the city."[101]

As he was writing *Self Portrait*, Man Ray was concerned with shaping his own legacy, drawing what he knew was a complex biographical profile without disclosing too much. Whatever the reasons that compelled him to write an autobiography—given the intricacy of his identity and the idiosyncratic trajectory of his career—there is in the very design of the book's jacket an ostensible aspect of expiation and confession, embodying a desire, perhaps, to seek redemption for having concealed so much and cutting off so many. He places himself between the arresting crosshairs (fig. 80), under the gun, implying that he has finally been fingered—and as in the Nick Carter detective stories he read as a child, that the "jig was up."[102]

This impulse toward disclosure is, of course, at best a struggle, its promise of candor eclipsed by guardedness, its revelation undermined by the ingrained habit of withholding. The fragments of fact that are divulged are compromised by the sketchiness of their extrapolation, which leaves the curious reader afloat in a harbor engulfed in fog, uncertain of where the shore is, but sensing it, perhaps, to be near.

Staged Domesticity

Almost nothing is known about the early years of Man Ray's family, and few documents exist. Even his birth certificate is available only as a transcript, the original obligingly destroyed or lost. A solitary extant photograph, taken in 1896, did not, as discussed above, make it unscathed into his *Self Portrait*, despite, or perhaps because of, its being the sole record of the Radnitzky family's seven years in Philadelphia. A typical late-nineteenth-century commercial-studio family portrait, it is an artifact of an era of immigration, with its infinitely varied tales of diverse social upheaval, dislocation, and sacrifice all endured in the quest for a new identity. Such documents served an evidentiary purpose, to mark the incipient fulfillment of such goals. Gathered in their finest dress, the casts of characters of this era often presented the bourgeois aspirations of the patriarch of the family, whose dominant presence, like that of Max Radnitzky, can be felt strongly in the photographs. Planted squarely in the middle of the photograph, this stocky man with dark features and powerful hands is pictured with his wife, Minnie, and their two children at the time, the artist, age five or six, and his one-year-old sister, Dora.[103] With his serious mien and upright posture, Max alone is seated, enthroned in an exotic chair, projecting the determination and pride of a hardworking individual who supplemented his daily earnings at a garment factory by working as a tailor at home at night. The solid reliability of this man is conveyed by his intractable presence, casting no doubt as to his protective role.

But the contrivance of such a scene only encourages the viewer to challenge that which appears to be, to notice any hint of contradiction: one is too aware of the artificiality and posturing of such staged domesticity. True, Max's intense features, his apparent strength and single-mindedness of character, are underscored by the elaborate chair on which he sits. Like the prop that it is, this imitation of a more serious, historical chair suggests an importance that belies its humble rattan composition. The sovereignty of Max's bearing is enhanced by the fact that while he is physically touched by both his wife and daughter, he remains impassive, his hands distinctly unoccupied. As sedentary guardian of the family, he assumes a monumental timelessness, becomes a signifier of the past, the upholder of a culture to be challenged by his son, in which individual needs were subordinated to those of the family. The differentiation is reinforced by the unique direction of his gaze, a divergence that also illuminates a contrast in personalities: one of the rare bits of information that one can glean from the artist's family is that his father was the conciliator, while his mother was temperamental and given to melodrama.[104] Max's eye was not on the everyday domestic details that preoccupied his wife but on the material realities of the world beyond his door. Further differences can be detected in the ways the parents interact with their children: Man Ray's mother stands protectively behind her son, with one hand resting on his shoulder, her other hand dutifully touching her husband. Solidly enthroned, feet rooted in front of him, Max seems indifferent to his tiny daughter, who perches unsurely on the seat next to his. Having emigrated from Russia in 1886, at the age of twenty-one, to escape the draft in Kiev, Max had wasted little time in trying to establish a legitimate family. The photograph reveals exactly the kind of stiff, patriarchal organization that Man Ray would spend his life fleeing or transforming. Any fact or object could be cathected and converted.

Against the Grain

Some photographers have traditionally demanded veracity from their craft, insisting on a process as pure and transparent as the negative it produces, and on the full-framed, unaltered image that the negative yields. Their photography reconstructs what was seen, as though the wonder, if not the purpose, of photography were to stand witness to truth itself. But for Man Ray, truthfulness or obligation had nothing to do with the making of art. He had jettisoned such parochial beliefs shortly after high school, when he abandoned plans to hone the mechanical skills of draftsmanship and become an architect. Neither did he subscribe to the idea that photography, or any medium of art-making, was necessarily a craft, a perfectible technique. He may have come to photography with no expectation or need other than that of utility, wanting simply to document his work. As a painter and an object maker, a bricoleur and an artisan of invention, he soon realized, under the influential spell of Stieglitz, that the camera could and should become a tool of discovery. Was he not already a practical artist, versed in the industrial arts in high school, capable of designing and drawing blueprints and mechanicals? Hadn't he already envisaged abstract paintings from fabric samples lying around his home, and pilfered what was necessary—whether wheels or crayons—to construct and make what he needed?

It was in the studio and the darkroom that Man Ray's images were realized. His was the antithesis of the practice of the "straight" photographer who insists the negative be printed full-frame. Of the 5,000 contact prints attributed to him in the Musée national d'art moderne archives, over 1,200 display cropping indications, the number according roughly with the number of pictures that Man Ray used. An analysis of the archives indicates that not a single negative of his was printed without some cropping. The artist downplayed his skills, referring to the effects of his photographs not only as chance discoveries made in the darkroom, but in terms that echoed his painterly sensibilities: "Some of the most effective photographs . . . were magnifications of a detail of the face and body. . . . I carried this idea further by giving such details a texture inherent in the medium itself, coarse grain, partial reversal of the negative and other technical variations; all frowned upon by straight photographers."[105]

By favoring a materialist understanding of his medium, Man Ray was going against the grain of those purists who, like Paul Strand, Charles Sheeler, and Alfred Stieglitz, had envisioned what was proper to ensure the autonomy of the medium. Far from ever supporting such an ideologically pure, or exclusive, approach to any medium, Man Ray proceeded to effectively dismantle photography's claim to transparent truth and, with the rayograph, its autonomous identity. While the rayograph dispensed entirely with the camera—in its simple exposure of the independent subject to light-sensitive paper, it conferred mystery upon ordinary objects, their contours merely circumscribed by light—photographers elsewhere were embracing a visionary potential for the camera of another, über order. Standing in contrast to the arbitrarily determined effects of the rayograph was the meticulously thorough and descriptive imagery of the technologically inspired Neue Sachlichkeit (New Objectivity) movement, which rapidly expanded throughout Western Europe, particularly in Germany during the Weimar years (1919–33). The technocratic ideology of optical precision was codified in Prague, where, in 1923, the avant-garde review *Disk* acclaimed this new sensibility with the slogan "PHOTOGRAPH: Objective truth and documentary clarity above all doubts."[106]

Belief in the virtue of the factual had its roots in Germany's longtime technically sophisticated printing industry, which had disseminated an unprecedented and brilliantly detailed set of images of the products of the new machine age.[107] These photographs had such compelling appeal that they were embraced by a generation of architects, writers, and artists, whose belief in the machine aesthetic was entirely positivist and futuristic in its social context. The elevated *neue Auge* (new eye or new perception) of the camera rejected the soft focus of the Pictorialists, and moreover announced that the camera was no longer in competition with painting. In precipitating an extraordinary range of formal exploration, Neue Sachlichkeit sought to incorporate the plastic concerns of modern painting—collage, simultaneity, spatial and temporal dislocation—and to supersede an illusionistic medium's ability to capture the modern world of pedestrian reality.

As practitioners of this new aesthetic positivism, including Karl Blossfeldt, Albert Renger-Patzsch, and August Sander, rejected extraneous (painterly or drawn) effects, even ceasing to use textured printing paper, Man Ray countered such German "factography" by assuming an antidocumentary position. He had already dismissed the camera with his rayographs and was using more textured paper; his work in the 1930s concentrated on more formal portraiture, elegantly enhanced, occasionally, by the solarization process. "I no longer tried out new cameras, but did go into the darkroom now and then to make *solarizations*, since it was a deviation from the principles of good photography: to work in the dark. *Solarizations* were made comfortably with the bright lights turned on."[108]

In addition to his investigations into the effects and properties of light in his new manner of photography, Man Ray provided endless evidence of his refusal to accept boundaries, with the constant employment of ulterior methods, such as framing or cropping, to illustrate how transformable any subject or object could be. Through such procedures of intervention and manipulation, he would conjure and enhance reality, the Surrealist in him imprinting matter upon thought in a way that only the unconscious could conceive it, as in the solarization *Primacy of Matter over Thought* (1929; fig. 81). The denaturalization of reality was, after all, the artist's prerogative, if not his Surrealist duty, and in the 1930s Man Ray exercised it freely, at times seeming to redefine the medium, to alter its character, as his crafty attenuation of form opened onto a kind of metamorphosis (figs. 82 and 83).

Even earlier, *Le violon d'Ingres* (1924; fig. 84), a photograph of the back of his first model and mistress in Paris, Kiki of Montparnasse (Alice Prin), her limbs hidden, becomes, with the slight addition of two f-holes that the artist "burned" into the image through cut-out templates, the evocation of the musical instrument.[109] Man Ray was naturally in a Francophile state during his first years in Paris, evident here in what might be referred to as a "post-Cubist" phase. While alluding to the collapsed, multiply spatial, fragmented, and punning coordinates (especially of the violin and the figure) of Cubism, Man Ray's ref-

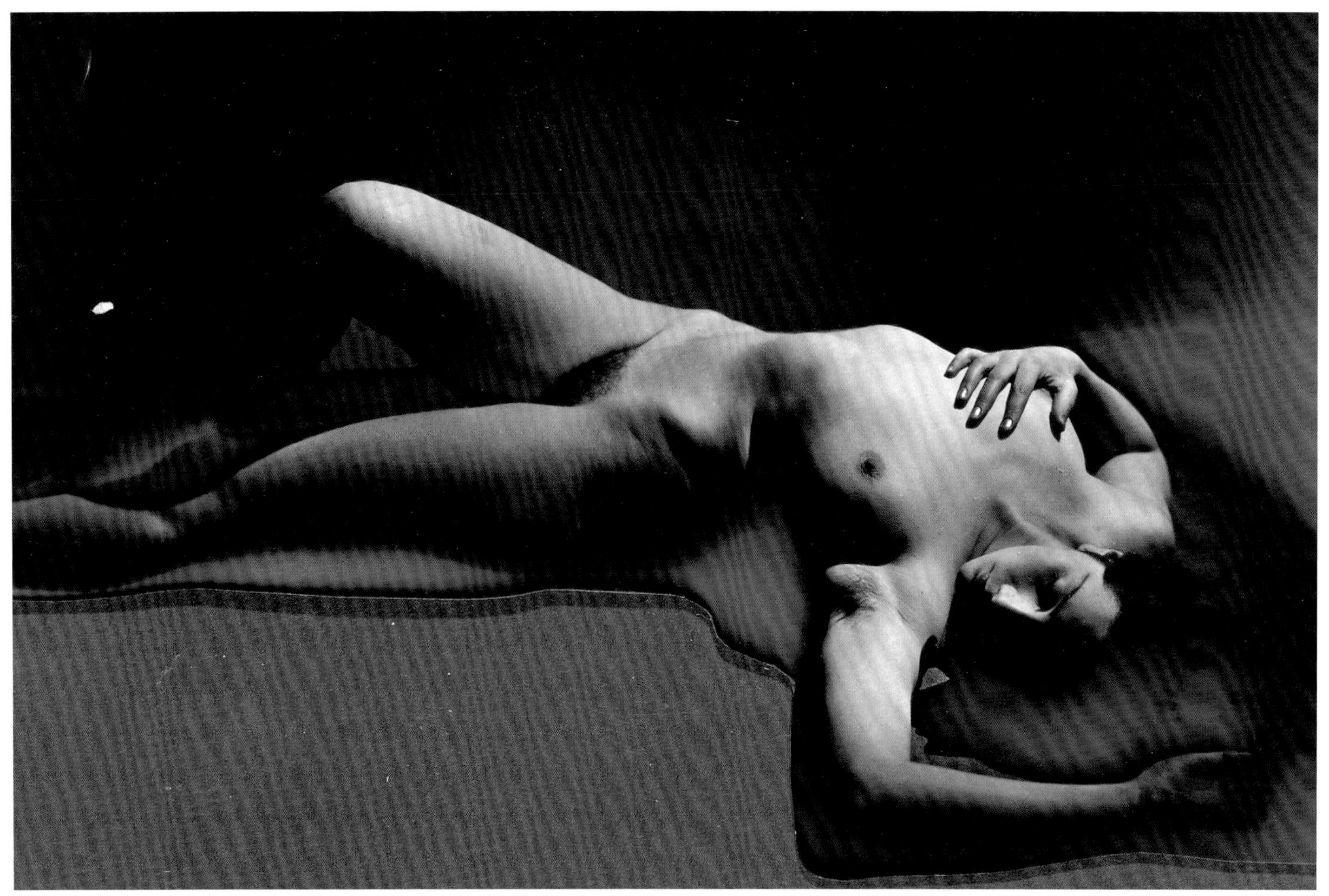

Fig. 81. *Primacy of Matter over Thought (Primat de la matière sur la pensée)*, 1929. Solarized gelatin silver print, cut out, 3 × 4⁹⁄₁₆ in. (7.6 × 11.6 cm). The Baltimore Museum of Art, Purchase with exchange funds from the Edward Joseph Gallagher III Memorial Collection, and partial gift of George H. Dalsheimer

Fig. 82. *Untitled*, 1931. Gelatin silver print, 11⅛ ×
8¹³⁄₁₆ in. (28.9 × 22.4 cm). The Museum of Modern
Art, New York, Gift of James Thrall Soby, 1941

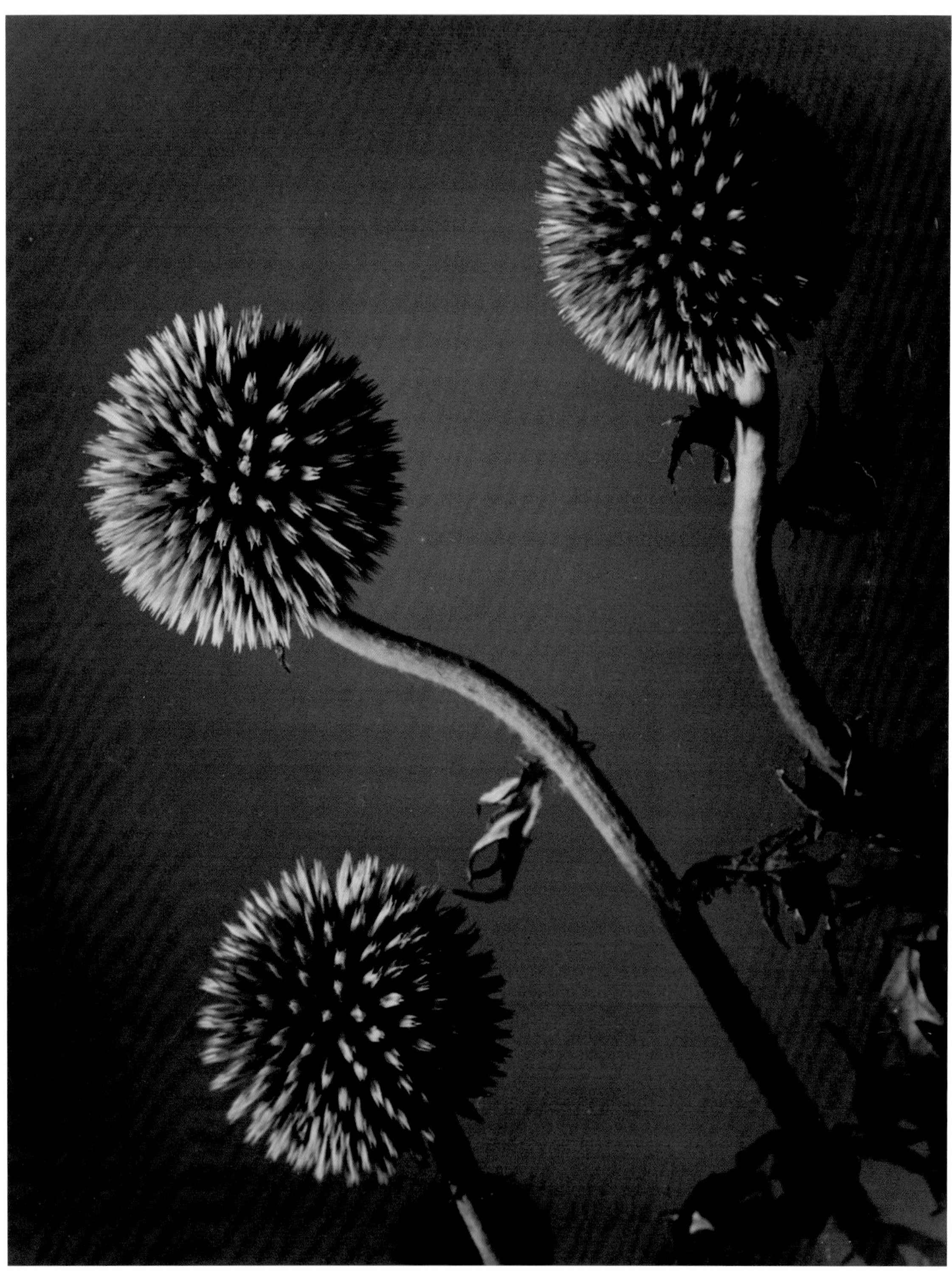

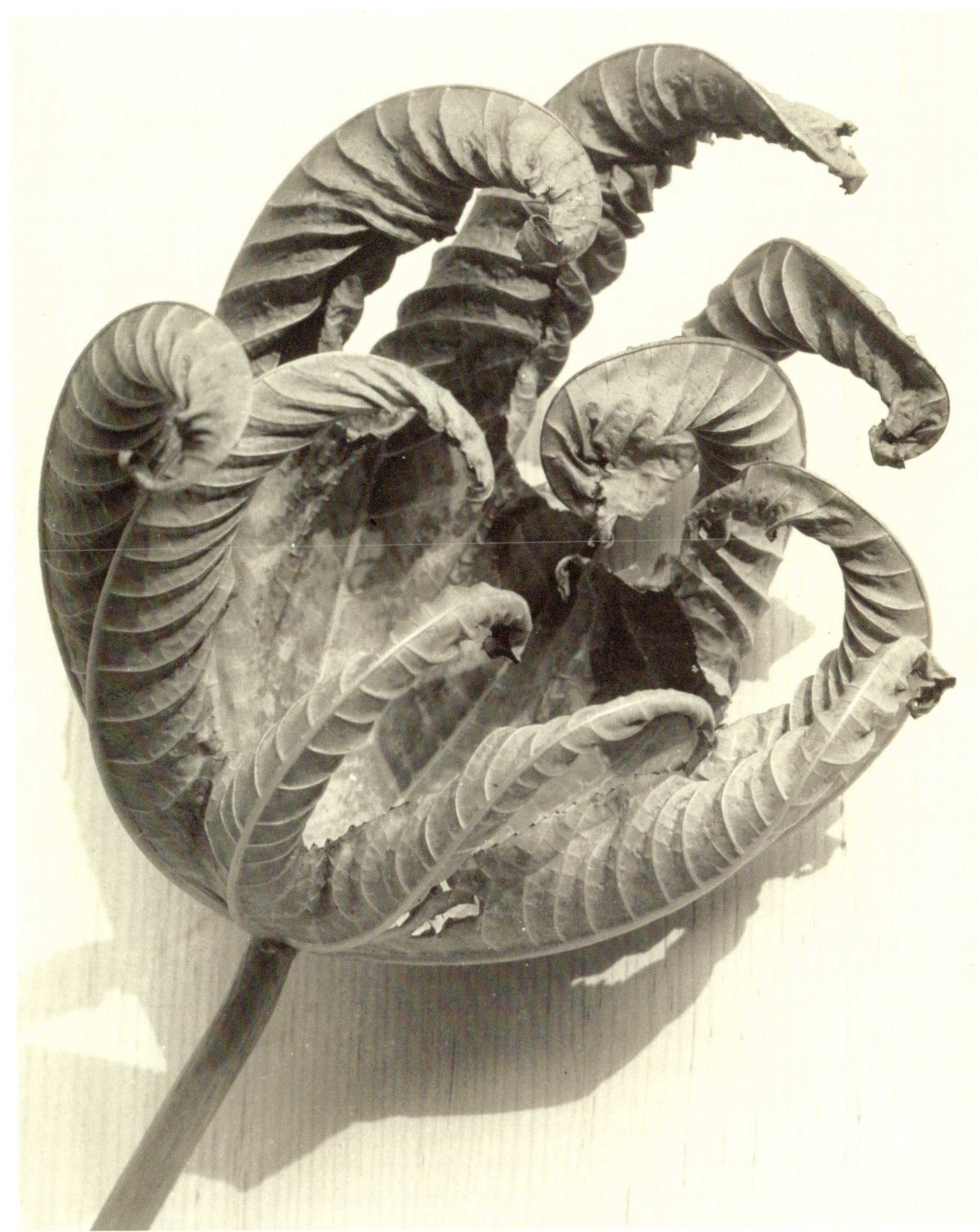

Fig. 83. *Untitled (Dead Leaf)*, 1942. Gelatin silver print, 9½ × 7¹³/₁₆ in. (24.1 × 19.8 cm). The J. Paul Getty Museum, Los Angeles

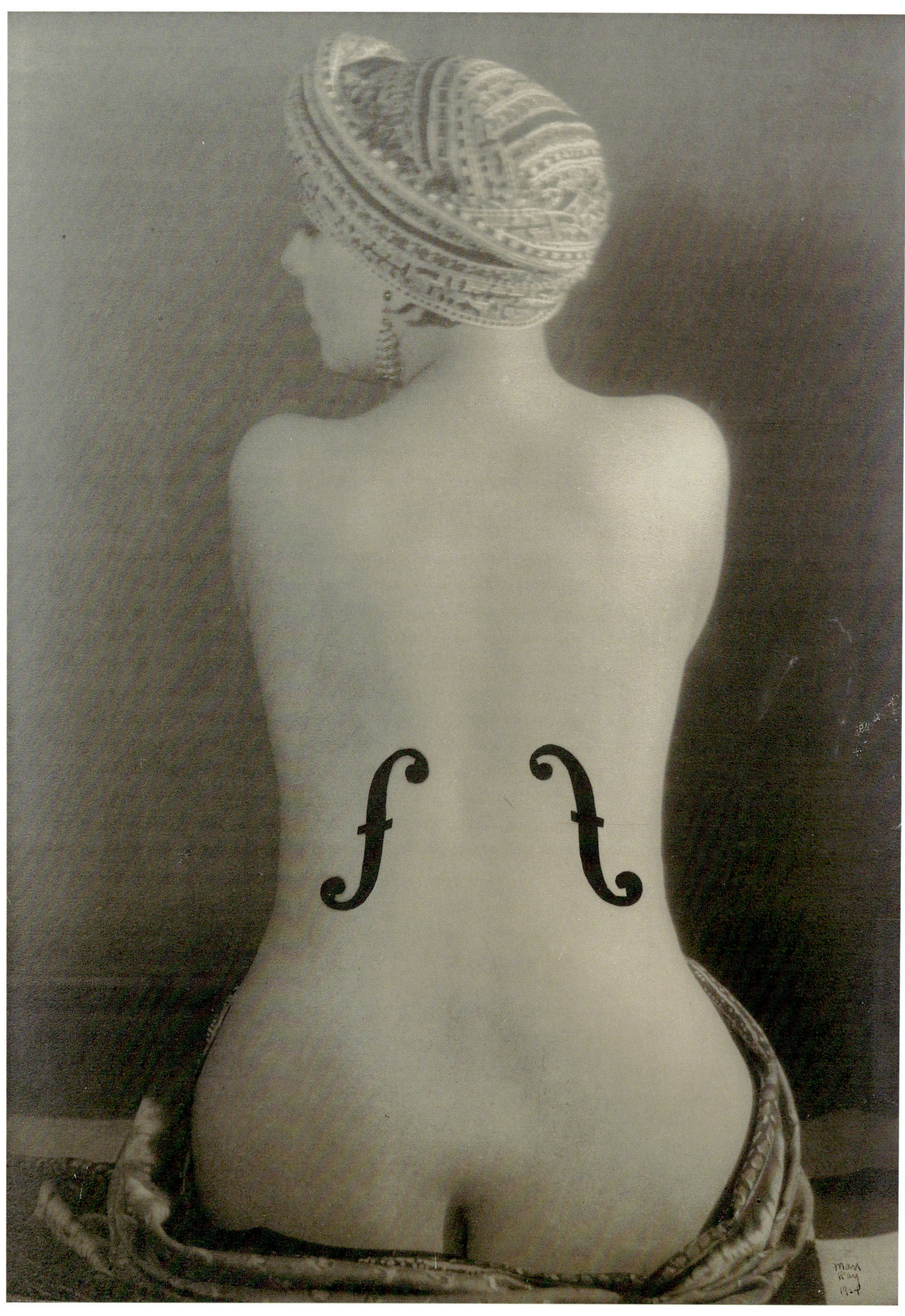

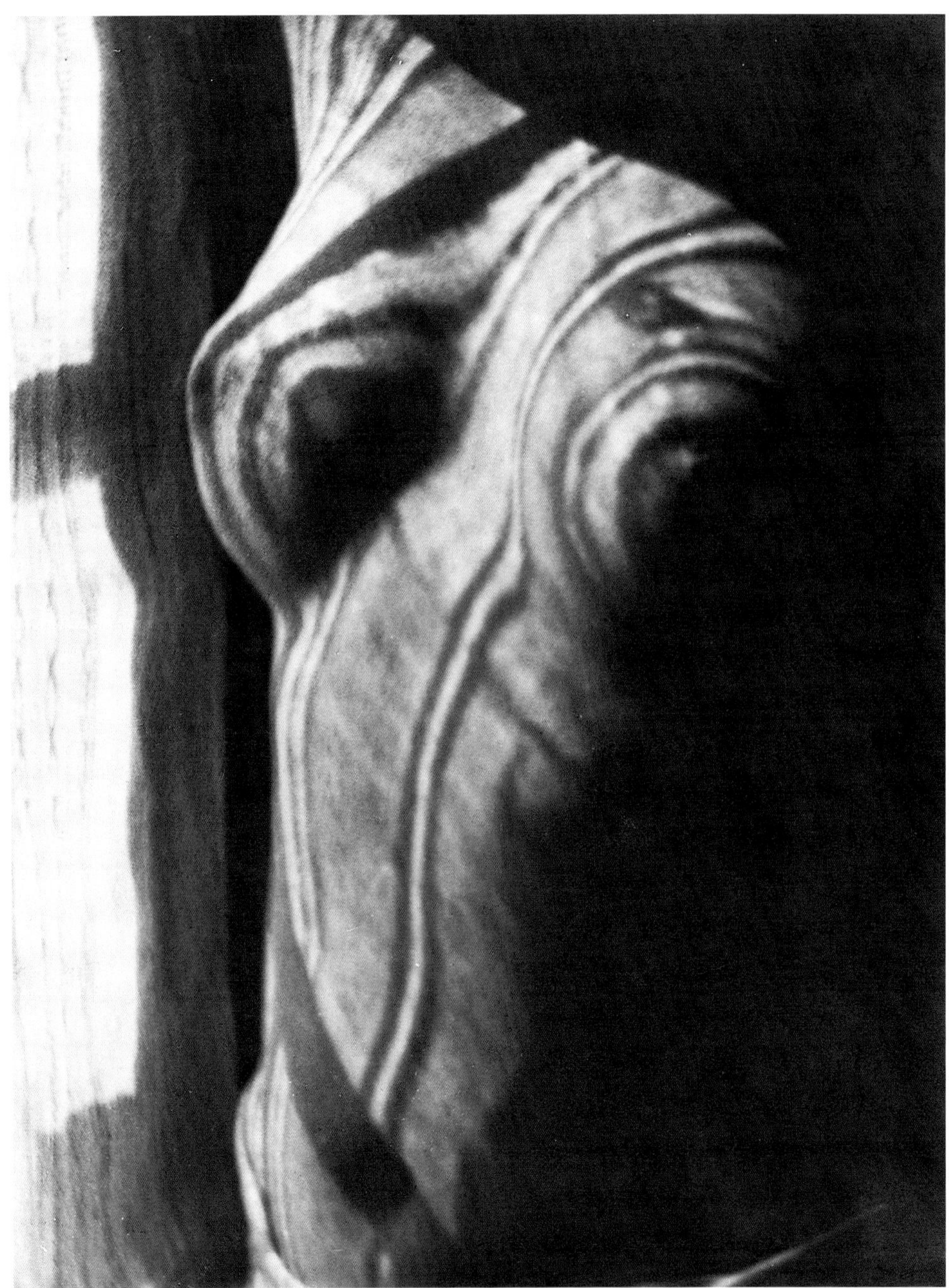

erence to Ingres's *La baigneuse de Valpinçon* was also a part of the institutional postwar *retour à l'ordre*, in which the neoclassicism of Ingres
played a major role (fig. 85).[110] The hyperrealism of the painter was
lauded even by Breton, who may have been the most immediate
source for Man Ray's renewed interest in Ingres. The painter had
been a standard for Man Ray much earlier, when he was first introduced to Ingres's work by Robert Henri at the Ferrer Center.[111] Yet
Le violon d'Ingres cannot be reduced simply to homage and the institutional embrace then being accorded Ingres.

Shortly before *Le violon d'Ingres* was published in Éluard and Breton's literary journal *Littérature*, in June 1924, a brief article called "Académisme" appeared in an issue of the same journal, signed with the initials F. P. (presumably Francis Picabia), in which the popular elevation and commodification of Ingres's art was ridiculed as the stuff of "salesrooms." It would have been far more intriguing to Man Ray to take the occasion to reconsider the Frenchman's art, recalling, no doubt, his youthful fascination with Ingres's idealization yet latent deformation of the body, that is, to rethink the body within the now normal, convulsive beauty of Surrealism—not to mention the appeal of joining Picabia and going against the grain of the popular, conservative restitution of Ingres's art. It is the fascination that such idealized figuration had held for him years before—as in *Nude* (1912; fig. 86), in the fig-

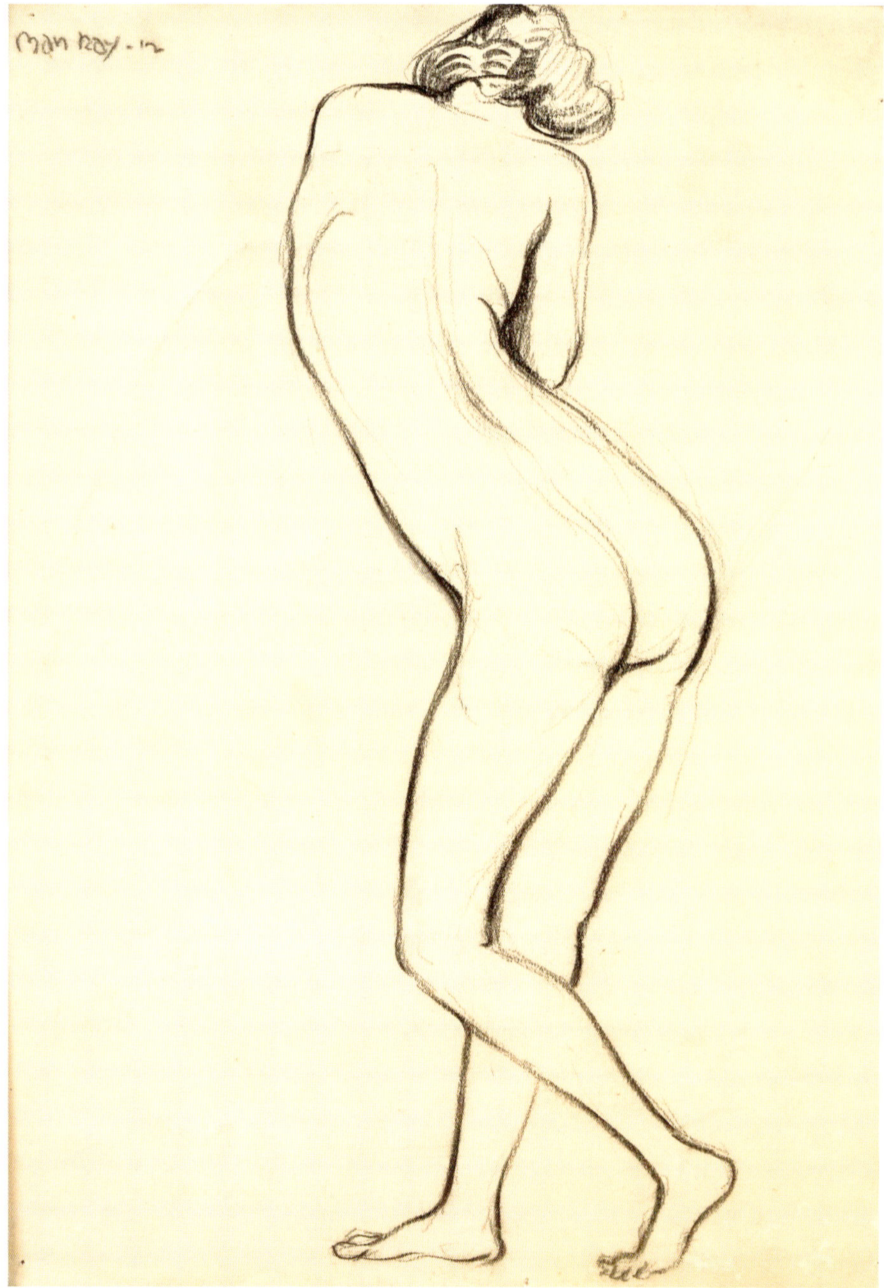

Fig. 86. *Nude*, 1912. Ink on paper, 20 × 15 in. (50.8 × 38.1 cm). Collection of Marion Meyer

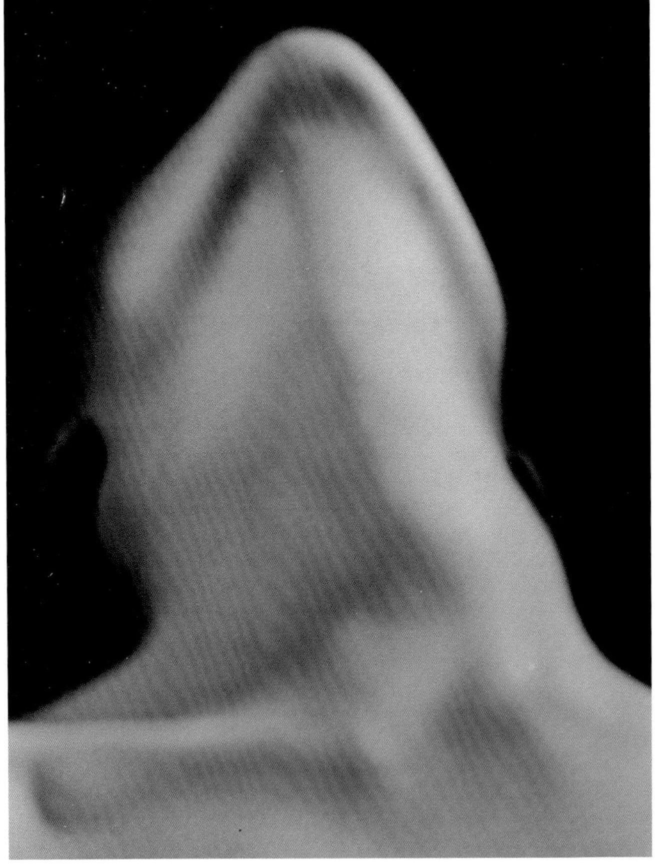

Fig. 87. *Anatomies*, 1929. Gelatin silver print, 8⅞ × 6¾ in. (22.5 × 17.2 cm). The Museum of Modern Art, New York, Gift of James Thrall Soby, 1941

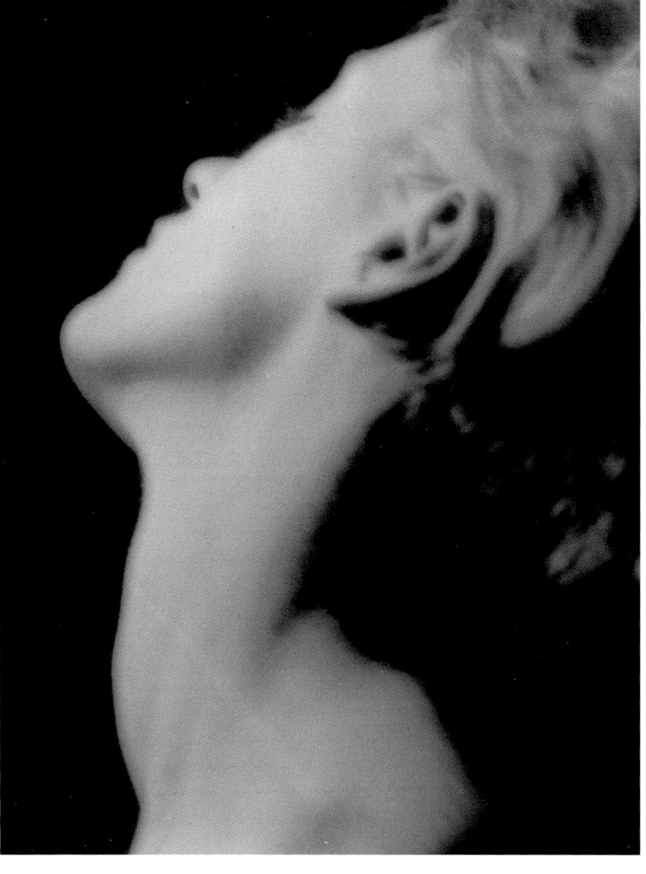

Fig. 88. *Neck (Portrait of Lee Miller)*, 1929. Gelatin silver print, 9¹/₁₆ × 7 in. (23 × 17.8 cm). The Penrose Collection, England

ure's elongated back—that Man Ray now chiefly resurrects. His youthful sexual response to Ingres's singular combination of the arabesque and the grotesque could now be the source of Man Ray's libidinal needs as prescriptive grist to reconfigure the body, fetishizing it far more than he ever could have dreamt as a young man.

One sees such effects in the elegant attenuation of form approaching its limits in the numerous concentrated, carnal examinations of Lee Miller's body, such as *Anatomies* and *Neck (Portrait of Lee Miller)* (both 1929; figs. 87 and 88), in which Man Ray attempts to eroticize the body by exacting from it its maximum plasticity—ultimately deforming it, by forcing it to conform to his will.[112] This sadistic tendency is, as I have mentioned above, a component of his desire or need to assert his control, the loss of which manifests in rage. For Man Ray to create, he must first destroy. While his rage toward Lee Miller's rejection resulted in *Object of Destruction*, it also yielded works that were published as full-page images in *Le Surréalisme au service de la révolution*, such as *Homage à D. A. F. Sade* (1930) and *Monument to Sade* (1933; fig. 89), both indicating the exalted position the Marquis de Sade had acquired by the end of the 1920s throughout the ranks of Surrealism (fig. 90).[113]

In *Monument to Sade*, one of the finest examples of Man Ray's manipulation of boundary, he inscribes an inverted, rigidly drawn cross on the close-up image of a woman's buttocks, which, thus reframed, metamorphoses the flesh into a phallus, itself doubled by the upside-down cross, to implement the Sadean anticlerical narrative of sodomy. Man Ray succeeds, in the year of Adolf Hitler's appointment as chancellor of Germany, in creating a powerful inversion of a traditional symbol of love and Christian good, deforming it, as does the sodomizing monk in Sade's *Justine*. In this assault on religion, or on the imposition of any dogmatic position, in whatever name of freedom, Man Ray overturns the static dimension of the ideal in favor of the formless, "desiring" state of the imagination.[114] Similarly juxtaposed is the ideal of geometry, represented by crosses, one hard-edged and the other, collapsed and deformed, composed of the creases of flesh within it. In this subtle positing of opposites, Man Ray invokes, as he had done with *Le violon d'Ingres* (or with *The Primacy of Matter over Thought*), the very dialectical condition that had long been associated with the neoclassicist. From his extreme perch of the ideal, overhanging the fulcrum of realistic anatomy, Ingres exercised what Théophile Silvestre described when he wrote of one of the painter's women: "The fingers of madame la princesse de Broglie are broken at every

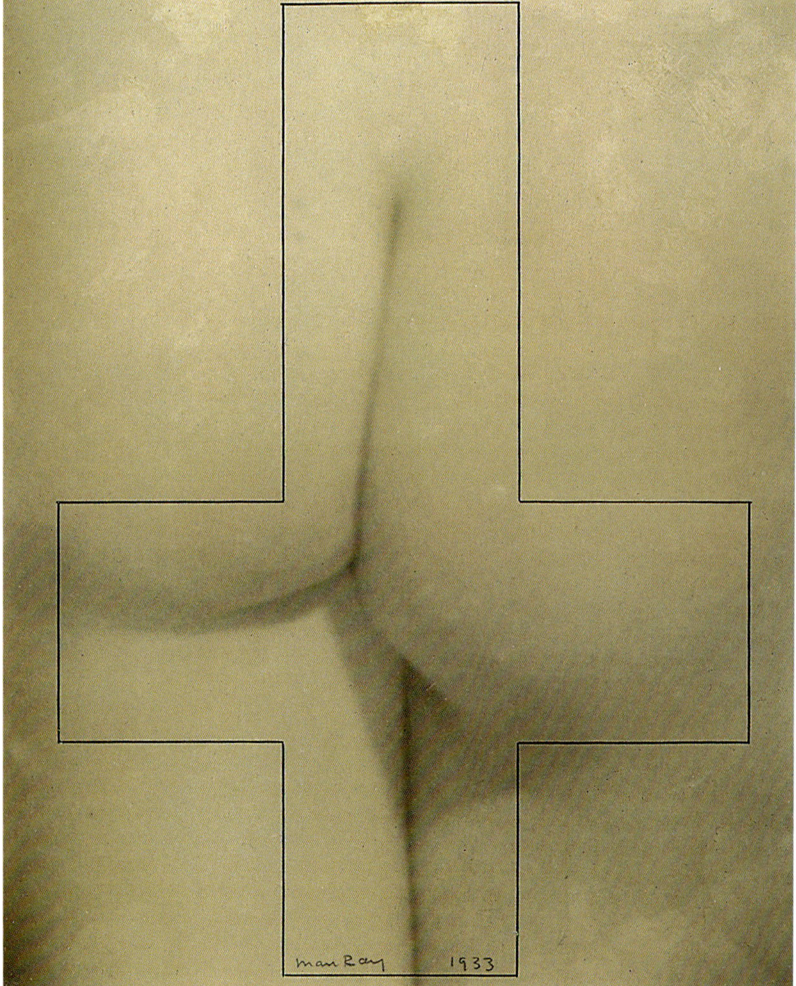

Fig. 89. *Monument to Sade*, 1933. Gelatin silver print and ink, 7⅞ × 6⁵⁄₁₆ in. (20 × 16 cm). Israel Museum, Jerusalem, Vera, Sylvia, and Arturo Schwarz Collection of Dada and Surrealist Art

opposite:
Fig. 90. *Portrait imaginaire de D. A. F. de Sade (Imaginary Portrait of the Marquis de Sade)*, 1938. Oil on canvas with painted wood panel, 24¼ × 18⅜ in. (61.7 × 46.6 cm). The Menil Collection, Houston

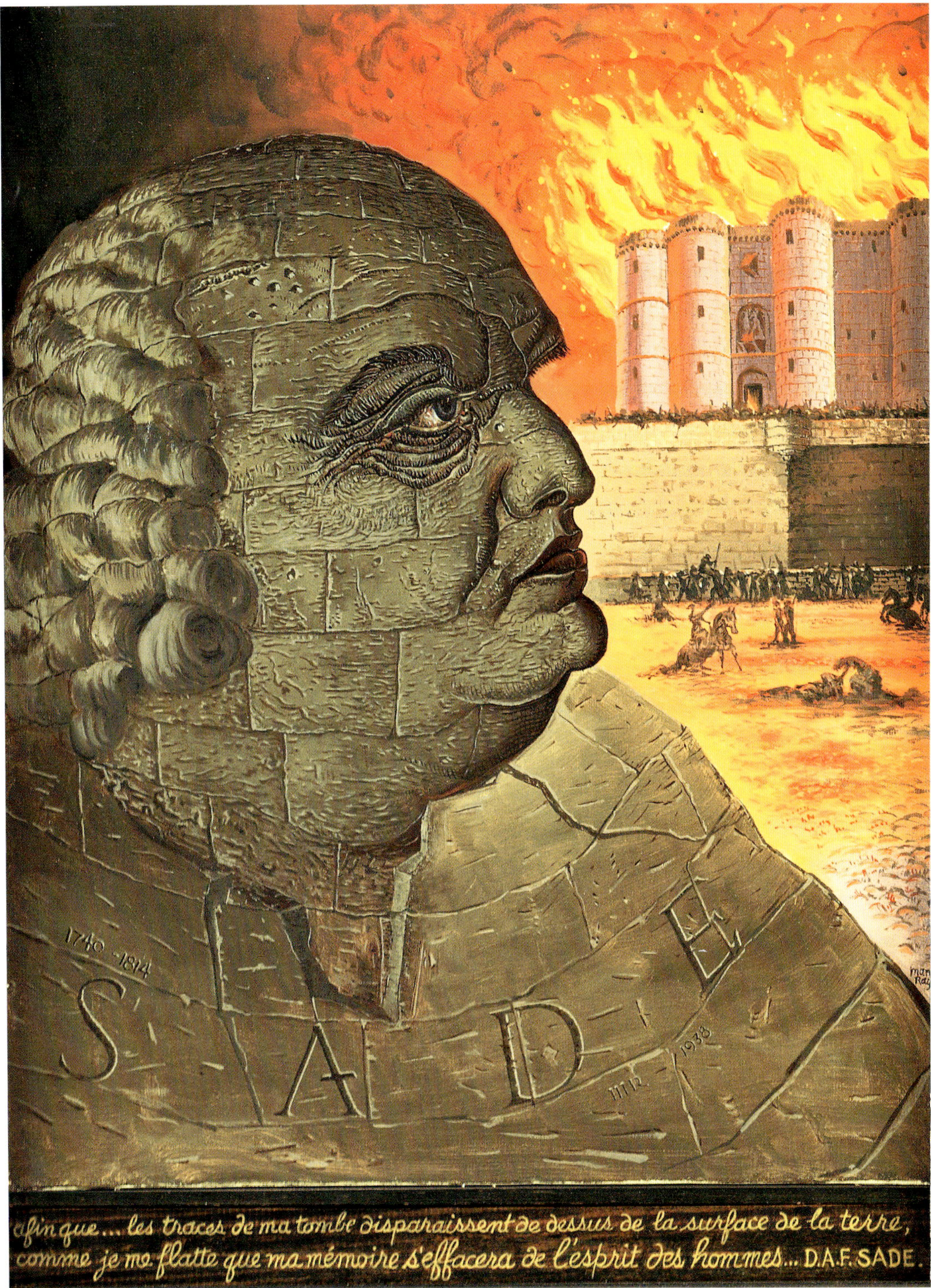

knuckle. . . . If M. Ingres's personages could feel and speak their pain, all the cries and moans of a battlefield would emerge from the depths of the paintings."[115]

Aside from the creation of such juxtapositions, Man Ray seemed to revel in incorporating a perceptual aspect that denied the factual. He understood perfectly what his friend Louis Aragon had written in 1926: "Reality is the apparent absence of contradiction. The marvelous is the eruption of contradiction within the real."[116] Man Ray's desire to juggle such dialectical components and his comfort with contradiction chiefly precipitated his attempt to achieve the Surrealists' ideal dissolution of the schism between the worlds of mind and material. Yet the state of such "ideal fusion," represented by the Surrealist understanding of the marvelous, is one that *Le violon d'Ingres* aspires to but cannot achieve. As David Bate writes of the work, it "reproduces oppositions . . . which cannot be resolved; oppositions in the pun of human figure and violin (flesh and wood, animate and inanimate). . . . In this respect, the image sets up what psychoanalysis describes as a 'psychical conflict.'"[117]

Man Ray's fascination with binaries relates to the temporal, as well as to the metamorphic Surrealist image. In *Space Writing (Self-*

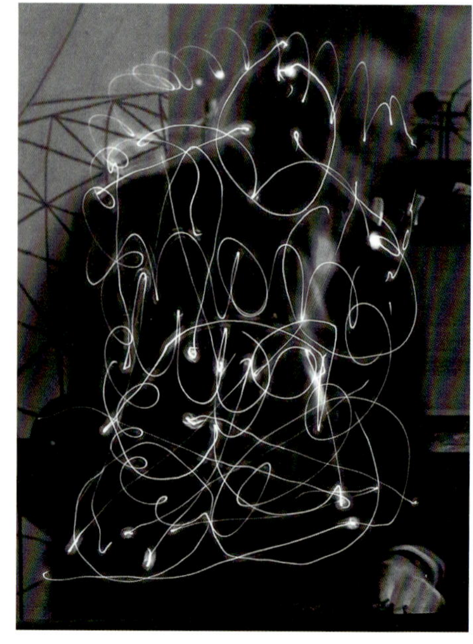

Fig. 91. *Space Writing (Self-Portrait)*, 1935. Gelatin silver print, 3³⁄₁₆ × 2⁵⁄₁₆ in. (8.1 × 5.87 cm). Bowdoin College Museum of Art, Brunswick, Maine, Museum Purchase, Lloyd O. and Marjorie Strong Coulter Fund

Portrait) (1935; fig. 91) he was able, by opening his camera's shutter in dim light, to seem to reverse the cinematic by extending the present and allowing the temporal process of choreographing with a flashlight to yield a drawing of light.[118] It was once again a matter of going against the grain, of rethinking the very potential of chemistry, as he had with his solarizations' reversal of the photographic process, and imbuing light with a dark, graphic presence while highlighting the tenuous immateriality of substance itself (fig. 92). Perhaps because of his territorial squabbling with Lee Miller over the claim to the discovery of this technique, Man Ray seemed to take great, almost proprietary pleasure in perfecting it. Throughout the 1930s he produced an array of daz-

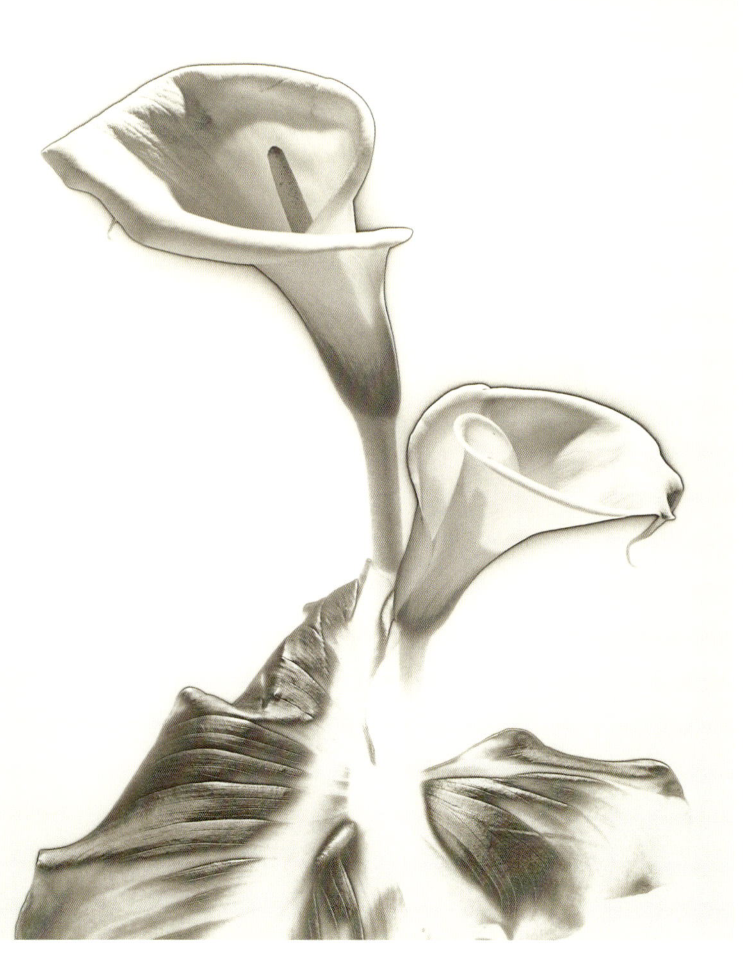

Fig. 92. *Calla Lillies*, c. 1930. Vintage solarized gelatin silver print, 13³⁄₈ × 10³⁄₈ in. (34 × 26.4 cm). Richard and Ellen Sandor Family Collection

zlingly sensuous still lifes, nudes, and portraits (fig. 93), each article or figure embraced by a dark, illusionistic shadowy line that lent an otherworldly, dreamlike mutability, as far removed as possible from the über-clarity and techno-idolatry of the German variety.[119]

Moving in the 1920s from the dark but poetic vagueness of his rayographs into the illuminated world of his solarized prints, Man Ray established a more visible presence as well in Paris, and seemed intent on synthesizing his earlier portraiture with the experimentation of his new technique. When he reflected on his rayographs years later he compared them to vanished objects: "like the undisturbed ashes of an object consumed by flames . . . oxidized residues fixed by light and chemical elements of an experience, an adventure, not an experiment."[120] Now he could stress both the experiential and the experimental, and this was important to an artist who lived as a work of art himself, whose persona was an integral part of the constellation of art in whose insular presence he lived. For Man Ray, there could be no boundary separating life from art.

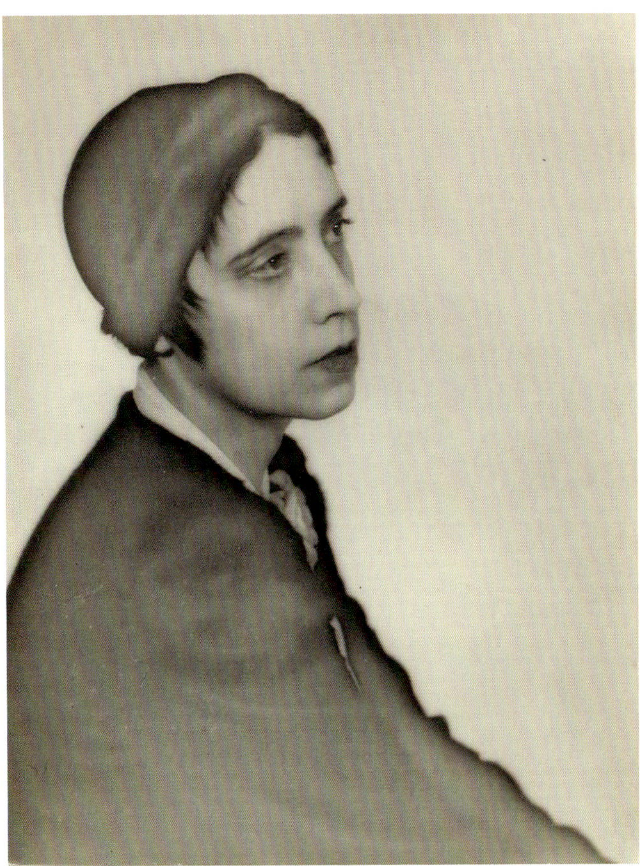

Fig. 93. *Elsa Schiaparelli*, 1934. Vintage solarized gelatin silver print, 9⁹⁄₁₆ × 6⅞ in. (23.0 × 17.5 cm). Collection of Timothy Baum, New York

prOjection

The epigraph to this essay comes from a brief story that Man Ray wrote in 1944 titled "Ruth, Roses, and Revolvers," which was published in *View* magazine that December. The German Dadaist painter and filmmaker Hans Richter had come upon it and invited his old friend to contribute it as a component of *Dreams That Money Can Buy*, a film he had conceived, which would include work by such mid-century art-world notables as Alexander Calder, Marcel Duchamp, Max Ernst, Fernand Léger, Darius Milhaud, and Richter himself.[121] Man Ray complied, stipulating, however, that his contribution "be realized by others" in order for him to take the idea of "projection . . . to a consistent end . . . so that I could get the same surprise out of it that any other spectator would have."[122] While Richter's movie is a classic Surrealist compendium of dreams, with Man Ray's contribution a consonant part, I will focus on those aspects of his film, and its initial published form, that extend beyond the classic dream-related Surrealist subject.

The significance of Man Ray's stipulation that his segment of the film be realized by others is clearer when framed by his use of the word "projection" in the program notes to the film. Man Ray's notion of taking "projection" to its logical conclusion ostensibly includes its submission to the mechanistic process by which a script is transformed and illuminated through cinematic presentation, as well as its realization by others—allowing for Man Ray to come upon the film as if for the first time. The alternative, psychological meaning of "projection" presents an altogether different set of terms, whose meaning hinges not on illumination but rather on concealment. From a psychoanalytic point of view, projection is a defense mechanism whereby emotions or impulses that one finds unacceptable (shameful, dangerous) are projected onto others, shielding one from having to tolerate or take responsibility for the content of the projected material.

It is specifically to such content that Man Ray, in a rare moment, in an obscure text, obliquely refers, articulating in "Ruth, Roses, and Revolvers" that his inescapable Jewish identity elicits in him the desire to become a "tree en espalier." "You see, I try to walk the tightrope of accomplishment between the chasms of notoriety and oblivion; were I not a product of my time, I should never be conscious of anything but my accomplishments. Hence the desire to become a tree en espalier!" This is the ulterior meaning of his stipulation that his "script" be realized by others—since he was unable to face it himself.[123]

Man Ray begins with the words "You see," an ironic emphasis on the problem of visibility central to an understanding of the man and his work. Desiring exposure and celebrity while still wishing that his identity remain private was a paradox, or "tightrope walk," to which he was quite accustomed. He had illustrated this narrative almost thirty years before in one of his most important works, *The Rope Dancer Accompanies Herself with Her Shadows*. The painting's initial subtext is explicated here, during the artist's repatriation in the United States during World War II, its earlier significance reverberating with renewed breadth. As a tree is trained *en espalier,* it grows into a vine; as it becomes entwined with others, its origins are disguised, yet within certain clipped bounds it is free to grow, discreetly, in any direction. Such conditional development, flourishing within self-imposed strictures, characterizes Man Ray and his work, perhaps more than any other artist of the twentieth century. What makes his particular manner of assimilation remarkable is how it manifests so thoroughly and symptomatically throughout his work for those who choose to recognize it.

"Ruth, Roses, and Revolvers" was written during the artist's interim stay in his homeland, where he had returned after twenty years in exile. He had fled Paris in June 1940, the same month as the Nazi conquest of France. After Man Ray's inevitable departure, the years of paranoia leading up to his repatriation are evident in the fleeting, shadowy figures and desperate, outstretched angular shards of beings that appear in countless drawings and paintings throughout the 1930s. In *Le dernier homme sur terre* (*The Last Man on Earth*; 1940), executed as he prepared to leave Paris, the artist depicted the nightmarish escape from which a barely identifiable human form struggles to remain standing on unstable ground, set against a disintegrating earth resembling the bleakest glacial terrain, whose blocks of ice are breaking off.

Man Ray, like many Parisians, had refused to believe the worst, choosing rather to settle down "impassively to face the future." Even in the fall and winter of 1939–40, shortly before he would be forced to leave, he remained, if not sanguine, at least determined to remain in Paris. His recollection years later suggests that even at this point his perspective never lost its artistic mooring: "If there were no immediate signs of war . . . new restrictions and laws were being promulgated to make for greater austerity. Sugar, tobacco, coffee and gas were rationed, and, naturally, hoarded, with a black market developing at once. Lines formed in front of groceries and food shops whose windows were crisscrossed with strips of paper, some very artistically. This, I think, depressed me the most, but I followed suit with my studio windows, using, however, transparent tape. It was quite invisible."[124]

Beyond the obvious need for light, he experienced an increasing sense of confinement and powerlessness, which is particularly evident in the dark figure in *Le rebus* (1938; see fig. 42). While his otherwise ghostly, rampant figures are hopelessly extended in distorted flight, this figure's pinched form is constituted from without—its body impinged upon by a sadistically eroticized, anatomically defined environment. As the figure veers toward extinction, in a world defined by an inverted sense of values, its shrinking nocturnal phantom presence is threatened by a glowing sun in the clutch of a morbid, skeletal hand. Dictated, perhaps, by Surrealism's preoccupation with rebuslike representations constructed of riddles, the painting exacts the artist's terrifying sense of impotence and dissolution.

The figures who inhabit *Le rebus, The Wall* (1938), and *Swiftly Walk over the Western Wave* (1940), which Man Ray made just before leaving Paris, exist in a world of unnatural, deadening light. He would write about the shadowless and dehumanizing effects of this light while in Los Angeles during the war:

Nothing is more detrimental to the eyes and to the spirit than this diffused indirect light. . . . It is against all the principles of our nature—of the construction of our two eyes which give us the sense [of] relief and three dimensions in conjunction with light and shade, this good old chiaroscuro. Beginning with the sun itself whose orientation determined our visual makeup—two eyes set under projecting brows emphasized by their lashes—beginning with the sun, a single point of light throwing shadows has always been a necessary adjunct to our complete understanding of our surroundings. . . . Throw out your inverted opaque lamps and your neon tubes carefully calculated to produce that monotonous confusion of even light without shadows.[125]

Man Ray's criticism of the dehumanizing effects of modern, industrial fluorescent lighting makes clear his symbolic investment in a world both illuminated and sheltered by a visible light, whose "necessary" cast shadows would allow one to comfortably, knowingly adjust to one's surroundings. In his persecuted wartime paintings, the elegance of the perfectly poised rope dancer (accompanied by her shadows) is replaced by the grossly teetering

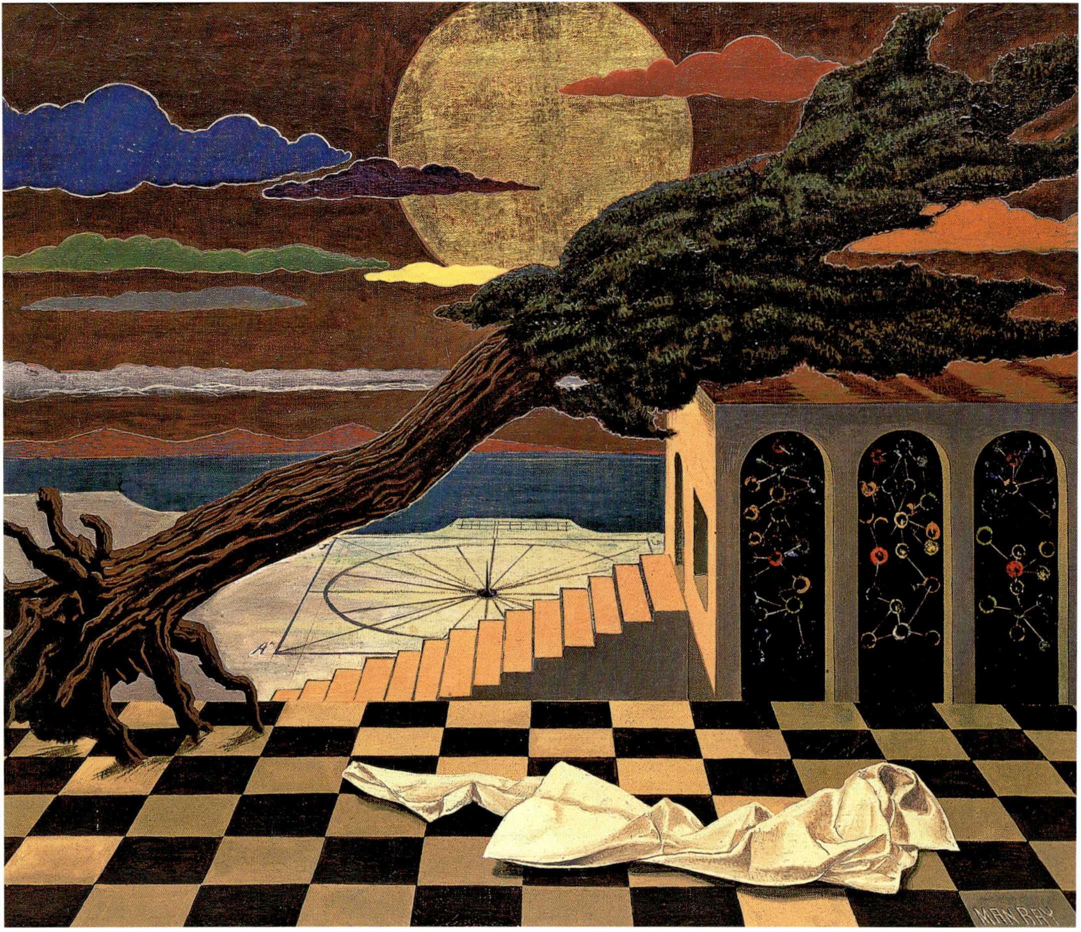

figure, harshly illuminated by the evil nocturnal sun of *Le rebus* or *Night Sun—Abandoned Play-*
ground (1943; fig. 94). Man Ray despised this kind of light, from which one could not hide, and which was no less ubiquitous than the relentless advance of the Third Reich.

Fig. 94. *Night Sun—Abandoned Playground*, 1943. Oil on canvas, 20⅛ × 24 in. (51 × 61 cm). Isidore Ducasse Fine Arts

For someone who maintained no traditional sense of Jewish identity, whose exis-
tence was defined entirely by his artistic persona, the impending Nazi invasion of Paris meant the imminent loss of a world that had provided him with an anonymous visibility. The immateriality of the figures that inhabit his work of the late 1930s bears an attenuated resemblance to the patternlike forms of such earlier works as *Promenade* (1916), one of numerous paintings that he, curiously, remade in California, not least because he feared that the originals, in Paris, would not survive the war, but also perhaps because he wanted to invest his earlier work with a new sensibility. In *Promenade II* (1941), for instance, a more modeled materiality replaces the kaleidoscopic transparency of the original, its reinvention possibly the result of being de facto in the world in a different way.

Man Ray felt professionally untethered in Los Angeles, where he quickly chose to go after returning to the States, clearly not wishing to settle in New York. Yet he adapted to this environment by creating theatrical works that reflected the illusionistic, performative world around him, Hollywood's brand of deliberate unreality. In *Night Sun—Abandoned*

Playground he attempted, characteristically, to meld into this environment by adopting a narrative-based, set-design format, toward which he had been gravitating in *La fortune* (1938; fig. 95) and *Le beau temps* (1939; fig. 96). As he attempted to respond to his new, unlikely setting, he was also invoking earlier works, not as copies but rather as "variations of the same subject."[126]

The articulated manikins of his wartime paintings (*Infinite Man*, 1942), photographs (*End Game*, 1942; fig. 97), and drawings (*The Fortunes of the Artist's Double, Drawings by Man Ray*, 1940; fig. 98) replace the harrowing specters Man Ray had painted in Paris—with their contours of negative space—made as his world was shattering and he was losing his guarded anonymity. As France was overrun by the Nazis he was compelled to confront a delimiting part of himself—his Jewishness—that he had assiduously denied, with cataclysmic and claustrophobic results. Works such as *The Wall* and *Le rebus*, both of 1938, reflect

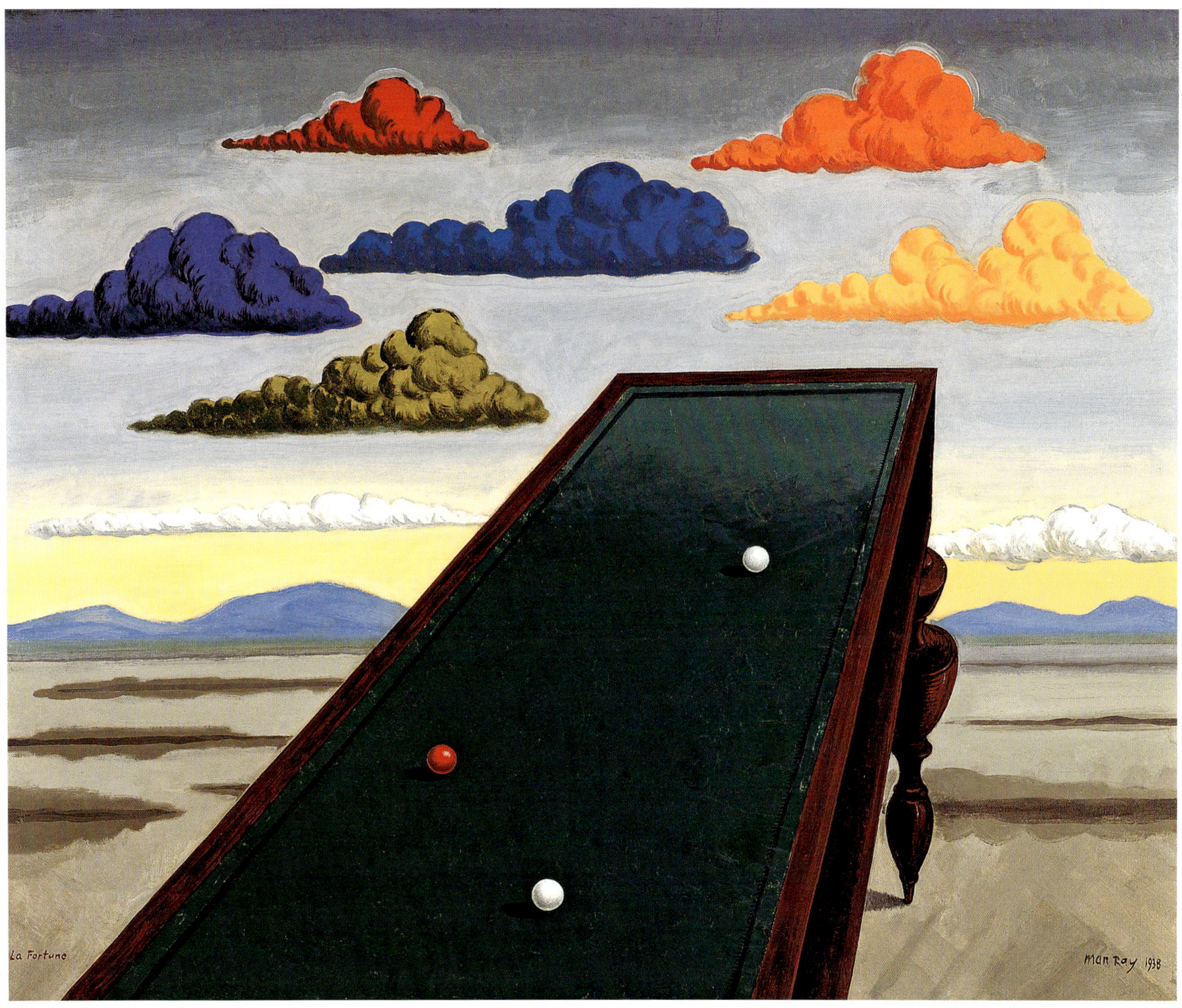

Fig. 95. *La fortune*, 1938. Oil on canvas, 24 × 29 in. (61 × 73.7 cm). Whitney Museum of American Art, New York, Purchase with funds from the Simon Foundation, Inc.

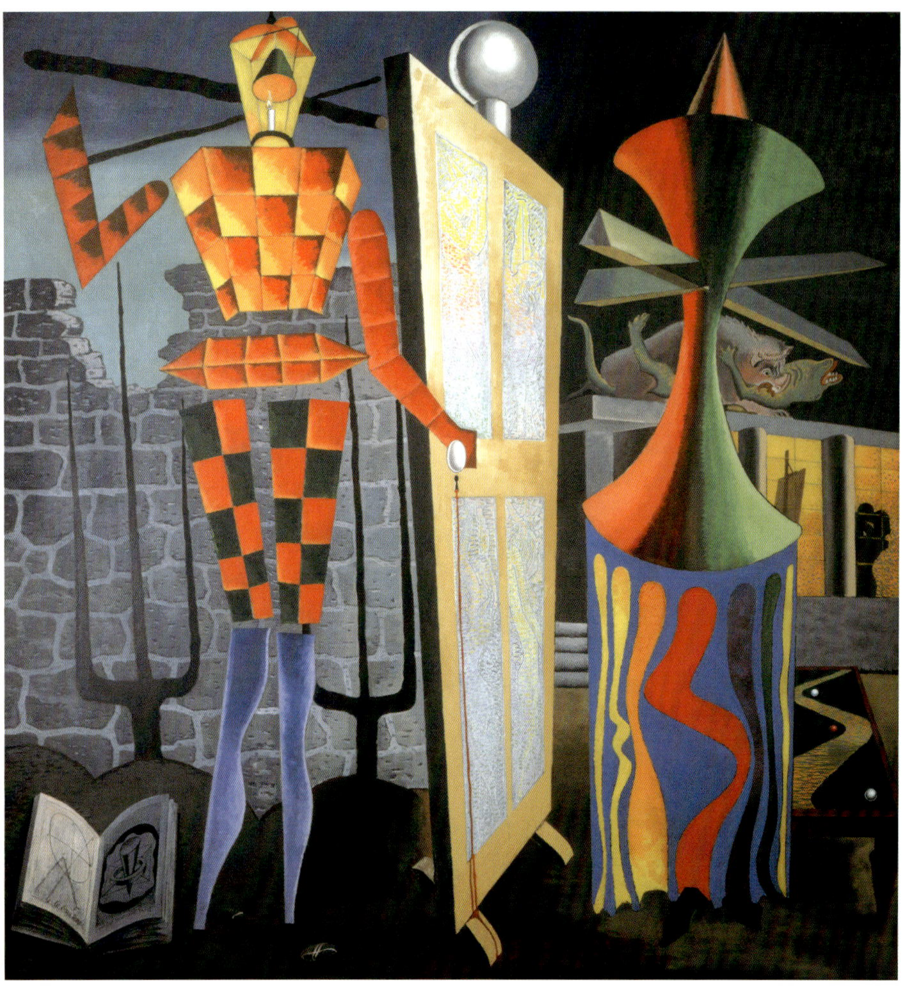

Fig. 96. *Le beau temps,* 1939. Oil on canvas, 82¾ × 78¼ in. (210.2 × 200 cm). Philadelphia Museum of Art, Promised gift of Sidney Kimmel

Fig. 97. *End Game,* 1942. Vintage gelatin silver print, 7⅝ × 9¾ in. (19.4 × 24.8 cm). Richard and Ellen Sandor Family Collection

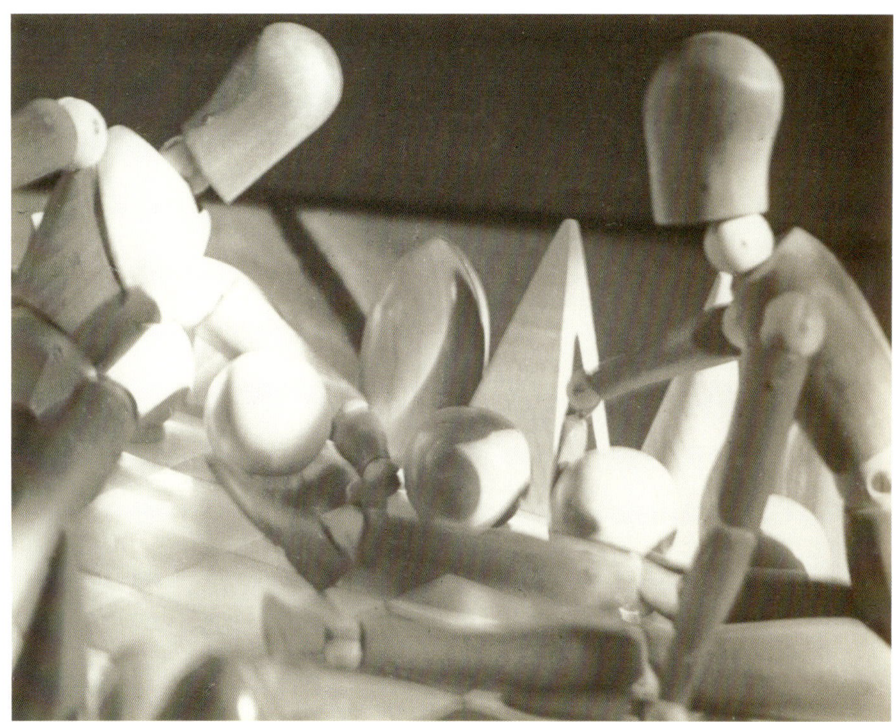

his mounting fear that his invisibility could no longer be sustained, that he, like the figures in these paintings, was being encroached upon by material reality. In *La fortune* and other works, he reinstates his earlier symbolic palette of primary and secondary colors, first used in *The Rope Dancer*, but now they assume new meaning: "A picture done in pure spectrum colors," Man Ray wrote, "could never be reconciled with its surroundings— it would even combat other rainbows."[127]

In *La fortune*, the primary-colored, densely cumulus storm clouds, their forms unsettlingly similar and evenly dispersed in the sky, suggest just how irreconcilable Man Ray felt the changing political "climate" in Europe had become. The dominating billiards table, a massive piece of mahogany that emerges in the foreground like a military tank, barges beyond the horizon into the sky. The table is a symbol of a dreaded, unforeseeable fate, and the perspective is such that one cannot tell whether it is inclined upward or downward. The outcome of the game is left up in the air.

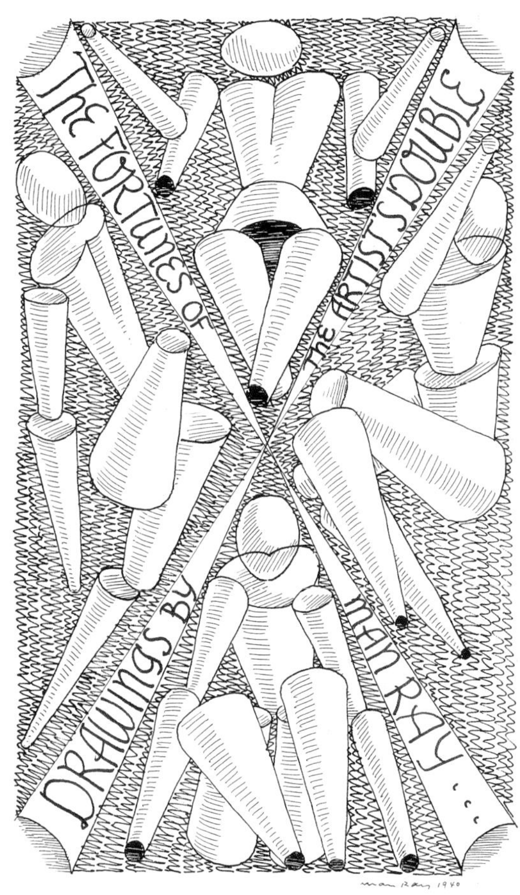

Fig. 98. *The Fortunes of the Artist's Double, Drawings by Man Ray*, 1940. Ink on paper, 18⅛ × 11¹¹⁄₁₆ in. (46 × 30 cm). Sylvio Perlstein Collection, Antwerp

"axiom: Because the Pyramid is a shadow—
it Cannot Have another shadow"

Man Ray's fondness for primary colors may be seen, in part, as another example of his constant desire to go against the grain, to remain *himself* irreconciled with his surroundings (fig. 99).[128] While early in life he found a balance in anonymity as a way to avoid being classified as "other," it was just such a tenuous equanimity that precipitated his enduring preoccupation with shadows. Whether in its analogical disengagement from its source, as in *6,396,78* (1922; fig. 100), metaphorically challenging the precision and expectation of mechanical movement, or in the ambiguity of the relation between light and shade in *Arrangement of Forms, No. 1* (1915; fig. 101), this symbol had retained its mythic but personal value since it first emerged in his earliest semiabstract works, beginning with *Tapestry* (1911).[129] It surfaces again in *La rue Férou* (1952; fig. 102), a painting that nostalgically depicts "strange people that were geometric forms walking in the street, or pushing a cart," that he had envisioned as a youth, "personages [that] were very colourful."[130] This combination of shadowy, geometric, but richly hued figures remained with the artist throughout his life, symbolizing his own contradiction.

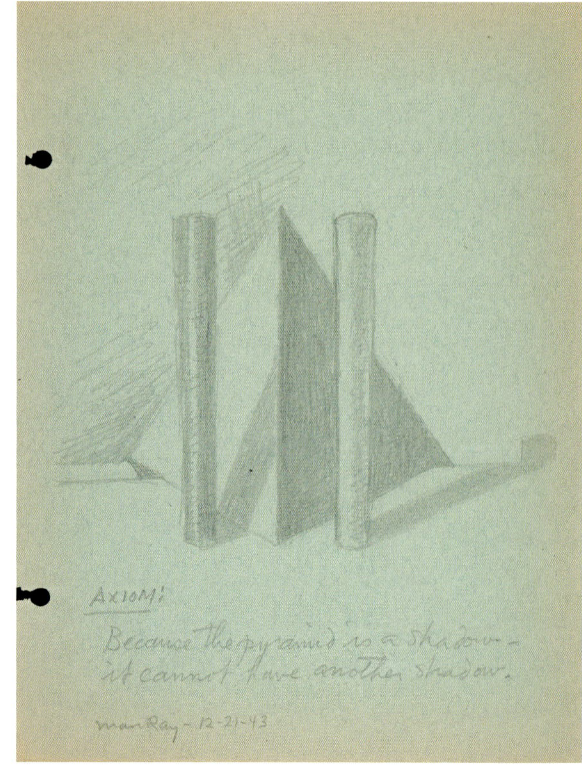

Fig. 99. *Axiom: Because the pyramid is a shadow—it cannot have another shadow,* 1943. Man Ray Letters and Album, 1922–76, Research Library, The Getty Research Institute, Los Angeles (930027)

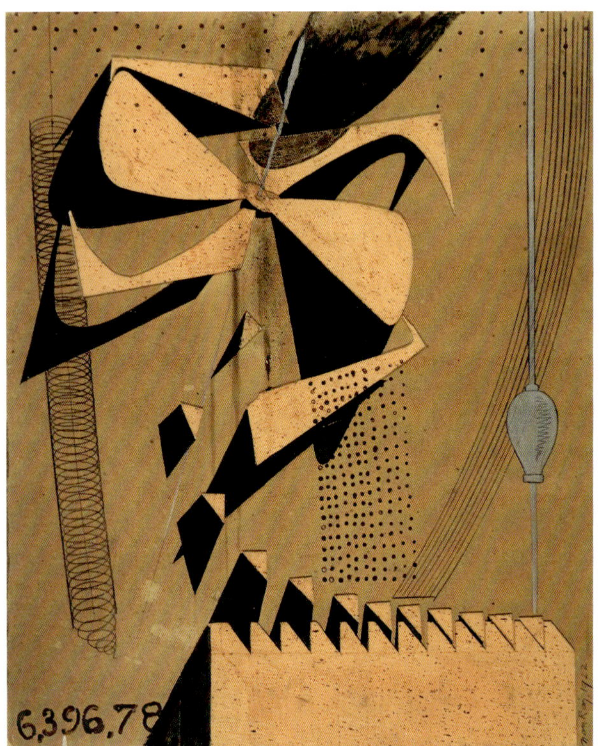

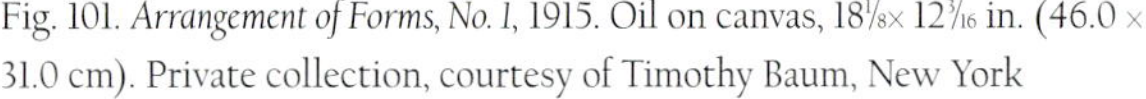

Fig. 100. *6,396,78,* 1922. Cork, gouache, graphite, and silver paint on brown paper, 25 × 20¼ in. (63.5 × 51.4 cm). New Orleans Museum of Art, Muriel Bultman Francis Collection

Fig. 101. *Arrangement of Forms, No. 1,* 1915. Oil on canvas, 18⅛ × 12³⁄₁₆ in. (46.0 × 31.0 cm). Private collection, courtesy of Timothy Baum, New York

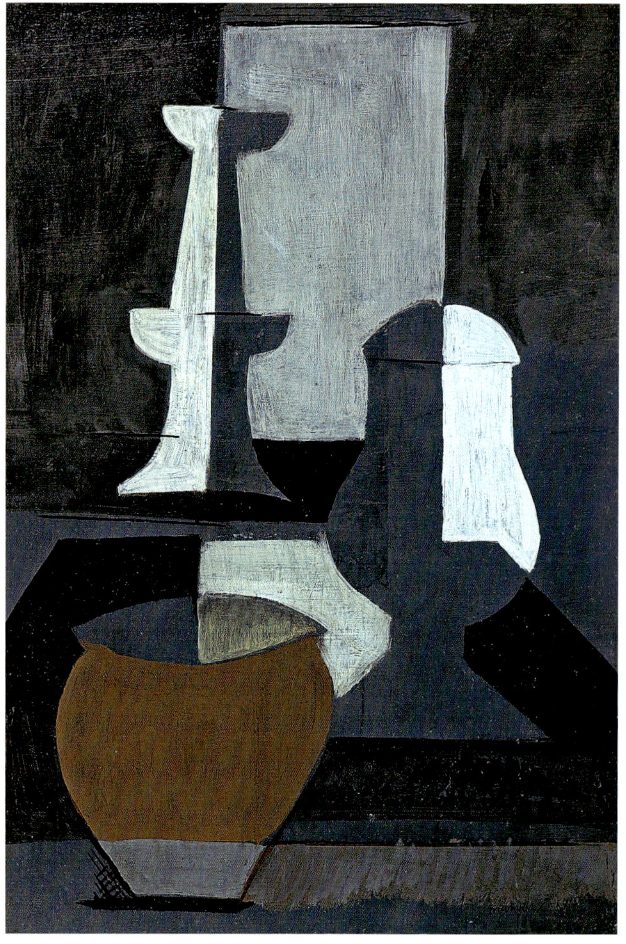

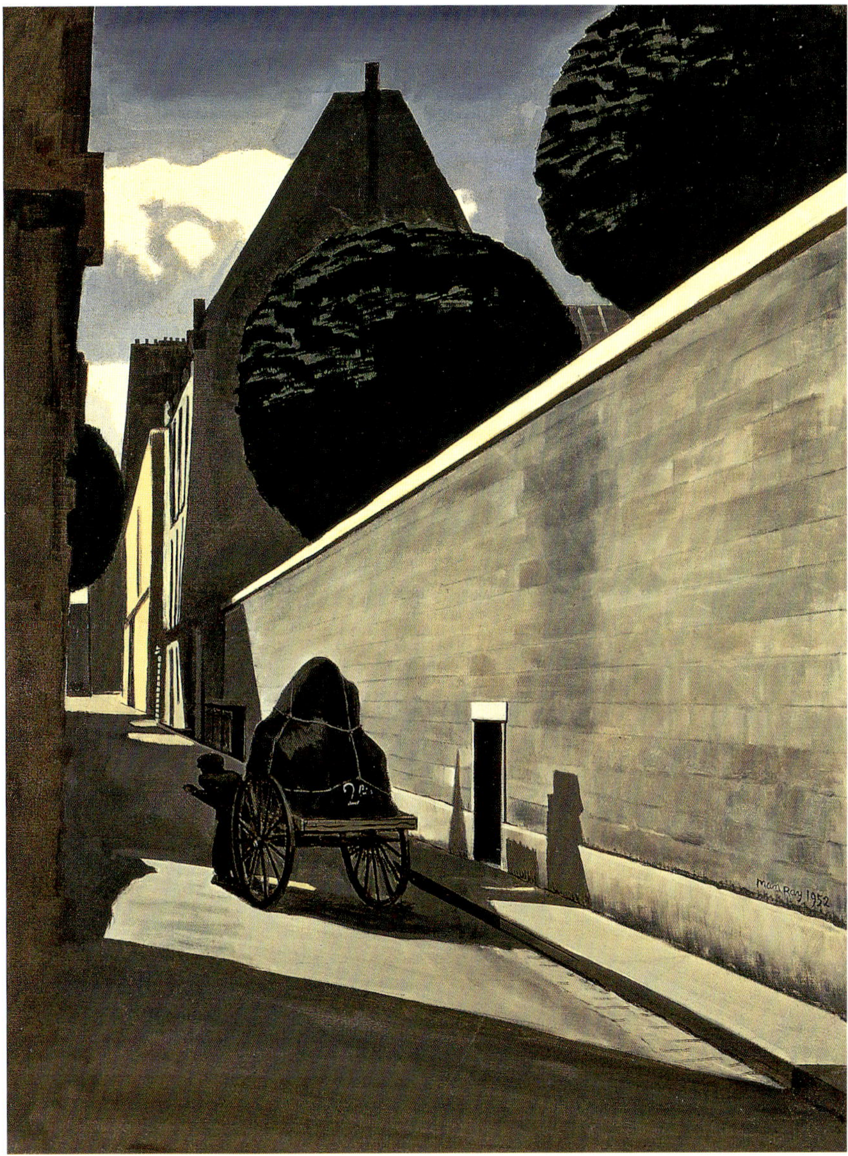

Fig. 102. *La rue Férou*, 1952. Oil on canvas, 31½ × 23⅝ in. (80 × 60 cm). Staff Stiftung, on permanent loan to Kunsthalle Bielefeld

In the last quarter of Man Ray's life the subject assumes a newly inflected gravity. The problem of not being seen, of being out of synch with the art world, of resisting falling into step with his times, became more pressing as his career in California and in the postwar years began to falter. The need to address his perceived complexity became unavoidable, as in *Self-Portrait with Half Beard* (1943; see Baker essay, fig. 29), an obvious attempt to humorously endure his dual identity as painter and photographer, not to mention his cloven Euro-American image. But as he confronted his amorphous profile with a new series of paintings, *Shakespearean Equations* (fig. 103), which represented yet another attempt to meld media by converting his 1936 photographic series *Mathematical Objects* into a painterly vision, he was also becoming more overtly defensive (fig. 104). The title of the exhibition where the *Equations* series was shown, in December 1948, at Copley Galleries in Beverly Hills, said it all: *To Be Continued Unnoticed*. Well, perhaps not quite all. In the catalogue essay

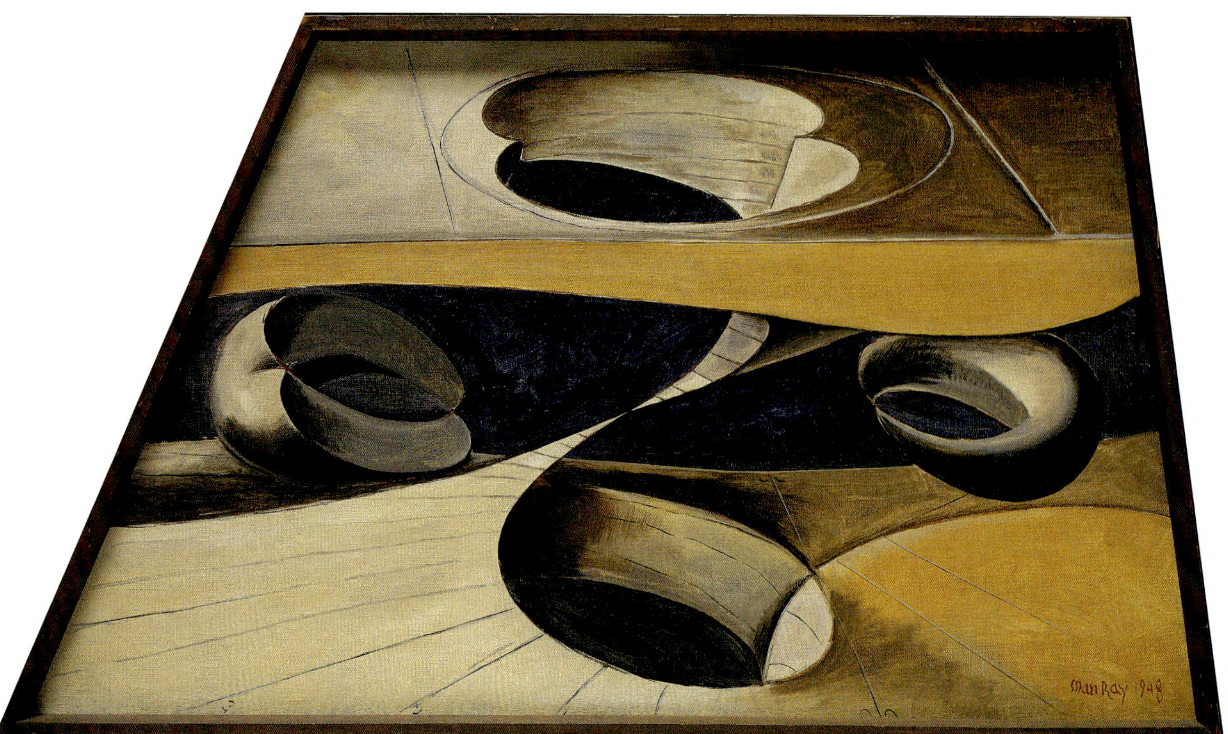

Fig. 103. *Shakespearean Equation: Measure for Measure*, 1948. Oil on canvas, 17¾ × 30¼ in. irregular (45.1 × 78.1 cm). Hirshhorn Museum and Sculpture Garden, Smithsonian Institution, Washington, D.C., Gift of Joseph H. Hirshhorn, 1972

"A Note on the Shakespearean Equations," Man Ray explicitly defended his poetic, late-Surrealist imagery and took issue with the "poverty of inventiveness and imagination" that he saw in new trends in abstract painting.[131]

It was a curious diatribe, and it reveals how insulated his mode of metamorphosis had become. As a Surrealist, but more so as an avant-garde provocateur, he had produced the kind of photography in the 1930s that led Surrealism to favor photography as the medium best equipped to render the real as fantastic. In the awkward, synthetic translation of his photography into dry, cerebral painting, Man Ray's work had lost that connection with the real. His painting lacked the sensual impact of his photographs, in which he had initially transformed mathematical models—originally constructed by a physicist attempting to portray algebraic formulas—into phenomenological, visionary scapes.[132] In the shift to the plastic domain of painting, Man Ray demanded more from the viewer than he offered. His new paintings lacked visual delectation, with their chalky, unsaturated colors, absence of finish, a strangely linear quality, and ambiguous Shakespearean titles—all of which seemed retrograde, a tiresome late-Surrealist ritual. He seemed to be simply coloring in his beloved drawings, hastily converting them into paintings.[133] Caught up in his own hermetic polemics, Man Ray failed to take notice of the advance of modernism as the next generation of post-Surrealist painters, led by Jackson Pollock, moved toward a more visceral engagement. Man Ray was still defending notions of originality and repetition: "The imitation of nature is our most advanced argument for merit. Pity we cannot stretch out this imitation as well as the argument for a period of time equal to that required by nature. The infinite variety of her (nature's) activity will always be the despair of the artist. And, only originality has the right to repeat itself. Only the artist who has created his own idiom can take pleasure in its repetition."[134]

His further distancing of object from origin paralleled the deepening of his own retreat—remaining ever the outsider, unable to see what was happening in the art world, eliding the real, presaging what he would soon do in *Self Portrait.*

Man Ray remained true to himself in the telling, or not telling, of his own story. He was comfortable being in the world only as an artist and choosing to connect to the world only from a carefully considered position; or rather, as a shadow, not just as metaphor for the relation between memoir and life but as the only way he could project himself in the world, one mysteriously lacking a footprint or trace, chronicling his life from the sole perspective of his artistic persona, and even then in dull light, obscured. "For who knows," Man Ray pondered, "but someday the shadow will be the dominating and condensed expression of our life. Throughout time this has been attempted, but it has remained only a fad of its period. Shadows in color—of three dimensions—that move and disappear, that speak and sing, collide with each other and embrace."[135]

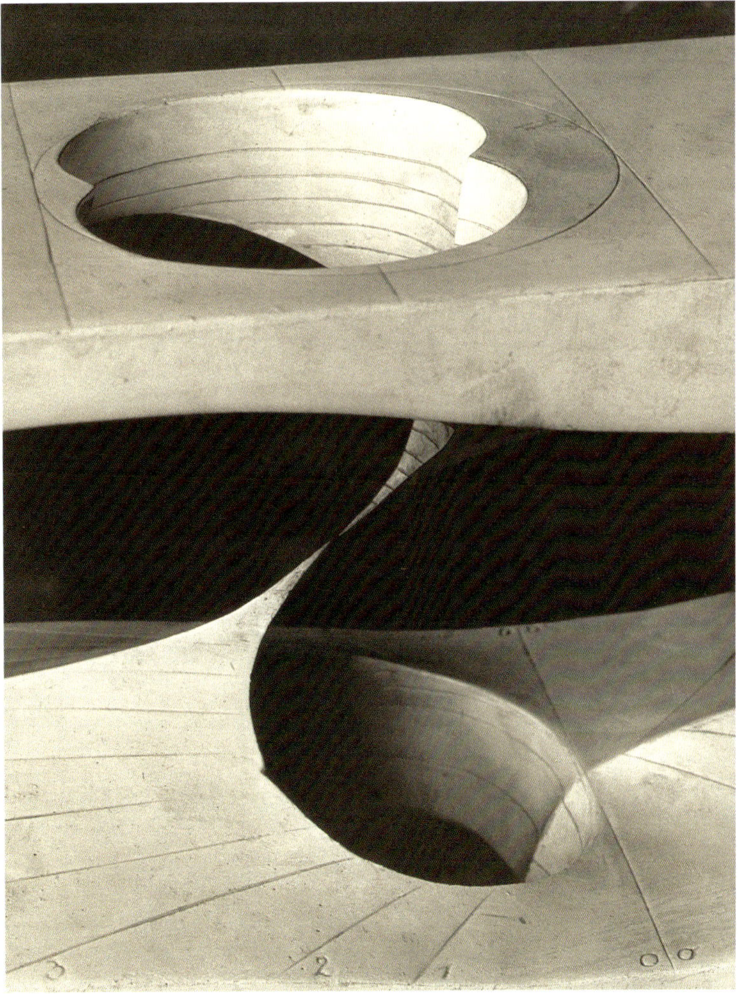

Fig. 104. *Equation, Poincaré Inst., Paris,* 1934. Gelatin silver print, 11¹³⁄₁₆ × 9⁹⁄₁₆ in. (30 × 23.3 cm). The J. Paul Getty Museum, Los Angeles

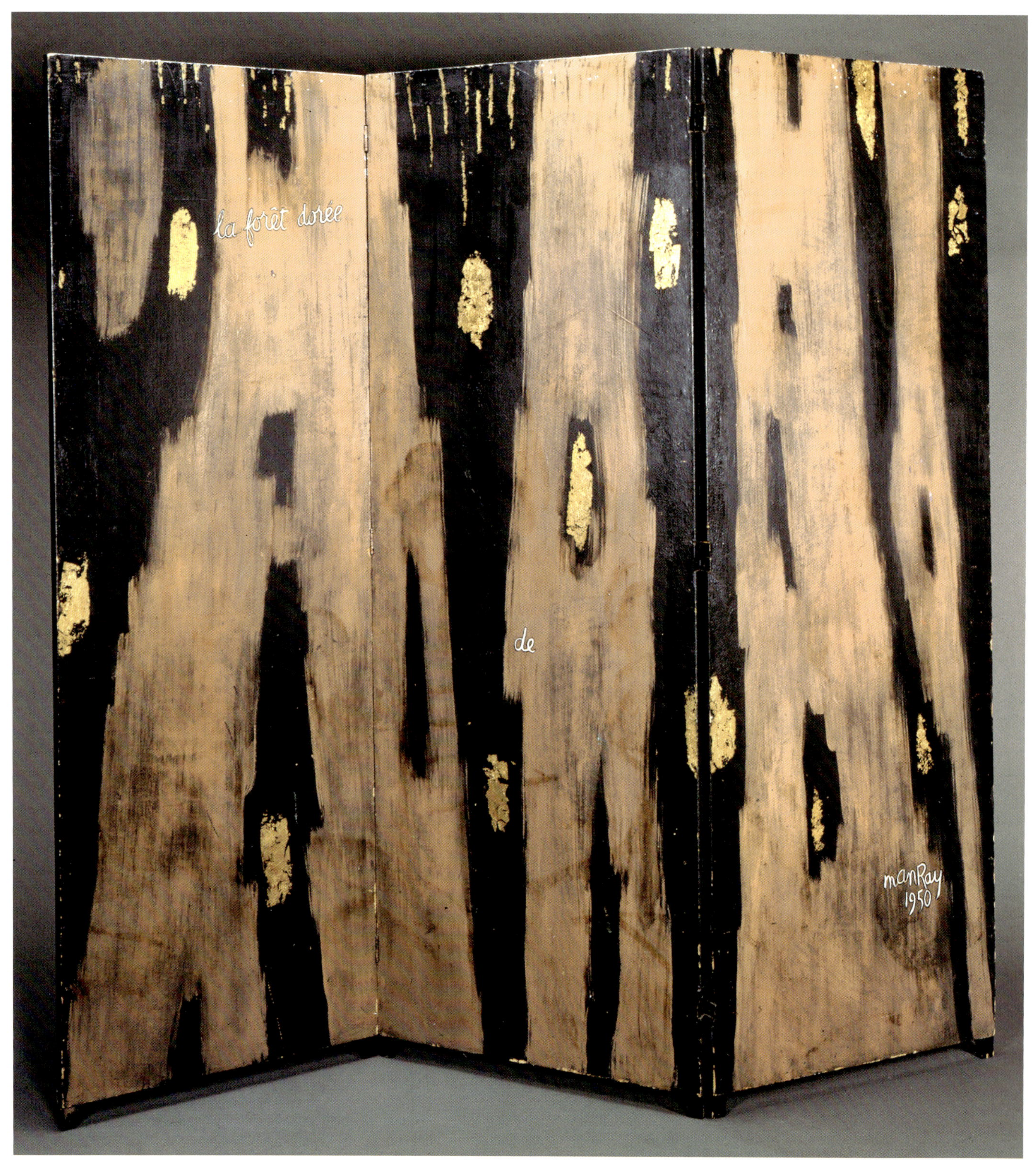

Fig. 105. *La forêt dorée de Man Ray*, 1950. Oil and gold leaf on panel, 67 × 70¾ in. (170 × 180 cm). Collection of Peter and Renate Nahum

The work that perhaps best illustrates Man Ray's desire to become one with his shadow, like his axiomatic pyramid—which, within Man Ray's idiosyncratic logic, *is* its shadow and therefore has no other—is a three-panel folding screen he painted in 1950 in California, called *La forêt dorée de Man Ray* (fig. 105). The painting was inspired by the giant sequoias that had overwhelmed him when he saw them, and whose effect he describes in his memoir:

> They are the oldest living things in nature, going back to Egyptian antiquity, their warm-colored, tender bark seems soft as flesh. Their silence is more eloquent than the roaring torrents and Niagaras, than the reverberating thunder in Grand Canyon, than the bursting of bombs; and is without menace. The gossiping leaves of the sequoias, one hundred yards above one's head, are too far away to be heard. I recalled a stroll in the Luxembourg Gardens during the first months of the outbreak of war, stopping under an old chestnut tree that had probably survived the French Revolution, a mere pygmy, wishing I could be transformed into a tree until peace came again.[136]

In an interview after her husband's death, Juliet Man Ray described the effect the artist had desired in the screen: "The brownish surface infused with vertical streaks of gold was Man Ray's vision of sunlight streaming through a redwood forest."[137] But one sees more than just sunlight in the relatively insignificant specks of gold that punctuate the treelike forms stretching from the base to the top of each panel; upon inspection, one detects three letters, subtly camouflaged, that spell out his name: MAN.

In calling the work *La forêt dorée de Man Ray*, the artist identifies, indeed becomes one, with his subject, once again employing the charged symbolism of trees. But the trees in his forest are so massive as to almost block out light, thus precluding their ability to cast a shadow. In his sixtieth year, at a time when he was feeling diminished if not unseen, Man Ray painted a subject he had been unable to render in a photograph, as, awestruck, he "fumbled with [his] inarticulate camera before the five-thousand-year-old, living patriarchs."[138] *La forêt dorée*, painted moreover on a screen, is an allegory of his own situation: He had become a forest one could not see for the trees.

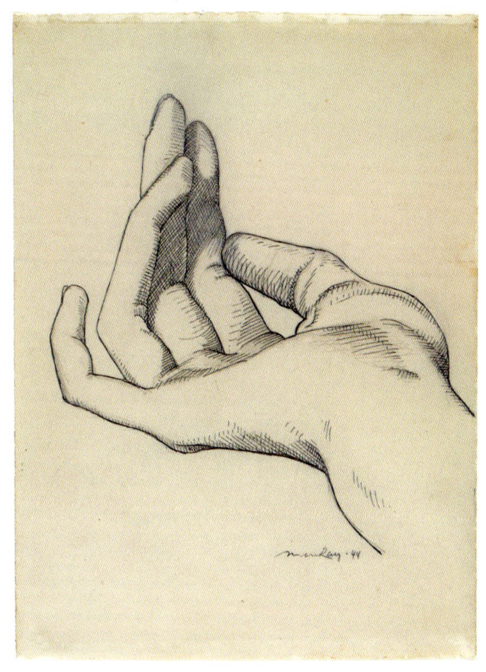

Fig. 106. *La main*, 1944. Pencil and ink on paper, 13⅛ × 9¾ in. (33.3 × 24.8 cm). Musée national d'art moderne, Centre Pompidou, Paris

Poetry and progress are like two ambitious men who hate one another with an instinctive hatred, and when they meet upon the same road, one of them has to give place.

— CHARLES BAUDELAIRE

*Everything is art. . . .
All this anti–art business
is nonsense. . . . If we must
have a word for it,
let's call it
Art.*

— MAN RAY

lost in translation
Man Ray and the Shifting Milieu of Modernism

Merry A. Foresta

It has become commonplace to think of Man Ray as someone who remained outside the mainstream of American art for his entire career. For most of the twentieth century, in the modernist milieus of New York, Paris, and Los Angeles, Man Ray's operating method was to shift in and out of media and movements. He encountered artistic styles and innovative media with energy and virtuosity, and then would break away in newer directions or circle back on ideas to recast them for the next, new audience. Like Baudelaire's *flâneur,* the observer who strolls through the crowd but is really not part of it, Man Ray navigated through the art movements of the twentieth century. His art represented, like photography for Baudelaire, a reordering of aesthetic experience, one inherently suspect for the new methods it harnessed for the expression of imagination. But if we think of him as someone who translated between the art of Europe and the art of the United States, between traditional modes of art and the desire for innovative practice, and as one who ultimately got lost in translation, we can get a more accurate picture of what his career was about and why his art remains critical to an understanding of our contemporary moment.

For most of the twentieth century Man Ray sampled from a variety of aesthetic ideas and critical precepts, including American modernism, Parisian Dada, and Surrealism on both sides of the Atlantic. As a result his art had no linear progression that would give it stylistic cohesion. He compensated by offering a body of work based on ideas rather than form, producing art in various media that could accommodate a range of interpretations. He was not a literal translator (he always carried both a French-English and a standard

French dictionary that enabled him linguistically), but insofar as his work was made in response to the critical climate of his times, his art was itself a form of criticism.

During his career, public reaction to his work was often somewhat mixed. Though John Russell, in his review of the artist's 1974 retrospective at the New York Cultural Center, declared that Man Ray was "one of the most remarkable Americans of his generation," he also pointed out that most followers of Man Ray's art would be hard pressed to say who Man Ray was.[1] A reviewer of his London exhibition of 1959 noted what he felt to be Man Ray's "meager talent for painting."[2] Most critics believed that the artist was better evaluated through the lens of Marcel Duchamp. Art historians who have studied Man Ray's career have struggled to come to terms with the discontinuity of his style and the multiple media in which he worked. The French writer and sometime Dadaist Georges Ribemont-Dessaignes, who produced in 1929 the first monograph about Man Ray's painting, suggested that the American had "unlocked a shocking universe with his rayographs" while continuing to "pursue journalistic fidelity in his photographs" and "maintain a pleasing facility" in his paintings.[3] American critic Lewis Mumford thought about it differently: "Man Ray has done almost everything with a camera except use it to take photographs. . . . A photographer who can deal intelligently with the human face should not waste his time photographing calla lilies so that they will look like a drawing by a second-rate academician."[4]

Man Ray himself often believed that he was neither appreciated nor understood, especially in America. During an interview late in his life he related an incident that occurred at the Société Anonyme in New York City in the early 1920s before he left for Paris. He had delivered a lecture on art, he recounted, and afterward "Miss Dreier [President and Founder of the organization] got up and declared: 'Now I shall say a few *serious* words.'"[5] He also recalled that by request he had supplied a photograph of one of the paintings from a 1917 exhibit of his work at the Charles Daniel Gallery to be used as an illustration in a publication on the history of art up to Matisse. Along with it, Man Ray remembered, was a caption that described the painting as "a picture by a painter whom I don't know and don't wish to know, but the man must be a drug-fiend, a sexual pervert and perhaps a criminal. 'And that,' Man Ray suggested, 'sums up the attitude of most people there [in America].'"[6]

If only an embroidered remembrance, the statement does contain some spirit of the critical moment. In America, modern art encountered its most vocal and vociferous criticism in the early years of the century, and Man Ray, along with other vanguard artists in and around New York, certainly felt the sting of this antagonism to the new. Still, he persevered on a course that embraced the most advanced painting of the day, starting with Cubism. Works such as *War (A.D. MCMXIV)*, for example, painted the year after the 1913 Armory Show, exhibit typical Cubist elements similar to those found in works by a number of young American artists who had just encountered contemporary European art. But if the Armory Show brought America into the loop and ultimately tempered the terms of

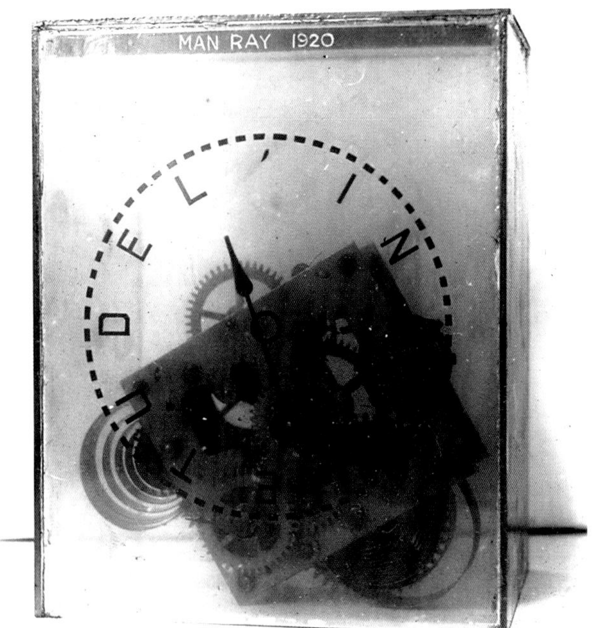

Fig. 1. *L'Inquiétude (Anxiety)*, 1920. Gelatin silver print, 4⅜ × 3⅝ in. (11.1 × 9.2 cm). Collection Goldberg/d'Afflitto

the argument with modern painting, assemblage and collage works like *Self-Portrait* (see Klein essay, fig. 31), shown at Man Ray's second Daniel Gallery exhibition in 1916, seemed to have puzzled the reviewers who were now intent on discussing the work in Cubist terms: "Such artificial devices as electric bells, push buttons, filter paper, darning silk and finger prints, which are plastered about his canvases, do not create any divergency of surface material."[7]

Rather than holding the line of Cubism, like most of his American colleagues, Man Ray adopted the iconography of the mechanized New World, which held such attraction for Europeans including Francis Picabia, Duchamp, and Jean Crotti. He abandoned painted Cubist angles for flat colored-paper cutouts in mechanomorphic shapes attached to revolving panels (*The Revolving Doors*). He substituted the mechanical airbrush for a paintbrush. He appropriated everyday objects and remade them into sculpture: eggbeaters, ball bearings in a jar, a carpenter's brace, the contents of an overturned ashtray. And then he photographed them, and in so doing began a practice of conceptual transference between media that would animate his entire career (fig. 1). Perhaps most important of all, Man Ray's involvement with Dada in New York made him more cognizant of a larger, more receptive audience abroad. In Europe, Man Ray made the most of his Americanness: the avant-garde celebrated the very traits of innovatively engineered can-do that at home made him odd man out.

In retrospect, one of the most intriguing talents that Man Ray had as an artist was an ability to travel from one place and from one artistic circle to another. When he arrived in Paris in 1921 at the age of thirty, he brought with him a trunk full of artworks, an advance of a few hundred dollars on some paintings yet to be realized, no working knowledge of the language, and hopes that his friendship with a few avant-garde European artists would open doors for him in the Old World's capital of art. Indeed, by the end of his first year in Paris, Man Ray was fully part of Montparnasse, which had replaced Montmartre as the center of the Parisian avant-garde. His trick, it seemed, was not to become the center of any

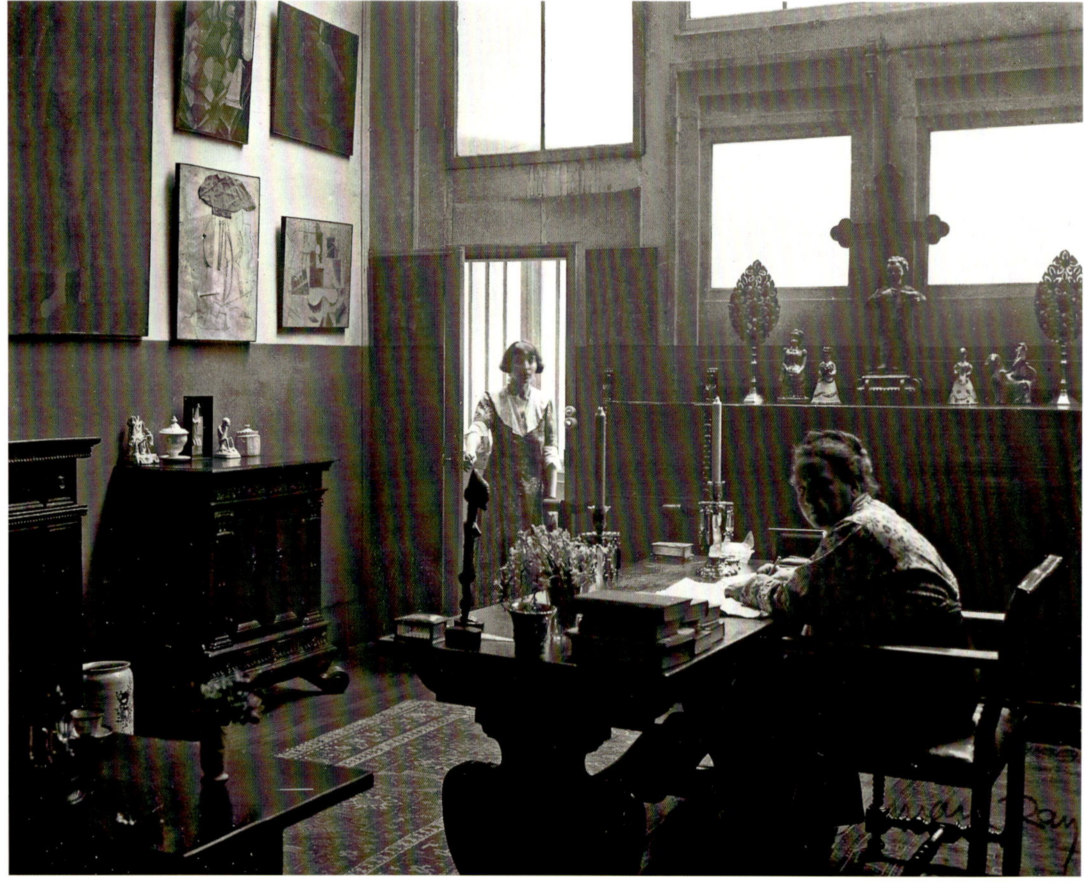

Fig. 2. *Alice B. Toklas and Gertrude Stein, 27 rue de Fleurus*, 1922. Gelatin silver print, 7⅛ × 9 in. (18 × 22.9 cm). Isidore Ducasse Fine Arts

one group but to belong to all of them: he was for a time Gertrude Stein's house photographer, but he did not attend her Saturday receptions (fig. 2); he did not sit with André Breton's Surrealist group at the café Certa, nor did he join any of the Americans who regularly gathered at cafés on the Boulevard Saint-Germaine. He was as likely to make a date with Tristan Tzara at the Rotonde as with Jean Cocteau (of whose social and stylish connections the Dadaists violently disapproved), who lived with his mother on the Right Bank (fig. 3).[8] He was on call as an artist for hire for European aristocrats and as a fashion photographer for New York magazines. Though he lost his privileges as the American in Paris when he left for Los Angeles during the Second World War, Man Ray maintained his popularity on the boulevards of Hollywood among the vanguard European filmmakers,

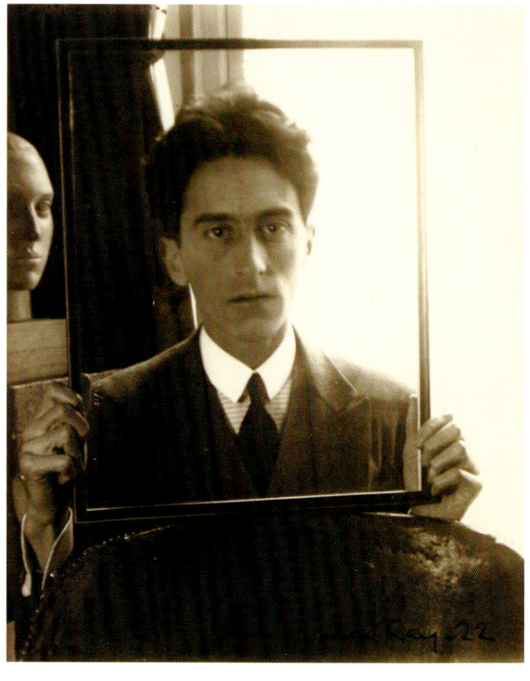

Fig. 3. *Portrait of Jean Cocteau with Empty Picture Frame*, 1922. Gelatin silver print, 4¾ × 3¾ inches (12.1 × 9.5 cm). High Museum of Art, Atlanta; Purchase with funds from Georgia-Pacific Corporation

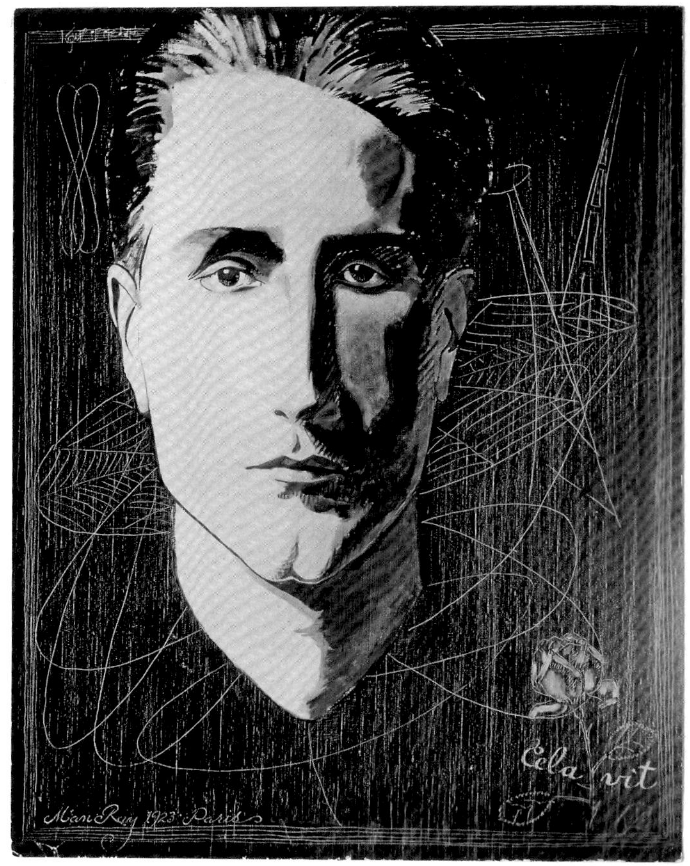

Fig. 4. *Portrait of Marcel Duchamp "Cela vit,"* 1923. Photograph of lost painting (vintage print), 7⅞ × 6⁵⁄₁₆ in. (20 × 16 cm). Kunsthaus Zürich

writers, and musicians who created an improbable café society during the war. If there was any constant, it was his relationship with the equally peripatetic Marcel Duchamp (fig. 4). That friendship and collaboration lasted over fifty years, winding in and out of America and France, forming and reforming within the history of art of the twentieth century.

Man Ray's art (sent parcel post) and his reputation arrived in Paris before he did. At the beginning of June 1921, Tzara, who himself had officially carried Dada into France just a year before, organized *Salon Dada: Exposition Internationale,* an exhibition and series of readings and theater performances at the Théâtre des Champs-Elysées. The bulk of the show was made up of objects, collages, and slogan-bearing signs, including many works made and provocatively installed expressly for the exhibition by Tzara and the French Dadaists (fig. 5).[9]

Man Ray's contribution came in the form of photographs of two Dada constructions, *Man* and *Woman. Man* was the photographic record of an eggbeater and the shadows it cast onto a blank wall. *Woman* was the document of an assembly of objects from his darkroom—two metal light reflectors and six clothespins attached to the edge of a plate of glass—illuminated in such a way that they duplicated their shapes as distinct shadows. Just as the eggbeater can be read for its distinctly male characteristic, the arrangement of objects in *Woman* can be read as female attributes. Initially sent by Man Ray from New York at Tzara's request for his planned but never realized publication *Dadaglobe*, the pictures efficiently represented and transported Man Ray's work across the Atlantic for one purpose, and then to the lobby of the exhibition space for another. The witty images were, in fact, many things in one: photographs and objects, illustrations and works of art. In fact, the images were purposely mistranslated by Tzara for the occasion. Appropriately for Man Ray's entrance into Paris Dada, *Man* became *Woman*, and *Woman* became *Man*.

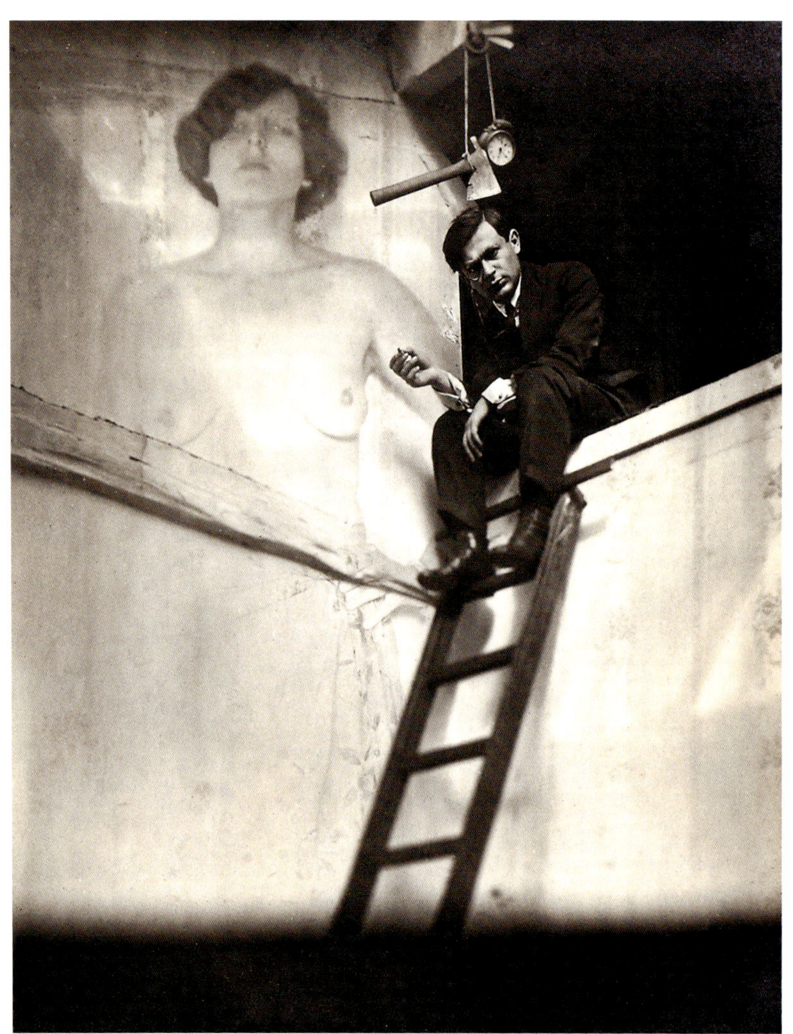

Other artistic translations followed. Staged as another Dada event symbolizing Paris receiving New York, Man Ray's first solo show in Paris included thirty-five works that he had brought with him. The show included the spiral paper *Lampshade*, Cubist-styled paintings like *Legend*, *Love Fingers*, and *Percolator*, as well as several examples of his airbrush paintings. *Aviary*, an aerograph painting from 1919, which featured the dressmaker's dummy that had stood in the corner of Man Ray's New York studio, became in Paris in 1921 *La Volière*. Slang for brothel, the French title expanded to include the larger definition of *le bordel*, which popularly referred to any confusing situation as well as a prostitute's place of employment. Tzara's note of welcome in the catalogue proclaimed: "New York sends us one of its love fingers, which will not be long in taking the susceptibilities of the French painters. Let us hope that this titillation will again indicate the already well-known wound which marks the closed somnolence of art."[10]

Adding to the Dada-inspired confusion of the day was still another work of art. During the opening, Man Ray was inspired by meeting Erik Satie, an avant-garde composer and a Dadaist favorite. With Satie's help as interpreter (he spoke fluent English) Man Ray dashed to a hardware store and purchased a flatiron, a box of tacks, and a tube of glue. Back at the gallery he glued a row of tacks to the smooth surface of the iron, titled it *Cadeau* (Gift), and added it to the exhibition (fig. 6). "This," declared Man Ray in his autobiography, "was my first Dada object in France."[11]

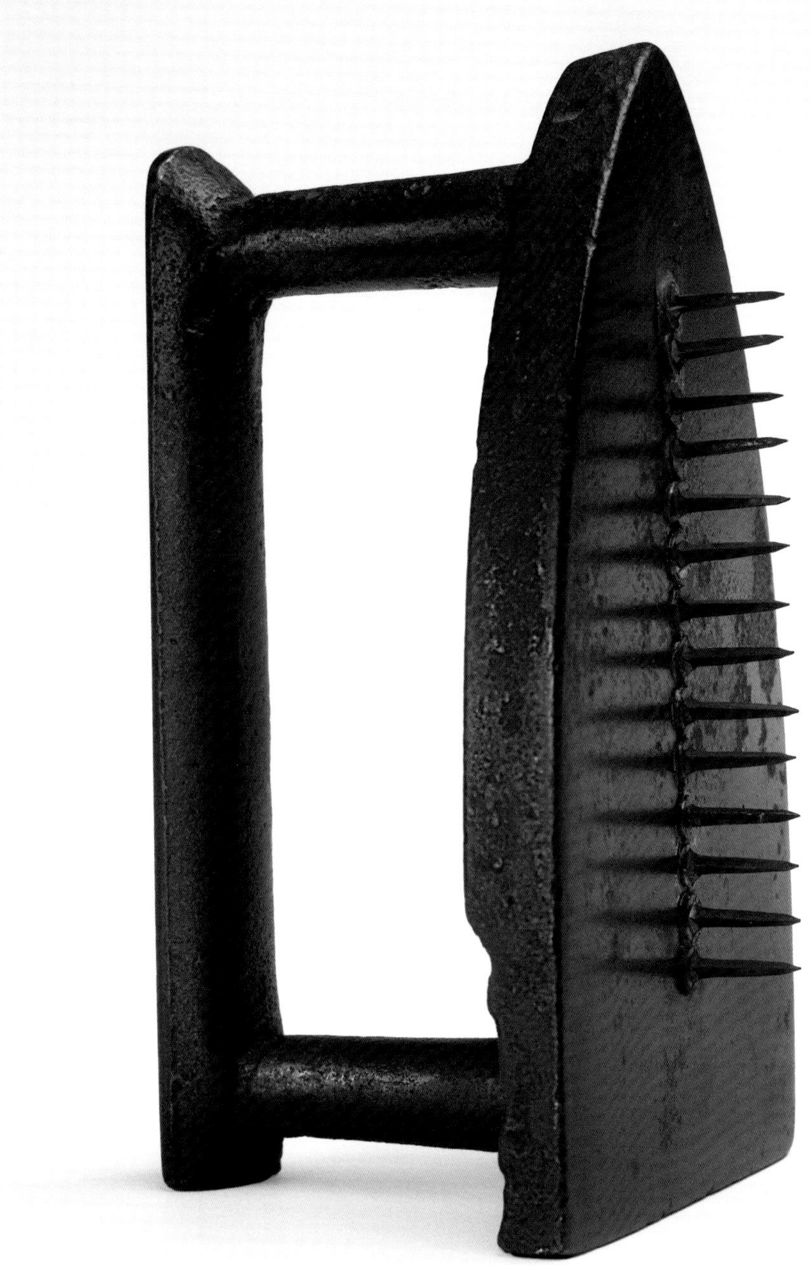

Fig. 6. *Cadeau (Gift)*, 1963 replica of lost 1921 original. Cast iron, brass tacks, 6⅛ × 3⅝ × 4 in. (15.3 × 9 × 11.4 cm). Philadelphia Museum of Art. Purchased with the Henry P. McIlhenny Fund in memory of Frances P. McIlhenny, 2005

While the concept of *Cadeau* derived from Man Ray's New York experiences with Duchamp, his vocabulary extended well beyond that of the French artist. Man Ray also photographed the iron. Thus documented, the object quickly disappeared, likely snatched by one of the Dada group.[12] Shot as a close-up, filling the frame of the photograph, the jagged surface of the iron looms menacingly. Thus transformed, the object's meaning could be translated on several levels: it was an everyday object subverted into a dark joke about utility; it was an announcement of independence from home and family (certainly an iron adorned with tacks would have

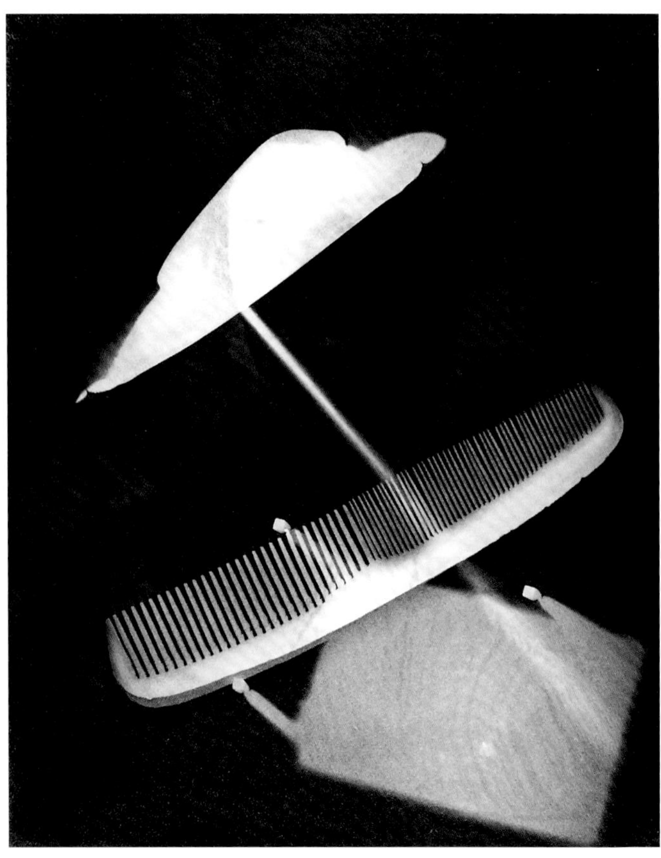

Fig. 7. *Untitled*, 1923. Gelatin silver print, 9$^{15}/_{16}$ × 8 in. (25.2 × 20.3 cm). Baltimore Museum of Art. Purchase with exchange funds from the Edward Joseph Gallagher III Memorial Collection, and partial gift of George H. Dalsheimer

been a dubious gift for his father, a tailor); and it suggested his freedom from what he now perceived as the provincial modernism of America, and the limits of American art photographers like Edward Steichen and Alfred Stiegltiz, who had in photograph after photograph made a modernist icon of New York's Flatiron Building. Man Ray's skyscraper-like *Cadeau* was a step beyond. Surviving finally as a photograph, the image made the translation between object and its double as artwork complete. If the object was made in the spirit of Dada subversion, at a moment when the Dada group itself was splintering into warring factions, the photograph also carried with it the opportunities for a more purposeful program of artistic survival and continuance.

Amid the laughter and buffoonery at the Librairie Six, the avant-garde of Europe made it clear that the measure for the American artist in Paris had little to do with French mastery or precedent, surely not with his New York Cubist-style paintings. Quite the opposite: the faltering movement of Dada was relying on Man Ray to demonstrate an art bred in the New World, not the Old, an art for a new age, one that could function in a variety of situations, something that moved the argument forward. *Cadeau*, the photograph, was literally and figuratively Man Ray's gift to the avant-garde endeavor.

In general, photography freed Man Ray to function on both sides of the barricade separating conventional expression from the imperatives of the avant-garde. Man Ray's prints seem to have convinced the Dada group almost overnight that the unpredictable results he obtained from a partially mechanical process were particularly appropriate to their anti-art stance. Ephemeral constructions were given the gravitas of permanence when converted to the silvery tonalities of the photographic print. Paintings, converted to photographs for publicity or catalogues, took on a different life—perhaps also becoming dispensable once reproduced. Photographs made years before in New York could also be retitled and redated (his 1918 photograph of dust on Duchamp's *Large Glass* became *Vue prise en aéroplane* in 1921, for example, when it was published in *Littérature* in October 1922) to assume new meaning as complements to Surrealist texts.

Rayographs were Man Ray's solution to being both a painter and photographer. Writing in his preface to *Les champs délicieux*, a collection of rayographs published in December 1922, Tzara proclaimed that Man Ray had "invented a new method."[13] To paint without using a brush was one thing, but to photograph without a camera and call it art was a whole new program. Created in the darkroom sans camera, populated with a mixture of machinery parts, bits and pieces of everyday life, even incorporating a human face or hand, these images kept faith with Dada irreverence even as they evidenced an aesthetic sensibility. Cocteau evocatively dubbed them "paintings with light."[14] All at once Man Ray had introduced into the anti-art Dadaist avant-garde an art that obliquely or covertly incorporated principles of design, form, and style (figs. 7–9).

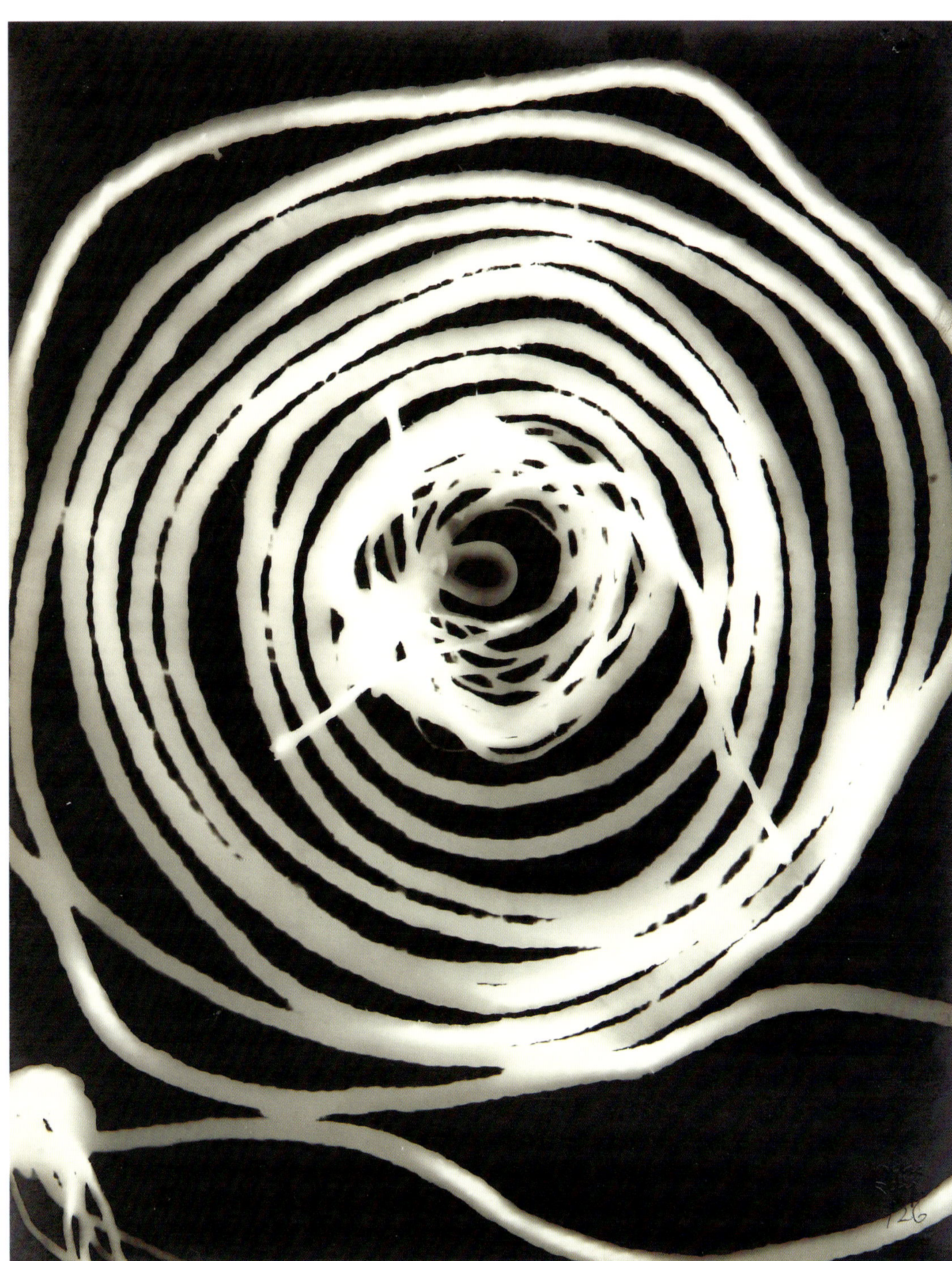

Fig. 8. *Rayograph*, 1926. Gelatin silver print, 10⅞ × 8½ in. (26.7 × 21.6 cm). Private collection, New York

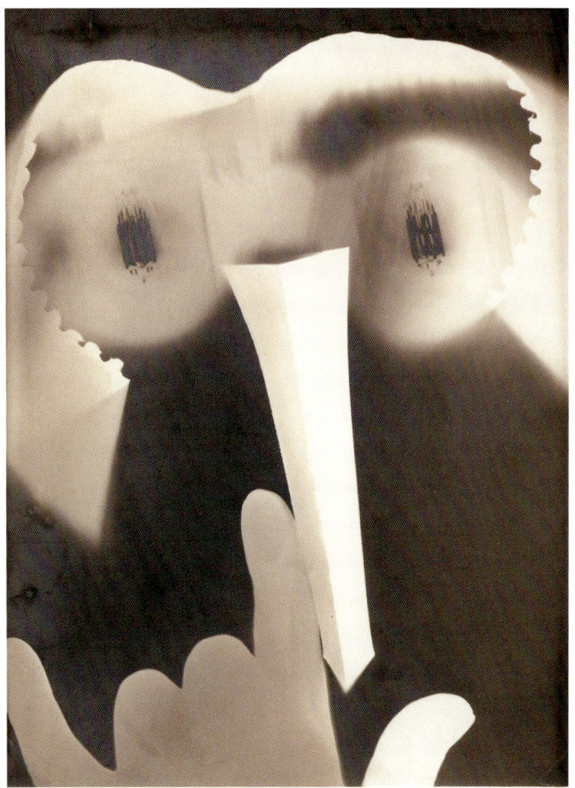

Fig. 9. *Monsieur . . . , Inventeur, Constructeur, 6 Seconds,* 1928. Gelatin silver print, 9½ × 7 in. (24.1 × 17.8 cm). Richard and Ronnie Grosbard Collection

In France, Man Ray's very point became the obscuring of boundaries between media. Even the difficult-to-please Breton paid homage to Man Ray's unique ability to move in so many directions so well (fig. 10). Smudging the distinctions between high and low art had been at the very heart of a program of transformative creativity at which Man Ray excelled. In Paris, his first photographs of his lover Kiki had pleased him because "they really looked like studies for paintings, or might even be mistaken at a casual glance for reproductions of academic paintings" (fig. 11). He had been satisfied too, when his aerographs were mistaken for photographs, because that matched the confusion the Dadaists had been after. About the relationship between painting and photography he was adamant: "It was perfectly normal," he insisted, "that one should influence the other."[15]

At home it was a different story. Only the fashionable magazine *Vanity Fair* featured his work with a page of rayographs, "Experiments in Abstract Form, Made Without a Camera Lens, by Man Ray," along with a quotation from Cocteau saying that Man Ray had "set painting free again."[16] The question "Can a photograph have the significance of art?" was still at the center of most American debates about the relationship between media; cameraless photography was particularly not welcomed in circles that had so lately won a place for the art of photography. Among the several artists responding to the question for the December 1922 issue of MSS, only Georgia O'Keeffe acknowledged that the best photographers were those who did not separate photography from other media.[17] And it was she who mentioned Man Ray as a "young painter of ultra modern tendencies and of varied experiments." O'Keeffe thought Man Ray "seems to be broadening the field of work." Submitting his answer from Paris, poet and critic Marius De Zayas thought otherwise. The rayographs and Man Ray's status as a photographer-artist, cast as part of a European program, did not interest him.[18]

What kind of art was this? Installed in Paris, Man Ray saw himself charting a new course worthy of America's technological superiority. America, in fact, had no name for what he was doing, few sympathetic artists or critics to establish a dialogue about the

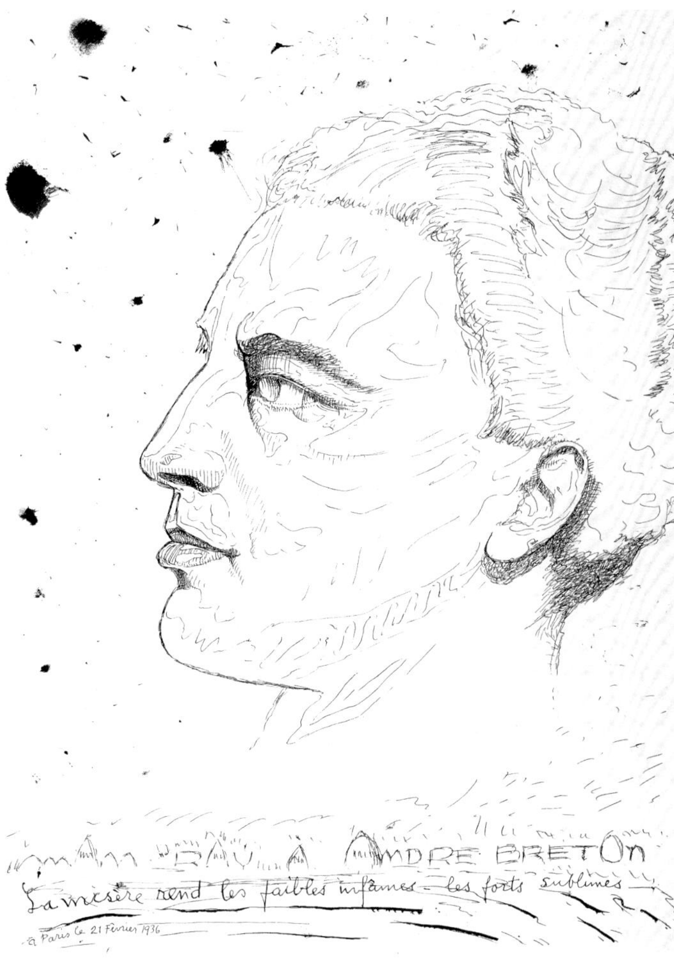

Fig. 10. *Portrait of André Breton*, 1936. India ink on paper, 14⅛ × 10¼ in. (36 × 26 cm). Original art for an illustration in *Les mains libres* (1937) by Man Ray and Paul Éluard. Collection of André Baum, New York

Fig. 11. *Untitled (Kiki)*, c. 1924. Gelatin silver print, 11⅛ × 8¹⁵⁄₁₆ in. (28.3 × 22.7 cm). The Baltimore Museum of Art. Purchase with exchange funds from the Edward Joseph Gallagher III Memorial Collection, and partial gift of George H. Dalsheimer

work, and no real audience. Except for a few machine-age enthusiasts such as Jane Heap and Margaret Anderson, who kept the conversation going with illustrations, reviews, and opinions in their small press publication *Little Review*, the modern-art community shied away, abhorring the commercial taint of photography and film.[19] Little notice was taken of his 1927 exhibition at the Daniel Gallery that combined both paintings and photographs. Of his film *Emak-Bakia*, which had no script and incorporated moving rayographs, street-scene montages, and Surrealist sequences, a critic declared after the New York premiere in March 1927 that the film had "gone straight to hell with good intentions."[20] Fair enough, America. But in the eyes of his French critics and artist colleagues old questions concerning the hierarchy of media were no longer of interest. As he spoke of it in 1928, Man Ray's tone still matched the optimism of dis-

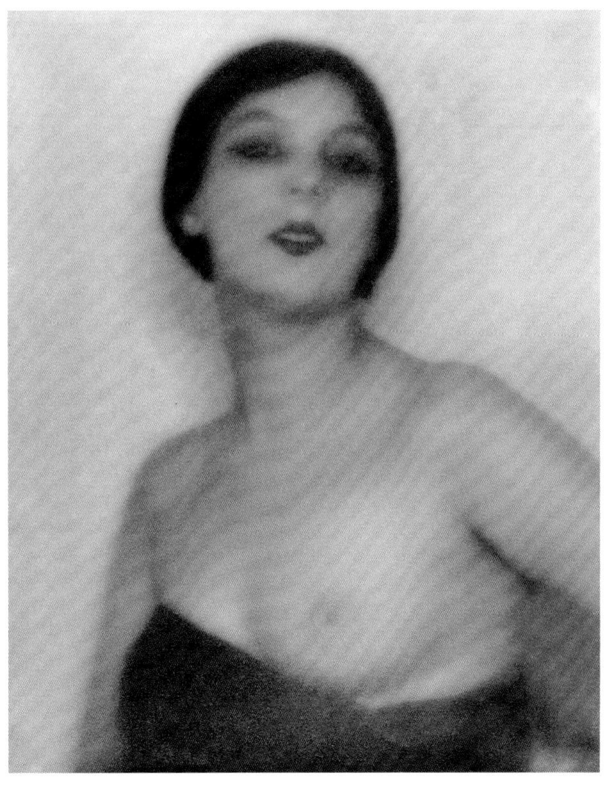

covery: "Is photography an art? One should not ask that question. Art is obsolete. We need something else. . . . I sit before a sheet of sensitive paper and I think."[21]

While few galleries in the United States or Europe showed Man Ray's paintings during the 1920s and 1930s, and few if any paintings were sold to important collectors or museums, Man Ray adopted a different kind of exhibition space: the printed page. He reached his audience on both sides of the Atlantic through magazines, both popular and intellectual. Fashionable readers of *Vanity Fair* and *Vogue* regularly saw Man Ray's portraits of the chic and celebrated. In the 1930s Man Ray's photographs, along with art by Salvador Dalí, Jean Cocteau, Marc Chagall, and other European Surrealists, regularly appeared in the pages of *Harper's Bazaar.* The first Surrealist journal, *La révolution surréaliste*, which began publication in 1924, featured Man Ray's images prominently and often. Indeed, his photograph of his object *The Enigma of Isidore Ducasse*, first made and photographed in 1920 in New York, was on the cover.[22] In the later and more doctrinaire Surrealist magazines, especially *Le Surréalisme au service de la révolution*, which began in 1930, Man Ray's photographs became more disturbing, their spirit more political. *Transition*, an elegant avant-garde journal that featured experimental and Surrealist work, published in Paris by the Americans Eugene and Maria Jolas, reproduced Man Ray's work extensively.[23]

Man Ray also found that the best critic to explain his work was often himself. Indeed, throughout his career in various self-published manifestos, catalogue statements, and radio and publication interviews he expounded on the purpose and meaning of his art. A comparison of two publications describes the range of Man Ray's production in the medium of photography. It also describes how Man Ray used the practice of photography to define the conditions upon which his entire career could be understood. On the one hand is *Photographs by Man Ray 1920 Paris 1934*, containing photographs and text by a variety of well-known artists. On the other is *La photographie n'est pas l'art*, published in collaboration with Breton. In both cases the reader is treated to a combination of words and text, and in both this combination has a meaning greater than the contents of the individual images.

Intended for an American more than a European audience, *Photographs by Man Ray 1920 Paris 1934* was Man Ray's way of presenting his career to a homeland that had rarely seen his work.[24] The book was subsidized by James Thrall Soby, a wealthy publisher whose connections to New York's newly opened Museum of Modern Art must have given Man Ray some hope that this book might impress the individuals helping to shape the museum's program. Overall it was a kind of grand promotional catalogue. With 105 photographs, a cover in glossy color, a portrait of Man Ray by Picasso for the frontispiece, and short texts in English and French by Man Ray, Paul Éluard, Breton, Tzara, and Duchamp, Man Ray's published collection was a virtuoso presentation of modern European-style photography (fig. 12). Close-up views, distorted angles, double exposures, night photography, negative prints, rayographs, still lifes, nudes, portraits, and fashion photographs were reproduced. References to his painting were included—the silvery toned *Gens du monde* was featured as

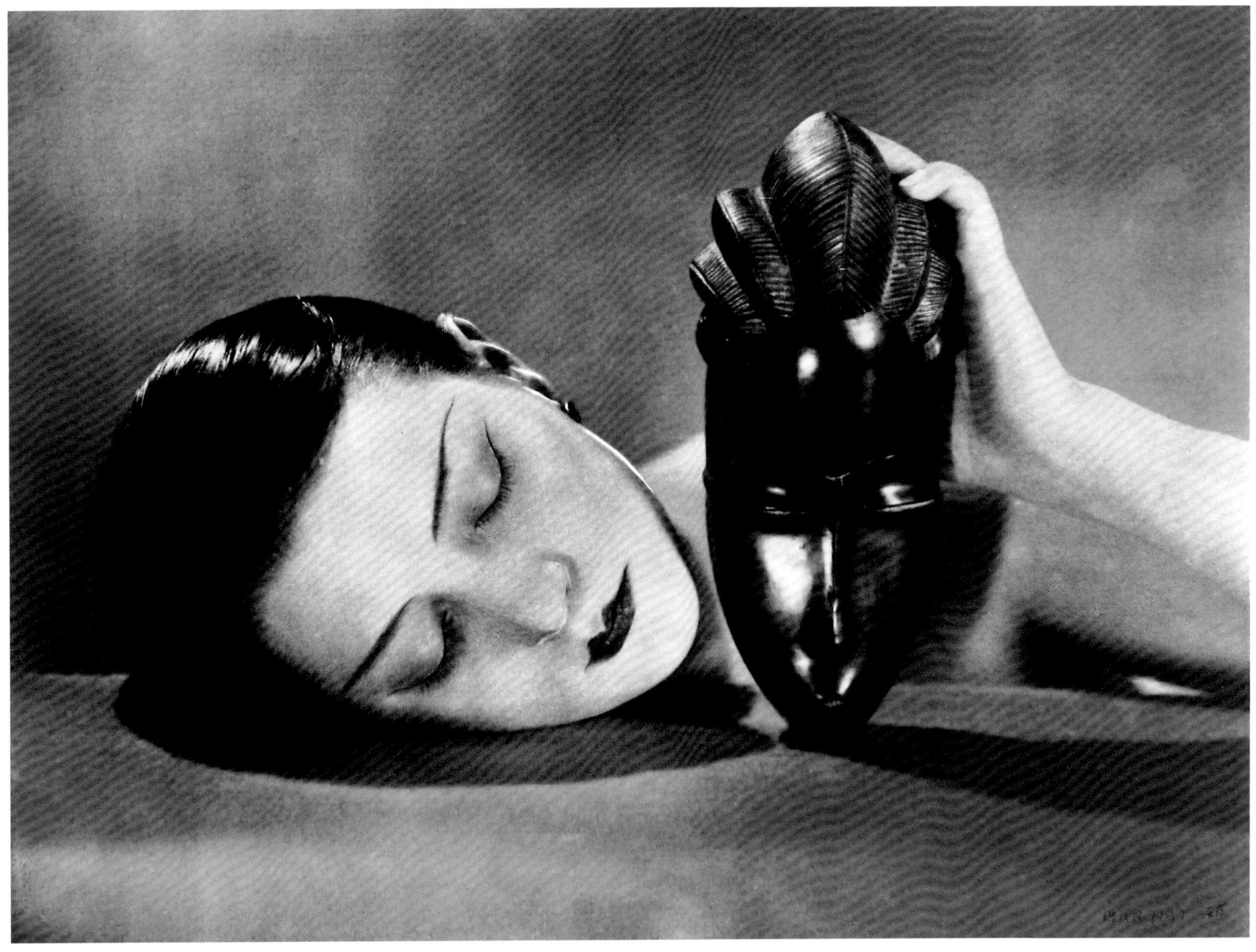

Fig. 12. *Noire et Blanche*, 1926. Gelatin silver print, 8⅜ × 10¾ in. (21.3 × 27.3 cm). Private collection of Thomas and Janine Koerfer-Weill

the subject in an interior view—and several of his object sculptures were arrayed on a table in front of a model for the cover image. Slyly, Man Ray also included himself on the cover, in the form of a plaster bust that stands in for the artist. In reproduction much of the work, especially the rayographs and solarized prints, with faces and forms outlined in dark and chiaroscuro shading, approached the textures and impression of watercolors, drawings, and paintings. Thus, the book was also a calculated assay on the connections between photography, art, and fashion. "The Age of Light," Man Ray's introductory essay, makes it clear that he has applied himself to testing conventional limits.

La photographie n'est pas l'art, a portfolio of twelve photographs that Man Ray made with Breton in 1937, also presents a catalogue of the types of art that photography had become.[25] Less an upbeat promotion than a statement of purpose, the small book continued the debate that had existed since photography's invention. Rather than argue photography versus painting, the book uses images to argue that photography might not be art, or only art, because it is able to mean so much else—poetry, for example. Breton had a curious tolerance for photography. Of the first two artists that he claimed for Surrealism proper—

Max Ernst and Man Ray—one was a photographer, and Breton had placed photography at the very heart of Surrealist publication. Breton had asked in his 1925 treatise *Surrealism and Painting,* "When will all the books that are worth anything stop being illustrated with drawings and appear only with photographs?"[26] Here, ten years later, more obviously subscribing to a Surrealist effort to effect a poetry in art, Man Ray demonstrated a medium that can describe real things and also transform them into appealing or appalling images: fashion pictures, portraits, nature studies.

One of the images is a picture of frogs mating; another is a fashion picture entitled (or retitled) *Le sex-appeal.* Other titles are more biting. A close-up of an ant colony is titled *Cerveau bien ordonné* (Well-ordered brain). A rayograph is treated like a product advertisement: *Photographie intégrale et cent pour cent automatique* (Completely and one hundred per cent automatic photography) (fig. 13). One of the images might be a reference to Man Ray's own situation: *Photo de mode "collection d'hiver"* (New winter fashion) depicts a fruit tree, its pro-

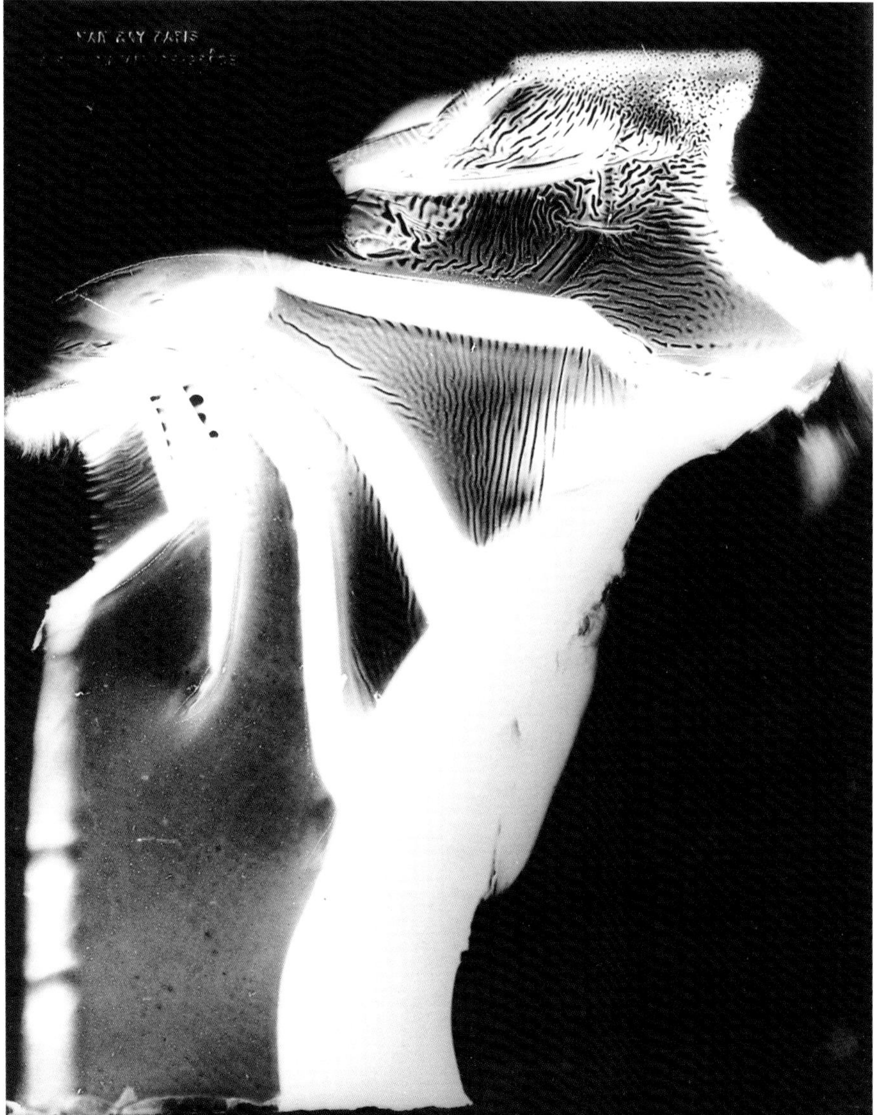

Fig. 13. *Rayograph "Photographie intégrale et cent pour cent automatique,"* 1937. Gelatin silver print, 11¹/₁₆ × 8⁷/₈ in. (28 × 22.5 cm). The Penrose Collection, England

Fig. 14. Leaf 17, *Dans les yeux des autres,* from *La photographie n'est pas l'art,* 1937. Rare Books Division, The New York Public Library, Astor, Lenox and Tilden Foundations

Fig. 15. Leaf 9, *Passage entre deux prises de vues,* from *La photographie n'est pas l'art,* 1937. Rare Books Division, The New York Public Library, Astor, Lenox and Tilden Foundations

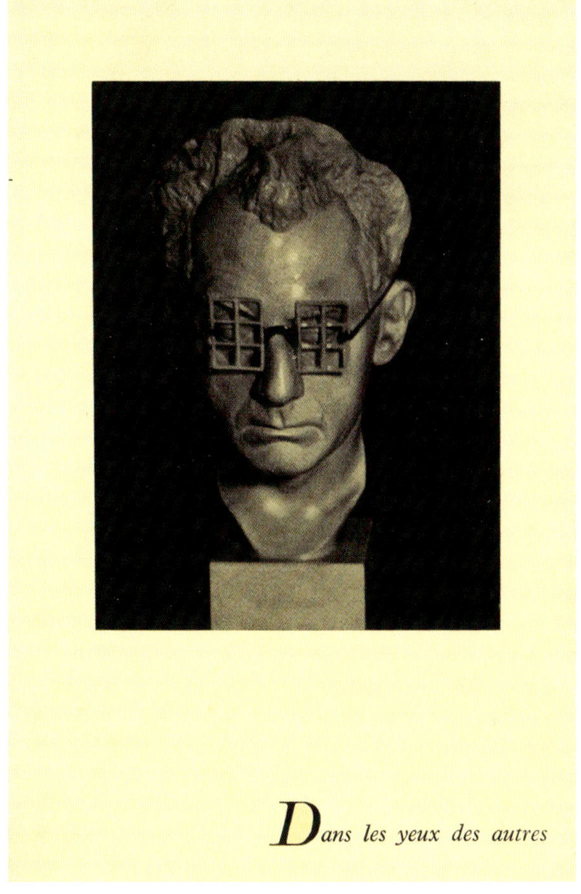

Dans les yeux des autres

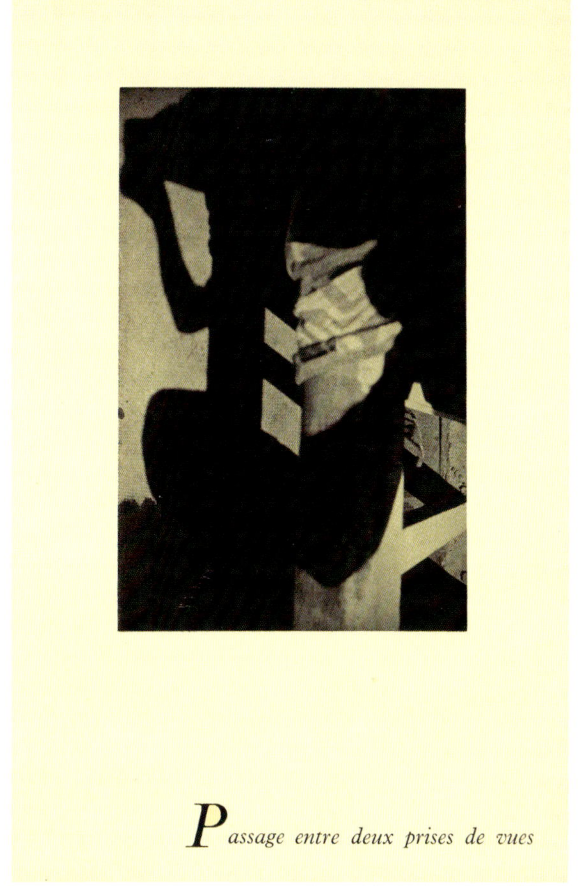

Passage entre deux prises de vues

duce wrapped against insects and cold. Though Man Ray had supplied a small retrospective of his works in all media to the Museum of Modern Art's enormous 1936 exhibition *Fantastic Art, Dada, Surrealism*, the experience had been less than a grand homecoming. The exhibition as a whole was greeted for the most part with comic derision by America; Man Ray's greatest success in the United States remained with the fashion magazines, which were eager to hire him as a photographer. The book is Man Ray's reply. This time when he makes an appearance via a photograph, called *Dans les yeux des autres* (In the Eyes of Others), of his plaster cast bust, he is wearing windowpaned spectacles (fig. 14). *Dans les yeux des autres* takes account of the two sides of Man Ray: the precise, encyclopedic appetite to get it all in, and the exquisitist urge to make art out of sensation and intelligence. The book is both a virtuoso performance of his practice of recast image and repurposed meaning and a vehicle to promote a Surrealist agenda (fig. 15). The theories that had begun as part of a significant revolutionary engagement with the terms of aesthetic evaluation had, thanks to Man Ray, been reintentioned as art.

In "Photography Is Not Art," published in two issues of *View* magazine in 1943, Man Ray makes an even stronger case for using photography as a vehicle for artistic ideas.[27] As if summoning strength from enigmatic references to the past he listed the images from the earlier publication and declared them the ten best photographs he had produced. It was also a retort to those who preferred to discuss his photographs to the exclusion of his work in other media. Photography was not to be confused with painting or drawing. Rather, he emphasized the importance of "concern with how the thing is to be done, instead of what is to be done."

What stands out most clearly in both publications, however, is how out of fashion Man Ray's vision of photography—as conveyed by his imagery and espoused by the texts he included—had become. By the mid-1930s a new style of photography was being practiced in Europe by young photographers such as Robert Capa, Brassaï, and Henri Cartier-Bresson. Capa's vivid and engrossing photographs of war and social unrest and Brassaï's reportage on the Paris demimonde were being published in picture magazines such as *Vu*. Street photography of the sort practiced by Cartier-Bresson seemed to many to be more compelling than Man Ray's studio-bound work, and no less Surrealistic in terms of mak-

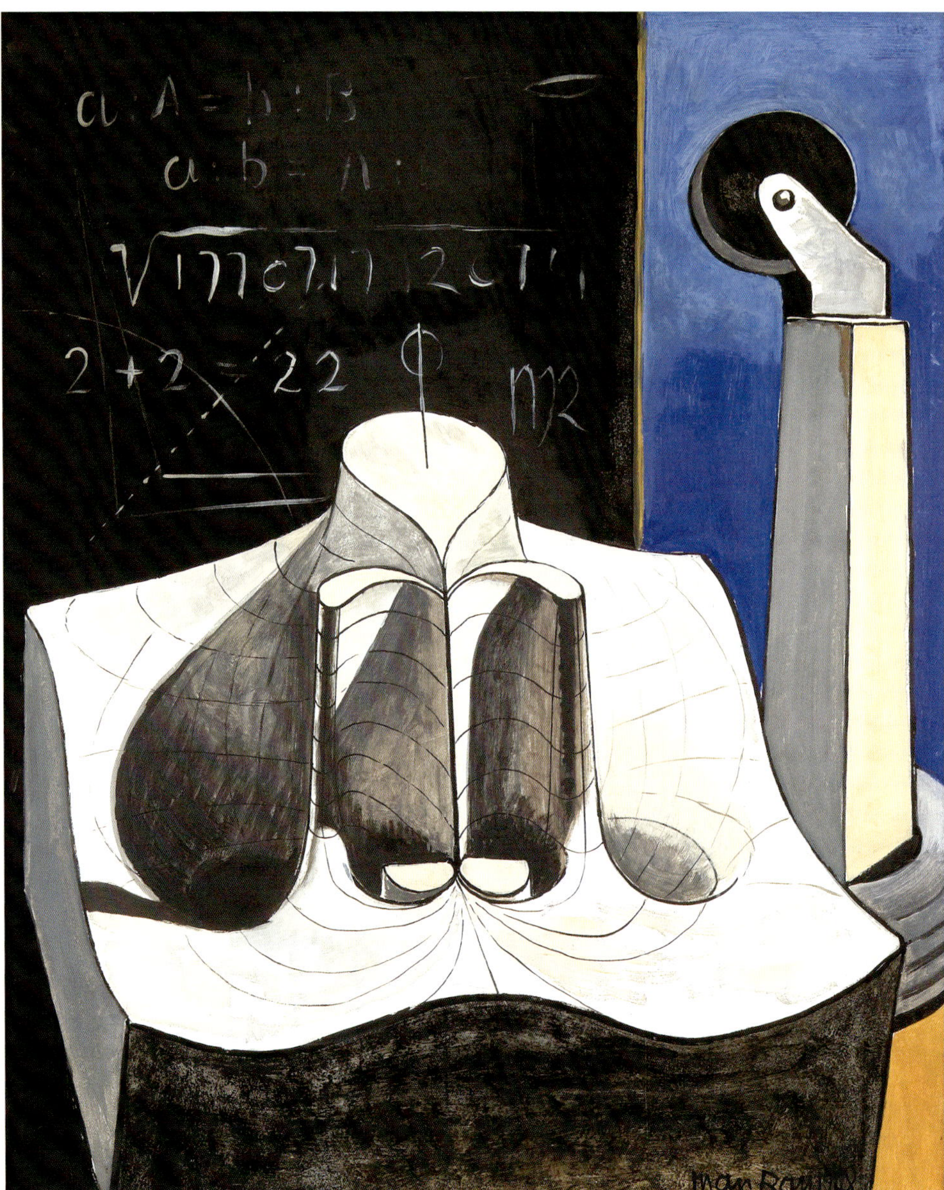

Fig. 16. *Shakespearean Equation: Julius Caesar,* 1948. Oil on Masonite, 24 × 20 in. (61 × 50.8 cm). Rosalind and Melvin Jacobs Collection

ing the world seem full of strange, uncanny incident. Man Ray was not unaware. In 1933, to shore up his own presence in the mix, Man Ray wrote an essay, "On Photographic Realism," in which he compared and contrasted the timelessness of painting and photography's need for social interaction and its reliance on actuality.[28]

The American art world that Man Ray returned to in 1940, shortly before the Nazis occupied Paris, was vastly different from the one he had left nineteen years earlier. The influence of a new generation of curators, critics, and gallerists, as well as the presence of the Museum of Modern Art, made for a much more sympathetic climate for modern art than had existed when the artist packed up for Paris. But the type of modern art that Americans were interested in was distinctly different from the transgressive, border-crossing kind that had made Man Ray stand out in Paris. Surrealism had established a beachhead among younger painters, including future stars such as Jackson Pollock, and among a few idiosyncratic collage artists, most notably Joseph Cornell. But Surrealism's other presence, in photography and writing and other art forms, and especially the fertile territory between media, was virtually invisible.

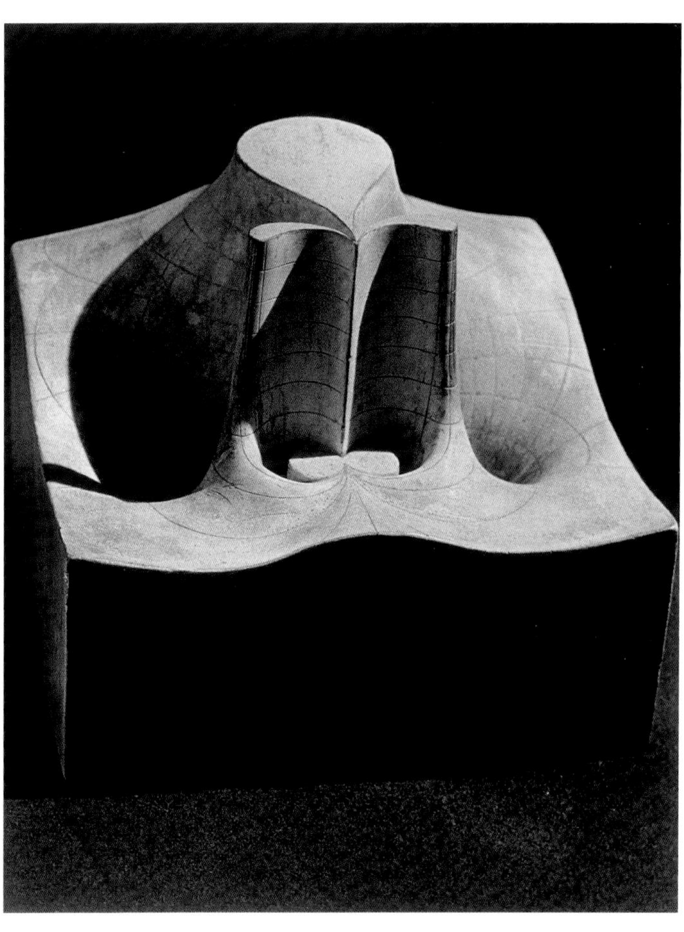

Fig. 17. *Mathematical Object, Modular expression of an elliptical function*, 1934–36. Gelatin silver print, 11¾ × 9½ in. (29.9 × 24.1 cm). Musée national d'art moderne, Centre Pompidou, Paris

Man Ray once again dug into his suitcase for inspiration, though this time he used photographs and reproductions that he had managed to bring to America from Paris as the basis for his paintings. *Equations for Shakespeare* (or *Shakespearean Equations*, as the series of paintings is sometimes called), completed in 1948, was the end product of a project begun in Paris more than ten years earlier. Man Ray had photographed displays of mathematical objects at the Poincaré Institute, and the photographs then became the centerpiece of a 1936 issue of *Cahiers d'art* devoted to the Surrealist object (figs. 16 and 17). In 1948, Man Ray used the images to once again confront issues of painting. Most obviously, the paintings from photographs point out the relationship possible between the two media. In addition to addressing this, *Shakespearean Equations* also confronted contemporary issues of abstraction. In a catalogue for a 1948 exhibition at the Copley Gallery in Los Angeles, which took the form of an unbound folio of essays and reproductions of drawings, objects, and photographs, Man Ray once again outlined his methodology. Evoking the Dada flavor of his Librairie Six brochure, one catalogue page was devoted to nonsensical reviews of Man Ray's work, and another page featured an exact painted reproduction of a photographic portrait of his wife, Juliet. In the artist statement, which took the form of a letter to Breton, Man Ray defended himself and his abstract paintings. He argued that the paintings were never intended as a justification for abstraction, but rather for the "discomfiture and impotence they worked on the exponents of nonobjective art with whom my principal quarrel is the poverty of inventiveness and imagination."[29] These words, however, held no sway in a postwar American art world.

The problem for Man Ray in 1940s America, which he may not have recognized or understood until later, was the growing influence of a modernist critical climate that sought to locate avant-garde activity within the differentiating characteristics of individual art media. For example, the task of painting was defined not as representation, which the camera could achieve perfectly well, but as an investigation of its own materiality: paint and canvas. The leading critics of this inherently formalist approach were Clement Greenberg, who embraced the term Abstract Expressionism to define the art he supported, and Harold Rosenberg, who preferred Action Painting as the key term of the new aesthetic. Both critics championed Jackson Pollock's "drip" paintings, albeit for different reasons, as representative of painting's new possibilities, and supported as well as Willem de Kooning, Mark Rothko, Barnett Newman, Franz Kline, and other abstract painters.

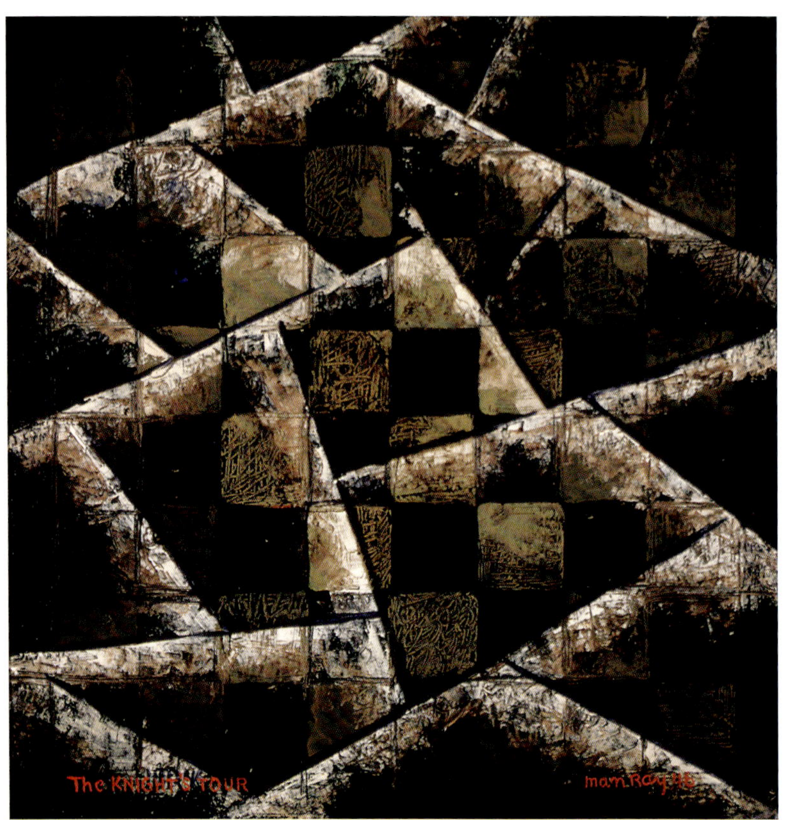

Fig. 18. *The Knight's Tour,* 1946. Oil on board, 13½ × 13½ in. (34.4 × 34.4 cm). The Penrose Collection, England

Definitions for the medium of photography had also become strict. The aesthetic of an equivalency—that photographs, besides being documents, are expressions of the photographer's vision—as it developed from Stieglitz through Ansel Adams to Minor White became a credo for American photographic modernist practice. Its assumptions were enshrined not only in the work of photographers but in the histories of photography, such as Beaumont Newhall's *History of Photography from 1839 to the Present,* which by the mid-twentieth century were being written to celebrate the medium's centenary. Photography developed a discourse as formalist, in its own way, as that for painting and sculpture.

In Man Ray's Parisian vanguard milieu, the medium hardly mattered, or it mattered only to the extent that its conventions were upset, usurped, or transformed. Greenberg's explicit emphasis on the medium of painting and its materiality set the stage for the revalidation of traditional studio practices, even though what was being produced in the painter's studio was abstract and therefore radical. The idea that art found its territory between media, or in the conceptual notion underlying a visual expression, was eclipsed by a critical climate that differentiated the tasks of each medium and privileged art that reflected on its own making.

Man Ray was not ignored by the American critics of the day, but they periodized him as a relic of a much earlier episode in American modernism. When Harold Rosenberg wrote of Man Ray as an American vanguardist as late as 1976, he grouped him with Charles Demuth, Marsden Hartley, and Stuart Davis.[30] The strict categories of museum structures that evolved in the postwar years did not suit Man Ray either. Paintings were hung in one place, photographs stored and exhibited in another. There was no opportunity or encouragement to present art as interwoven media. The critical literature pointed to Stieglitz's strict definitions, not Man Ray's extra-pictorial aesthetics. In America, Man Ray was more a conduit to Surrealism's past than a harbinger of its contemporary usefulness in post–World War II American art.

The paintings that Man Ray produced during his Hollywood years confound critics to this day; for the most part they recapitulate tropes and themes of his Paris years in an overtly Surrealist style recognizable from Dalí, René Magritte, Paul Delvaux, Ernst, and early Pollock (fig. 18). He did not follow Pollock's example and make the transition from painting discontinuous Surrealist scenes to making abstract art; the temptation to jump on the Greenbergian bandwagon either did not strike him or struck him as repulsive. The paradox, of course, is that aside from making replicas of works from his early Paris years he chose to present himself as a painter, not as the boundary-crossing artist of multiple media who had made such an impression abroad (figs. 19 and 20). By the time he returned to Paris, in short, he seemed complicit in his growing marginalization within the avant-garde.

Today Man Ray's decisions to live in California instead of New York and to virtually abandon photography in favor of painting appear confounding and even tragic, given the brilliance of his first two decades in Paris. On the other hand, it may be unreasonable to expect any artist to maintain a place on the cutting edge of contemporary art for more than thirty years. The conservatism of his late paintings only makes us appreciate more the radical boldness of works like *Cadeau*, the cameraless rayographs, and the sophisticated translation of painting and objects into photography. Along with Duchamp, his reputation managed to persevere long enough to catch the eye of the generation of artists in the late 1960s and the 1970s, artists in rebellion against Greenberg's formalism and intent on trespassing the autonomous domains of painting and sculpture. When postmodernism struck the art world in the late 1970s and the 1980s, it marked another moment when photography

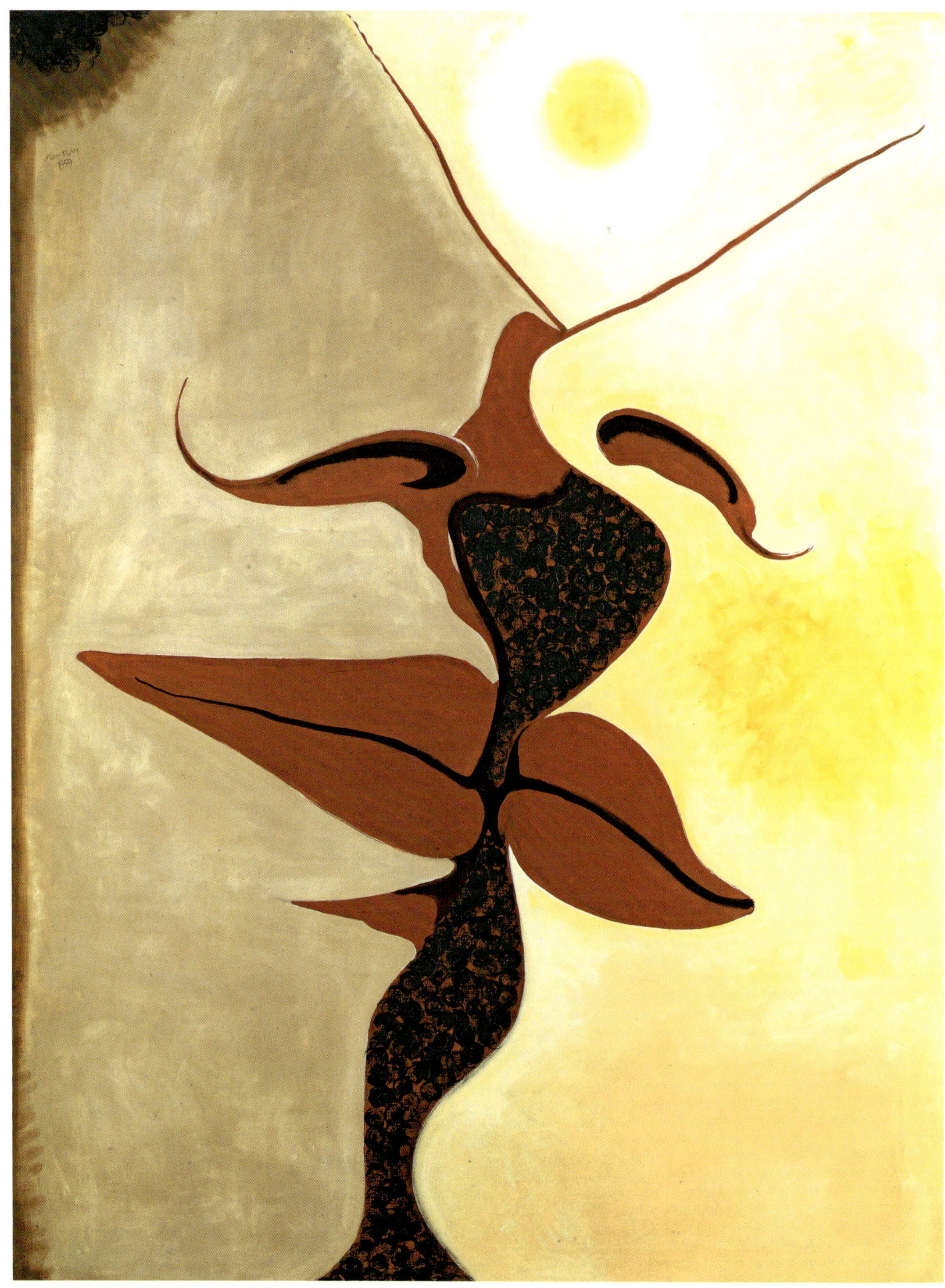

became an instrument with which to critique conventional approaches and attitudes toward art. In this more recent milieu, Man Ray once again emerged as an influential modern artist. That influence is still being felt today.

Man Ray's rediscovery in the postmodernist climate of the 1980s, in exhibitions like *L'Amour fou: Photography and Surrealism*, a 1985 group show of Surrealist photographs at

Fig. 19. *Image à deux faces*, 1959. Oil on canvas, 78¾ × 59 in. (200 × 149.9 cm). Collection of Mr. and Mrs. George L. Lindemann, Florida

the Corcoran Gallery of Art, and *Perpetual Motif: The Art of Man Ray,* his 1988 retrospective at the Smithsonian's American Art Museum, was in part a validation of Man Ray's long-held belief that photography was as important a medium as painting and sculpture. By the 1980s photography had been widely institutionalized in museums and university art departments and had developed a presence in commercial art galleries; it also had become a favored medium, along with film and video, of contemporary artists. More importantly, though, it was the example of Man Ray's hybrid approach to art-making that served as a beacon for young artists. Following in the footsteps of the early Conceptual artists of the late 1960s and early 1970s, these new-generation artists saw themselves not as painters, sculptors, or photographers but simply as artists. By refusing to align with any particular medium, they allowed themselves the freedom to use any materials of their choosing and focused critical attention on the quality of their ideas. Greenberg's formalist approach ceased to hold sway in this artistic climate, and Man Ray's reputation consequently flourished.

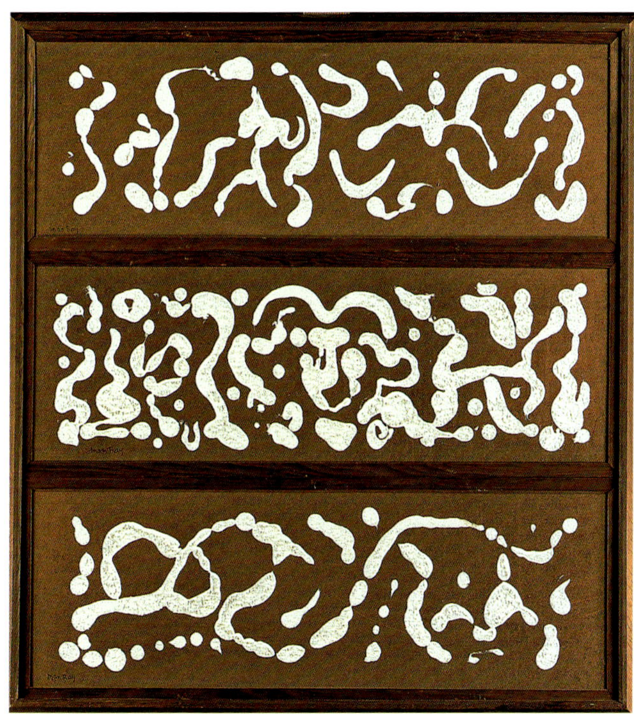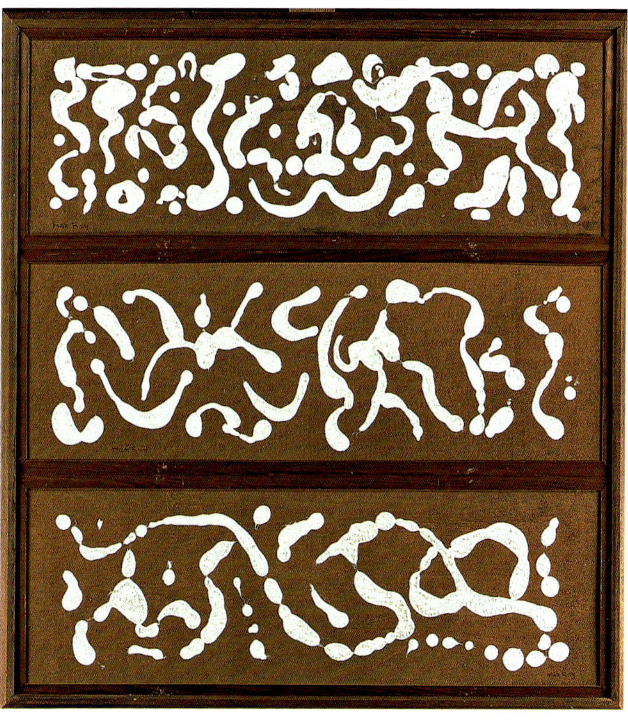

One also could argue that the artist's transatlantic career provided a model for a new art world that was not centered in New York or Paris but in capitals across the world. The current global condition of contemporary art favors artists who, like Man Ray, can reach across cultures and fit readily into a variety of artistic milieus. Perhaps today's artists no longer function, as Man Ray did, as translators of another culture's aesthetic innovations, but like him they provide a bridge to seeing art as an activity without geographic or aesthetic limits.

Fig. 20. *Message to Marcia,* 1958–65. Acrylic on Masonite, two panels, each 48 × 49⅛ in. (122 × 126 cm). Collection of Joan and Michael Salke, Naples, Florida

And none of the artists
I have [worked] for have become rich like the French
artists so lovingly supported by art loving America!
Why aren't you and Marin and O'Keeffe
and Dove Frenchmen?
— and I at least a Man Ray in Paris?

Some may call
your work tricky — I tell them that
the tricks of today
are the truths of tomorrow.

Man Ray's Culture industry

George Baker

In 1981, some five years after Man Ray's death, Juliet Man Ray was asked to speak about her husband's past. Obviously nervous, chain-smoking, still upset over her loss—the interview constantly interrupted so that she might catch her breath—Juliet could answer no questions about the origins or family history of her husband of thirty years. To the question, "How did his father earn a living?" she responded: "I don't know because he never talked about his family. I only met his sister." To the question "Did Man Ray also have a brother?" she admitted: "Yes, yes, he had a brother. I think he was a poet, but I don't know anything about him because Man Ray never wanted to talk about his family to me, or to anybody." The interviewer wanted to know more about the "obvious question," as he put it, "about his name." Juliet's response: "As [Man Ray] said, it's a personal question, so leave it there."[1]

It is now well known that Man Ray was born Emmanuel Radnitzky in 1890, the eldest child in a family of immigrant Russian Jews who settled in Philadelphia. If Man Ray's complex relation to his Jewish identity has recently become a topic of art-historical discussion, the artist's silence and evasion regarding his origins has not been entirely broken.[2] For, alone among the major Dada and Surrealist figures, Man Ray was an artist whose roots were in the working class. His father, Melach (Max) Radnitzky, was a tailor who worked in a garment factory by day and at a workspace in his home by night. Indeed, within the central Dada trio of Marcel Duchamp, Man Ray, and Francis Picabia, we face a tripartite division in terms of class: Picabia from an almost aristocratic, haute bourgeois Parisian family;

Duchamp from the provincial French middle class; Man Ray an American from the immigrant working class. And this class history remains unspoken, a nontopic even in the face of
the major museum retrospective that recently served as an apotheosis of the trio's dialogue.[3]

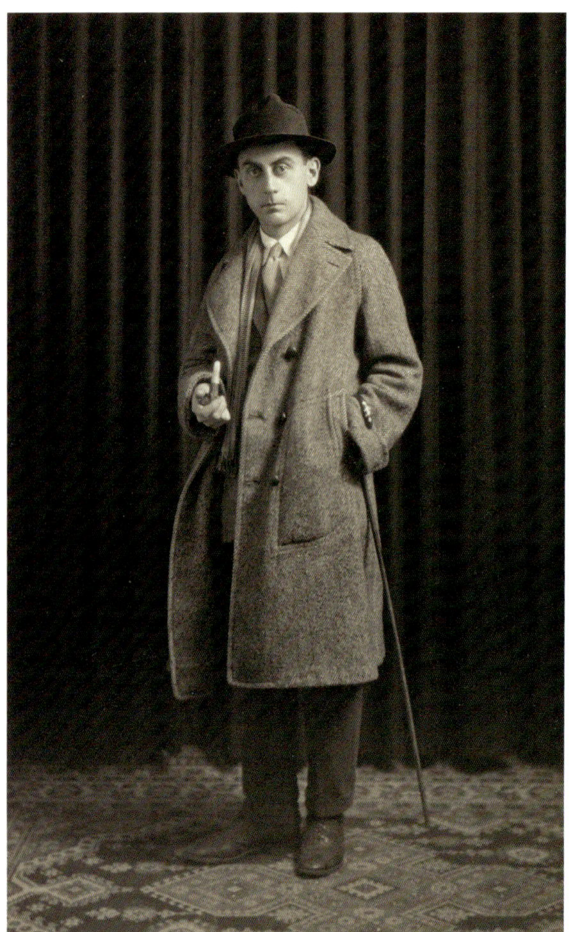

Man Ray, working-class artist: The incongruity of such a label speaks to the fact that art history's silence about the import of Man Ray's class origins obviously has its roots in the artist's own evasions—in other words, such evasion might be deemed structural to Man Ray's reinvention as a central figure within the historical avant-garde (fig. 1). In this, one silence recalls another: the inability or unwillingness of art history to broach any discussion of the intimate relation of Man Ray's avant-garde production to the commodity culture of the 1920s and 1930s.[4] We have celebrations of Man Ray's fashion photography and hagiographies of his Surrealist photography but hardly any consideration of the shared landscape of his commercial and avant-garde work (fig. 2). For if Man Ray as house photographer to the Surrealist movement was publishing his photographs during the 1920s and 1930s in *La révolution*

Fig.1. *Self-Portrait with Pipe, Paris,* 1921. Gelatin silver print, 5³⁄₁₆ × 3¹⁄₄ in. (13.2 × 8.3 cm). The J. Paul Getty Museum, Los Angeles

surréaliste and *Minotaure,* his work was just as central during these years to the magazines *Harper's Bazaar, Vanity Fair,* and *Vogue.* Man Ray again lies at the origins of the silence around this issue: While he set himself up in the portrait and fashion photography business upon his arrival in Paris to join the French avant-garde in 1921, the artist would always radically distinguish his commercial activities from his artistic ambitions, going so far as to

Fig. 2. *Die Unmöglichkeit (Danger),* 1920. Photograph (vintage print) of the assemblage *Dancer/Danger* (1920), 6¹³⁄₁₆ × 4⁷⁄₁₆ in. (17.3 × 11.3 cm). Kunsthaus Zürich

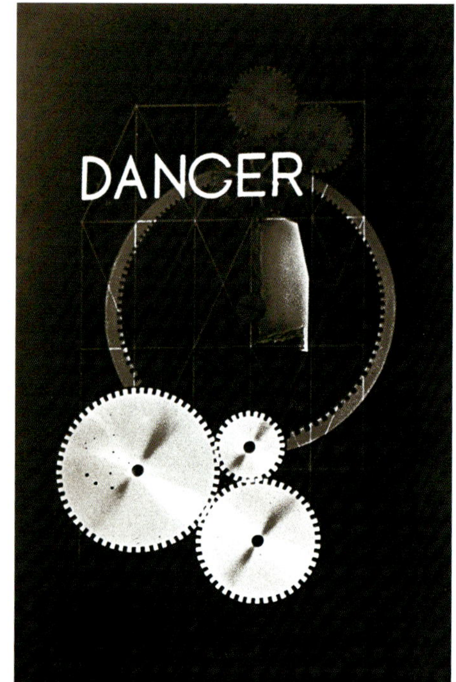

reject his innovative photographic oeuvre later in his life for the way in which it had over-
shadowed the reception of his painting (figs. 3 and 4).

But the task is to begin to trace the connections between Man Ray's involvement
in art and in commerce, his work within Dada and Surrealism and his labors for the indus-

tries of fashion, advertising, and, ultimately, Hollywood celebrity. To what degree is Man Ray's Surrealist articulation of photographic images of desire a precursor to postwar consumer culture and the advertising and fashion industries' ever-increasing control of desire? It will be my gambit in what follows that the only way of broaching such an issue within Man Ray's work is to break the silence surrounding both the artist's class background and his later work's position between the avant-garde and capital. If one silence recalls the other, perhaps their dual repression stems from their historical and conceptual linkage. Unlike so many of his artist friends, Man Ray in his early years always needed a job; in his later years he would play a central role in defining new forms of the radical merger of art and business, the collision of aristocratic "high" culture and "low" forms of mass entertainment that Theodor Adorno long ago named the "culture industry."[5] Indeed, with Man Ray we move directly from an early

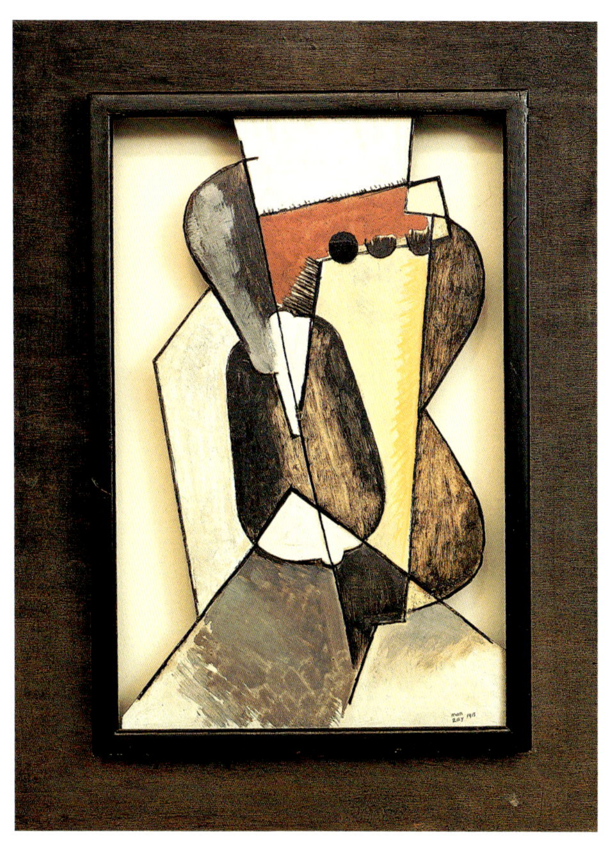

Fig. 3. *Cut Out*, 1915. Oil on cut cardboard, 17¹¹⁄₁₆ × 11⅝ in. (45.1 × 29.5 cm). Collection of Joel and Paula Friedland

Fig. 4. *Spanish Dancers*, 1918. Oil on cement board covered with paper, 32¾ × 36 in. (83.2 × 91.4 cm). Tokyo Fuji Art Museum

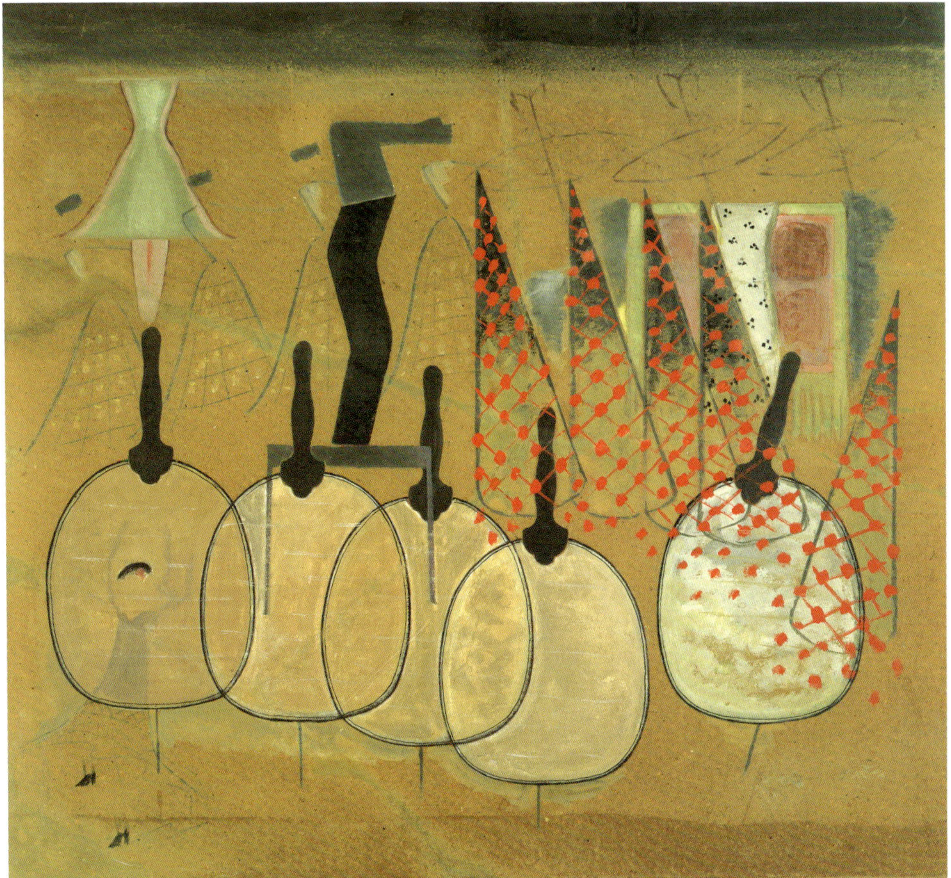

Dada aesthetic of industry to what might be called the beginnings of the industrialization of the aesthetic field. To trace such a history is not necessarily to ignore the transgressive claims that have been made for Man Ray's avant-garde work, to turn instead to a reduced narrative of complicity and compromise. We face an artistic oeuvre suspended—often in the most critical and self-conscious of ways—between an older world of work and labor and the new tasks of the culture industry.

get a job

"No more painting," Marcel Duchamp wrote in a note to himself in 1912. "Get a job."[6] It was an odd thought for an artist who, like his two older brothers and eventually a sister, would be generously supported by his father in his artistic ambitions, the father ticking off advances to his son against the total sum of his future inheritance. But for Duchamp, such a note attested to the young artist's abandonment of Cubism and opened onto his selection of the industrially produced "readymades" just one year later. Duchamp indeed did get a job during the following years—he would work first as a librarian, then as a language tutor. But his shift from painting to work seems, in retrospect, intentionally to prepare the industrial model of artistic production represented by the readymade.

If the readymade signaled the abandonment of painting, as well as the critique of elitist concepts of artistic training and skill, art history has not registered forcefully enough the manner in which Duchamp's transition away from painting in fact entailed the acquisition of a whole range of entirely new skills. And these were skills of a very specific kind. We face this phenomenon in the dialectic of indolence and invention that characterizes Duchamp's promulgation of the readymades simultaneously with his intermittent and yet painstaking work on the *Large Glass (The Bride Stripped Bare by Her Bachelors, Even)*. But consider Duchamp's two versions of the painting *Chocolate Grinder*. The first version, completed in 1913, turns away from fine art traditions of drawing to inhabit a functional pictorial language, what has been called the "language of industry" or of work, the technical skills of the mechanical drawing.[7] Remaking the image just one year later, Duchamp seemed to intensify and multiply his "anti-aesthetic" procedures, layering one new device upon the other. But Duchamp's anti-aesthetic turn in *Chocolate Grinder No. 2* was simultaneously a turn toward a whole range of social forms of work as they exist in the larger world. The act of painting would become a labor not unlike mechanical repetition and industrial assembly, with Duchamp's serial image now produced using the "skills" of nonpainterly labor. The residual brushwork of *Chocolate Grinder No. 1* cedes in the second version to the use of the graphic artist's airbrush, and a bookbinder was asked to emboss the work's title upon the bottom of the painting. Most extraordinary of all, Duchamp methodically laid down the individual, shimmering lines within his second depiction of the grinder by actually sewing thread from the back to the front of the canvas. Line and drawing literally become string, a readymade, but only by transforming the work of the work of art into the manual labor of sewing. Get a job, indeed.

We can only imagine the effect that seeing *Chocolate Grinder No. 2* must have had upon Man Ray in the wake of his first encounters with Marcel Duchamp by 1915.[8] We do not need to imagine the effect within Man Ray's work, as his dalliance with painterly procedures culled from the realm of everyday work and labor, as well as his eventual turn to tools such as the airbrush, are well known. But what has not been noted is the way in which *Chocolate Grinder No. 2*, or related works such as Duchamp's *Three Standard Stoppages*—the term "stoppage" coming from the profession of the French tailor or seamstress—would have engaged Man Ray in relation to his class background: his father's and mother's work as tailor and seamstress, or his own set of labors making a living during the 1910s. For unlike Duchamp's decidedly middle-class "jobs" in what we might call the knowledge industry—librarian, teacher—Man Ray worked in a variety of capacities, often in ways related to physically making things, or, ultimately, to applied versions of art and design. After high school, we know that Man Ray worked briefly as a newsstand attendant, and just as briefly as an engraver of handles in an umbrella and cane factory. Eventually he would come to land a job producing layout in an advertising office on Fourteenth Street. For some six years, he would work for the McGraw Book Company on Thirty-Ninth Street, using his graphic skills to design maps and atlases. And Man Ray's jobs extended into his first forays within his career as an exhibiting artist: he would be tapped to produce catalogue covers and to do layout for his first major gallery in New York, the Daniel Gallery, for several seasons in the wake of his first show.[9]

There was thus an unexpected but shared terrain between the form of Duchamp's "anti-aesthetic" turn and the actual lived experiences and class identity of Man Ray during these same years, producing an identification and exacerbation of earlier endeavors that seemed to herald—if not to produce—the conditions of Man Ray's entrance into the center of the avant-garde.[10] From this perspective, formerly incomprehensible "works" by Man Ray can now be understood, such as the functional *Tapestry* of 1911 (see Klein essay, fig. 35), a collection of some 110 fabric samples, perhaps culled from his father's work materials, sewn into an all-over but randomly articulated grid. The incongruity of the piece—anticipating by some five years the noncompositional grids of European abstraction from Zurich Dada to De Stijl, but at a moment when Man Ray had not yet even been exposed to Cubism—points to a retrospective claiming for art, from the later vantage of Dada's concerns, of an object made within the horizon of function and decoration (and through the skills of sewing and embroidery that all of the children in Man Ray's family were proudly taught).[11] And yet *Tapestry*'s incongruity sets up the place of work and labor within Man Ray's production: a persistent outside that would serve to challenge modernist form. For here the grid does not map the painterly field itself, as modernist abstraction would come to do: as a blanket or a wall hanging, *Tapestry* is a covering, a skin, that takes the form of that to which it is applied. And it is deformed by this in the process, its warp and woof testifying to a process of direct displacement from a concrete world of practical work, labor, and class identity.

Already in 1914, Man Ray described his manifesto-piece *War (A.D. MCMXIV)* (see Klein essay, fig. 41) as worked on "with palette-knives like a mason building a house with bricks."[12] Suspended between the themes of Italian Futurism or its "lines of force," and his experience at the Armory Show the year before of Duchamp's "explosion in a shingle factory," the *Nude Descending a Staircase No. 2*, Man Ray's painting concatenates a repetitive array of robotic bodies, transformed into faceless color fields and shorn of any trace of hands or feet.[13] While the work's facture may turn against the finesse of the artist's brush in order to seize upon an analogy from the domain of social labor, its de-individuated figures present the viewer not with the serial bricks and mortar of the mason, but with flat patterns that seem characteristic of the sheaths of material that a tailor uses to produce a garment. This is precisely the metaphor that Man Ray will work with throughout 1915, the year of his encounter with Duchamp. In the painting *Dance*, we witness bodies reduced to off-white patterns as if sliced from cloth; a dressmaker's dummy appears to dominate the multiple versions of *Promenade* (see Klein essay, fig. 48); and *Black Widow* touts a central form that folds open before us less like a body than a headless "template" traced upon a swatch of fabric. As Francis Naumann has observed of the latter painting, the articulations of limbs appear upon the black form like the chalk lines a tailor makes during a garment's alteration; background color fields resemble nothing more than another selection of fabric swatches; and serrated lines make their way through this and many of the other works of 1915, "as if cut by a pair of seamstress's pinking shears."[14] Lines seem traced repeatedly from outsize pins and needles now used as readymade stencils in *Black Widow*; scissors and other tool-like forms erupt from within the flat patterns of *Promenade*. Critics at the time seemed to recognize such references to labor. Man Ray's gestures were disparaged but legible: *Dance* was described by a disgruntled journalist as "some tailor's patterns . . . having a gay time," and Man Ray's work in general at this moment as resembling "the work of a drunken patternmaker."[15] By 1915, Man Ray had positioned his painting in relation to the issue of work, riding a line between art's purported uselessness and the world of objects that have a definite function, pressing to the full the incongruence of aesthetic desires and working-class realities. The labor of the tailor grounds (or haunts?) Man Ray's fantasy of the release of the body into pure pattern and flattened form, producing an aesthetic of collapsed physicality and ambivalent anonymity—threatening but ecstatic, depersonalized but universal—all at once.

In turning to the flat patterns of the tailor, Man Ray drew his painting close to a world from which it was otherwise barred, the world of mass production. In fact, the tailor's templates of Man Ray's painting in 1915 attest to a specific labor involved in the reproduction of forms. If Man Ray immediately began to mine the concept of reproducibility, making multiple versions of *Promenade*, for example, as had occurred simultaneously in Duchamp's work, the contradiction between unique painting and the objects of industrial production remains palpable—almost, at times, unbearable. For if work and reproducibility enter Man Ray's production through the tailor's template, labor thus enters Man Ray's painting only through the imperious formal logic of the stencil—the larger trajectory of Man Ray's subsequent deployment of contour, drawing, and line. The stencil produces form through iteration, through the trace and remnant of an initial object, but also, we might say, through the rigorous nonpresence of this original object itself. In this, the specific forms of labor that Man Ray appropriates—from his own lived experience and class background—enter his work after 1915 only as a kind of ghostly absence. The tailor's template, the stenciled form, implies that work continues to exist for Man Ray in this early period as an outside force. Work and labor—class as well—form a literal matrix for Man Ray's painterly forms during his Dada period, but presented via the logic of the stencil, work becomes the structuring condition that as a matrix cannot literally enter the painting that it otherwise founds or makes possible. In other words, work and labor enter Man Ray's painting only to be presented in displaced form, distanced and absent from the scene. More, Man Ray seizes upon modalities of labor—understands the work of his own father—as a specific technique that produces displacement. Work will be understood not as a form of production but of reproduction, not as a modality of gain but of loss, not as a technique of self-creation and fulfillment but as the depersonalized logic of the ghost—threatened now as much as threatening.

Man Ray seemed at pains to intensify this experience of absence and displacement in the major work that immediately followed the "tailor" paintings, the monument of his early period's production: *The Rope Dancer Accompanies Herself with Her Shadows* (see Klein essay, fig. 20). Dissatisfied with the multiple images he had constructed of the work's central figure, Man Ray was gripped during the work's production by the discarded scraps of paper from which he had cut this figure, dispersed across his studio floor. Seizing upon these discards and remnants, Man Ray replicated them in his final painting, working away from the body toward an array of "abstract" color fields, each of which, however, retains the negative trace of some fragment of the original figure's body: a tubular arm, the siphon of a skirt and the arc of its hem, the remains of the scissor-blade legs or tomahawk head. A devastating negation of the productive building of form in Synthetic Cubism, Man Ray's exploration of negative space simultaneously builds upon the memory of "his father's similar attitude toward materials," the fallen scraps of fabric that the tailor's template produced and that the frugal worker obsessively recycled and reused.[16] And so now Man Ray weds the ghost logic of the template to an explicit celebration of the remnant, both in terms of the production of aesthetic form and practical objects. He marries art to labor—formal abstraction to the tailor's procedures, the incision of collage to the cutting of the garment industry—only to push their shared processes into the realm of the waste product and of detritus. Work remains an outside force pressuring modernist form, but not toward some utopian or productivist future, the imagined unification of labor and aesthetic activity. Instead, work turns art against itself, toward the negative images that it cannot represent; and art fixates on labor as precisely useless, the endless piling up of trash: senseless garbage and incomprehensible forms.

With this, Man Ray shows himself to be in dialogue but also dissonance with what has been called Duchamp's techniques of "work avoidance" during the Dada period.[17] Through the dialectics of their differing class identities we discover that altered relations of work to readymade come to bear upon Duchamp and Man Ray's Dada production. Work was precisely *unavoidable* for Man Ray; he would face the impossibility of its negation, the necessity instead of its transformation—to change the very character of what we call work, industry, and labor. A first reaction would be to render labor vestigial, or, conversely, to make it an engine of excess. Indeed, Man Ray's relation to work at the height of the New York Dada moment becomes the prodigal labor of what has been called the "wastrel."[18] Forms of manual labor and regimes of industrial production come into play within Man Ray's art, but only to give rise to images of labor's displacement, to give issue to accumulations of labor's remnants. Labors pile up one upon the other, in excess of any realm of function, leading it astray. In the wake of *The Rope Dancer,* the year 1916 also sees Man Ray producing a series of paintings in which he began to attach readymade objects to the canvas surface, such as the now-lost work *Self-Portrait* (see Klein essay, fig. 31), an image of a door replete with an imposing handprint and two electric bells with a push button. And here, painting's eruption into readymade objects heralds the model of what Man Ray himself named the strategy of the "bad workman." The button called upon the participation—the work—of the audience, but when it was pressed, nothing at all happened. "That made them livid," Man Ray remembered, "and they said I was a bad workman."[19] And so the wastrel attaches wooden furniture knobs (and another fabric sample) to the picture plane in *Boardwalk* (1917); the very same hairpins that had been stenciled onto the surface of *Black Widow* appear again as actual objects tacked down onto the work *Decollage* (1917), but now holding nothing at all in place. Man Ray seems to have added furniture maker and barber to his roster of imagined social labors gone awry.

Shortly thereafter, Man Ray quits his actual job to begin to support himself as a photographer. Simultaneously, he begins to use one of the tools of what had formerly been his commercial work, the airbrush, to trace so many absent industrial objects upon his canvases, from carpenter's clamps and other work implements to detritus located in the street. He photographs garbage, a crushed tin can, and calls it *8th Street.* He slices open a lampshade and submits this to an exhibition (only to have a janitor throw the useless, lovely thing away, taking it out with the trash). He prepares to leave New York, to join the French avant-garde, and photographs the contents of an ashtray, dumped—like the discards of the tailor—onto his studio floor. He combines the photograph with a map in the collage *Trans atlantique,* recalling his job producing maps and atlases during the 1910s, at the same time as he now prepares to leave behind the world of work and labor from which he came. The wastrel—the collage seems to announce to the artist's new friends among the French avant-garde—the wastrel has arrived. But the very character of work within Man Ray's production was about to undergo the most radical change.

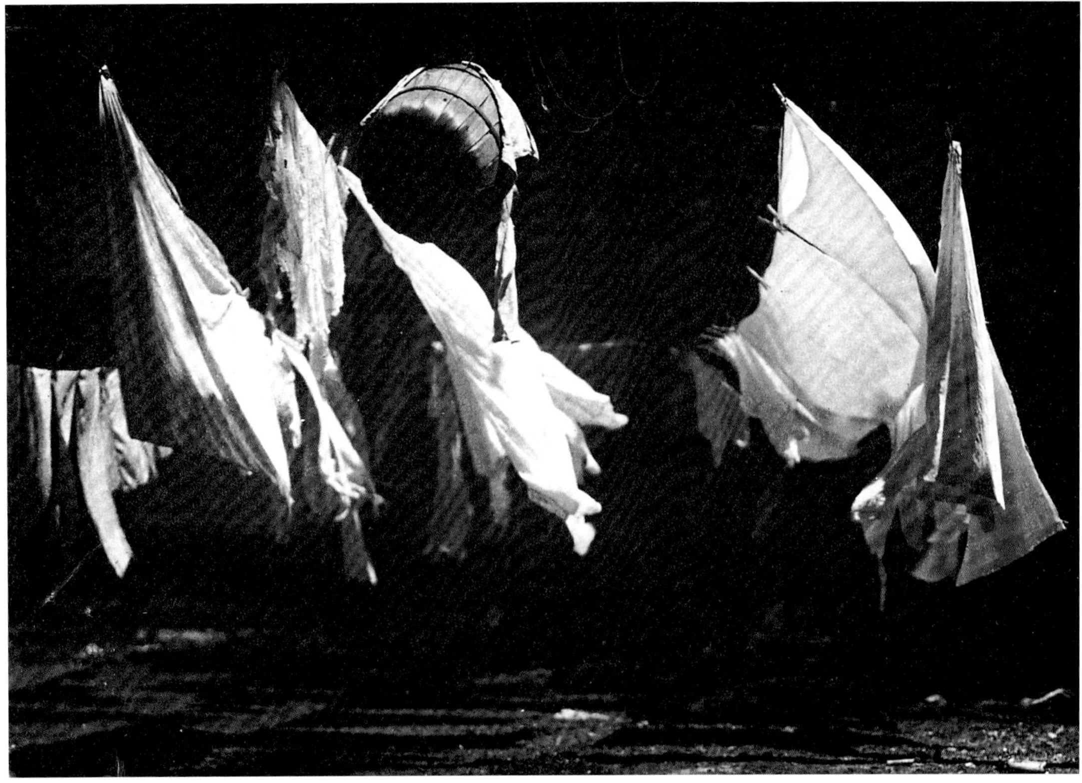

Fig. 5. *Moving Sculpture*, 1920. Gelatin silver print, 6¾ × 9⅜ in. (17.2 × 23.9 cm). The Baltimore Museum of Art, Purchase with exchange funds from the Edward Joseph Gallagher III Memorial Collection, and partial gift of George H. Dalsheimer

war on **Work**

Just before leaving for Paris, Man Ray consolidates his aesthetic of industry in at least three of the major works of 1920. In dialogue with Duchamp's procedures incorporating chance and physical conditions in the production of his *Large Glass*, Man Ray locates—typically, and even quite radically, we now can see—a parallel proposal in the heart of the world of domestic labor. Focusing on "women's work," Man Ray takes a photograph of laundry billowing in the wind in what seems a New York tenement courtyard, and entitles the composition *Moving Sculpture* (fig. 5). Duchamp's exploration of chance and physical properties emerges for Man Ray only in relation to one of the few forthright working-class spaces that Dada will ever admit into its collective representations. With the photograph's focus on ropes, as well as its sheets and undergarments billowing into so many unique, unrepeatable shapes, *Moving Sculpture* evidently also seeks to update the earlier *Rope Dancer*, as Man Ray's recent seizure upon chance and photography provides new fodder for the labors of the wastrel.

Work similarly edges into excess in Man Ray's *Obstruction* of the same year (fig. 6), an accumulation of clothes hangers, but now absent the lumpen garments of *Moving Sculpture*. The hangers hold only more examples of themselves, like a parody of modernist self-reflexivity, multiplying the original object into a serial construction that could fill a room, creating a physical barrier. And in the photograph *The Enigma of Isidore Ducasse* (see Klein

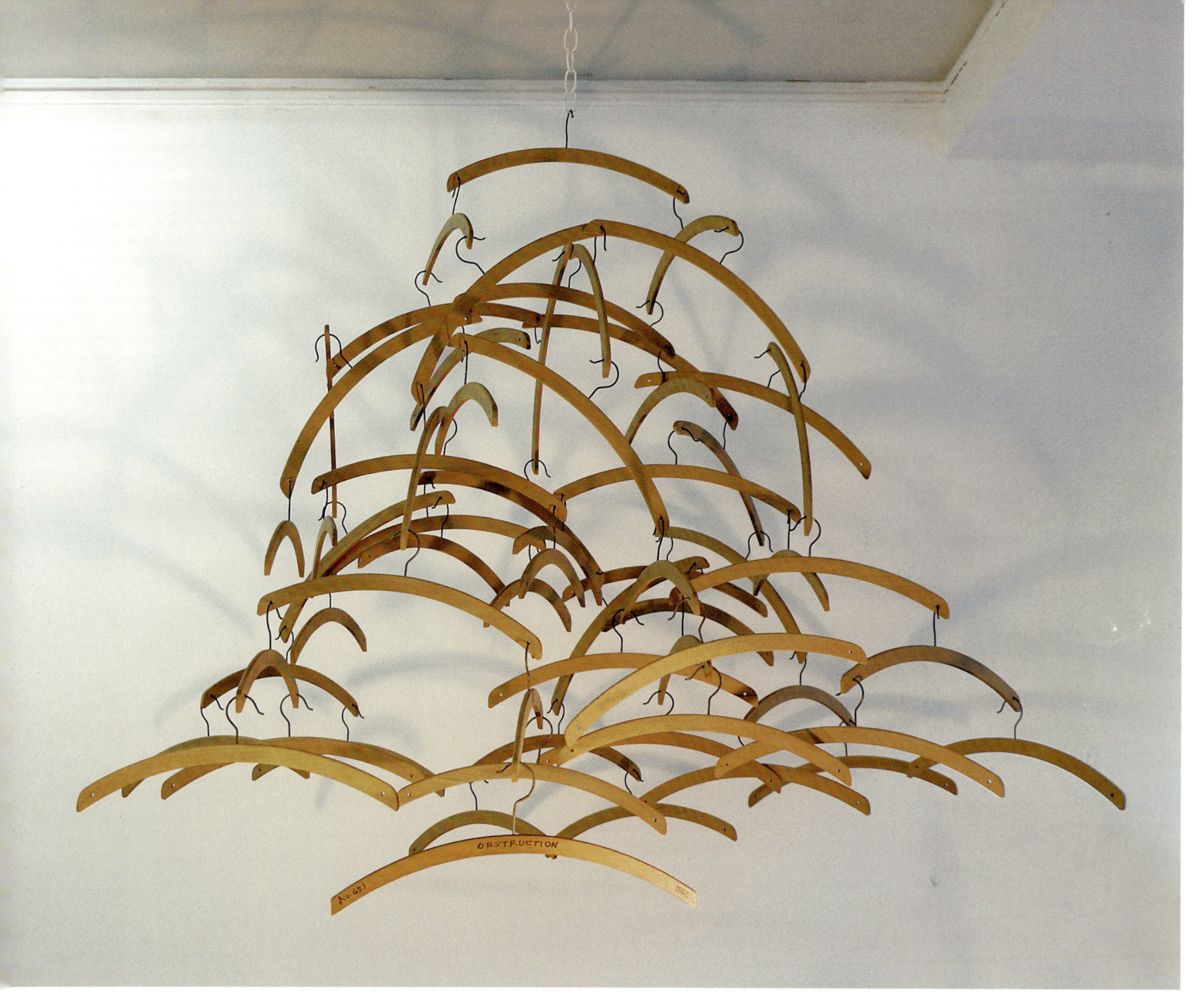

essay, fig. 52), Man Ray captures an object always assumed to be a sewing machine wrapped in an army blanket. The image manages to position work as both vestigial and excessive at once, another slightly menacing but ultimately abstract form, like the sheets in *Moving Sculpture* or the color fields of *The Rope Dancer*, produced from the specific site of labor and the textiles so crucial to the artist's origins. Labor, it seems, will now be block-aded, laboriously (excessively) so; it will be forced into the condition of displacement that produces the visual experience, for Man Ray, of abstraction. But we might also begin to wonder here whether we face an image of labor now itself become abstract, in the social-historical or materialist sense—in other words, whether labor for Man Ray will henceforth evince the process of its utter transformation. We face an "enigma" provoked by a photo-graph that presents work as both buried and sublated, lifted onto another plane.[20]

By the time of Man Ray's arrival in Paris in 1921, the signs of this transformation begin to appear throughout his production. Just before his first exhibition in Paris that winter, Man Ray produces a portrait photograph of most of the Paris Dada group (fig. 7). In some versions of the print, we see Man Ray's face as part of the group image, seemingly

Fig. 6. *Obstruction*, 1920/1964. 63 wooden coat hangers, 43⅝ × 47¼ × 47¼ in.
(110 × 120 × 120 cm). Collection of Marion Meyer, Paris

Fig. 7. The Group Dada, c. 1922. Gelatin silver print with collaged photograph, 5⅜ × 10¼ in. (13.7 × 26 cm). Musée national d'art moderne, Centre Pompidou, Paris. Back row, from left: Paul Chadourne, Tristan Tzara, Phillippe Soupault, Serge Charchoune; front row: Man Ray, Paul Éluard, Jacques Rigaut, Mick Soupault, Georges Ribemont-Dessaignes.

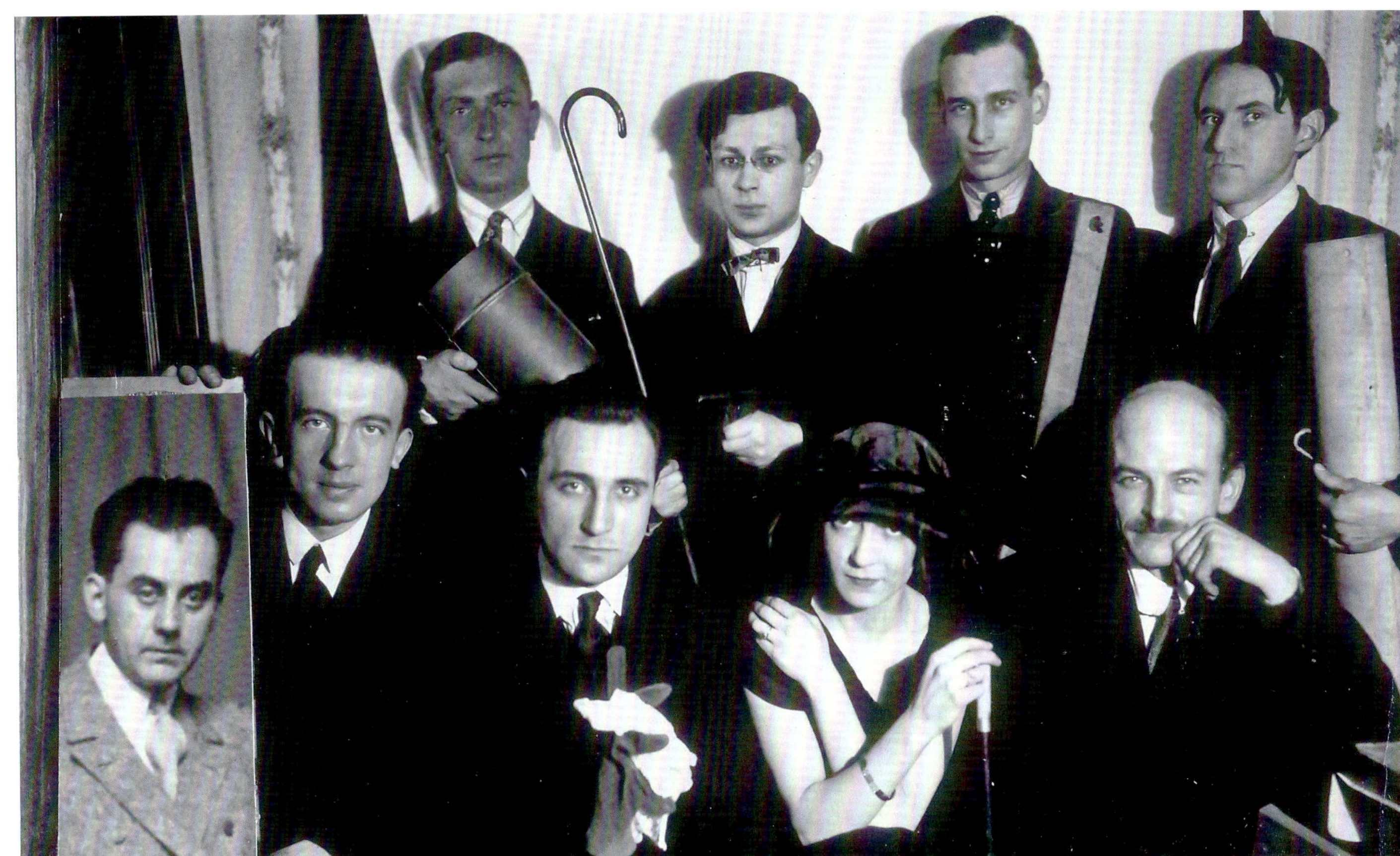

reflected in a mirror held by Paul Éluard to the far left of the scene. But each of the Dadaists holds some form of prop or attribute, and these objects—chosen, one imagines, from things lying around the photographer's living space—enact a résumé of Man Ray's former jobs: a cane, a carved handle, perhaps a scissor or razor blade, a T-square, a wooden plank, a canister for a mechanical diagram. It is as if by producing this catalogue Man Ray were once again saying farewell to a world he had left behind. Some attributes, however, speak to imagined or fantasy "professions": Tzara holds a revolver, recalling Man Ray's repeated assertion that he would have preferred to make his living as a gangster. And some attributes—the gloves, for example, associated with the dandy Jacques Rigaut—speak to Man Ray's future jobs, both his later association with Surrealism and his entrance into the world

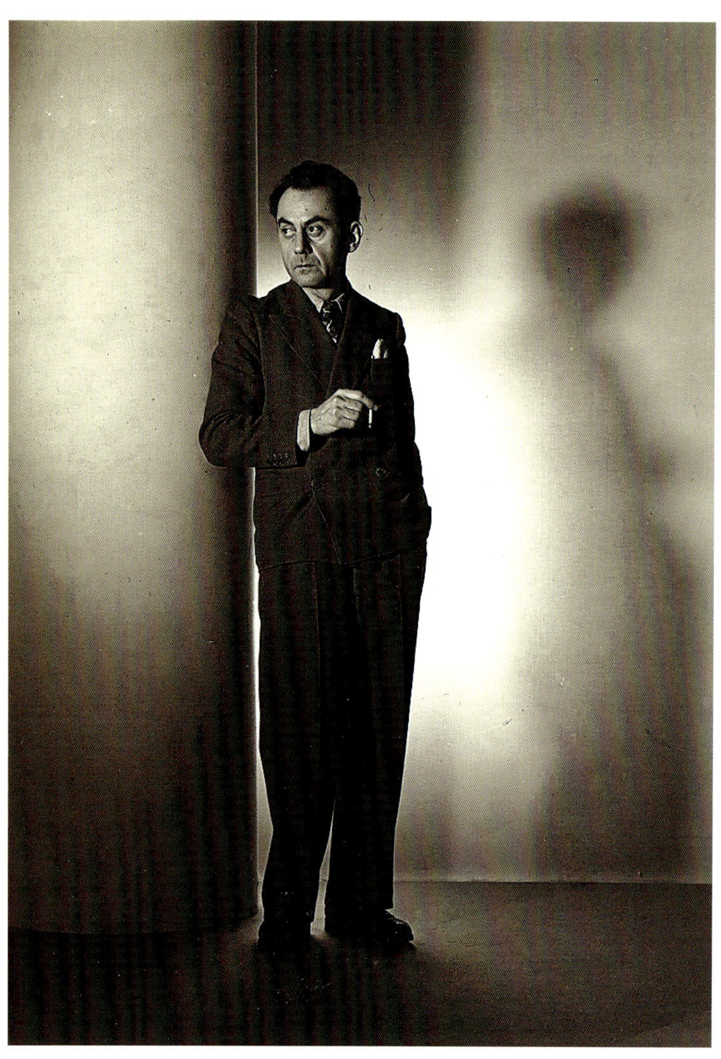

Fig. 8. *Self-Portrait as a Fashion Photographer*, 1936. Gelatin silver print on warm-toned, matte-surface paper, 8¼ × 6 in. (21 × 15.2 cm). Collection of Steven M. Sumberg

of high fashion by the summer of 1922, in the wake of the commercial failure of his Paris Dada exhibition the previous winter (fig. 8).

Man Ray's first Paris exhibition had also been a résumé of sorts, filled with his past production, and the one new object notoriously created for the show—the assemblage *Cadeau*, an iron to which Man Ray attached a line of razor-sharp tacks—continued the strategies of the wastrel Man Ray had carved out during his New York Dada years. But the newfound intensity of this object's violence toward work and labor perhaps testifies, despite itself, to a crisis of sorts, and to the transformed place that labor would now take up within Man Ray's artistic project. The Paris Dada group pointed to this shift in the collective verbal portrait of Man Ray they in turn produced and published in the few pages of his exhibition pamphlet. "One no longer remembers where Mr. Ray was born," the catalogue intones. "After having been a coal merchant, a millionaire several times over, and the chairman of a chewing-gum trust, he decided he was open to the Dadaists' invitation to show his latest paintings in Paris."[21] Fantasies again: The Dadaists explicitly elide Man Ray's origins and the actual conditions of his class background; as the description privileges the association of Man Ray's art to work instead of aesthetics, it shifts to associations with big business and administrative roles as opposed to working-class labor. And yet the fantasies contain the glint of the real, as Man Ray had in fact just been appointed "Vice-President" of the Société Anonyme, Katherine Dreier's idea for a museum of modern art—an institution that Man Ray also named, supposedly choosing in ignorance the French term for a "corporation" because of its verbal association with "anonymity," the condition explored in almost all of his New York Dada paintings.[22] Indeed, by the time of Man Ray's Paris Dada exhibition the artist had begun setting up his own business, organized around his recently acquired skills as a photographer.

From anonymity and labor to the administrator and the corporation: such is the shift that Man Ray now enacts within his work. It is an alteration that closely follows the artist's well-known move from an early focus on painting to his becoming the most important photographer working in France during the interwar years (figs. 9–11). But this change of medium also produced a change in Man Ray's manner of working, and consequently it was paralleled by a whole series of other, conceptual shifts in which an earlier relationship to labor would now be transformed. These shifts have never been mapped, but their direc-

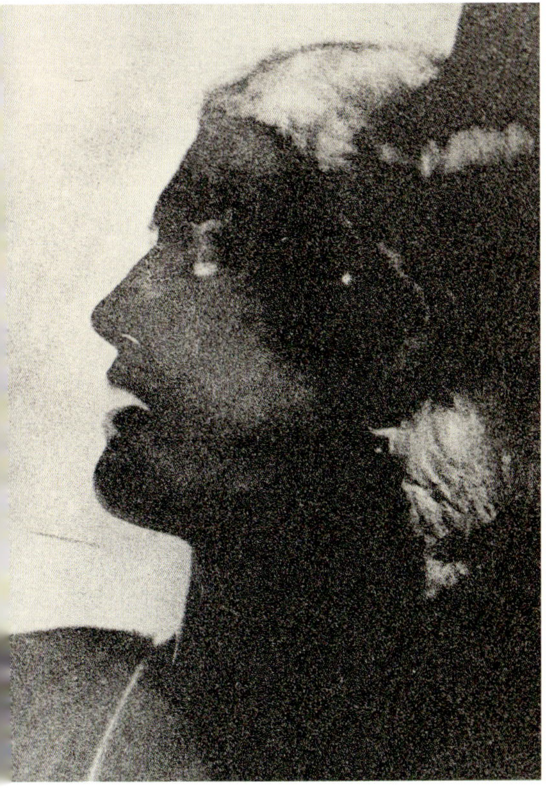

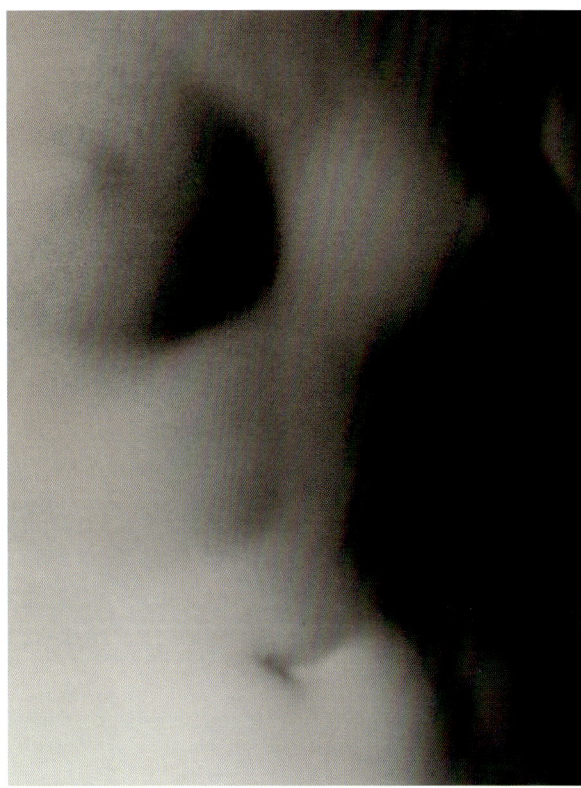

Fig. 9. *Untitled (Silhouette)*, 1930. Gelatin silver print, 11⅝ × 8⅞ in. (29.3 × 22.5 cm). The Museum of Modern Art, New York, Gift of James Thrall Soby, 1941

Fig. 10. *Untitled*, 1933. Gelatin silver print, 11½ × 8⅞ in. (29.3 × 22.6 cm). The Museum of Modern Art, New York, Gift of James Thrall Soby, 1941

Fig. 11. *Hier (Kiki de Montparnasse)*, 1931; *Demain (Kiki de Montparnasse)*, 1930/1965; *Aujourd'hui (Kiki de Montparnasse)*, 1932. Vintage gelatin silver prints and collage, 23 × 15¼ in. (57 × 38 cm); 15⅛ × 10¼ in. (37.5 × 25.5 cm); 23 × 15¼ in. (57 × 38 cm). Private collection of Thomas and Janine Koerfer-Weill

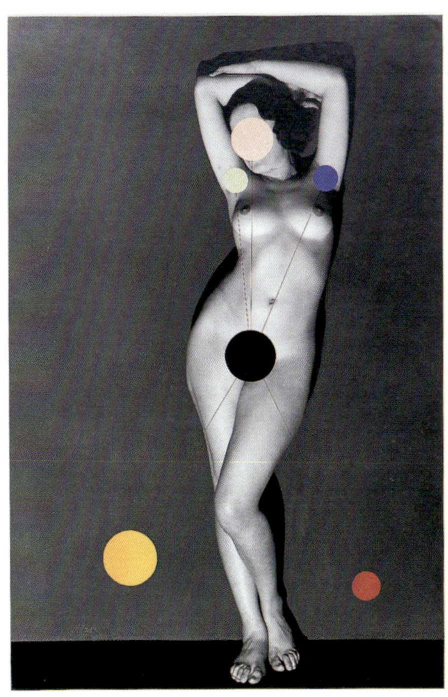

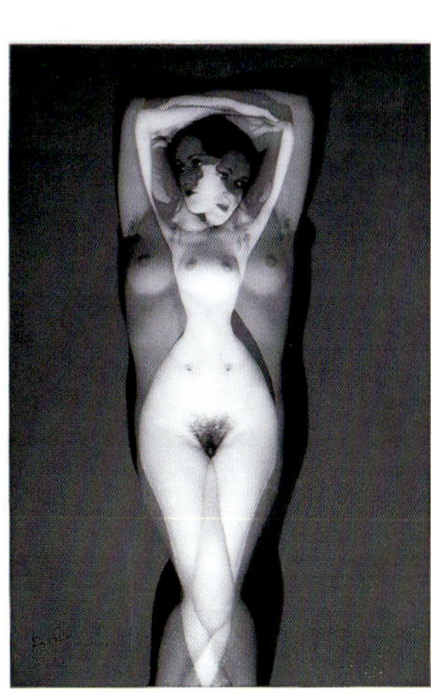

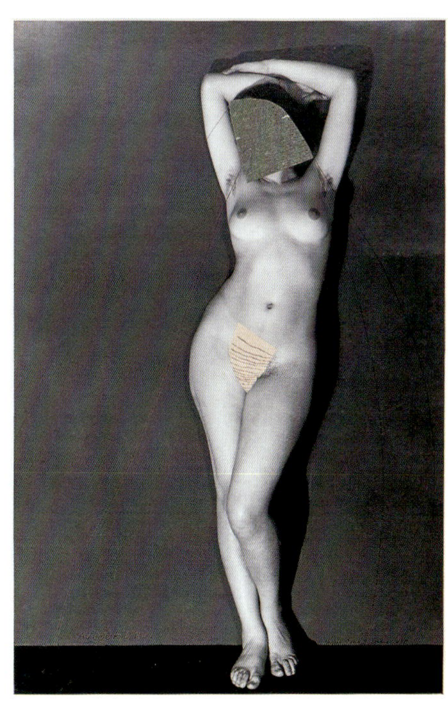

tion seems clear. In every instance, a manual or working-class labor with which Man Ray had experimented during his New York Dada period would be elevated—sublated—into an aesthetic transvaluation of that trade. Rather than "work avoidance," Man Ray's art is transformed into a kind of work, and we move from an early aesthetic of industry to the intimation of a set of fully industrialized aesthetic activities, linked in each case to business. Man Ray lays down his brush to take up the camera, and he switches from the work of the tailor to the image styling of the fashion photographer. He moves from early works that evoked the labor of the carpenter (*Boardwalk,* or *New York;* fig. 12) to experiments with interior design and decoration. He shifts from his actual job as a typographer to an imagined role as an "adman," collaborating with Duchamp on the design and layout of the journal *New York Dada* and on their joint "product," the perfume bottle *Belle Haleine, Eau de Voilette* with its (Jewish) spokeswoman, Rrose Sélavy (fig. 13).[23] Even in the realm of the image a transformation comes into play: Man Ray moves from the work of "cameraman" as an assistant to Duchamp during the 1910s, to the role of "director" in the 1920s— even if the wastrel sticks around, and Man Ray proclaims himself a director of "mauvais movies."[24]

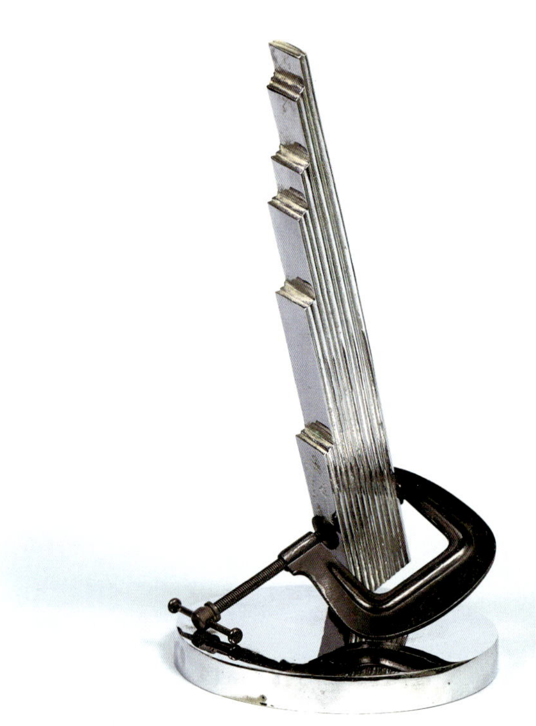

Fig. 12. *New York,* 1917/1966. Chrome-plated metal and metal clamp, 17½ in. high (44.5 cm). Whitney Museum of American Art, New York

Or consider the following shift, again enacted in close proximity to Duchamp: Many of Man Ray's works in the 1910s evoke the labor of the barber, whether in the context of equating the cut of collage not only with the template of the tailor but the work of the hairdresser, as in the clump of hair attached to *Decollage;* or in relation to what could be called Duchamp's pornographic version of *The Bride Stripped Bare,* his lost film of the shaving of the Baroness Elsa von Freytag-Loringhoven's pubic hair, in which Man Ray was cast as "barber" and cameraman. A 1920 portrait of Duchamp, sitting with Joseph Stella—in a sense, the beginning of Man Ray's career as a major portrait photographer, launched in Paris the following year—shows the artist seated beneath another "attribute," a startling photograph of a woman's inverted head, chin and cigarette rising toward the top of the frame as her hair spreads out in a tangle at the image's base (fig. 14). This second, untitled photograph seems paired specifically with Duchamp's face, their inverted directions perhaps a play on the latter's theme of the "bride" and her "bachelors," the woman's excessive hair seeming to take the place of the near-lack of Duchamp's own. And yet this image has always presented some major stum-

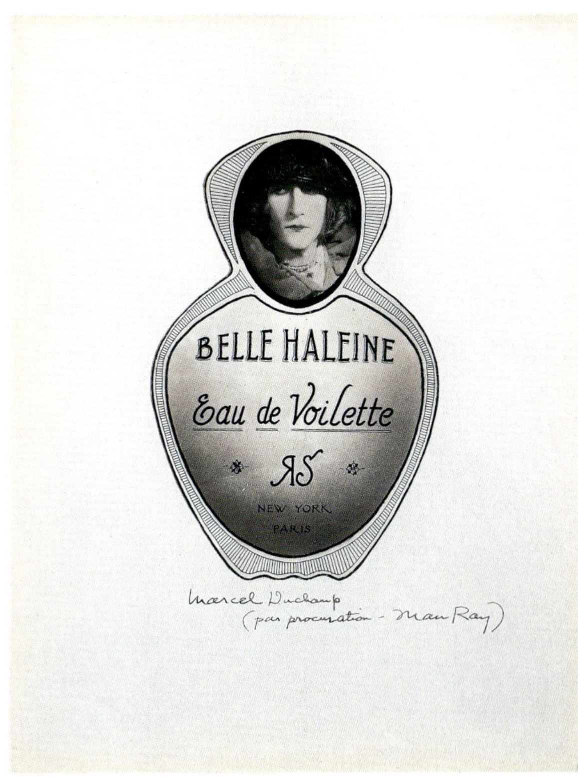

Fig. 13. Man Ray and Marcel Duchamp, *Belle Haleine, Eau de Voilette*, 1921. Gelatin silver print, 11¹¹/₁₆ × 7⅞ in. (29.6 × 20 cm). Private collection, New York

Fig. 14. *Untitled (Woman with Cigarette, New York)*, 1920. Vintage silver gelatin print, 3⅞ × 2⅝ in. (9.8 × 6.7 cm). Bruce Silverstein Gallery, New York

bling blocks to interpretation, its radically oblique angle occurring years before the onset of the photographic techniques of the New Vision, its reorientation of the human form anachronistically linked by some critics to the philosophies of Georges Bataille, ideas that emerge within Surrealist debates that will not occur for another decade.[25] The image seems more comprehensible—and yet still remains, I would say, startling—if seen in the context of work and of class: Man Ray appropriates here the gaze of the barber, the way in which a head is seen under quite specific conditions of labor, associated with the photographer's own.[26]

A decade later—in 1930—the photographer makes another untitled image of a woman's face in which he fixates on cutting once more, showing a model with a modern bob surrounded by the wayward strands of hair from which her hairstyle has been carved. It is as if Man Ray now wished to compare the cutting of hair to the cropping of the photographic image, another transformed labor of the cut quite distant from the residual painterly world of collage. But the 1930 image emerges from Man Ray's work within the fashion industry. We seem to be confronted with a self-reflexive acknowledgment of Man Ray's shift from the productive labor of the barber to the consumerist fashionings of the stylist. From barber to stylist: this shift was already predicted within Man Ray's role in the elaboration of Duchamp's image as Rrose Sélavy (fig. 15), dressed up in hat, furs, and makeup (and with some of the photographic prints signed "by procuration Man Ray"). It would be a role Man Ray explores in the wake of his work for the fashion

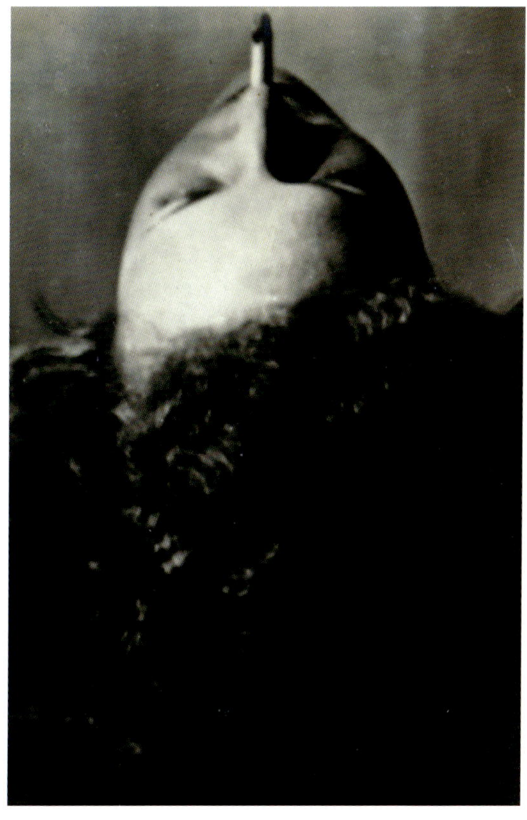

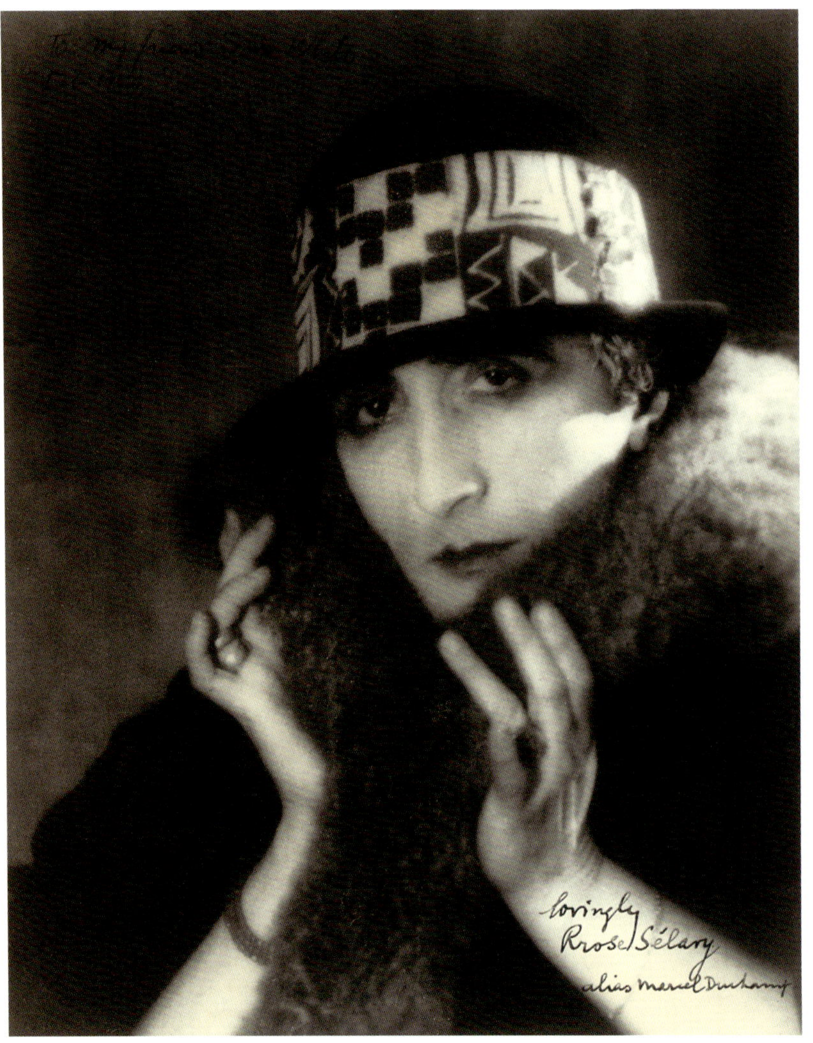

Fig. 15. *Marcel Duchamp as Rrose Sélavy*, c. 1920–21. Gelatin silver print, 8½ × 6¹³⁄₁₆ in. (21.6 × 17.3 cm). Philadelphia Museum of Art: Samuel S. White 3rd and Vera White Collection, 1957

magazines as he temporarily lays aside his painting to work obsessively, for example, on the makeup and visual "image" of his lover Kiki de Montparnasse during the 1920s. Every night before they would go out, Man Ray meticulously applied her cosmetics and assisted in the choice of her clothes, creating a visual style that is as much a part of his oeuvre as any of his signed paintings, and that he would then immortalize in his portrait photographs.[27]

This shift within Man Ray's work was announced, proclaimed by the avant-garde, even if no one has bothered to listen in the ensuing years. In 1925, commissioned by *Vogue* magazine to document the Pavillon de l'Élégance at the Exposition Internationale des Arts Décoratifs, Man Ray photographed a series of mannequins dressed in the fashions of Lanvin, Worth, and many others. The mannequins had startled contemporary viewers due to their overly lifelike appearance and their outlandish styling, painted silver, gold, or "Egyptian red." They startled the Surrealists as well, for one of Man Ray's *Vogue* photographs would wind up on the cover of the fourth issue of *La révolution surréaliste*. There, the Surrealists gave Man Ray's photograph a caption unlike any that it had acquired in *Vogue*. "AND WAR," the image now was made to proclaim, "ON WORK."

Man Ray's aesthetic of industry had been turned around, like the woman's head in his anonymous, untitled image of 1920. The task that remains is to trace the formal shifts that follow from Man Ray's sublation of the place of labor within his early work. From tailor to fashion photographer, from barber to stylist, from carpenter to designer: these paradigmatic shifts in the status of work determine a number of formal developments within Man Ray's photography of the 1920s and 1930s. And to the extent that art history has failed to narrate the larger paradigmatic shifts of his relation to his former labors and his own class, the formal logic of Man Ray's industry of the image has remained unspoken. If once work had provided him with an aesthetic modality of excess, now excess itself would become a form of industry. If once labor had functioned as an outside force in his painterly production, now the outside would be invited into the center of the image, undoing the very boundaries of the aesthetic and the real.

from Index to aura

One understanding of Man Ray's turn to photography stresses the artist's dialogue with Duchamp, who envisioned the *Large Glass* as a kind of metaphorical photograph, produced by the physical trace of objects. Duchamp was everywhere concerned with the modality of what has been called the "index," a sign physically caused by that to which it refers, tying art insistently to the realm of matter, anchoring it to the world from which it came: cast shadow, traced stencil, imprint or mold, photography itself.[28] Thus can Man Ray's entire dedication to photography be explained, as well as the artist's self-reflexive understanding of the photograph as trace, the indexes of indexes that he would ceaselessly produce—photographs of cast shadow, burnt objects, crushed cans, mirror reflections. Seen in this way, Man Ray's use of photography builds logically to the initiation of the so-called rayographs by 1922, cameraless images that stress the physical imprint of things, that understand photography as nothing more than the naked chemical trace of light and the object, an apotheosis of the indexical sign (figs. 16 and 17)

But the paradoxical dialectics of Man Ray's rayographs can be ascertained by registering how utterly dematerialized the physical indexes that they record have become. If

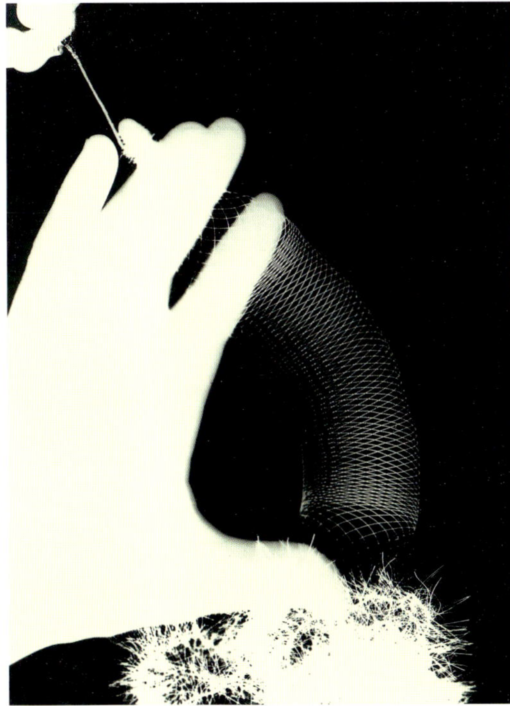

Fig. 16. *Untitled (Hand)*, 1922. Gelatin silver print, 9¼ × 6⅞ in. (23.6 × 17.5 cm). Collection of Gérard Lévy, Paris

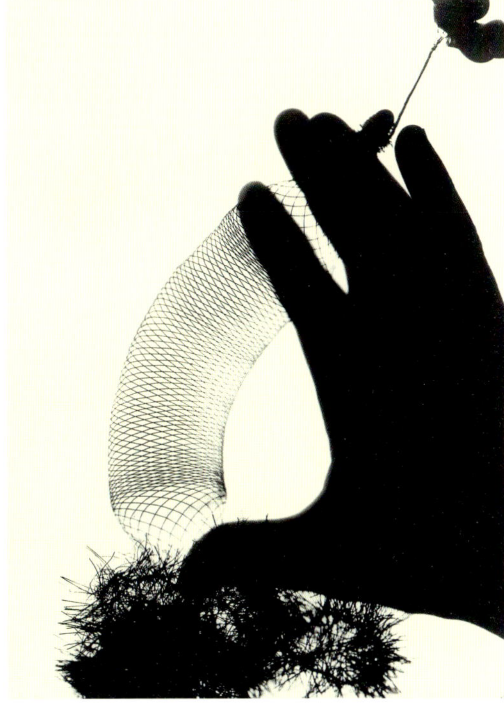

Fig. 17. *Untitled (Hand)*, 1922. Gelatin silver print, 9¼ × 6⅞ in. (23.6 × 17.5 cm). Collection of Gérard Lévy, Paris

the indexical procedure recasts the work of art as insistently earthbound, the antitranscendental fusion of making and mark, procedure and product, Man Ray's rayographs emerge as the culmination of what could be called the dematerialization of the index within the artist's work. We move from the textured imprint of the artist's hand in *Self-Portrait*, thick with paint, to the elimination of tactility and the trace of the body in the airbrush paintings, to the flat shadows of photographs such as *Man* and *Woman* (also called *Integration of Shadows* in another of its versions). The index is transformed from a physical thing into an image, its "integration" a function of the flat field of the visual and its fusion with the voided mass of the object. The rayograph culminates in images of sheer contour and negative delineation, the outline as the apex of visual form.

Rather than a triumph of the physical trace over the optical apparatus of the camera, the rayographs reinvigorate the visual field on the other side of its obliteration. They are another sublation.[29] Many of the rayographs thus portray substitutes for the absent lens of the camera: the magnifying glass, lightbulbs, spectacles, or drinking glasses that repeated images record. And freed of the bonds of the physical in this way, the "integration" of objects within the rayographs can proceed apace, with so many of Man Ray's images contemplating the irrational fusion of disparate things via the interpenetration of contour and field, a collage aesthetic without the heterogeneity of material to act as a force of disruption— like diagrammatic vectors, or the combinatory structure of the Surrealists' later game of "exquisite corpse." Such "integration" would often be thematized by Man Ray as erotic, the fusion or melding of objects that was synthesized in one of the most famous of the early rayographs, two profiles seized in the gesture of a kiss. But this rayograph is also an image of the fusion of the tactile hand with the site of vision that is the face, as well as the interpenetration of human being and inanimate object in the form of two pillows that were evidently laid upon the paper in the wake of its first exposure. The rayograph presents a "world

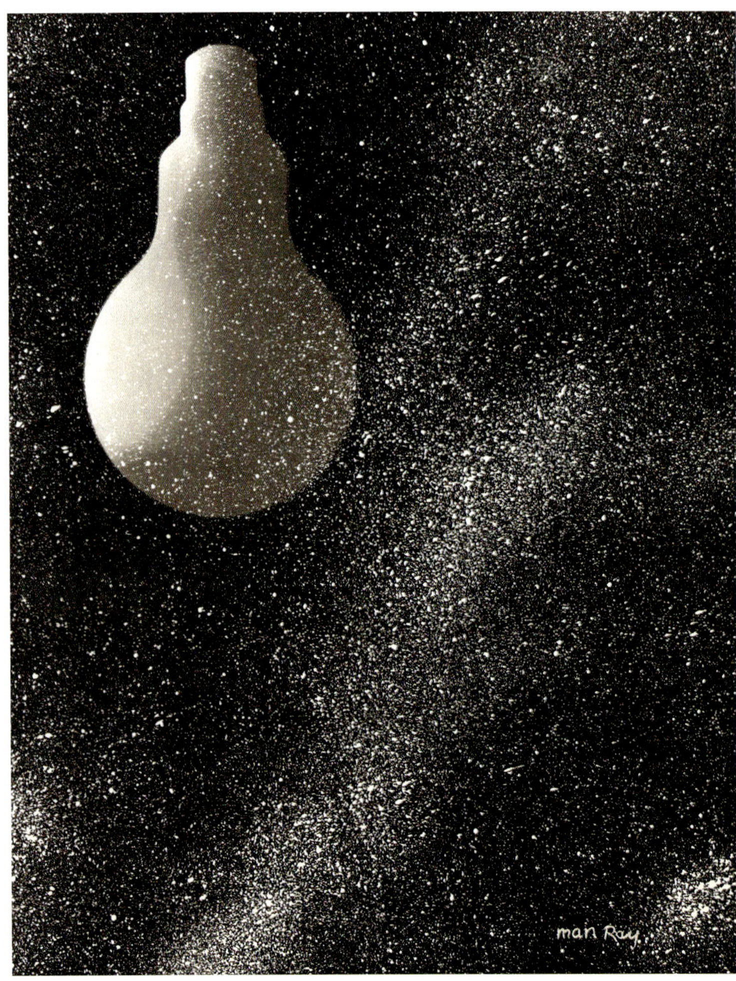

Fig. 18. *Electricité*, from the portfolio *Electricité*, 1931. Photogravure from rayograph, 10⅛ × 8 in. (25.7 × 20.3 cm). Heckscher Museum of Art, Huntington, New York, Museum purchase with funds provided by Andrea B. and Peter D. Klein

Fig. 19. *Le souffle (The Fan)*, from the portfolio *Electricité*, 1931. Photogravure from rayograph, 10⅛ × 8 in. (25.7 × 20.3 cm). Heckscher Museum of Art, Huntington, New York, Museum purchase with funds provided by Andrea B. and Peter D. Klein

Fig. 20. *Untitled*, from the portfolio *Electricité*, 1931. Photogravure from rayograph, 10⅛ × 8 in. (25.7 × 20.3 cm). Heckscher Museum of Art, Huntington, New York, Museum purchase with funds provided by Andrea B. and Peter D. Klein

upside down": a reversal of tonal values but also in this case a pair of hands held by the shadows of the face, not the other way around; the human countenance hardly perched upon a cushion but instead encased in the contours of the object, one imprint laid upon and binding the other.

We might imagine that it was the rayograph's capture of the human body by the object, combined (paradoxically) with its vision of transformation unconcerned with the physical limits of things, that made the images so immediately attractive to the world of fashion. For the rayograph was born from a fashion assignment: Having been introduced by Gabrielle Buffet-Picabia to Paul Poiret, Man Ray made his first rayograph accidentally in the darkroom while developing images of the designer's work. And while some accounts would then prioritize the rayographs' anti-instrumental nature, their embrace of chance and accident, their unproductive erosion from within Man Ray's commercial practice of photography, such images were immediately taken up by the fashion world.[30] Frank Crowninshield, then editor of *Vanity Fair* (and eventual member of the board of directors of the Museum of Modern Art), had by November 1922 published a selection of the rayographs in his magazine.[31] A decade later Man Ray would be using the rayograph technique in an advertising campaign for a Parisian electricity company (figs. 18–20).[32]

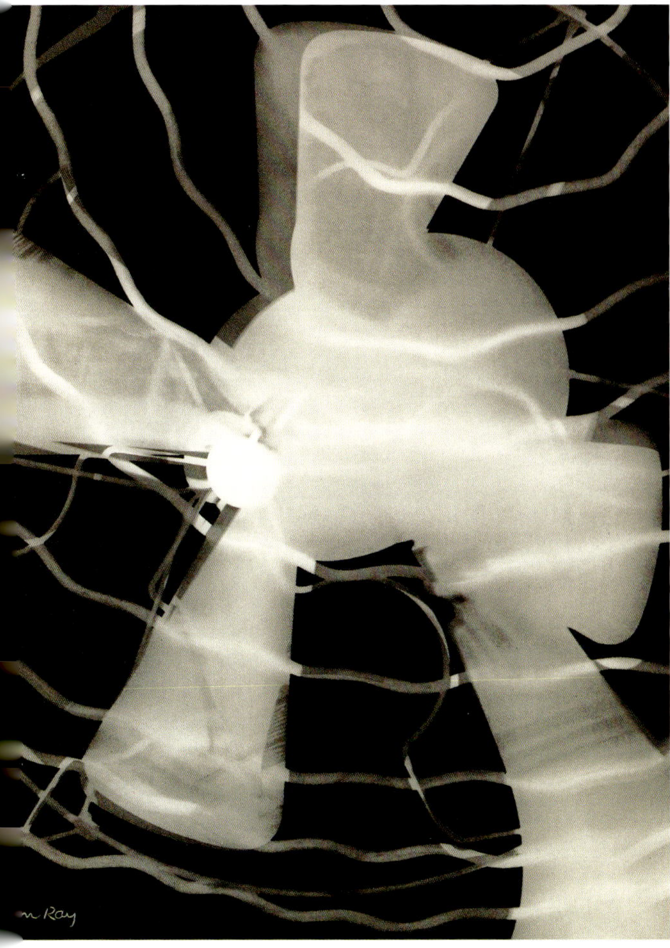

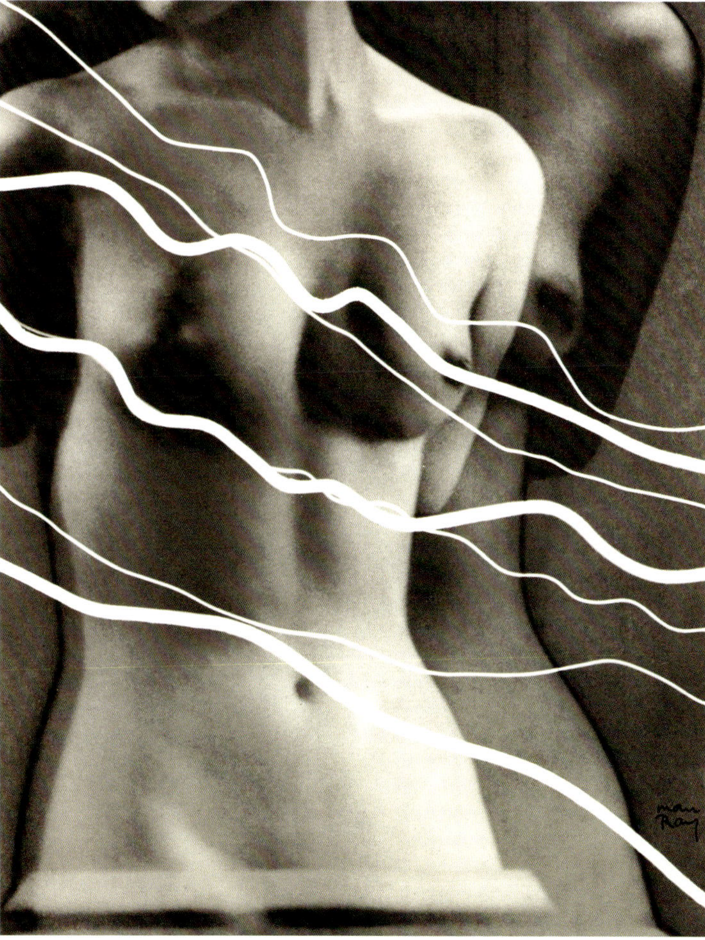

A transvaluation of the object and the physical trace, the rayographs hardly "suck the aura out of reality like water from a sinking ship," to use Walter Benjamin's famous description of the work of Eugène Atget.[33] Instead, Man Ray's things now seem to glow with an uncanny penumbra—to have *become* that penumbra—the physical object ceding its place to the wavering ghost of its previous material form. "What is aura, actually?" Benjamin once asked. "A strange weave of space and time: the unique appearance or semblance of a distance, no matter how close it may be." Aura would be linked for Benjamin to "uniqueness and duration," opposed to the "transience and reproducibility" of the mechanical copy, the photographic reproductions that the critic saw as rupturing aura within modernity by bringing objects insistently "*closer* to us."[34] It must immediately be admitted that the rayograph's perverse relation to photography involved its temporal regression to

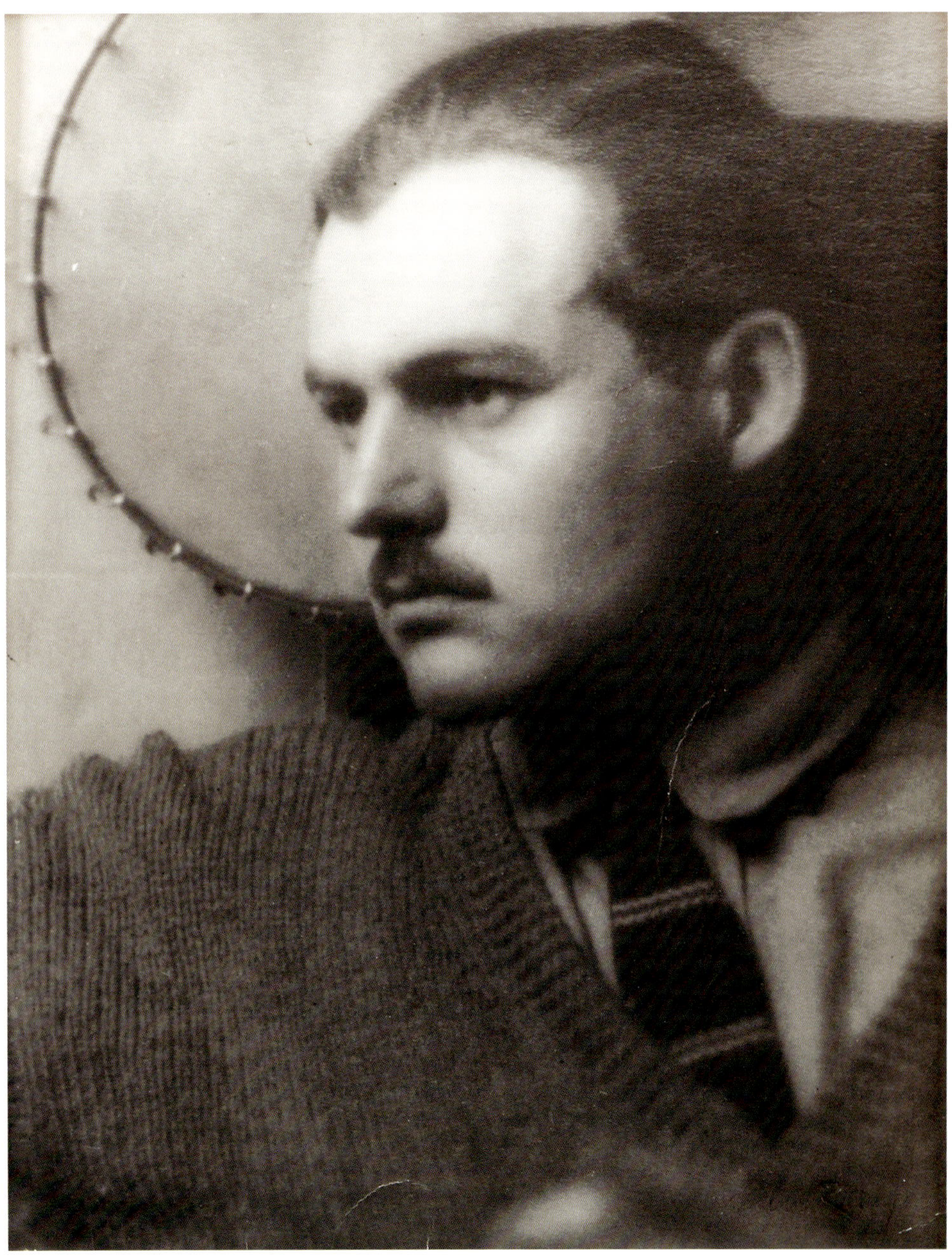

the origins of the medium, a resurrection of the photogram—an image that while photographic was still unique, not created as a negative but inscribed directly onto the paper of the print, a singular image. And many of the rayographs produce the effect of an incalculable distance, their ghost images floating in a space of utter inaccessibility. An untitled rayograph from 1923 depicts a single wine glass standing upright upon the photographic print. The base of the glass becomes a circular nonobject, an eye or lens directing vision toward the receding body of the glass positioned as if "above" us, ever retreating from the scene, in flight from the picture plane, dissolved in a haze of light. The rayographs do not bring us

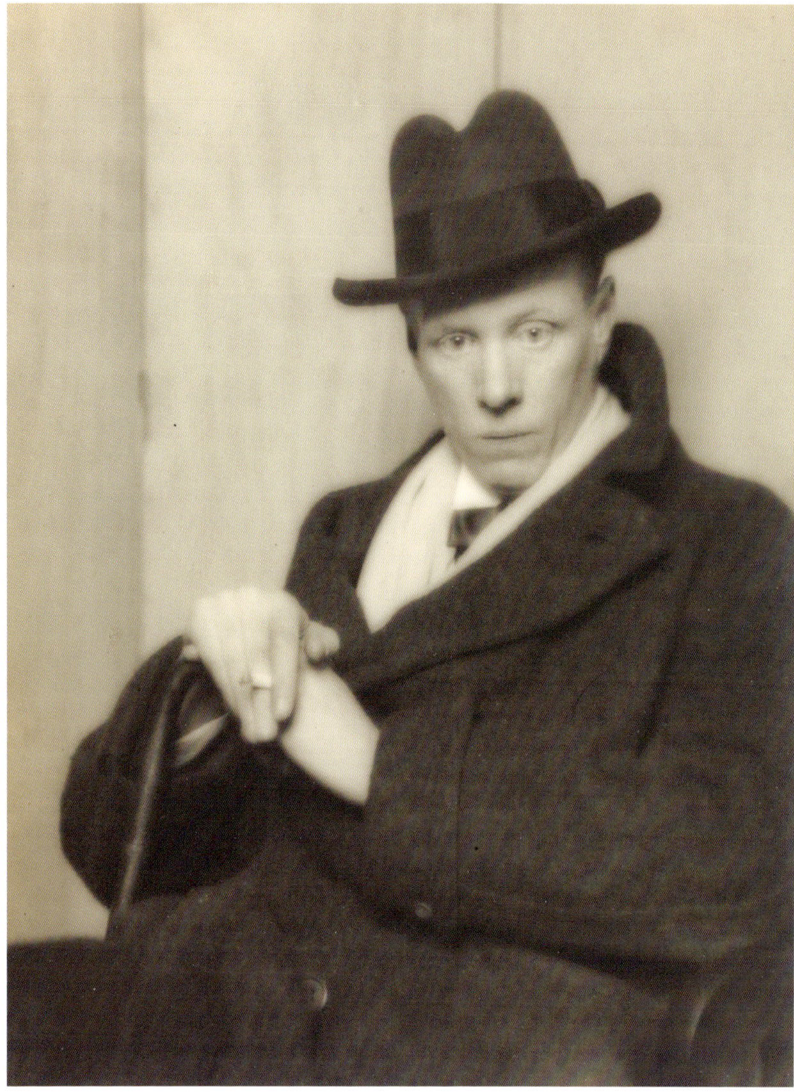

closer to the object, grounding vision in the here-and-now, the index and the trace. We seem to gaze at the indistinct penumbra of things as if through the fog of ages, the expanse of miles, a "strange weave of space and time."

It becomes the paradoxical achievement of Man Ray's photography in the 1920s and 1930s to deploy the medium in the service of an aesthetic of the aura, a visual technique of distance and mythification, the singular and exceptional erupting from the reproductive machine of the visual. We confront a sublation of the index and the trace, spawned by the rayograph's earlier overcoming of the opposition between eye and hand, vision and tactility, subject and object, painting and photography. This explains the regressive effect of Man Ray's portrait photography, his return to the impact of the early portraits produced by photographers in the nineteenth century, like the pantheon of Nadar—precisely the era and images whose passing Benjamin would later mourn, and whose revival he would advocate (figs. 21 and 22). In part, the aura of Man Ray's portraits was an effect that the artist achieved by taking his images at some distance from his subjects, using a long focal length,

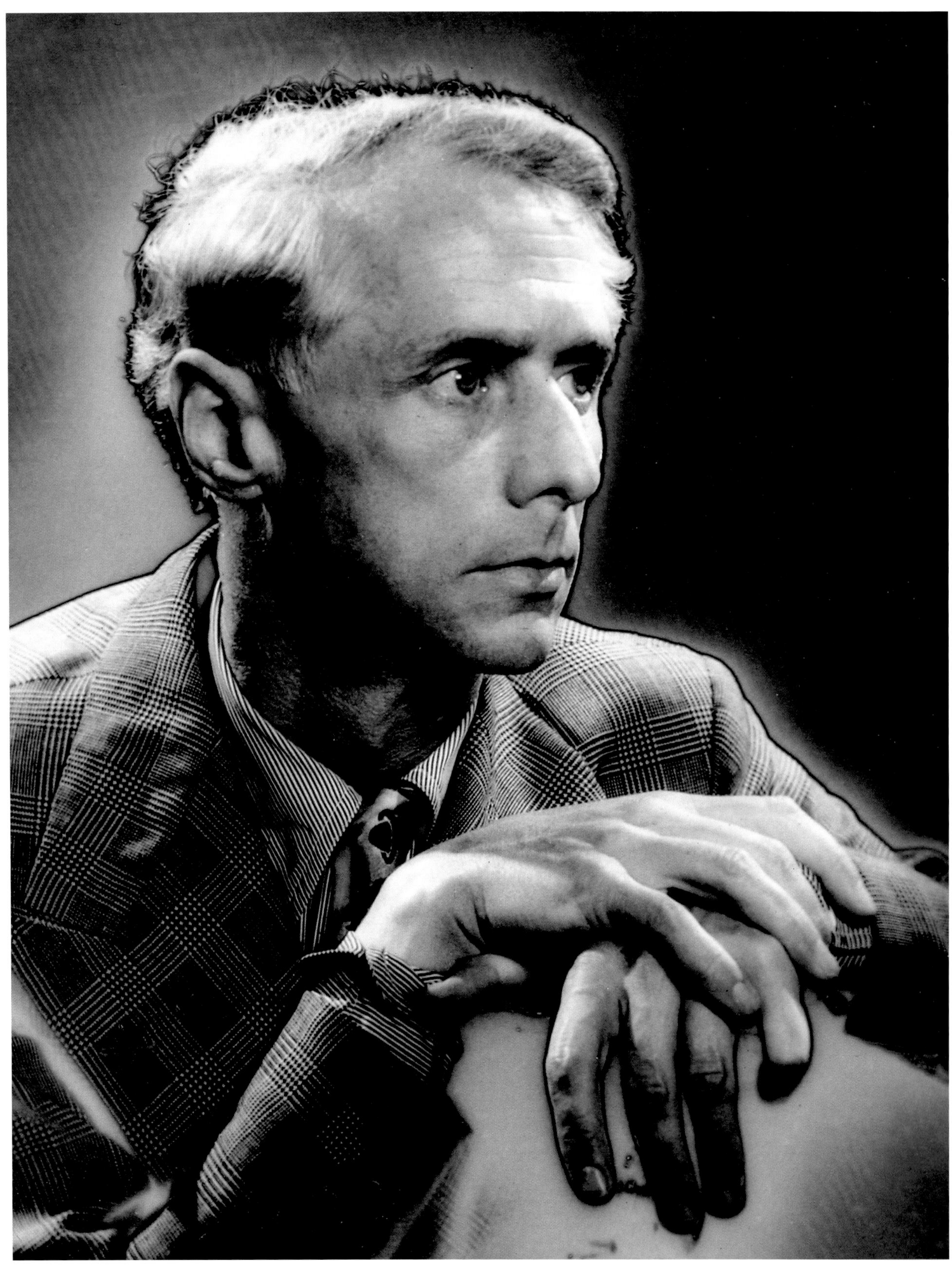

Fig. 23. *Max Ernst*, 1935. Gelatin silver print,
11½ × 9 in. (29.2 × 22.9 cm). High Museum of
Art, Atlanta, Purchase with funds from
Georgia-Pacific Corporation, 1984.228

and then cropping and enlarging from the negatives, producing the penumbra of the inaccessible in what otherwise seems a series of images that borrow the cinematic conventions of the close-up.[35] Similarly, distance and inaccessibility would be the great experience of all those photographs manipulated by Man Ray so that we attempt to see the object through some form of scrim or screen—behind bubbles, or a shade, or overprinted with a stubbly textile—enacted most uncannily in Man Ray's Duchampian film *L'étoile de mer*, with the majority of its scenes filmed through a plate of glass. And aura becomes the literal effect of Man Ray's other great manipulation of the photographic image during these decades, another device fallen upon by accident, the technique of solarization, which we can now see as the sublation and apotheosis in turn of Man Ray's earlier aesthetic of the rayograph.

The solarized image surrounds its objects with the most insistent of contour lines. Whereas once the physical object had been superseded in the rayograph, now in the solarized photographs of the 1930s the body follows suit, achieving a penumbra, a linear echo that most often punches out the subject against a blank background space (fig. 23). The visual halo of the technique removes the body from its surroundings, erasing the ties of context like the disconsolate readymades that had floated through the nonspaces of the mechanomorphs of Duchamp, Man Ray, and Picabia during the 1910s.[36] From index to aura: Rendered singular and distinct, unique and unrepeatable, the solarized body languishes in an empty space where it is simultaneously inaccessible and displaced, like a dream image, or a commodity available for exchange. This paradox of inaccessibility and availability, of uniqueness and exchange, would be one of the great promises the new regimes of consumer culture and fashion would now explore. "The use of contour to mark the object as a discrete presence is of great use to commerce," Julian Stallabrass writes of Man Ray's solarizations. "Figures are often transformed into objects, as cold and classical as statuary."[37] Rather than rendering art physical, rather than a triumph of the index, Man Ray in the aftermath of Dada renders the physical aesthetic, lending objects and bodies the glow of the singular and distanced effect of art, their reversal, their sublation: their aura, as Man Ray almost names his aesthetic in a 1937 essay published in the Surrealist journal *Minotaure*.[38]

from **d**ocument to pro**P**

The story that is always told about Man Ray's turn to photography begins with the artist's need for documents of his paintings, and his realization that if he could teach himself how to use a camera his photographs would serve this purpose better than those of anyone else. The photograph we retain of *Self-Portrait* from 1916 amounts to a good example of this practice by Man Ray, and documenting works of art would become one of the artist's first photographic "jobs." After photographing Duchamp's *Large Glass* in New York, Man Ray will document a number of Picabia's paintings upon his arrival in Paris, a commission that then blossomed into others, as Picabia spread the word of Man Ray's skills among the French avant-garde.

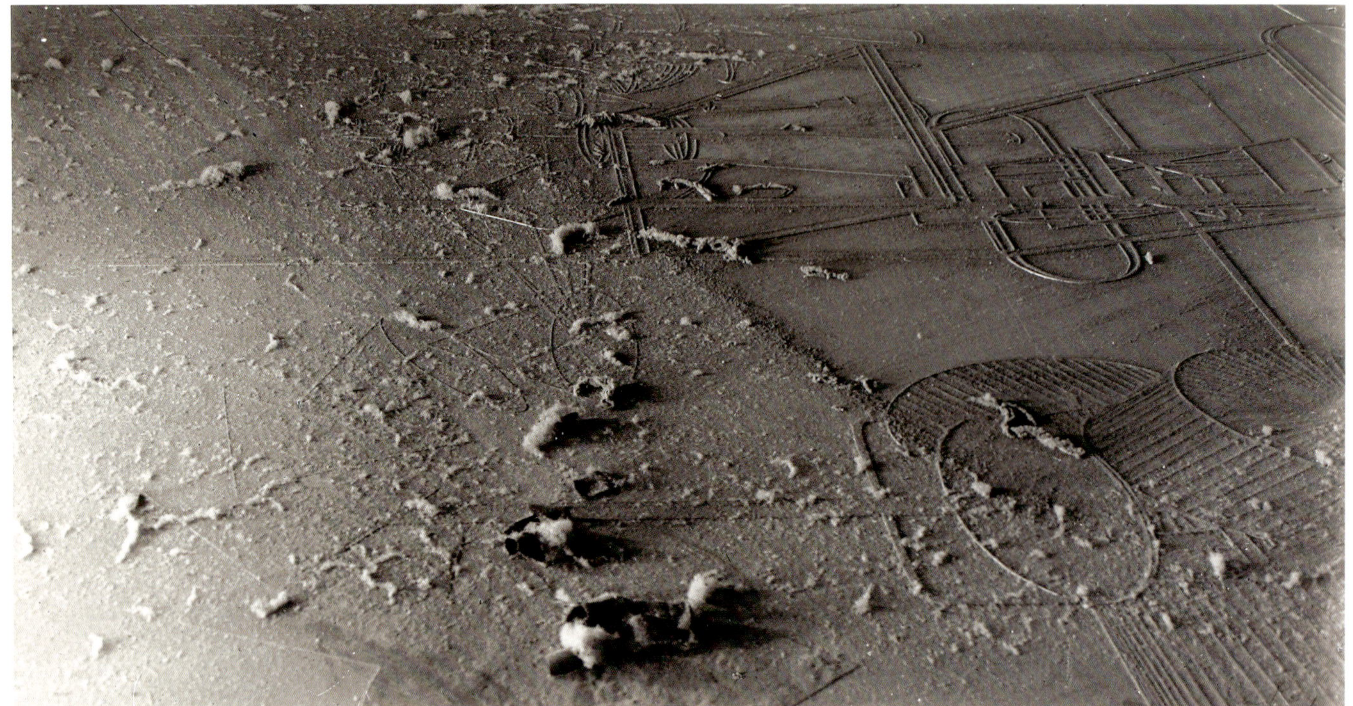

Fig. 24. *Dust Breeding*, 1920. Gelatin silver print, 7⅞ × 9⁹⁄₁₆ in. (19.3 × 24.3 cm). High Museum of Art, Atlanta, Purchase with funds from GeorgiaPacific Corporation

But this origin story hardly speaks to the charged status that Man Ray's "documents" of art immediately obtain, as his images of the *Large Glass* like *Dust Breeding* (1920; fig. 24) operate more as collaborative works than as functional records. Moreover, Man Ray immediately begins photographing objects that do not function for the artist as documents of readymades or of prior works —the photograph becomes the form of the work itself, the only modality in which the work exists. *Man* of 1918, or *Woman* of the same year, deploy readymade objects but only within the context of the photograph, submitting the work of art to the regime of the copy, the industrial object fused with the reproducible image.

And it is a story further complicated by the way in which Man Ray begins to photograph works of art in the wake of his entrance into the fashion industry. Consider one of the earliest of Man Ray's fashion photographs, "*Mythe*" (1922), made for Paul Poiret, an image of the designer's wife, Denise, wearing a Poiret dress. With the dress seemingly made from feathers, Man

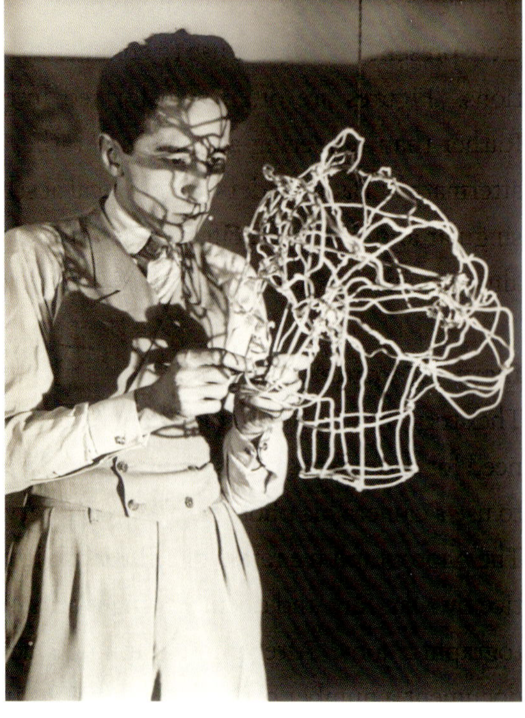

Fig. 25. *Jean Cocteau, Sculpting His Own Head in Wire*, 1926. Gelatin silver print, 9¼ × 7 in. (23.5 × 17.8 cm). Richard and Ronnie Grosbard Collection

Ray had his model stand before the birdlike form of Brancusi's sculpture *Maiastra*, a work acquired by the fashion designer in 1912. Immediately, in fashion photography, Man Ray's images of works of art move from the condition of document to the status of prop—another "attribute," like those used in the portrait photographs he began at this same time (fig. 25). This prop functions in a specific way: matched with Poiret's fashion design on the level of resemblance, the work of art plunges into the operations of myth, setting off a series of regressive analogies between human and natural forms. The work of art simultaneously seeks to elevate that which it resembles, to extend the status of art from the Brancusi sculpture to Poiret's shimmering dress. Echoed in the double of the mirror against which all is posed, and capturing the room's reflections in its bright metallic surface, Brancusi's sculpture also claims photography for this chain of mythic resemblance, collapsing art and fashion and different mediums all at once.

Already in the same year of 1922, Man Ray had begun to use his own works of art as props within his portrait photographs. The strategy of the prop within these two types of image—portrait and fashion—was shared. From 1922 dates Man Ray's double portrait of Tristan Tzara and Jean Cocteau, the two sitters draped in dark fabric so that only their decontextualized faces would show, with Man Ray's sculpture *Lampshade* snaking its way from Cocteau's chin to Tzara's head below (fig. 26). As a prop, Man Ray's sculpture decoratively frames the sitter's heads, but it also takes on a set of functions, as aggressively as did *Maiastra*. Linking Cocteau to Tzara, the prop creates a new form of the collective or group portrait, acting like the diagrammatic lines that connected words and images in the Dada mechanomorph. Simultaneously, Man Ray's prop suggests not just the diagram, but the cut—of collage or montage, to be sure, but also presenting an image staged as if Cocteau's and Tzara's heads had been decapitated, or were about to be, like the menacing hatchet the photographer would include in one of his other early portraits of Tzara. The prop links and displaces simultaneously, transforming the

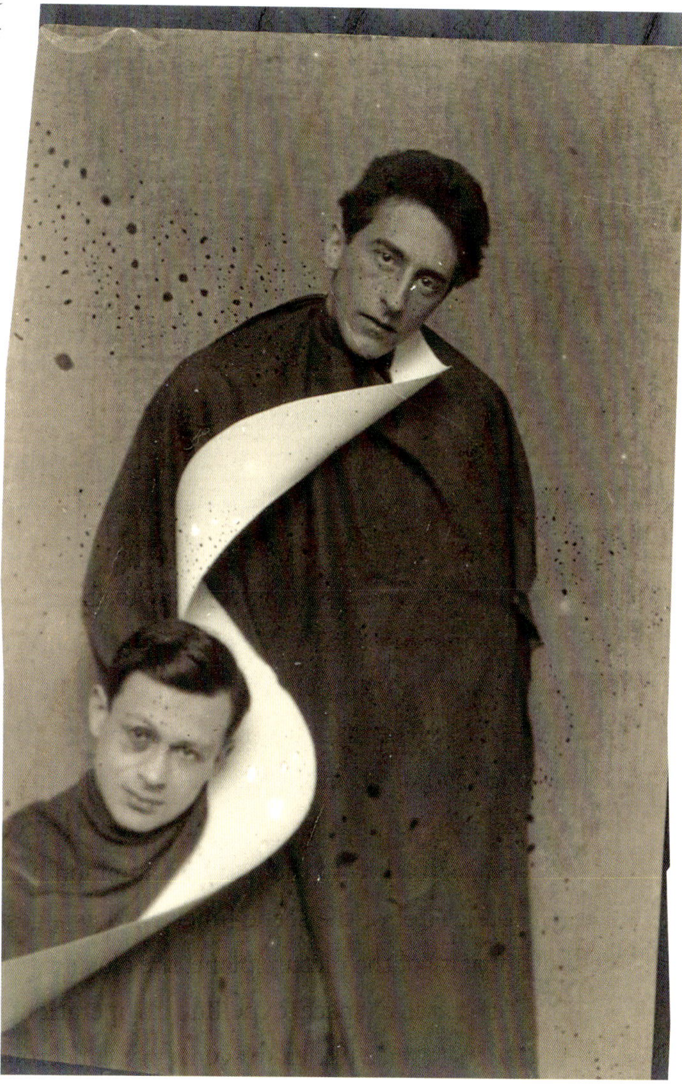

Fig. 26. *Cocteau and Tzara with Spiral*, 1922. Gelatin silver print, 4½ × 2½ in. (8.8 × 6.4 cm). Private collection, France

status of both the art object and the self-contained image of the (here threatened) subject, an operation tied to the prop's more general transformation from object into image, the work of art's role in defining Man Ray's portrait images and his fashion photographs.

Inevitably, this portrait calls up an image from a decade later of another work of art—another sculpture—Man Ray's photograph of a seminude model grasping the phallic bladelike form of Alberto Giacometti's *Objet désagréable* (*Disagreeable Object*). While Man Ray documents Giacometti's artistic production, here sculpture at the height of Surrealist activities has been self-consciously conceived as a prop—an object to be taken off its pedestal, touched and handled by the viewer, now become a participant with the work of art. Surrealism by 1930 understands sculpture as a prop, its logic one that contemplates the fusion of subject and object: every object presented as an extension of the subject, and the subject attached to all of its objects.[39]

If such were one of Giacometti's crucial contributions to the Surrealist aesthetic, Man Ray had been involved in the logic of the prop since his entrance into fashion and portraiture a decade before. In 1925, Man Ray photographs Giorgio de Chirico's *L'engime d'une journée* (*The Enigma of a Day*). Rather than a simple document, the work of art again mutates into a prop, in this case a backdrop for the body of André Breton, a portrait in the form of a manifesto declaring the interpenetration of the space of art and the space of the real, painted bodies and real ones (fig. 27). It was another statement of the Surrealist aesthetic, linking subject and object, the imagined and the real, but what needs to be realized is the manner in which this transformation had been worked out by Man Ray in relation to his larger body of commercial work, his portrait and fashion images.[40]

The distance traveled from an early "document" like Man Ray's photograph of his *Self-Portrait* seems immense. For *Self-Portrait* presented an image of a door (transformed into a face), but it was manifestly a door that could not be entered. The nonfunctional electric bells attached to the painting summon no opening, and Man Ray's indexical handprint at the center of the scene functioned as a gesture of interdiction. *Self-Portrait* underlined the opacity of the picture plane, the closure of the conception of the art object as an interior or "expressive" space, expelling its operations outward into the world, attaching readymades to its surface like excrescences or cancerous growths. In this, *Self-Portrait* presented the art object as a model of subjectivity, a "public" subject built around the collapse of the art-work's metaphorical interiority, a personhood built from the outside, all surface, imprint,

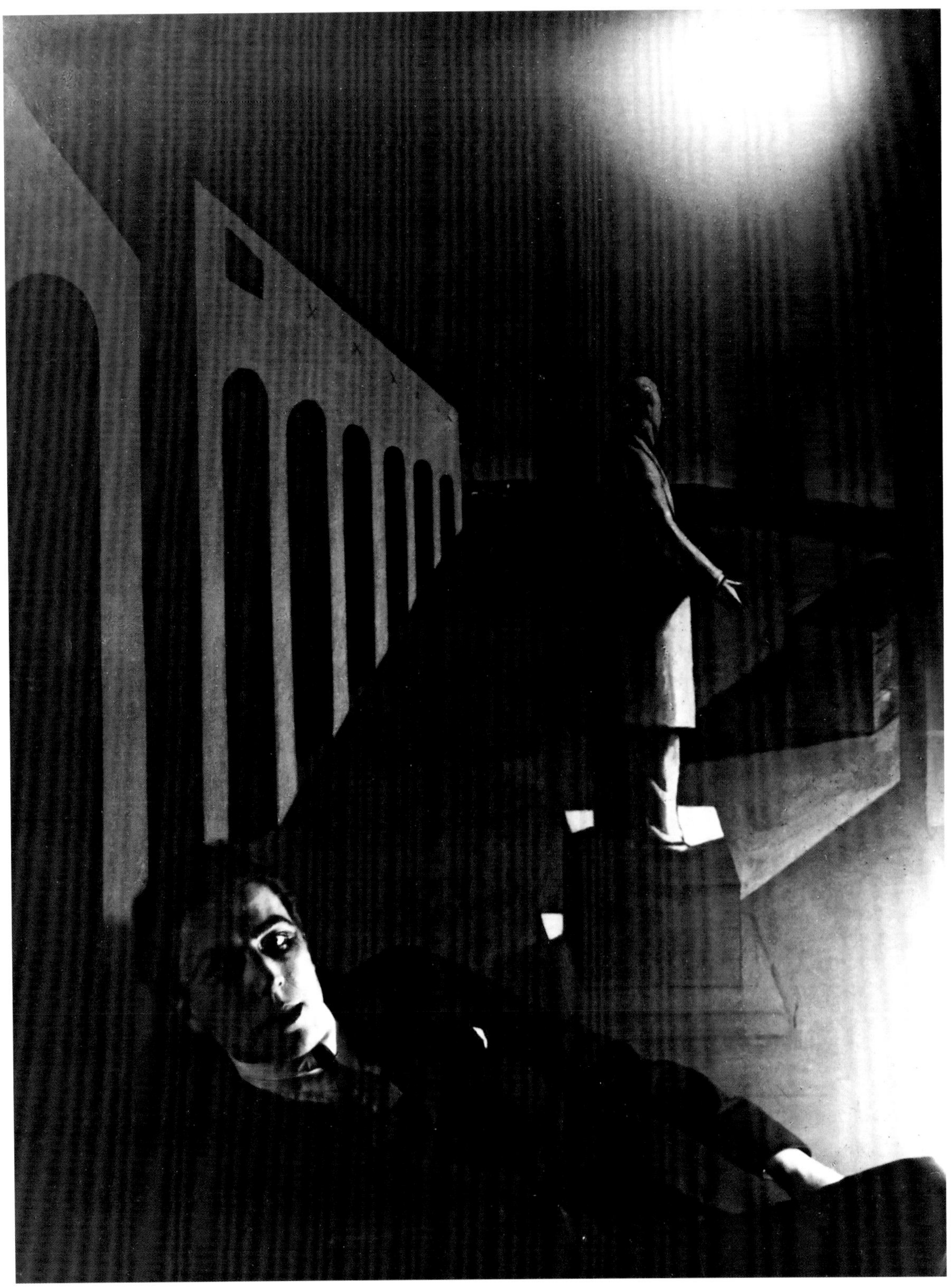

Fig. 27. *André Breton in Front of Giorgio de Chirico's "L'engime d'une journée,"* 1925. Gelatin silver print, 8⅝ × 6⁷⁄₁₆ in. (22 × 16.4 cm). Isidore Ducasse Fine Arts

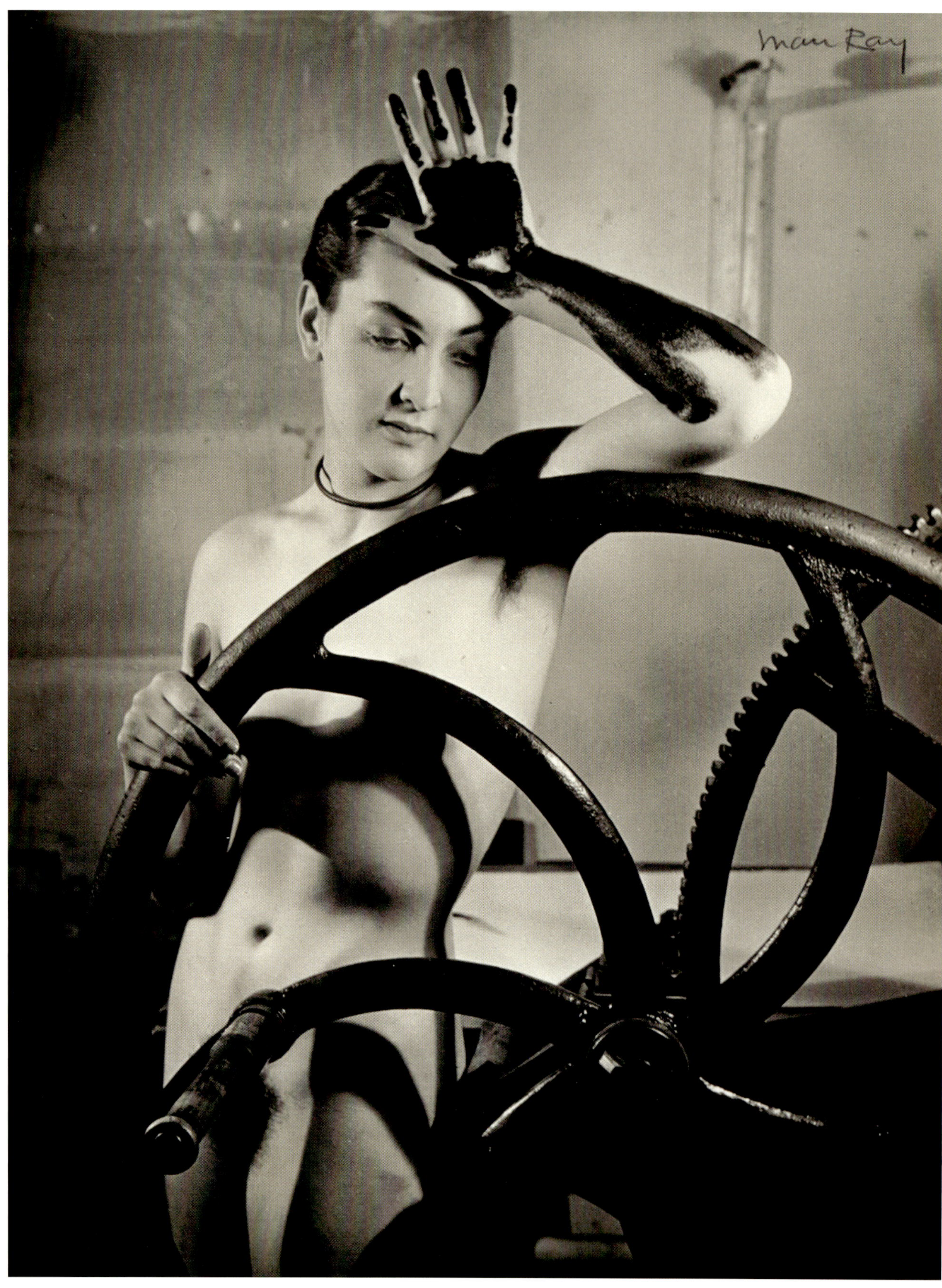

Fig. 28. *Érotique-Voilée*, 1933. Gelatin silver print, 11½ × 8¹⁵⁄₁₆ in. (29.2 × 22.7 cm). Museum of Fine Arts, Houston, Museum purchase with funds provided by the Caroline Wiess Law Accessions Endowment Fund, The Manfred Heiting Collection

and exterior.[41] Consequently the painting called not for the expressive visions of the artist but the activation of its public, the shared condition of all its viewers on the external side of its inscrutable scene.

The logic of the prop relates to this external model of the work of art, but it also transcends it. We face, yet again, another sublation. On the other side of the closure of the interior space of art, the extermination of the expressive model of the artist, there exists a different form of interiority. It would be a model the avant-garde enthusiastically embraced, and that the culture industry never ceased to mine. It entails the involution of the space of the aesthetic and the real. In 1934, Man Ray creates a series of photographs of his recently completed painting *A l'heure d'observatoire—les amoureux* (*Observatory Time—The Lovers*). They are interior shots, taken in Man Ray's living space, the painting hung upon a wall. Beneath it, Man Ray will photograph a nude woman from behind, the curves of her body taken up by the painting's own, the latter's outsize lips matched to the arc of hip, mouth aligned with posterior, the body as passive (anal) object for the gaze. Man Ray also photographed himself beneath the work, his head just touching the bottom of the painting's frame, and in another version, casts of classical sculpture—a bust and torso—that he had been using in his fashion photographs. In the most striking image of the series, Man Ray photographs a woman prostrate beneath the painting, modeling "a beach coat by Heim of white silk painted with little brown foxes," as the image was captioned upon its publication in the November 1936 issue of *Harper's Bazaar*.[42] Cropped so that the painting exactly bifurcates the scene, and so that its edges stretch to the limits of the photographic print, the image now seems to assert that painted space and the space of the real have become one, an effect of fusion amplified by the pointed transgression of the model's languid fingers breaking into the arena of the painting. Her hands rise up to the painting in a gesture unlike the interdiction of *Self-Portrait*, her outstretched palm all invitation, submission, and reverence, a summons to worship or to communion, a gesture of acquiescence.

Such is the logic of the prop within Man Ray's photographs of works of art, a logic determined by the more general relation of his (commercial) photography to his (artistic) project as a painter. The prop opens up an involution of subject and object, the real and the imaginary, actual space and the image world. It reveals a spectacle logic, we might say, of the real becoming an image, and the image world becoming real (fig. 28). By the 1930s, Man Ray would not just photograph Giacometti's *objets sans base*, his sculptural aesthetic of the prop, he would commission Giacometti to produce actual props for the photographer's fashion labors (a background screen of abstract birds in flight, the heavy sculptural object taken to the air, so many shades of Brancusi's *Maiastra*). Simultaneously, he would return to Brancusi, requesting Brancusi's large abstract sculptural bases, upon which Man Ray would pose the actual bodies of his fashion models, the ultimate fusion of body with art object, fashion with sculpture. For the logic of the prop was not just a Surrealist imperative. The prop fused the Surrealist revolution with the needs of the culture industry, if it were not in fact discovered in the latter domain. The image pushed out into the space of the world not only opened onto the transgressive becoming-real of the aesthetic, it also implied the eventual aestheticization of the real. Its fusion opened up a logic of dependency, the logic of the prop, linking the hopes of the avant-garde—the merger of "art and life"—to the radical undoing of any distinction between the realm of the image and the real.

to be Continued unnoticed

We could continue to trace the transformations within Man Ray's photography, as the aesthetic of industry mutated into the industrialization of the aesthetic. We have only just begun: For example, one could point to Man Ray's early assertion of the "birth" of the object at the time of Dada (*My First Born, First Object*), inverted in his later acceptance of what he called his *Last Object*, the "indestructible object," a move from the physical thing to the dissemination of the image: from First Object to Last. Or one could explore his Nadar-like pantheon of portrait photographs of artists and intellectuals, the great interwar assertion of the exceptional subject—an early project of what we now call celebrity—transformed in the 1930s by Man Ray's taking up of many of these images as part of his own "self-portrait" in the publication *Photographs by Man Ray 1920 Paris 1934.*[43] Here, the images would be associated with Man Ray's self-image as classical bust, entering the project into his larger concern at this point with classicism's rendering of the body and the subject as a deadened, passive object: from Exceptional to Damaged Subject.

We could continue, but Man Ray did not. Fleeing the rising tide of war and fascism, Man Ray left Paris to return to New York in 1940. There his primary welcome and recognition—much to his dismay—came from advertising agencies; he was received as a commercial photographer.[44] Fleeing this welcome in turn, Man Ray made the only logical move for someone seeking to elude his usefulness to the industries of culture: he settled in Los Angeles. There, like so many other European exiles and émigrés, he was confronted by the true onset of the culture industry, by the machine of Hollywood.[45] But faced with the realities of the culture industry in the site of its greatest early development—in the place of its new-found "capital"—Man Ray's entire model of artistic production collapses, or (once again) utterly shifts. For the most part, the greatest avant-garde photographer in France abandons photography in the ensuing years, and for the rest of his life, dedicating himself instead to the Duchampian hermeticism of the visual-verbal pun, a Magritte-like unworking of the very ground of representation. He abandons all work with the fashion magazines. Faced with the films of Hollywood, he ceases his cinematic production as well. He returns to painting. He will accept a photographic commission from time to time, but he proceeds to mock his renown as a portrait photographer, refusing to sign in any traditional way, for example, his portrait of a new friend, the Dutch painter Knud Merrild, insisting instead when it is reproduced that it be labeled "Trial for television makeup on Knud Merrild by Man Ray."[46] From this point begin his denigrations of the culture industry roles he had earlier enthusiastically embraced—advertising, fashion designer, decorator.[47] And his conclusions about Hollywood were equally severe: "There was more Surrealism rampant in Hollywood than all the Surrealists could invent in a lifetime," Man Ray would conclude. When asked if he would want to make a Hollywood movie, he replied: "It is like asking me to set up a new religion in a country swarming with cults and temples."[48]

Man Ray had entered into his culture industry activities as a set of performative *roles*, an advance diagnosis of the reality of the interplay of art and commerce, and a critical transformation of the limits and traditional forms of art. But faced with the full colonization of the spaces and functions he had himself carved out, he retreated. Or rather, he created another apotheosis, yet one more sublation. For in fact, Man Ray did make at least one major contribution to a film during his Hollywood years. It was a film that turned the culture industry against itself, destroyed Man Ray's earlier destruction of the autonomy of the avant-garde, an assault as if from within: a self-annihilation of Man Ray's culture industry model. Asked to participate in Hans Richter's 1947 collective film project *Dreams that Money Can Buy*—a "story of dreams mixed with reality"—Man Ray submits the scenario "Ruth, Roses, and Revolvers." And here, as realized by Richter, we watch a movie about movies. We watch an audience enter a movie theater. They are told that they will have "the privilege tonight of witnessing one of the most unusual films ever produced." Whatever "it may lack in the way of sound and color," they are instructed, "you may supply out of your own conversations." They are then implored, however, "to collaborate even more actively." As the film within the film begins, an actor appears on-screen, sitting before an image of the glaring eyes of Man Ray himself, staring at the audience within the film and the audience outside of that too, a panoptic assertion of the author's cultural power (cropped from the artist's "Hollywood" self-portrait, an image of the artist under the crosshairs of a gun). The actor beneath Man Ray's eyes begins to move, to strike a series of ludicrous poses. And the audience within the film moves too, following him, imitating his every action, laying head on hand in thought, standing on their chairs, kneeling down when he kneels down to pray, eventually leaving the theater altogether as the actor exits the scene.

As opposed to the gesture Man Ray had made years earlier when, in 1930, he had been asked to produce "special effects" for an aristocrat's ball and projected some found Méliès films onto the dancing guests all dressed in white, as if they were a screen—fusing the cinema and its audience, the primitive and the modern, the popular and the aristocratic, the image and the space of the real—now Man Ray desiccates the space of cinema.[49] He has the audience, like the actor, abandon the scene, emptying out the image he had formerly been concerned to fill, and to excess. Furthermore, the avant-garde hopes of Man Ray's earlier decades—the Surrealist strategy of the double, the Dada activation of the viewer— come to be utterly turned around. These earlier avant-garde dreams now erupt in the reality of a mimetic image of conformism, the passive identification of the audience with the products of the screen—precisely the totality and control that would bring writers like

Adorno to focus on the imperatives of the culture industry in connection to their larger wartime analysis of the rise of fascism.

It is thus only wrapped in bitter irony that we can hear Man Ray assert, in an unpublished note, that having had Richter produce his scenario, he had enjoyed exploring "the combined role of entertainer and entertained." For such was the dystopic vision of his film, not just its method of production. He would conclude, enigmatically: "To wear a beard and not wear one at the same time is indeed an achievement."[50] Man Ray seems to connect "Ruth, Roses, and Revolvers" to a self-image he produced at this same time, returning to the labor of the barber: *Self-Portrait with Half Beard* (fig. 29). It was an image that depicted Man Ray as the title described, his face bifurcated by a half-beard, split down the middle as if in memory of Léo Malet's *objets reflets* of the late 1930s, advertising images upon which Malet perched a mirror at a perpendicular angle, splitting the image in two, multiplying the space of advertisement into the space of the Surrealist double and the dream. Man Ray's image, if a mirror were placed at its center, would erupt in two complete self-images, but utterly at odds, "wearing a beard and not wearing one at the same time."[51] And it was not a dream. More a nightmare: The split and the contradiction here speak to a vision that could no longer be sustained. We see Man Ray not just as bearded and shaved, as entertainer and entertained, as painter and photographer, as ethnic (Jewish) and assimilated, as working class and bourgeois at once. We see the model of the artist as Man Ray had hoped to sustain it. We see the terminus of an exploration. We see the decimated option of what had once been Man Ray's culture industry, the ambivalent attempt to suspend art between two realms that would broach no resolution in the aesthetic sphere, nor their sublation. We see the artist suspended between labor and capital. We see Man Ray caught between the jobs of the working class and the tasks of the culture industry.

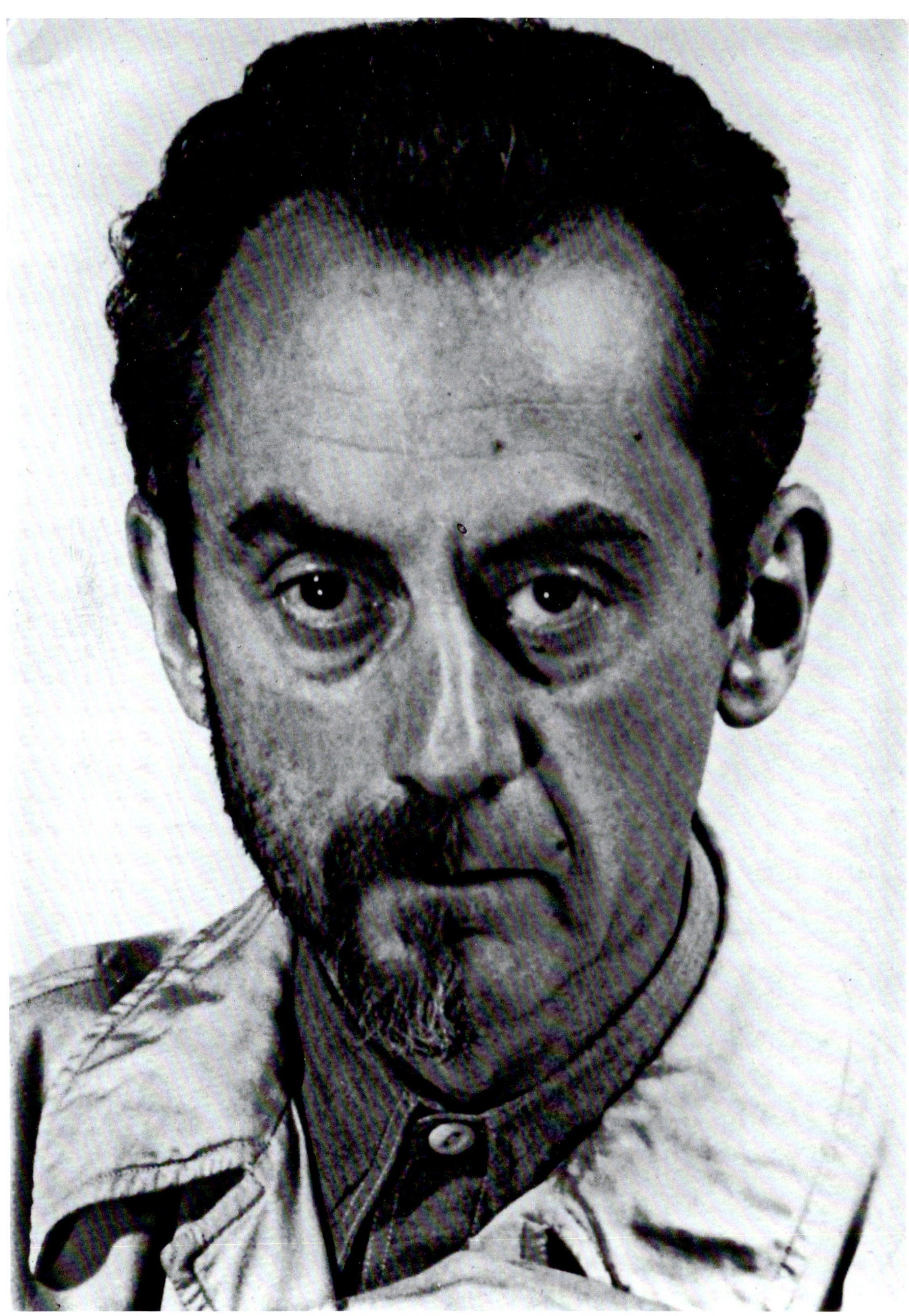

Fig. 29. *Self-Portrait with Half Beard,*
1948. Gelatin silver print, 7⅛ × 5⅛ in.
(18.1 × 13 cm). Naomi Savage Estate

Man Ray

A Cultural Timeline, 1890–1976

> "When exactly were you born, Man Ray?"
>
> "Read my book."
>
> "But people who have read your book say that there are no dates in it."
>
> "As far as I am concerned, everything happened simultaneously—like scenery seen from a fast train."
>
> —INTERVIEW WITH MAN RAY, 1964

Lauren Schell Dickens

On August 27, Emmanuel Radnitzky is born, the first child of Melach (Max) and Manya (Minnie) Radnitzky, recent émigrés from Russia to Philadelphia.

In December, Man Ray participates in
the first group exhibition organized by
artists associated with the Ferrer Center.

Man Ray enrolls in evening art classes at the Francisco Ferrer Center, the leading anarchist center in New York City and a gathering place for political radicals like Alexander Berkman, Emma Goldman, and John Weichsel. The Modern School, as it is also called, seeks to create an atmosphere of freedom and self-discovery: it is a forum for discussions about socialism, birth control, free love, Cubism, Futurism, psychoanalysis, feminism, and anarchism. Man Ray later remembers his Ferrer Center art instructor Robert Henri saying, "We should try to assert our individuality even at the risk of being misunderstood."

1912

Anarchism describes a variety of revolutionary social agendas that play an important role in social and labor movements in the United States during the early twentieth century. Emma Goldman, the nation's most famous anarchist, often cites Henry David Thoreau and Walt Whitman for their anarchistic belief in individualism and self-reliance. For many artists and poets associated with the Ferrer Center, anarchism is not only a political philosophy, but also a belief in individual liberation that encompasses lifestyle, literature, and art. Radical politics merge with artistic goals, giving value to individual expression, and urging personal liberation from the traditions of academic painting.

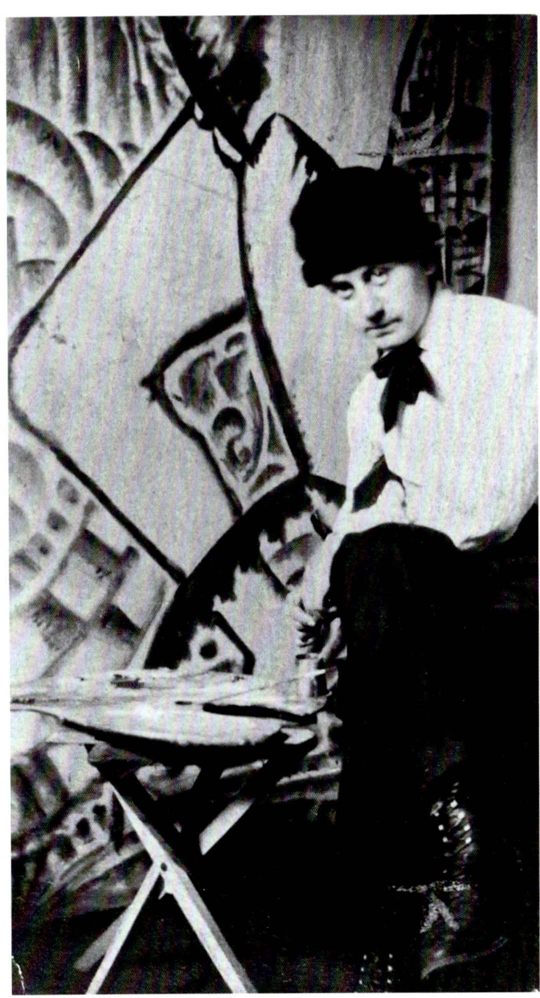

Fig. 7. Man Ray in front of his *Tapestry Painting*, c. 1913. Collection of Constance and Albert Wang

Works by marginalized authors—James Weldon Johnson's anonymously published *Autobiography of an Ex-Colored Man* (1912), Chinese-American Sui Sin Far's (Edith Eaton) *Leaves from the Mental Portfolio of an Eurasian* (1909), and the Santee Sioux Charles Eastman's (Ohiyesa) *Indian Boyhood* (1902) and *From the Deep Woods to Civilization* (1916)— explore the concept of racial "passing," and reflect the strong assimilationist pressures of the period.

1913

In the spring, Man Ray moves to a small artists' colony in Ridgefield, New Jersey, where he shares a cottage with fellow Ferrer Center student Samuel Halpert. They are later joined by the writer Alfred Kreymborg.

On February 17, the *International Exhibition of Modern Art* opens at the Sixty-Ninth Regiment Armory in New York, showcasing more than sixteen hundred works by mostly European artists. The exhibition exposes an estimated seventy-five thousand New York visitors to the concept of modern art—including former President Theodore Roosevelt, who skips Woodrow Wilson's inauguration to see it. While conservative critics view the Armory Show as an attack on the fundamental laws of art, morality, and society, the exhibition also spurs the opening of galleries specializing in modern art, and the emergence of new collectors. The exhibition has a profound effect on many artists, including Man Ray: "I did nothing for six months. It took me that time to digest what I'd seen."

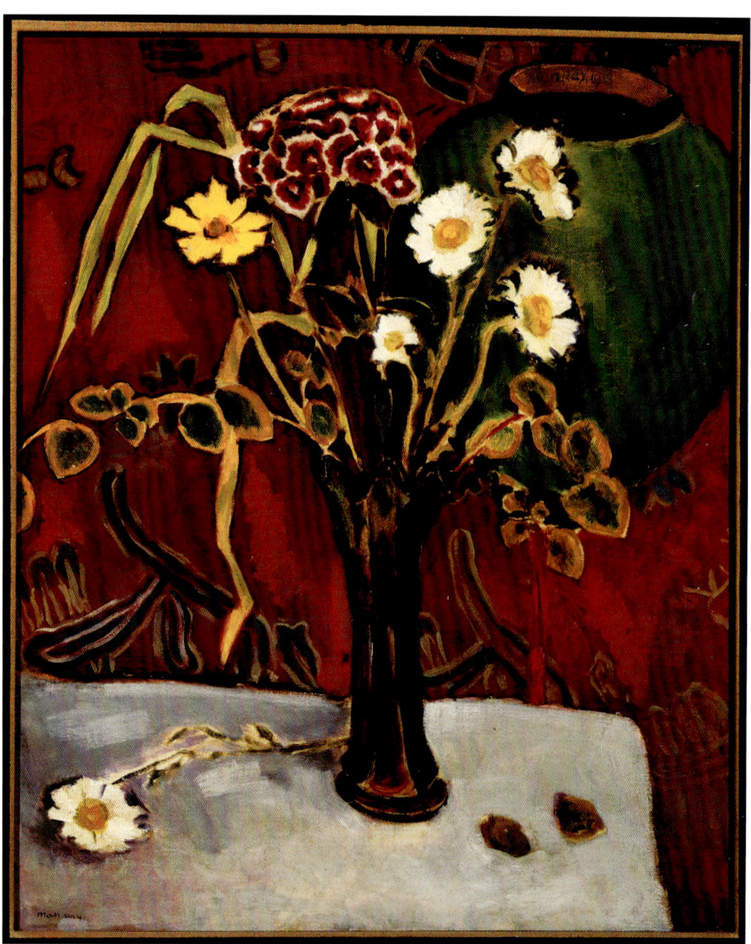

Fig. 8. *Flowers with Red Background*, 1913. Oil on canvas, 24 × 20 in. (61 × 50.8 cm). Collection of Mr. and Mrs. Edward A. Fuller

On a camping trip, Man Ray decides that he will "no longer paint from nature. In fact," he later recounts, "I . . . decided that sitting in front of the subject might be a hindrance to really creative work. . . . After the imaginary landscapes I would paint as inspired by the trip, not only would I cease to look for inspiration in nature; I would turn more and more to man-made sources."

1913

In August, Man Ray meets the Belgian poet Adon Lacroix (then living with Ferrer Center student Adolf Wolff), who introduces him to the writings of Guillaume Apollinaire, Charles Baudelaire, Stéphane Mallarmé, Arthur Rimbaud, and to the Comte de Lautréamont's *Les chants de Maldoror.* Lacroix and her daughter move into Man Ray's Ridgefield cottage, and he and Lacroix marry the following year.

"A man shall never have to take more than one step. . . . The application of these principles is the reduction of the necessity for thought on the part of the worker and the reduction of his movements to a minimum." —Henry Ford, on his invention of the assembly line

As it nears the sixtieth anniversary of its publication, Walt Whitman's *Leaves of Grass* is considered with renewed interest by the artistic community. Inspired by the poet's emphasis on individuality, his overt sexuality, and free verse, Adolf Wolff hails Whitman's work as "A gesture of revolt . . . /A declaration of the right of all/To live, to love, to dare and to do" in the initial issue of the *Glebe.* Throughout his life, Man Ray treasures his own copy of *Leaves of Grass*—a reward for highest marks in a high school English class.

"Little magazines," though often limited in circulation, constitute a primary means for sharing ideas and forging group identities among the avant-garde. These journals are produced mostly in collaboration, combining poetry, essays, and visual art, to voice a group's literary, political, and artistic preoccupations. Some of the important little magazines of the early 1900s focus on discussions of anarchism, nationalism, gender and sexuality, modern poetry, photography, and visual art.

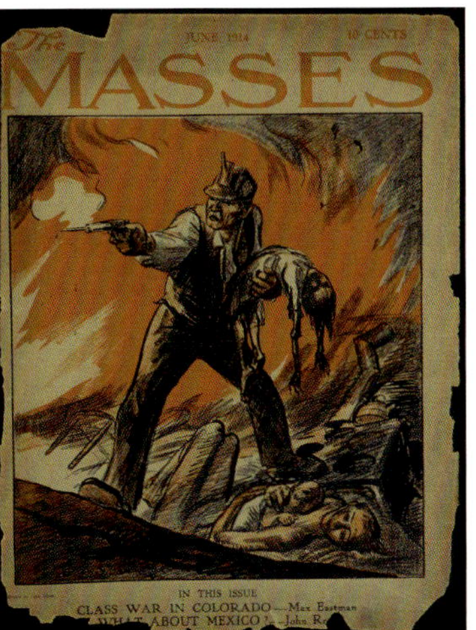

Fig. 9. John Sloan, *Miner at Ludlow, Colorado.* Cover of *The Masses,* June 1914. Tamiment Library, New York University

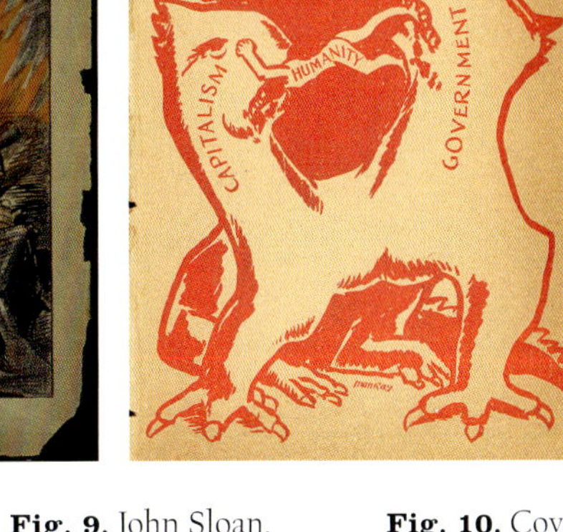

Fig. 10. Cover of *Mother Earth* with drawing by Man Ray, August 1914. Widener Library, Harvard University, Cambridge, Massachusetts

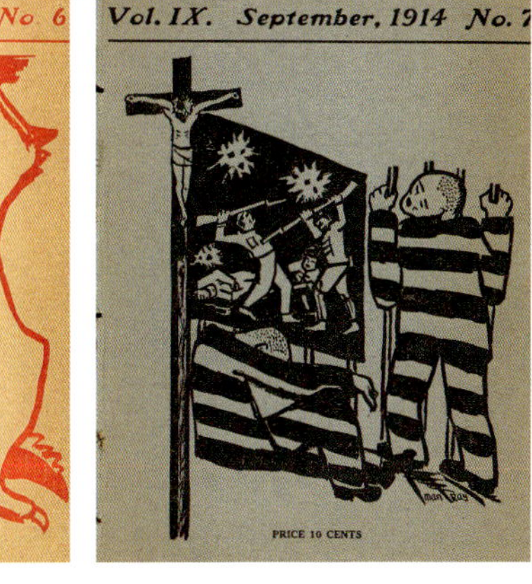

Fig. 11. Cover of *Mother Earth,* with drawing by Man Ray, September 1914. Widener Library, Harvard University, Cambridge, Massachusetts

1913

Man Ray's first published poem, "Travail," appears in the fall issue of the Ferrer Center's publication, the *Modern School*. Inspired by the shock of the Armory Show, Alfred Kreymborg hopes to catalyze similar poetic experimentation in America. Together he and Man Ray produce the first issue of the literary journal *Glebe* (1913–14).

1914

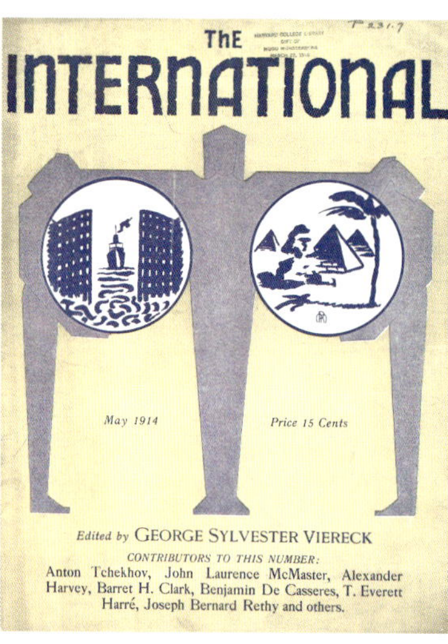

Fig. 13. Cover of *The International*, with drawing by Man Ray, May 1914. Widener Library, Harvard University, Cambridge, Massachusetts

"Man Ray is a youthful alchemist forever in quest of the painter's philosopher's stone. May he never find it, as this would bring an end to his experimentations which are the very condition of living art expression."—Adolf Wolff, "Art Notes" in *International*

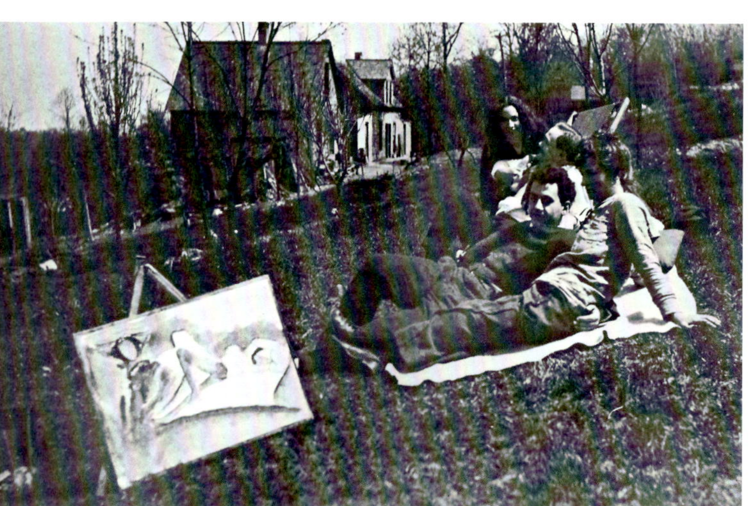

Fig. 12. Wedding day in Ridgefield, New Jersey, May 1914. Collection of Neil Baldwin. Front to back: Adon Lacroix, Man Ray, Alanson Hartpence, Helen Slade. Photographed with a painting Man Ray made to commemorate the occasion

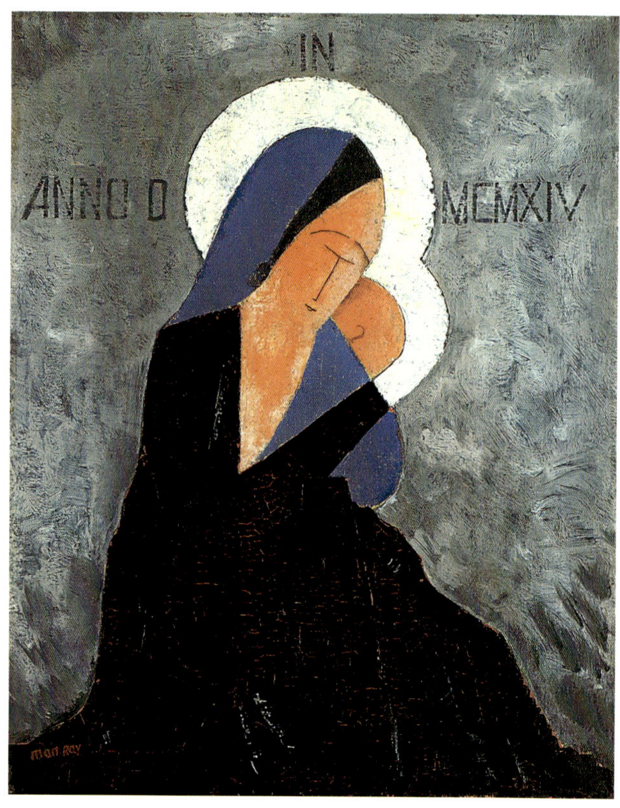

Fig. 14. *Madonna*, 1914. Oil on canvas, 20¹⁄₁₆ × 16⅛ in. (50.9 × 41 cm). Columbus Museum of Art, Ohio, Gift of Ferdinand Howald

World War I erupts in Europe, driving many European artists to New York during the following years.

1914

Arensberg Salon: Walter and Louise Arensberg host evenings at their Manhattan apartment, which becomes the informal meeting place for avant-garde and Dada activities in New York. Surrounded by the Arensbergs' collection of works by Constantin Brancusi, Georges Braque, Matisse, and Henri Rousseau, as well as African and pre-Columbian sculptures, Gabrielle Buffet-Picabia describes a "motley international band" that turns "night into day, conscientious objectors of all nationalities and walks of life living in an inconceivable orgy of sexuality, jazz, and alcohol."

Among those in regular attendance are John Covert, Arthur Cravan, Jean Crotti, Charles Demuth, Marcel Duchamp, the Baroness Elsa von Freytag-Loringhoven, Alfred Kreymborg, Mina Loy, Man Ray, Picabia, and Morton Schamberg.

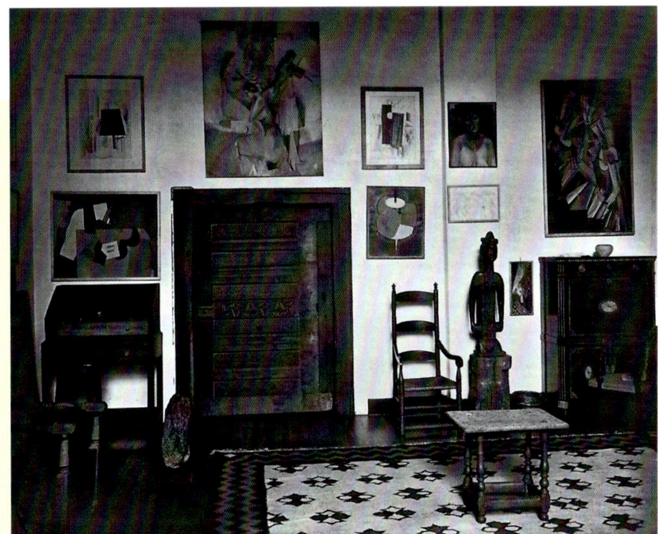

Fig. 16. Living room of apartment of Louise and Walter Arensberg, New York, 1918. Photograph by Charles Sheeler. Philadelphia Museum of Art, Louise and Walter Arensberg Collection, 1950

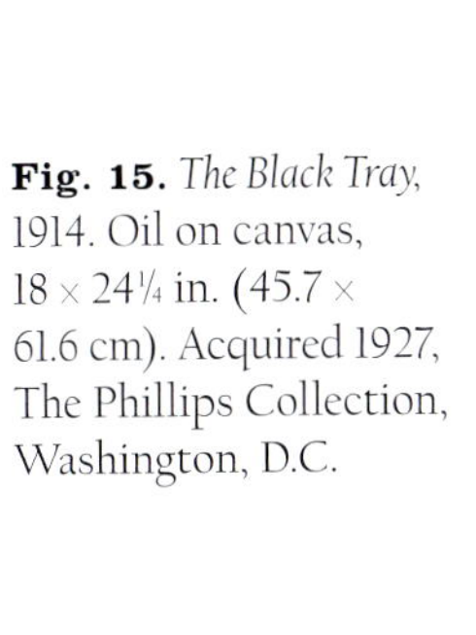

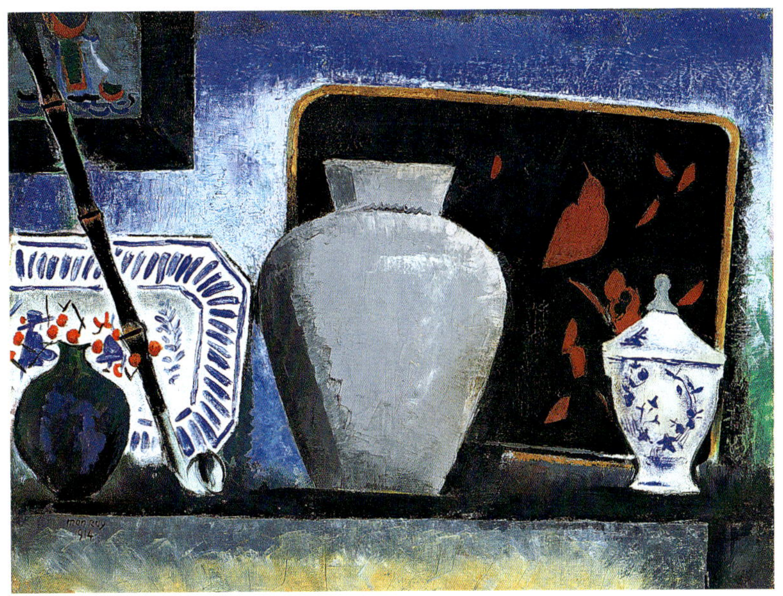

Fig. 15. *The Black Tray*, 1914. Oil on canvas, 18 × 24¼ in. (45.7 × 61.6 cm). Acquired 1927, The Phillips Collection, Washington, D.C.

A Book of Divers Writings, a selection of poems by Adon Lacroix, is designed, calligraphed, and hand-printed by Man Ray. It is followed by the first and only issue of the *Ridgefield Gazook*, designed and produced entirely by Man Ray.

Feminism: The so-called New Woman plays a key role in Greenwich Village life, promoting contraceptives, sexual parity, progressive education, and women's suffrage. Prominent feminist Village activists include Berenice Abbott, Djuna Barnes, Willa Cather, Mabel Dodge, Baroness Elsa von Freytag-Loringhoven, Charlotte Perkins Gilman, Susan Glaspell, Emma Goldman, Mina Loy, Margaret Sanger, and Beatrice Wood, many of whom are known as artists and writers.

John Weichsel, a prominent art critic who champions the positive social role of art in Jewish communities, founds the People's Art Guild. Early participants include Stuart Davis, Robert Henri, Maurice Prendergast, and John Sloan; Man Ray declines, citing the obscurity of exhibition venues. Through its final season in 1918, the Guild shows hundreds of artists and broadens its mission to reach all immigrant communities.

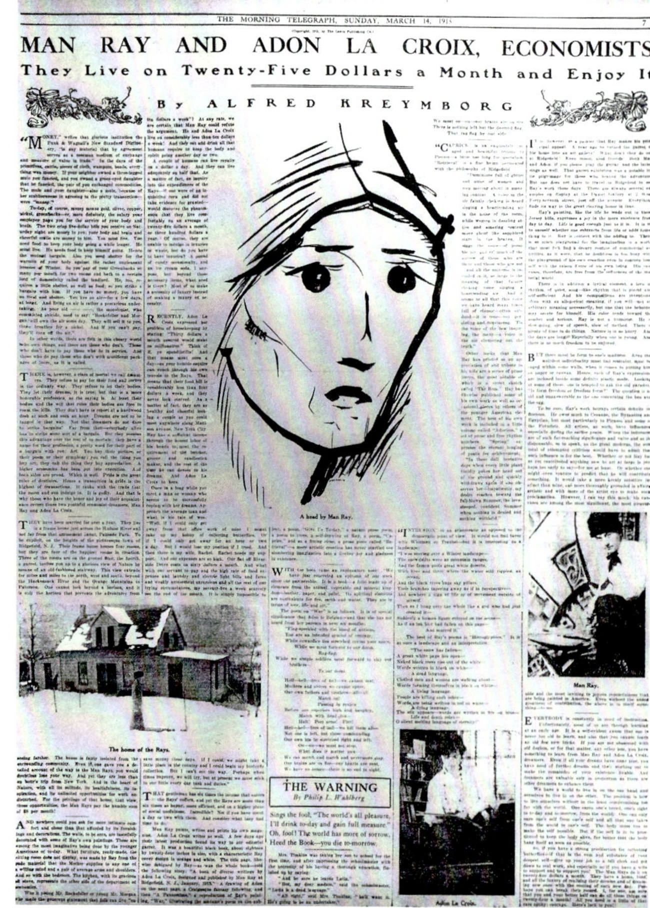

Fig. 17. Alfred Kreymborg "Man Ray and Adon La Croix, Economists," *Morning Telegraph*, New York, March 14, 1915, p. 7. General Research Division, The New York Public Library, Astor, Lenox and Tilden Foundations

1915

Duchamp accompanies Walter Arensberg on an autumn visit to Ridgefield and is introduced to Man Ray. The American and the Frenchman play a game of tennis, without a net and without a common language—their first collaborative Dada performance. "I called out the strokes to make conversation: fifteen, thirty, forty, love," Man Ray later recounts, "to which [Duchamp] replied each time with the same word: yes." The two will continue their friendship and artistic dialogue for more than fifty years.

1915

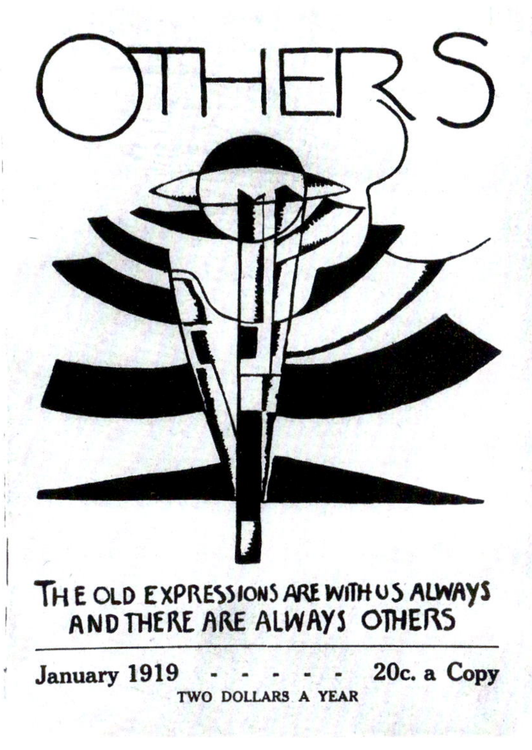

Fig. 18. Cover of *Others*, January 1919

The experimental poetry magazine *Others* (1915–19) is launched by Alfred Kreymborg. The magazine publishes modernists such as Mina Loy, Marianne Moore, Carl Sandburg, and William Carlos Williams, many of whom participate in the Ridgefield colony. Man Ray's poem "Three Dimensions" appears in the magazine's second issue.

"Psycho-analysis is the greatest discovery made by intellectual conversationalists since [Henri] Bergson and the [International Workers of the World]," Floyd Dell writes in *Vanity Fair.* Psychoanalysis, or Freudianism, is a term widely used to describe a variety of psychological explorations. Freud is embraced, however inaccurately, as an advocate of sexual and political reform, and psychoanalysis is an increasingly fashionable part of the intellectual movement against convention, censorship, and traditional conceptions of human behavior. The psychoanalytic interest in dreams and the subconscious will be central to Surrealism as it develops in Europe in the 1920s.

John Weichsel writes an article for the Jewish cultural journal *East and West* arguing that great art can emerge from the Jewish community only when common cultural values give way to individualism as the dominant principle. In November, in "New Art and Man Ray," he describes the artist's work as part of a general trend away from traditional mimetic painting, toward a self-created reality: "Notwithstanding numerous affiliations in his work, Man Ray is distinctly himself. . . . His deepest self will, I believe, eventually furnish a wholly personal manifestation for his strong feeling of form and poetry in color."

In December, Man Ray and Adon Lacroix move into a studio near Grand Central Terminal. As he later recalls, "The racket of concrete mixers and steam drills was constant. It was music to me and even a source of inspiration." The couple will separate in 1918.

In preparation for his first one-man exhibition at the Daniel Gallery in Manhattan, Man Ray photographs his paintings for reproduction in the catalogue. The Chicago collector Arthur J. Eddy purchases six canvases for a total of $2,000.

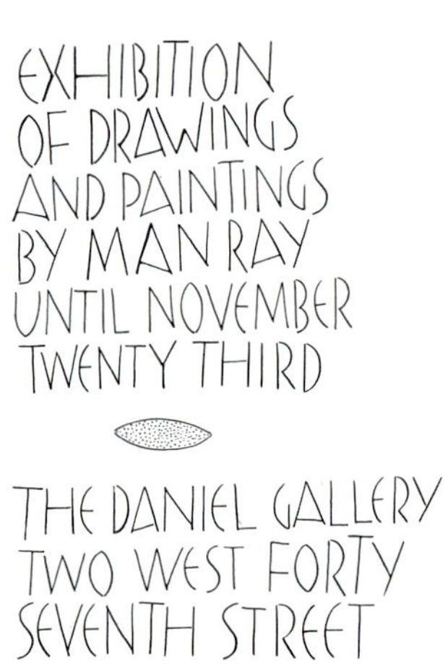

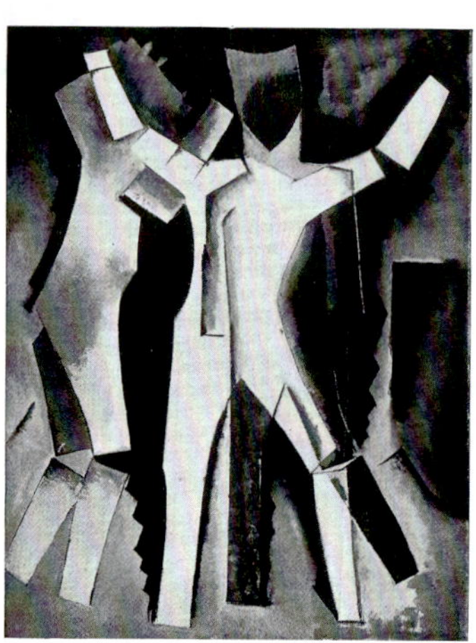

Fig. 19. *Exhibition of Drawings and Paintings by Man Ray,* 1915. Cover and page spread of catalogue for the Daniel Gallery, New York. Collection of Teruo Ishihara, Kyoto

"The machine has become more than a mere adjunct of human life. It is really a part of human life—perhaps the very soul." —Francis Picabia

"A Man, the lover of all through himself stands in his little gray room. His eyes have no sparks—they burn within. . . . The Man is inevitable. Everyone moves him and no one moves him. The Man through all expresses himself.
—Man Ray, homage to Alfred Stieglitz, in "Impressions of 291" in *Camera Work*

Fig. 20. *The Mime*, 1916. Oil on Masonite, 24¼ × 18⅛ in. (61.6 × 46 cm). The Metropolitan Museum of Art, New York, Gift of Everett B. Birch, 1982

Man Ray writes and publishes *A Primer of the New Art of Two Dimensions*, a formalist text that establishes the flat plane as a common basis for all art—music, litera-ture, dance, architecture, painting, and sculpture. A belief in this fundamental unity among media supports Man Ray's lifelong refusal to categorize himself as a painter or a photographer, and his privileging of the idea overall.

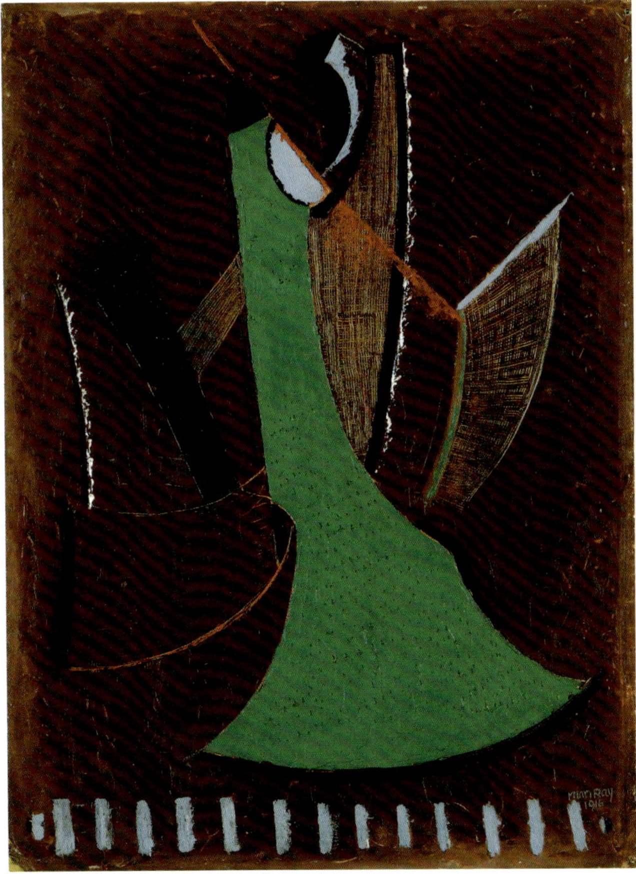

The *Forum Exhibition of Modern American Painters* at the Anderson Galleries in Manhattan is organized to chal-lenge the artistic dominance of Europe evident in the Armory Show. It is the first major exhibition devoted solely to American modern art. In his foreword to the catalogue, Stieglitz comments: "Art as it is looked upon in America to-day is the equivalent in society to what the appendix is to the human body. Scientists are still differing as to whether the appendix is of value or not to the human organism." Man Ray has ten paint-ings and three drawings in the exhibition.

Nationalism in the arts: When, in 1918, the critic Van Wyck Brooks charges artists to dig into America's "usable past," he is one of many voices urging for a national art. William Carlos Williams calls for contact with local culture to create new forms of art, and Robert Coady praises popular culture as the spirit of America. In unison, they encourage artists to ignore Europe and look to their own shores for inspiration, but in a nation of immigrants the substance of popu-lar and local cultures is hotly debated. While the magazine *Seven Arts* recognizes the contribution of immigrants, and Jews in particular, to developing a rich national tra-dition, a more commonly held view is artic-ulated in the 1923 article "Ellis Island Art" by the conservative critic Royal Cortissoz: "The United States is invaded by aliens, thousands of whom constitute so many acute perils to the health of the body politic. Modernism is precisely of the same hetero-geneous alien origin and is imperiling the republic of art in the same way."

Man Ray has a second one-man show at the Daniel Gallery.

1916

1917

The committee for the first exhibition of the Society of Independent Artists, a supposedly jury-free exercise, rejects a urinal that Duchamp has submitted under a pseudonym. The scandal surrounding the rejection of this deliberately offensive object is orchestrated by Duchamp to expose the hypocrisy of the committee, and introduce the notion of Dada into American art. In protest of the rejection, Man Ray removes his *Rope Dancer* from the exhibition, and he, Duchamp, and Walter Arensberg resign from the Society. (Man Ray will, however, show *The Ship "Narcissus"* in the Society exhibition the following year.)

"The fact remains that the greatest work [of art] must bear the stamp of originality. In exactly the same way, the greatest work must bear the stamp of nationalism. American work must smack of our own soil, mental and moral, or it will have little of permanent value."
—Former President Theodore Roosevelt, address to the eighth annual joint meeting of the American Academy of Arts and Letters and the National Institute of Arts and Letters, New York

Camera Work ceases publication and 291 closes. Stieglitz will open An American Place in 1929, and into the thirties and forties will develop a rhetoric of spirituality and national identity in art.

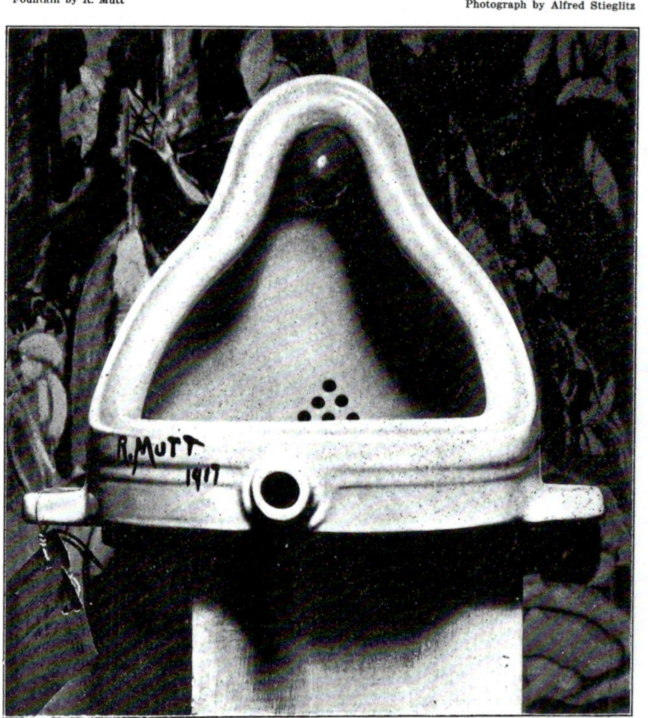

Fig. 21. "The Exhibit Refused by the Independents," page from *The Blind Man (No. 2)*, May 1917, with photograph by Alfred Stieglitz of Marcel Duchamp's *Fountain* (1917), attributed to R. Mutt. Philadelphia Museum of Art, Louise and Walter Arensberg Collection, 1950

The Espionage Act is passed, outlawing public opposition to the war. By the end of the summer, the U.S. postmaster will suppress circulation of eighteen radical magazines, and Alexander Berkman, Eugene Debs, Emma Goldman, Bill Haywood, and others will be arrested.

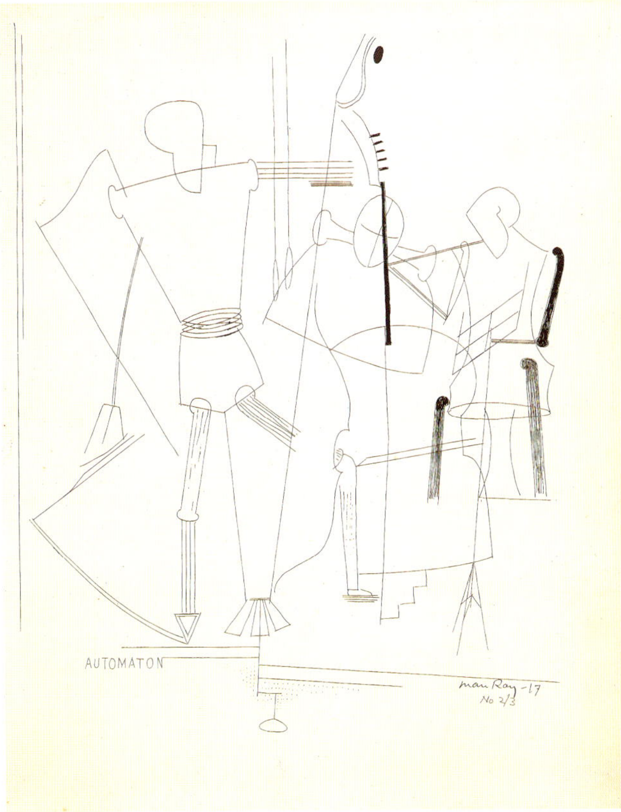

Fig. 22. *Automaton*, 1917. Cliché-verre, 9¼ × 7½ in. (23.5 × 19.1 cm). Private collection, New York

Fig. 23. *Destroy This Mad Brute*, c. 1917. Poster by H. R. Hopps. This anti-German propaganda poster was intended to motivate enlistment in the U.S. Army. Ann Ronan Picture Library, London

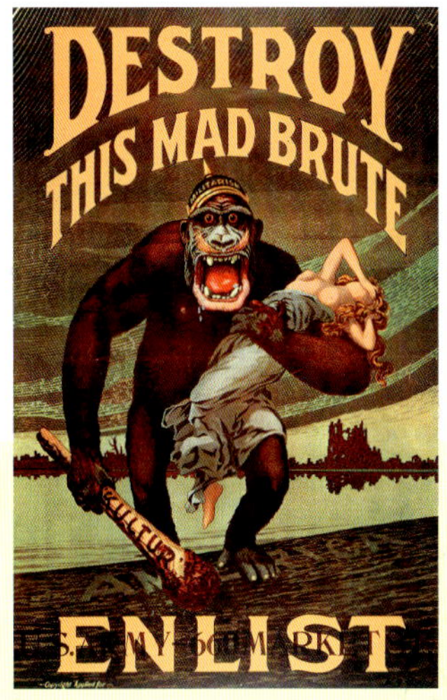

New York Dada, a group named in hindsight, includes American and European artists and poets who congregate at the Arensbergs' during the years of World War I. While Dada in Europe tends to deal directly with the horrors of the first industrialized war, New York Dada has a more playfully irreverent and antiacademic, though nonetheless political, approach. Joseph Stella, a frequent visitor to the Arensbergs' home, remarks that Dada is a "movement that does away with everything that has always been taken seriously. To poke fun at, to break down, to laugh at, that is Dadaism." By challenging accepted norms of art and culture, the New York Dadaists, many of whom are European transplants, also seek to liberate themselves from the increasingly oppressive social and patriotic constraints of wartime America.

The Anarchist Exclusion Act is passed, banning the immigration of anarchists into the United States, and legalizing deportation of alien anarchists. Emma Goldman and Alexander Berkman will be deported under this act in 1919.

With Adolf Wolff, Man Ray publishes the only issue of the anarchist journal *TNT*, which includes a reproduction of his first aerograph (airbrush painting), *My First Born*. "It was thrilling," he later says, "to paint a picture, hardly touching the surface—a purely cerebral act."

"Dada was born of a need for independence, of a distrust toward unity. Those who are with us preserve their freedom. We recognize no theory. We have enough cubist and futurist academies: laboratories of formal ideas."
—Tristan Tzara, First Dada Manifesto

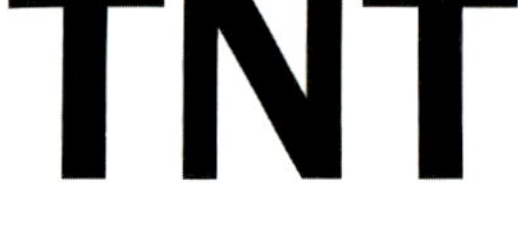
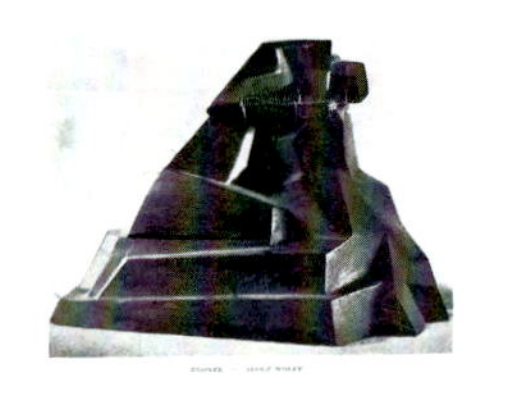

Fig. 25. Cover of *TNT*, March 1919. Lithograph (pamphlet). Philadelphia Museum of Art, The Louise and Walter Arensberg Collection

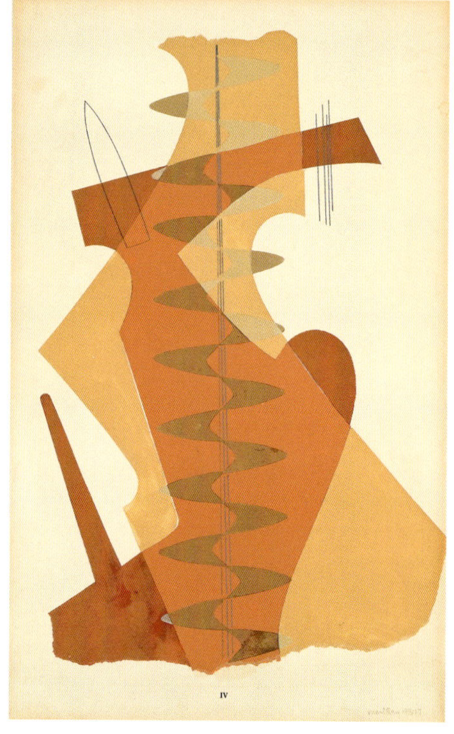

Fig. 26. *Revolving Door Series IV: The Meeting*, 1916–17. Collage on paper, 21¼ × 13¼ in. (51.4 × 33.7 cm). Whitney Museum of American Art, New York, Bequest of Richard S. Zeisler

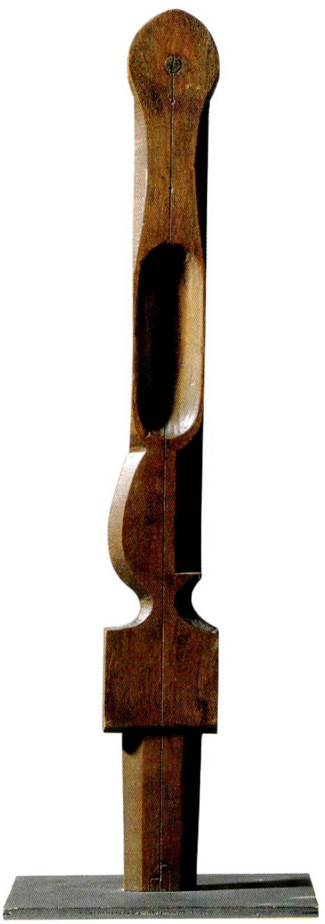

Fig. 24. *By Itself II*, 1918. Wood, 23⅜ × 8¼ × 7½ in. (60 × 21 × 19.1 cm). Kunsthaus Zürich

John Reed writes *Ten Days That Shook the World*, his widely read firsthand account of the Bolshevik rise to power in Russia.

1919

Man Ray: An Exhibition of Selected Drawings and Paintings Accomplished During the Period 1913–1919 opens at the Daniel Gallery to mixed reviews. On display are all ten collages of the *Revolving Doors* series.

1920

Société Anonyme, Inc., the nation's first "experimental museum" for art, is founded by Katherine Dreier, Man Ray, and Duchamp. Its initial exhibition includes Man Ray's *Lampshade*, *Portemanteau*, and *Dancer Danger*, in addition to works by Brancusi, Duchamp, Juan Gris, Picabia, Georges Ribemont-Dessaignes, Morton Schamberg, Joseph Stella, and Vincent van Gogh. Until 1941, the artist-driven institution will present exhibitions, lectures, and related educational programming to promote appreciation for avant-garde art in the United States. Its motto: "Traditions are beautiful—but to create them—not to follow."

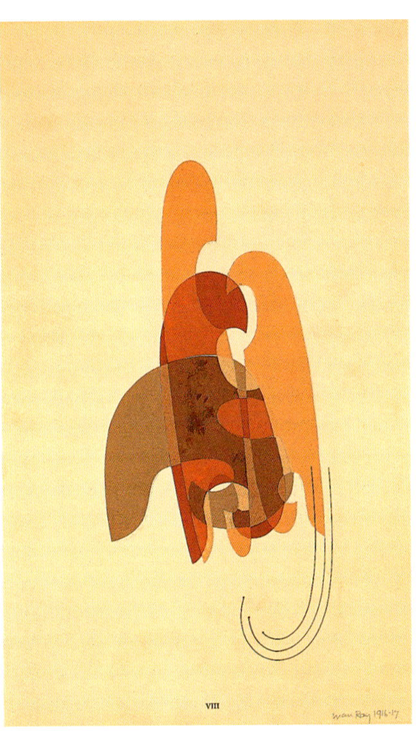

Fig. 27. *Revolving Door Series VII: Young Girl (Jeune Fille)*, 1916–17. Cut colored papers, colored threads, and stamp on paper mounted on cardboard, 22 1/16 × 14 in. (56 × 35.6 cm). Solomon R. Guggenheim Museum, New York, Gift, Estate of Geraldine Spreckles Fuller, 1999

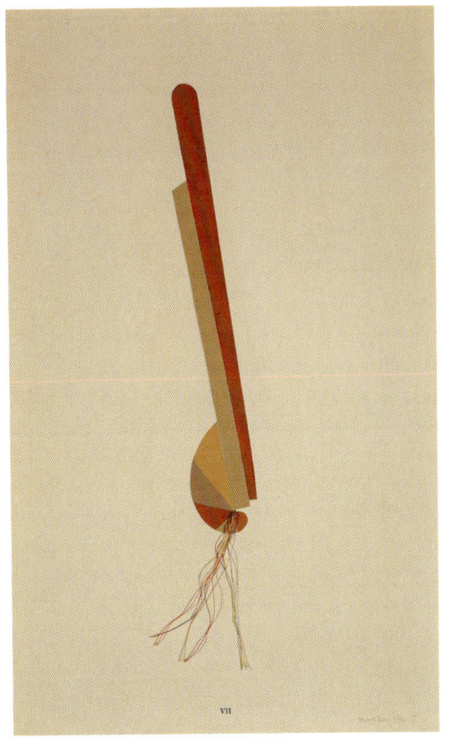

Fig. 28. *Revolving Door Series VIII: Shadows*, 1916–17. Collage on paper, 21 × 14 in. (53.3 × 35.6 cm). Private collection of Cornelia and Meredith Long

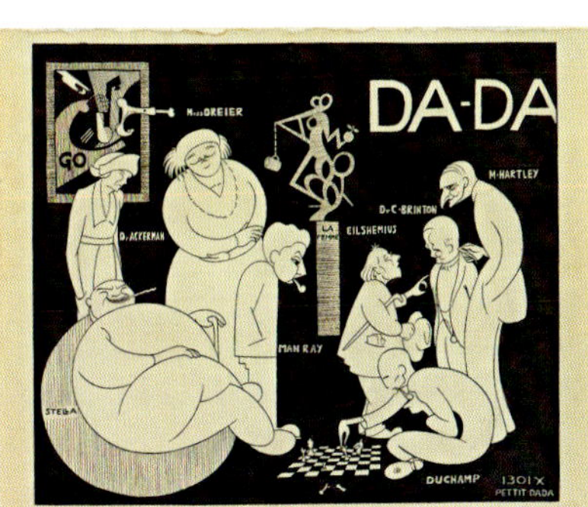

Fig. 29. Richard Boix, *DA-DA (New York Dada Group)*, 1921. Brush, pen, and ink on paper, 11 1/4 × 14 1/2 in. (28.6 × 36.8 cm). The Museum of Modern Art, New York, Katherine S. Dreier Bequest

1921

Man Ray's photograph of Berenice Abbott wins a ten-dollar prize at the *Fifteenth Annual Exhibition of Photographs* at John Wanamaker's department store in Philadelphia.

Man Ray and Duchamp collaborate on their first film (later destroyed) in which the Baroness Elsa von Freytag-Loringhoven shaves her pubic hair. A sculptor, poet, and street performer of sorts, the baroness is known to parade around Greenwich Village wearing a tomato-can brassiere and a birdcage hat with live canary. She exploits her aristocratic title, and her body, to challenge bourgeois notions of taste. In 1922, Jane Heap, who publishes the baroness's poems and essays in the *Little Review*, calls her "the first American dada. She is the only one living anywhere who dresses dada, loves dada, lives dada."

Man Ray and Duchamp collaborate on the creation of Duchamp's alter ego Rose (later Rrose) Sélavy. Though he considers adopting a Jewish persona, Duchamp instead aligns himself with two other marginalized groups: women and homosexuals. Androgyny, practiced in the form of costume balls, cross-dressing, and artistic personae, is a way of expressing a radical mobility by disrupting stable gender identities.

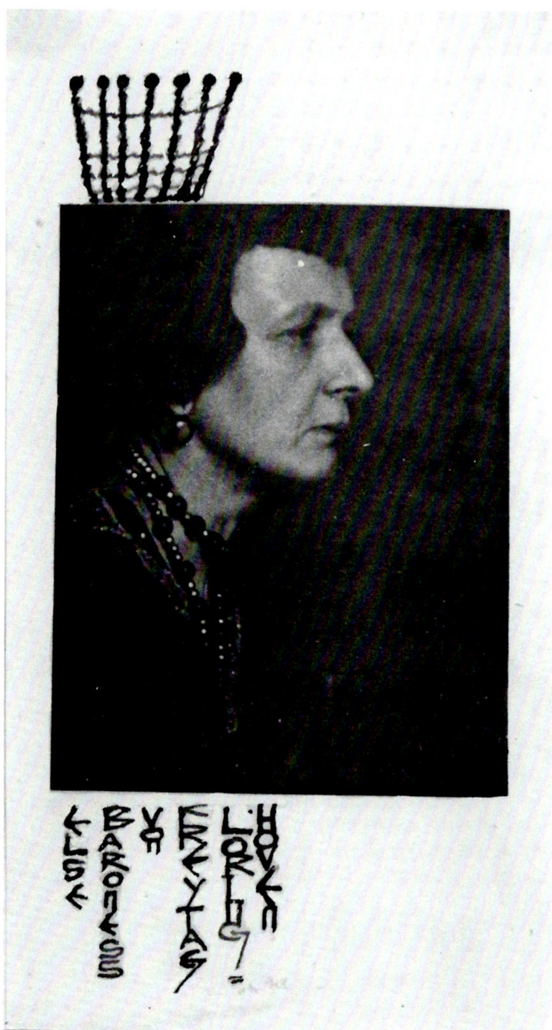

Fig. 30. *Else Baroness von Freytag-Loringhoven,* published in the *Little Review,* September–December 1920

Man Ray and Duchamp publish the first and only issue of *New York Dada.* Two months later Man Ray writes to Tzara: "Dada cannot live in New York. All New York is dada, and will not tolerate a rival."

Man Ray leaves New York on the SS *Savoie* for France. He will remain in Paris for the next nineteen years.

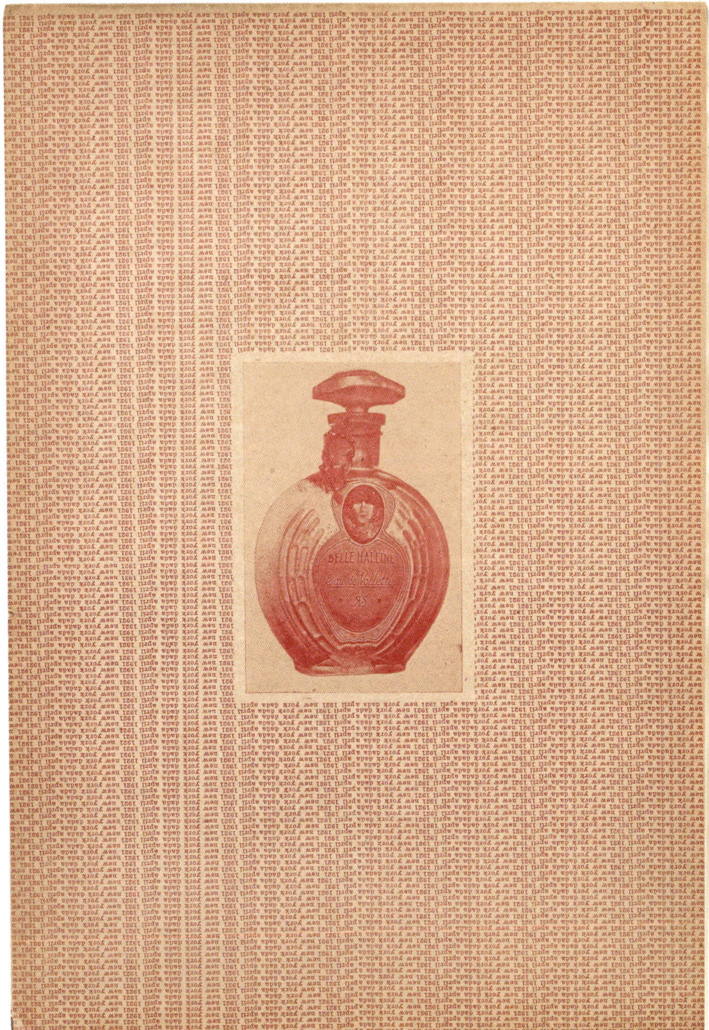

"The Dadaist may be a child with a new toy, but he is a perverse and destructive imp, a ruthless smasher of his own and every one else's Dada. His nursery breathes an atmosphere of decadence and dynamite. He is for the annihilation of logic, memory, archaeology, prophecy, and the absolute. He is anti-everything —except anti-Semitic." —Henry Tyrell, "DADA: The Cheerless Art of Idiocy," *World Magazine*

Fig. 31. Cover of *New York Dada*, 1921. Spencer Collection, Humanities and Social Services Library, New York Public Library. Man Ray and Duchamp's collaborative creation of Rrose Sélavy is shown on the cover

"Dada is a state of mind. It consists largely of negations. It is the tail of every other movement—Cubism, Futurism, Simultanism, the last being closely related."—Man Ray, quoted in "Dada Will Get You If You Don't Watch Out: It Is on the Way Here," *New York Evening Journal*

In his autobiography, Man Ray recounts that he reaches Paris on July 14, thus connecting his arrival with France's Independence Day; in fact, he arrives the following week. Duchamp takes him to the Café Certa, where he meets Dadaists Louis Aragon, André Breton, Jean Cocteau, Paul Éluard, Jacques Rigaut, and Philippe Soupault. "I came to Paris and suddenly ran into the Dada movement," he later recalls. "These were youngsters who really had an ideal . . . a violence, an enthusiasm, a conviction, which I'd never come across in America except amongst anarchists."

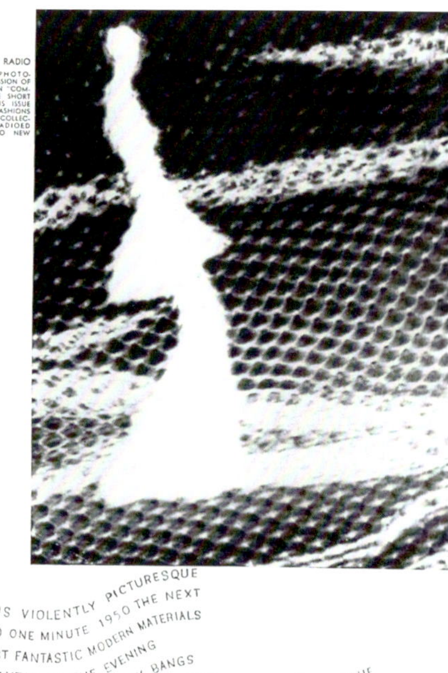

Fig. 33. "Fashions by Radio," with photograph by Man Ray, *Harper's Bazaar,* November 1936

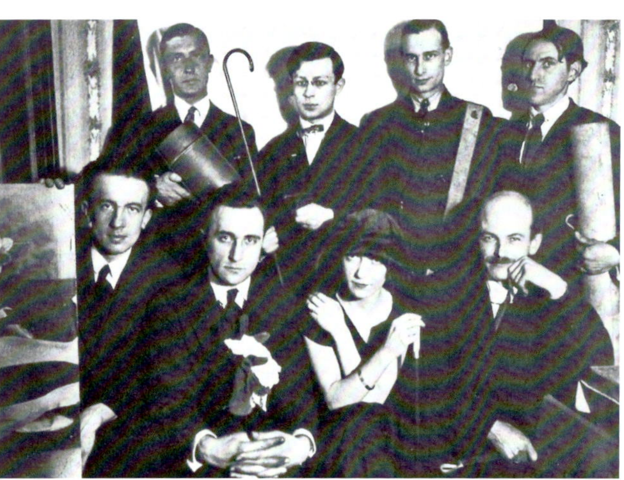

Fig. 32. A group of Dadaists, November 1921. Top row, from left: Paul Chadourne, Tristan Tzara, Philippe Soupault, Serge Charchoune; bottom row: Paul Éluard, Jacques Rigaut, Mick Soupault, Georges Ribemont-Dessaignes. Photograph by Man Ray

Man Ray meets the fashion designer Paul Poiret and begins a successful career in fashion photography. By the 1930s he is working regularly for *Vogue* and *Harper's Bazaar.*

1921

Man Ray moves into the Hôtel des Écoles in Mont-parnasse, the epicenter of artistic life in Paris, and meets Kiki de Montparnasse (Alice Prin). She will be his mistress and model for the next seven years.

Man Ray makes his first rayograph.

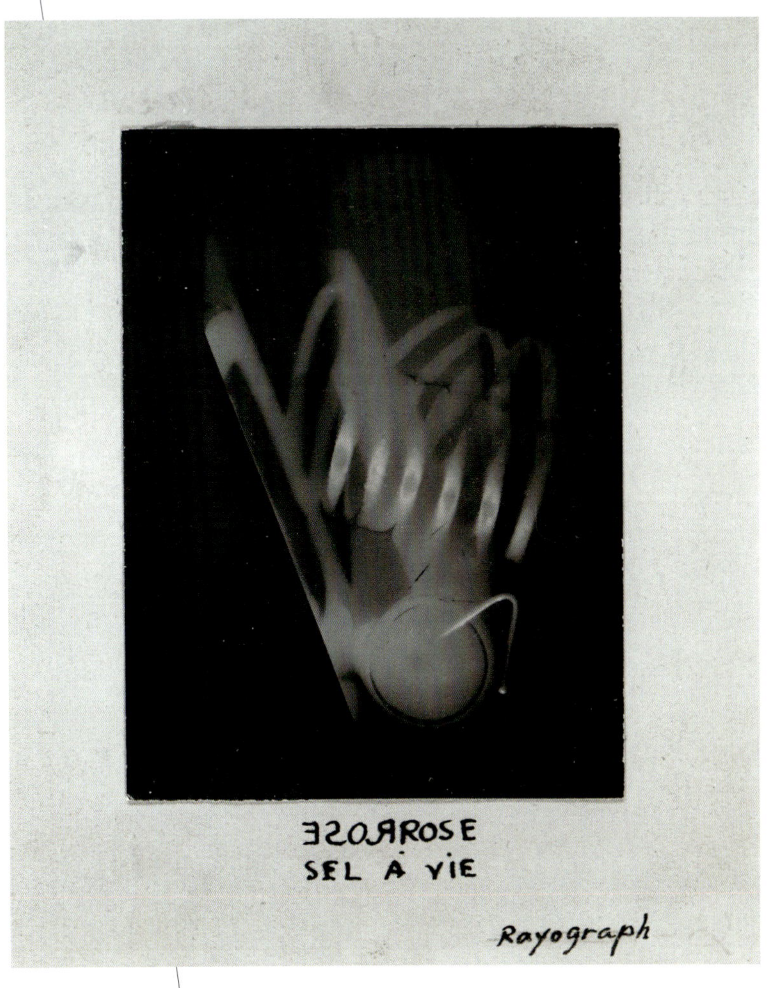

Paris Dada: In early 1920, the Dadaists are a succès de scandale, drawing hundreds of people to their spectacular exhibitions and performances. They are often portrayed in the press as spoiled, sexually perverted, left-leaning Jews and Bolsheviks intent on destruction and mayhem. "They ought to be burned at the stake. . . . Those who are at the head of this Dada movement are merchants of dementia and entrepreneurs of madness," one French critic writes in 1920. While the Dadaists are always more of a framework of shifting alliances than a unified movement, by the time Man Ray arrives, feuding has erupted and the group is collapsing.

The *Exposition dada Man Ray* opens at Librarie Six in Paris on December 3. The catalogue includes notes by the artist, as well as Aragon, Jean (Hans) Arp, Éluard, Max Ernst, Georges Ribemont-Dessaignes, and Soupault, and an introduction by Tzara: "One no longer remembers where Mr. Ray was born. After having been a coal merchant, a millionaire several times over, and the chairman of a chewing-gum trust, he decided he was open to the Dadaists' invitation to show his latest paintings in Paris."

"I now turned all my attention to getting myself organized as a professional photographer, getting a studio and installing it to do my work more efficiently," Man Ray recounts years later. "I was going to make money—not wait for recognition that might or might not come." He finds a place at 31 bis, rue Campagne-Première, one of the more expensive studio buildings in Paris.

The Salon des Indépendants exhibits three pieces by Man Ray. His work receives no attention and he vows to never again submit to the Salon (though he does the following year).

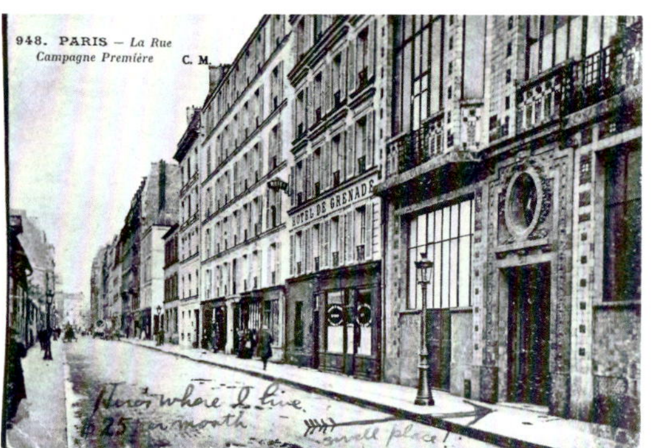

Fig. 35. Postcard from Man Ray to his parents announcing his move to 31 bis, rue Campagne-Première, July 1922: "Here's where I live, $25 a month—a swell place!" Collection of Neil Baldwin

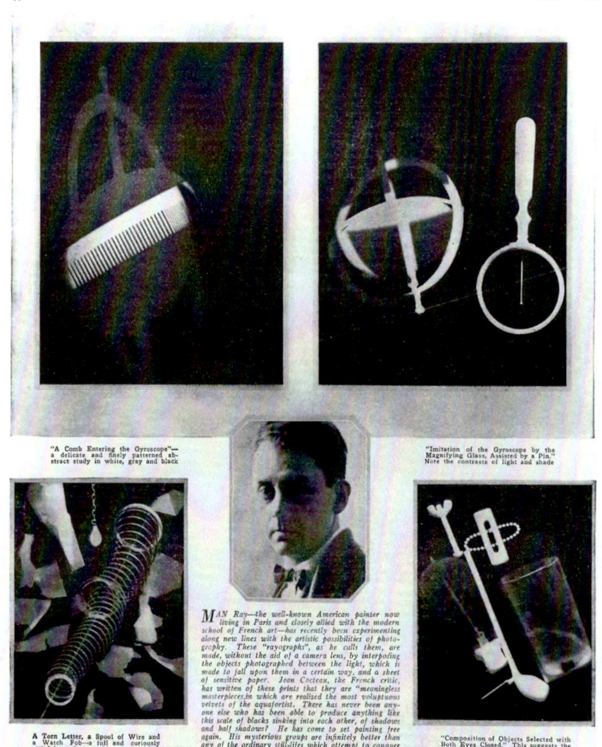

Fig. 36. "A New Method of Realizing the Artistic Possibilities of Photography," *Vanity Fair*, November 1922. Harvard Theatre Collection, Houghton Library, Harvard College Library, Harvard University, Cambridge, Massachusetts

Vanity Fair publishes Man Ray's first rayographs. Later in the year *Les champs délicieux*, featuring twelve rayographs, is published with a preface by Tzara. "Man Ray has delivered painting anew," Cocteau declares in the magazine *Les feuilles libres*.

Transatlantics:
A constant flow of American artists and writers cross the Atlantic after the war to stay in Paris, whether for a month or a few years, and absorb the European traditions of their craft. The numbers are so substantial that in 1924 the *American Review* jokingly pronounces Paris the "capital of America." Though he will live in the city for most of his life, Man Ray seeks neither acceptance in American circles of expatriates nor French citizenship. Instead, he embraces his role as a permanent foreigner, flitting around the margins of groups without belonging to any. "I like to be a foreigner," he later says. "Only a foreigner enjoys complete freedom from social conformity. . . . You are automatically granted the freedom to be different from the natives around you."

"I have finally freed myself from the sticky medium of paint, and am working directly with light itself. I have found a way of recording it. The subjects were never so near to life itself as in my new work, and never so completely translated into the medium." —Man Ray, letter to his patron Ferdinand Howald

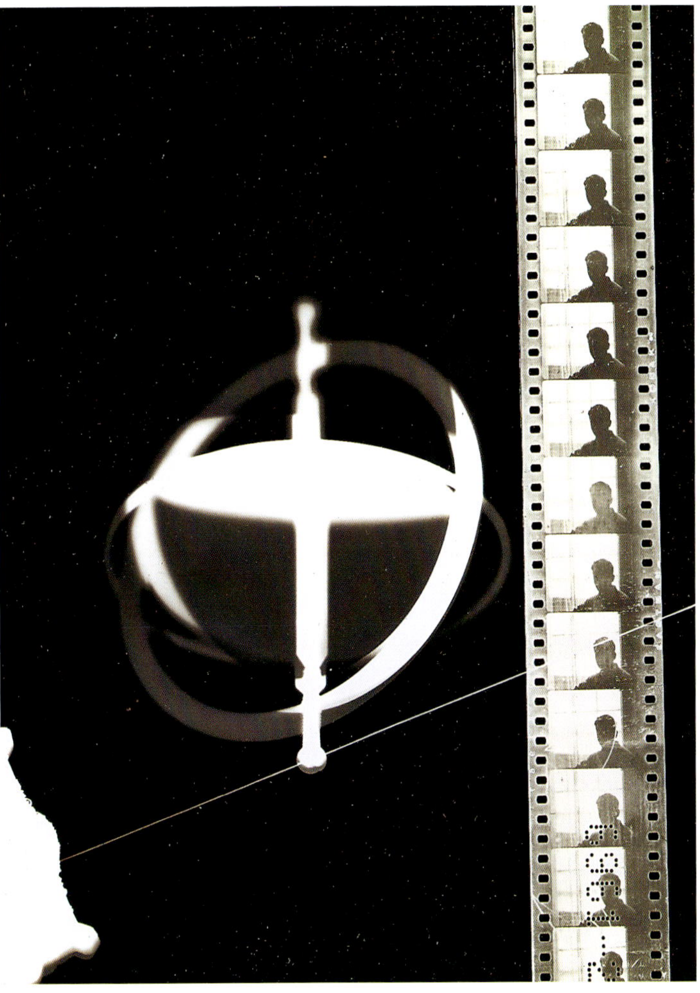

Fig. 37. *Rayograph (gyroscope & film)*, 1922. Vintage gelatin silver print, 9⅜ × 7 in. (23.9 × 17.8 cm). The Bluff Collection LP

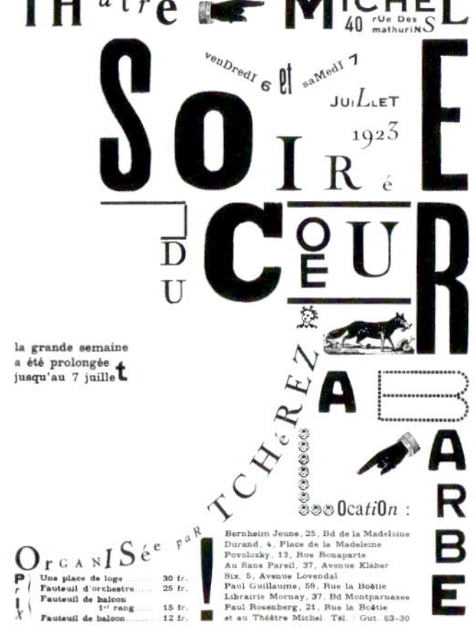

Fig. 38. Announcement for the Dada evening *La coeur à barbe* (*The Bearded Heart*), July 1923

The American nightclub Le Jockey opens in Montparnasse, one block from Man Ray's studio. To accommodate the growing expatriate population, the Dôme and La Rotonde cafés will be renovated and expanded the following year.

Fig. 39. *Painting*, 1918/1924. Oil on canvas, 17¼ × 14⅛ in. (43.8 × 35.9 cm). Courtesy of Forum Gallery, New York and Los Angeles

Fig. 40. *Abstraction*, 1924. Oil on canvas, 17¹⁄₁₆ × 14¹⁄₁₆ in. (43.3 × 35.7 cm). The Baltimore Museum of Art, Gift of Cory and Stanford Z. Rothschild

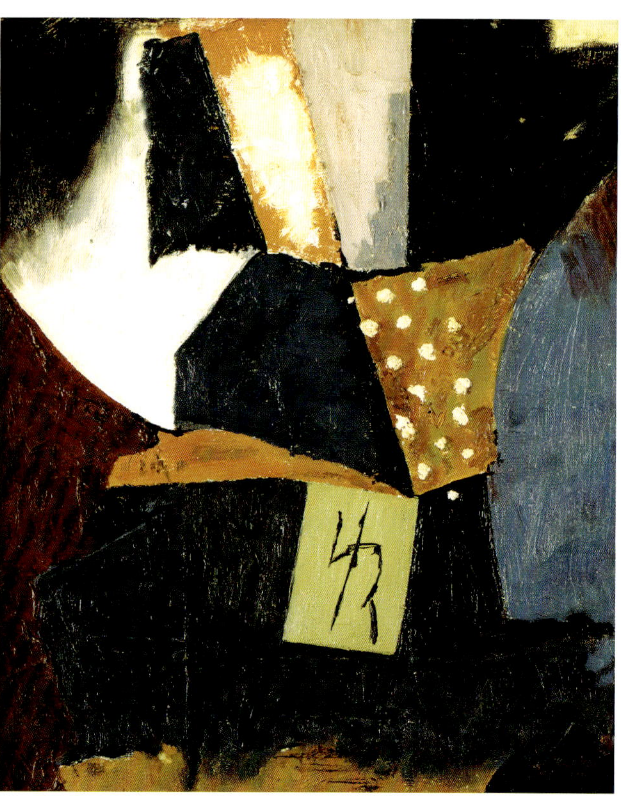

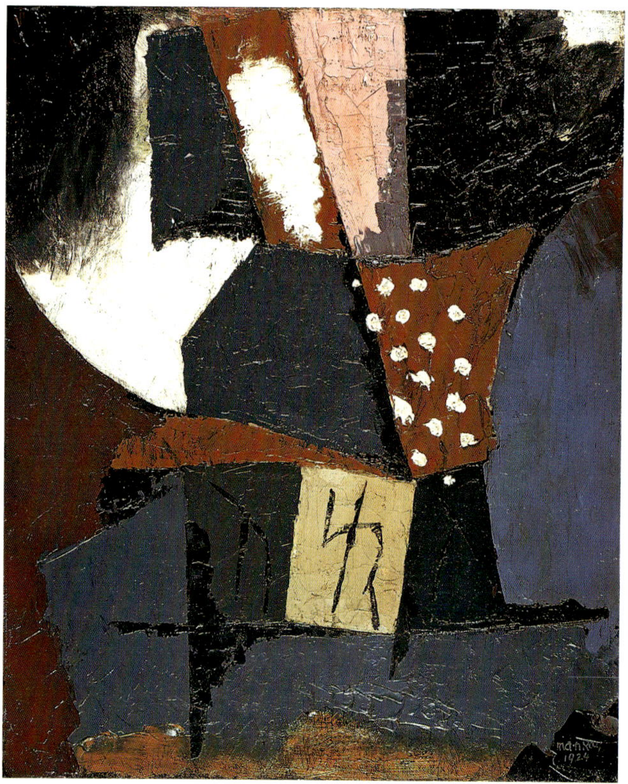

Man Ray hires Berenice Abbott to assist him in the darkroom. Their sitters include the expatriate writers who frequent Sylvia Beach's legendary Paris bookshop Shakespeare and Company: F. Scott Fitzgerald, Ernest Hemingway, James Joyce, Ezra Pound, and Gertrude Stein. Beach later writes in her memoirs: "Man Ray and his pupil Berenice Abbott . . . were the official portraitists of 'the Crowd.' The walls of my bookshop were covered with their photographs. To be 'done' by Man Ray and Berenice Abbott means that you were rated as somebody."

In October, Breton publishes his first Surrealist manifesto and defines Surrealism as: "n. Psychic automatism in its pure state, by which one proposes to express—verbally, by means of the written word, or in any other manner—the actual functioning of thought. Dictated by thought, in the absence of any control exercised by reason, exempt from any aesthetic or moral concern." Surrealism, drawing on Freudian ideas of the unconscious as driving sexual desire and aggression, emerges in part in response to postwar anxiety. By attacking traditional methods of seeing and thinking, Surrealism negates distinctions between states of consciousness, and interior and exterior realities, at a time when national boundaries and identities are in flux.

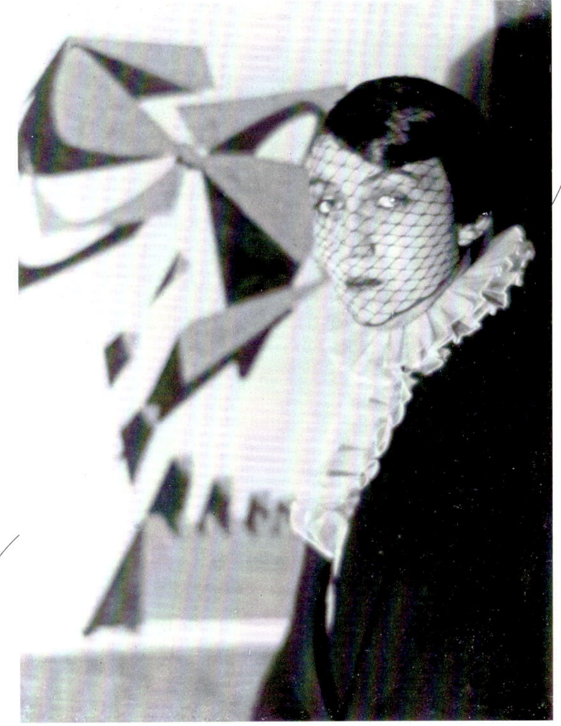

Fig. 43. *Harlequin Composition with Berenice Abbott*, 1922. Gelatin silver print, 8⅛ × 3¹/₁₆ in. (20.6 × 7.8 cm). New Orleans Museum of Art, Museum Purchase

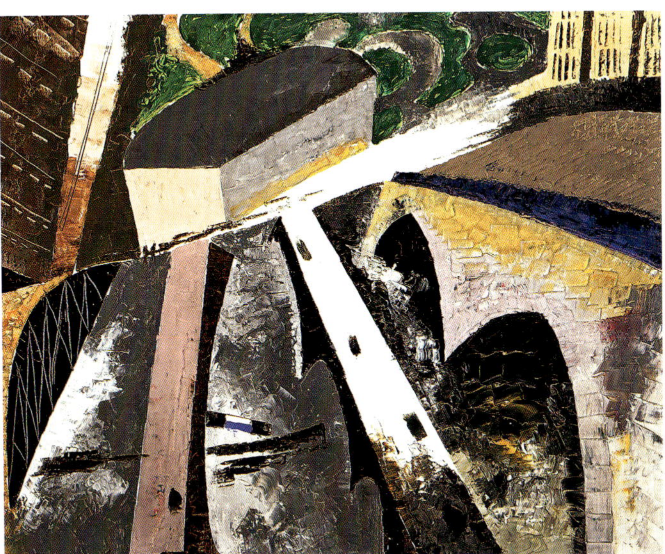

Fig. 41. *Le Grand Palais*, 1924. Oil on canvas, 19⅝ × 24 in. (49.9 × 61 cm). Columbus Museum of Art, Ohio, Gift of Ferdinand Howald

Fig. 42. Cover of *La révolution surréaliste* with *La France* (or *Moving Sculpture*; 1920), by Man Ray, March 1926. Brown University Library

The inaugural issue of Breton's journal *La révolution surréaliste* reproduces five of Man Ray's photographs. From this point on, Man Ray's photography is inextricably linked to the Surrealist movement.

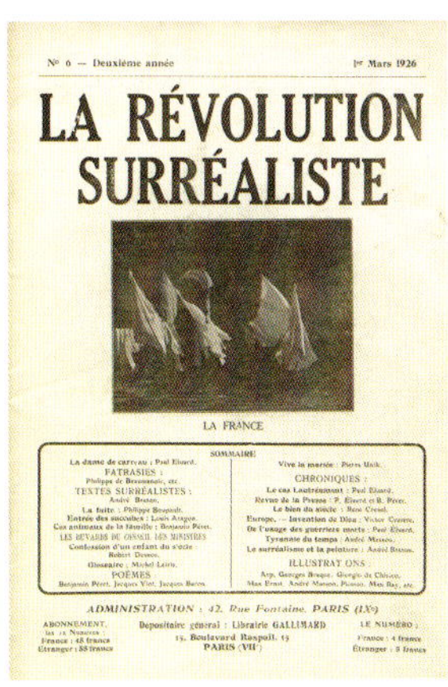

The inaugural exhibition at Galerie Surréaliste in Paris displays work by Man Ray alongside selections from Breton's collection of "primitive" objects from the Pacific Islands. Man Ray shows works mostly from his Dada period, which, he says, "fitted in just as well with the Surrealist idea."

Robert Desnos writes "Pamphlet Against Jerusalem" for *La révolution surréaliste*, expressing the Surrealists' antinationalist, and therefore anti-Zionist, agenda, and discussing the value of Jewish immigration to Paris for the social disorder it brings. The same year, in response to Franco-Spanish colonial intervention against the indigenous Rif fighters in Morocco, many Surrealists join the Communist Party.

"There are better things to do in life than copy. . . . Isn't it this perpetual mania of imitation that prevents man from being a god? . . . I prefer the poet. He creates, and every time man is raised in the moral order, he is a creator, whether of a machine, a poem, or a moral attitude. As far as painting goes, isn't it amazing that some painters still persist, a century after the invention of photography, in doing what a Kodak can do faster and better?"—Man Ray, "Deceiving Appearances," *Paris-Soir*

Man Ray and Duchamp make *Anémic Cinéma*, a study of optics. It is the only film they complete among several experiments during the 1920s. Marc Allégret also collaborates on the film.

The first group exhibition of Surrealist painters, presented at Galerie Pierre in Paris, includes work by Arp, Giorgio de Chirico, Ernst, Paul Klee, Masson, Joan Miró, Picasso, and Pierre Roy. Man Ray is the only American represented.

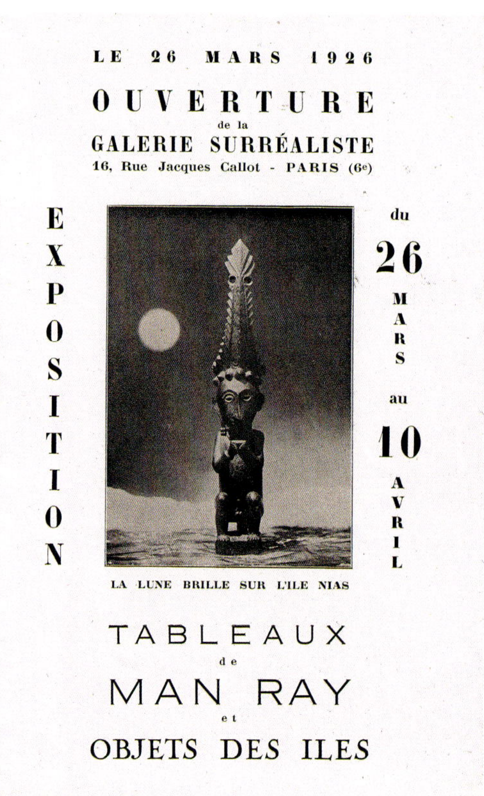

Fig. 44. Cover of Galerie Surréaliste exhibition catalogue with photograph by Man Ray, 1926. Francis M. Naumann Fine Art, New York

Man Ray's film *L'étoile de mer,* based on a poem by Robert Desnos, premieres in Paris. The critical response is largely confusion.

The first monograph on Man Ray, written by Georges Ribemont-Dessaignes, is published.

Man Ray visits New York for the U.S. premiere of *Emak-Bakia* and the opening of *Man Ray: Recent Paintings and Photographic Compositions* at the Daniel Gallery. The film runs briefly, garnering no critical attention; it later has an extended fourteen-week run in Paris. A *New York Times* review bluntly states, "Man Ray's paintings do not seem to be especially significant. His gift really is in the province of photography." Such criticism fuels what will be his lifelong struggle to justify his painting in light of his photographic practices.

"I've been in Paris all summer working. . . . What with abstract and portrait photography, movies and now and then a painting, I have plenty to do. But it's all one thing, in the end. Giving restlessness a material form!"—Man Ray, letter to Katherine Dreier

The "problem" of Jewish painting: By the end of the 1920s, France has the highest per capita population of immigrants of any country in the world. This influx of immigrants, combined with anxiety produced by shifting social roles, economic pressures, and the increasing prominence of Jewish artists and dealers, leads to heightened xenophobia. Attacks target the primarily foreign artistic contingent based in Montparnasse, and as early as 1925, articles address the "problem" of Jewish painting in Parisian salon culture. So-called Jewish painting is perceived as a threat to the purity of the French art-historical tradition.

Breton's pioneering novel *Nadja* draws on the psychoanalytic idea that the self is not a knowable entity. The book opens: "Who am I? If this once I were to rely on a proverb, then perhaps everything would amount to knowing whom I 'haunt.'"

Lee Miller, a young model from New York, arrives in Paris with the intention of learning photography from Man Ray. She will be his companion and assistant until 1932.

The international exhibition *Film und Foto* in Stuttgart addresses the variety of practices and debates surrounding photography, and marks the emergence of a new critical theory concerning the medium. Christian Zervos selects Man Ray and Eugène Atget to represent France. In response to the growing interest in photography, Man Ray takes a second studio, at 8 rue du Val-de-Grâce, for painting. Mornings are spent painting, and afternoons in the photography studio and darkroom.

A special erotic issue of the avant-garde journal *Varits* includes risqué poems by Louis Aragon and Benjamin Pret, and pornographic photographs by Man Ray of his lover Kiki and himself. Ostensibly created to boost sales for the failing journal, the issue is seized by officials, and few copies make it into circulation.

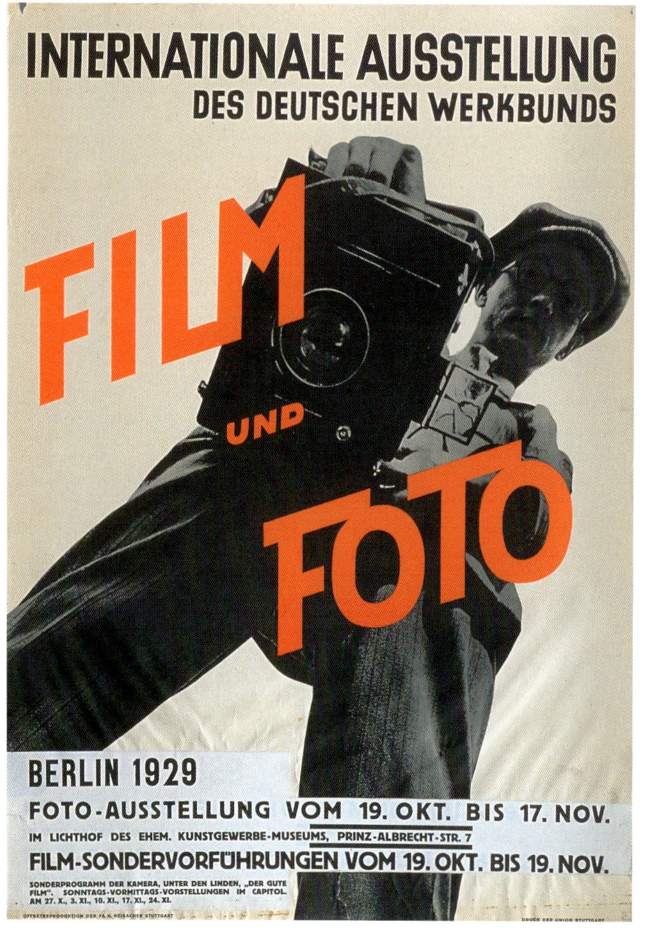

The Surrealists stage the exhibition *La verité sur les colonies* (*The Truth About the Colonies*) in response to the concurrent *Exposition coloniale internationale de Paris*'s celebration of colonialism. *Verité* brings together African masks, Christian iconographic objects, West Indian music, popular French songs, and photographs and texts explaining the forced labor of colonized peoples, in order to challenge European assumptions about cultural hierarchies.

Surréalisme at Julien Levy Gallery officially introduces New York to Surrealism. As Levy later wrote in his memoirs, the exhibition presented the movement enriched by American voices, a "paraphrase which would offer Surrealism in the language of the new world rather than a translation in the rhetoric of the old." Among the Americans included are Man Ray, Joseph Cornell, and the photographer George Platt Lynes.

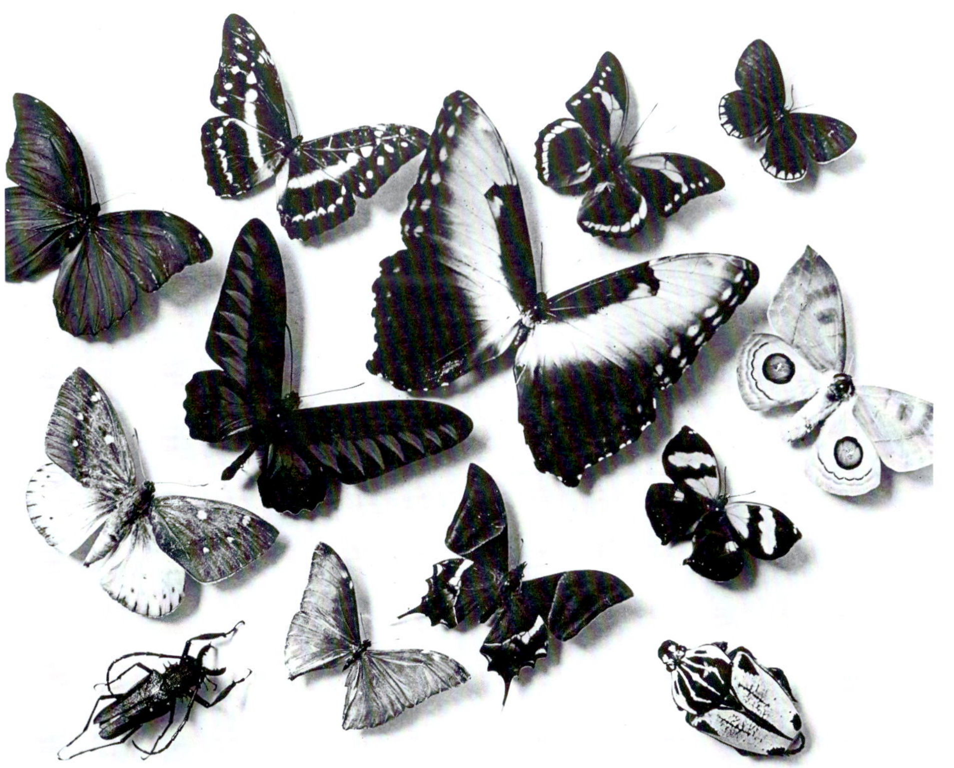

Fig. 46. *Untitled (Butterflies)*, c. 1930. Gelatin silver print, 10⁹⁄₁₆ × 13³⁄₁₆ in. (26.8 × 33.5 cm). The Metropolitan Museum of Art, New York, Warner Communications Inc. Purchase Fund, 1977

"For, whether a painter, emphasizing the importance of the idea he wishes to convey introduces bits of ready-made chromos alongside his handiwork, or whether another, working directly with light and chemistry, so deforms the subject as almost to hide the identity of the original, and creates a new form, the ensuing violation of the medium employed is the most perfect assurance of the author's convictions. A certain amount of contempt for the material employed to express an idea is indispensable to the purest realization of this idea." —Man Ray, "The Age of Light," *Photographs by Man Ray 1920 Paris 1934*, the first full survey of the artist's photography

Man Ray has one-man shows presented by the Art Center School in Los Angeles, Galeria d'Art Catalònia in Barcelona, and Galerie des Cahiers d'Art in Paris.

Man Ray's brother, Sam, dies of heart failure at age forty-two in New Jersey. Man Ray does not attend the funeral.

Au loin les fleurs fanées des vacances d'autrui
Un rien de paysage suffisant
Les prisons de la liberté s'effacent
Nous avons à jamais
Laissé derrière nous l'espoir qui se consume
Dans une ville pétrie de chair et de misère
De tyrannie

La paupière du soleil s'abaisse sur ton visage
Un rideau doux comme ta peau
Une aile salubre une végétation
Plus transparente que la lune du matin

Nos baisers et nos mains au niveau de nous-mêmes
Tout au delà ruiné
La jeunesse en amande se dénude et rêve
L'herbe se relève en sourdine
Sur d'innocentes nappes de petite terre

Premier dernière ardoise et craie
Fer et rouille seul à seule
Enlacés au rayon debout
Qui va comme un aveu
Ecorce et source redressée
L'un à l'autre dans le présent
Toute brume chassée
Deux autour de leur ardeur
Joints par des lieues et des années

Notre ombre n'éteint pas le feu
Nous nous perpétuons.

II

Au-dessous des sommets
Nos yeux ferment les fenêtres
Nous ne craignons pas la paix de l'hiver

Les quatre murs éteints par notre intimité
Quatre murs sur la terre
Le plancher le plafond
Sont des cibles faciles et rompues
A ton image alerte que j'ai dispersée
Et qui m'est toujours revenue

Un monotone abri
Un décor de partout

Mais c'est ici qu'en ce moment
Commencent et finissent nos voyages
Les meilleures folies
C'est ici que nous défendons notre vie
Que nous cherchons le monde

Un pic écervelé aux nuages fuyants au sourire éternel
Dans leurs cages les lacs au fond des trous la pluie
Le vent sa longue langue et les anneaux de la fraicheur
La verdure et la chair des femmes au printemps
La plus belle est un baume elle incline au repos
Dans des jardins tout neufs amortis d'ombres tendres
Leur mère est une feuille
Luisante et nue comme une linge mouillé

Fig. 47. Page spread from *Facile*, poems by Paul Éluard and photographs by Man Ray, 1935. Paris editions, GLM. Purchase, B. Osgood Pierce Fund, 1949, Houghton Library, Harvard University, Cambridge, Massachusetts

Salvador Dalí, as photographed by Man Ray, is on the cover of *Time* magazine.

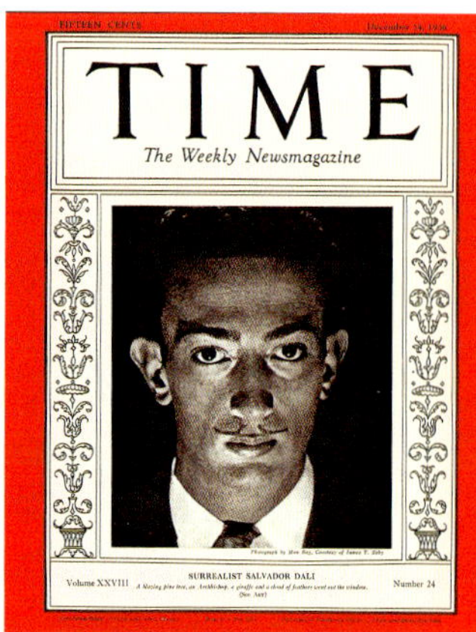

Fig. 48. Cover of *Time* magazine with photograph of Salvador Dalí by Man Ray, December 14, 1936

Maurice Heine (Man Ray's neighbor) publishes the Marquis de Sade's *Les cent vingt journées de Sodome* (*The One Hundred Twenty Days of Sodom*). The Surrealists glorify Sade as a political and sexual outlaw, a defiant individual who embodies complete and total liberty. Man Ray eventually reads all of Sade's novels.

La photographie n'est pas l'art, a small volume of photographs by Man Ray, is published with an introduction by Breton. Its title —photography is not art—typifies the sort of dismissive statement Man Ray will make about the status of photography in the ensuing years.

Fantastic Art, Dada, Surrealism opens at the Museum of Modern Art, New York, with more than seven hundred works on view. The exhibition will travel to five other cities in the United States, exposing a large public to Surrealist ideas. Man Ray's *A l'heure d'observatoire— les amoureux* (*Observatory Time —The Lovers*; 1934) is prominently displayed.

The Nazi's *Entartete Kunst* (*Degenerate Art*) exhibition opens in Munich, ridiculing artists associated with Dada, Cubism, Surrealism, and Expressionism. *Entartete Kunst* will travel to several major cities in Germany and be seen by nearly 3 million people.

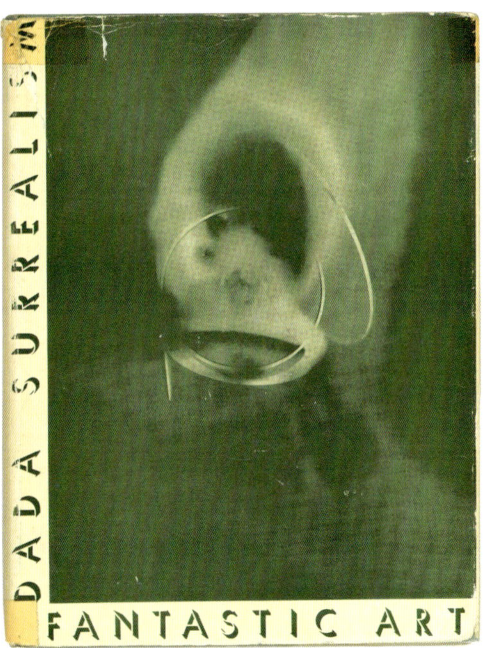

Fig. 49. Cover of *Fantastic Art, Dada, Surrealism* exhibition catalogue with rayograph by Man Ray, 1936. The Museum of Modern Art, New York

"I hate photography, and want to do only what is absolutely necessary to keep going, and produce something that interests me personally. . . . I have painted all these years . . . but these one-track minded Americans have now put me down as a photographer. . . . Do you wonder that I stay in Europe?" —Man Ray, letter to his sister Elsie

With his companion Adrienne Fidelin (Ady), Man Ray rents a flat in Antibes, in the south of France, so as to devote himself as much as possible to painting.

Les mains libres, a book of drawings by Man Ray illustrated with poems by Éluard, is published. In his introduction, Éluard refers to Man Ray as "a man who reveals himself, who gives us his eyes, his hands. . . . Man Ray draws so as not to forget himself."

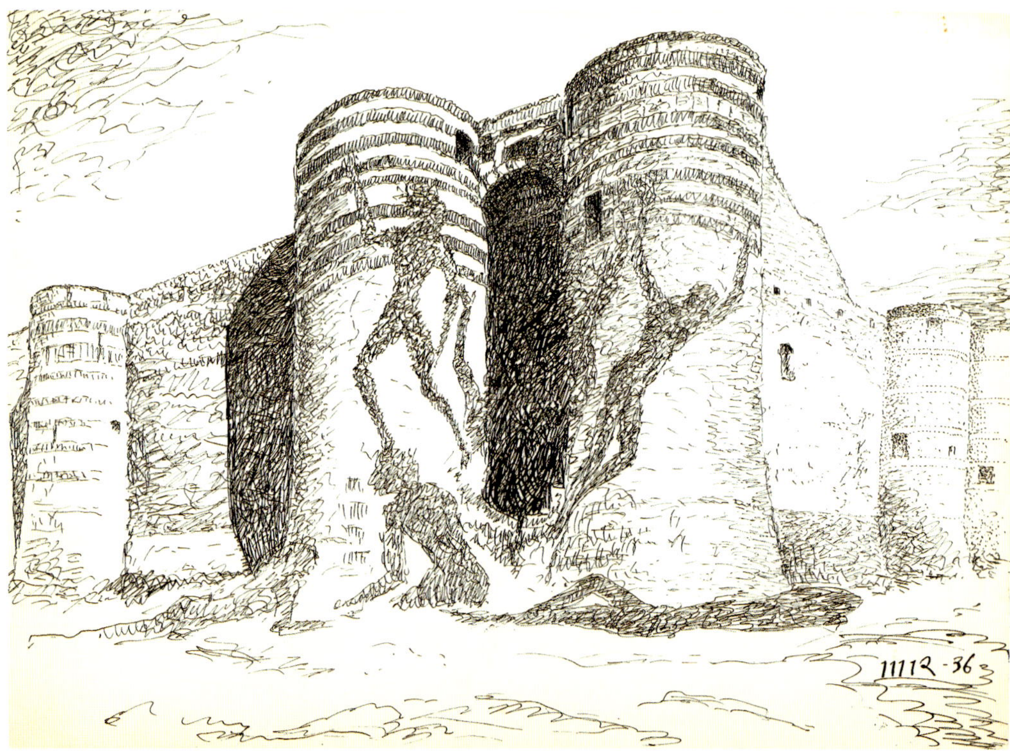

Fig. 50. *Les tours du silence*, 1936. Ink on paper, 11¹⁵⁄₁₆ × 15¹⁄₁₆ in. (30.3 × 38.2 cm). Original art for an illustration in *Les mains libres* (1937) by Man Ray and Paul Éluard. Collection of Mark Kelman, New York

Man Ray has a solo show at Paris's Galerie de Beaune. The catalogue includes an essay by the Marquis de Sade on imagination.

Man Ray claims his American citizenship and is granted repatriation mere days before German troops occupy Paris. He sails for New Jersey in late June, leaving behind almost twenty years of work.

The *Exposition Internationale du Surréalisme* (*International Surrealist Exhibition*) opens at the mainstream Galerie des Beaux-Arts in Paris, curated by Breton and Éluard and installed by Duchamp. Sixty artists from fourteen countries participate in this last collective project of the Surrealists before World War II. The installation is conceived to challenge the purity and stability of the conventional art gallery environment; Duchamp covers the ceiling with coal sacks, Man Ray distributes flashlights as the only source of illumination, and a hired dancer simulates "hysteria" to German marching music.

"Art in France seems above all anxious to throw a carpet of flowers over a mined world. Although a wind of destruction was blowing at all the gates, to judge by what many painters exhibited one would think that life was going on sweetly and even with ostentation. . . . The problem is no longer, as formerly, to know if a painting 'holds up' in a field of wheat, but whether it holds up beside the daily newspaper."
—André Breton, "Prestige d'André Masson," *Minotaure*

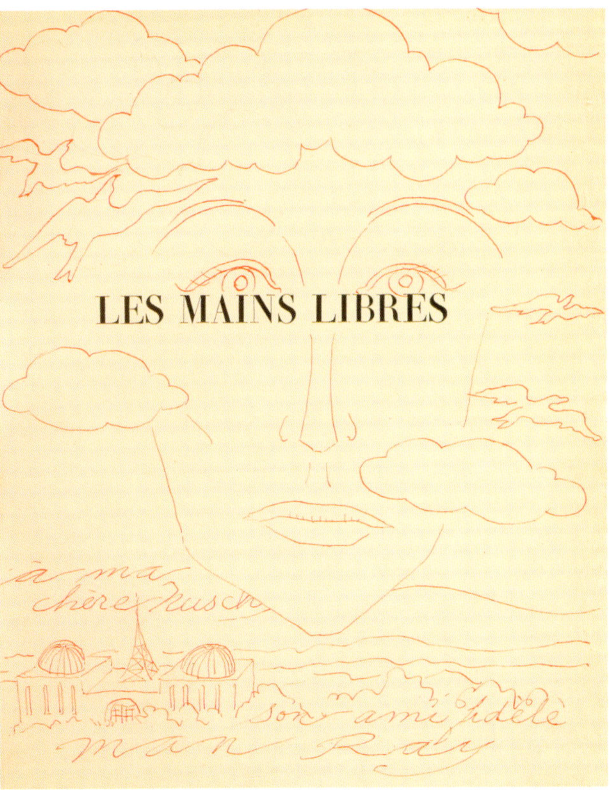

Fig. 51. Title page of *Les mains libres* (1937). Inscribed by Man Ray for Nusch Éluard. Collection of Timothy Baum, New York

Hollywood 1940–51

Man Ray heads to California in September. On his second day in Hollywood, he meets Juliet Browner, a dancer. She will be his companion and model for the rest of his life.

In August, the liner *Excambion* arrives in Hoboken, New Jersey, carrying among its passengers René Clair and his wife, Bronya Perlmutter; Salvador and Gala Dalí; Virgil Thomson; and Man Ray. A crowd of reporters gathers to meet Dalí, whose name is synonymous with Surrealism in America, while Man Ray slips away unnoticed: "The landing in New York was exciting and thrilling, especially for the European refugees. I was overcome with a feeling of intense depression. Leaving twenty years of progressive effort behind me, I felt it was a return to the days of my early struggles, when I had left the country under a cloud of misunderstanding and distrust."

Clement Greenberg's article "Towards a Newer Laocoon" in *Partisan Review* argues that the value of art is found in its form. Greenberg's formalism will promote Abstract Expressionist painting as the dominant American art.

The periodical *View* is first published by the poet Charles Henri Ford. Until 1947 it will be one of the primary vehicles for familiarizing the American public with Surrealism.

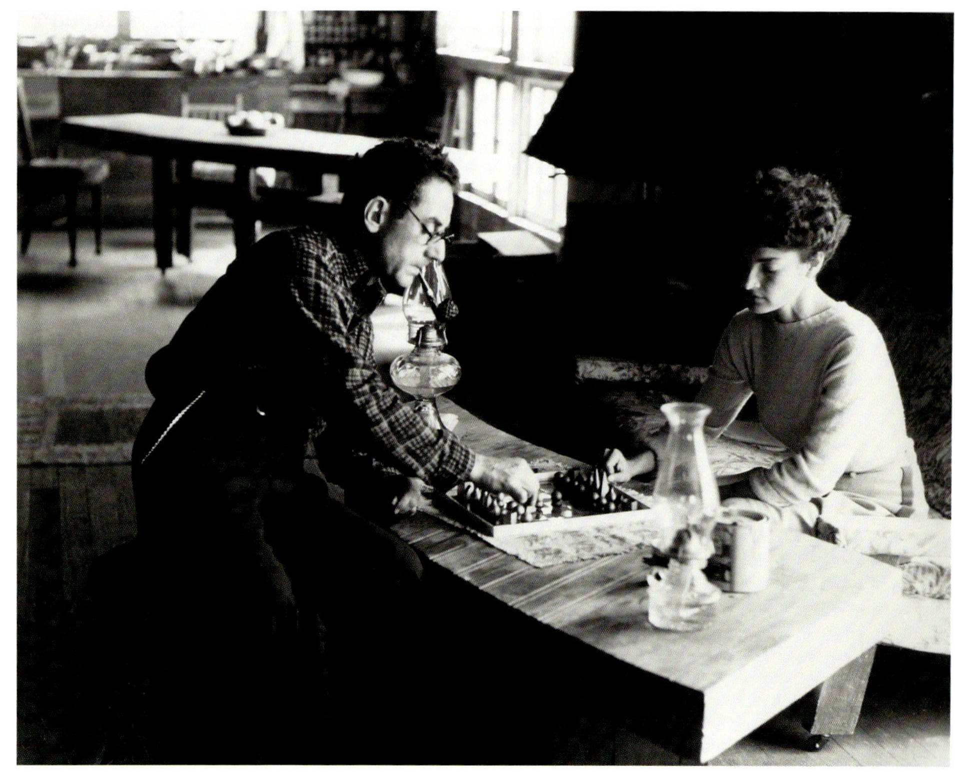

Fig. 52. Man Ray and Juliet playing chess, 1940s. Photograph by Naomi Savage. Collection of Neil Baldwin

Man Ray rents a large studio at 1245 Vine Street and re-creates some of the work he left behind in Paris. During his decade in Hollywood, he will produce more paintings, objects, and rayographs than he has made in the previous thirty years of his life.

In "Art in Sanity," published in *California Arts & Architecture*, Man Ray pokes fun at the right-wing Society for Sanity in Art, whose members equate modernism and abstraction with communism: "In former times art had no country. . . . Only by laying aside ulterior motives, by accepting the unfamiliar and the unknown, by intensifying individual effort, can the artist hope to produce a great and healthy art."

In a review of Man Ray's solo show at Frank Perls Gallery in Los Angeles, Henry Millier, critic for the *Los Angeles Times*, dismisses the artist: "Man Ray's aesthetic psychological exercises, while done with evident artistry, seem products of a period which was more exciting than substantial; a period, to us, remote in feeling and in time. . . . America is on a different track."

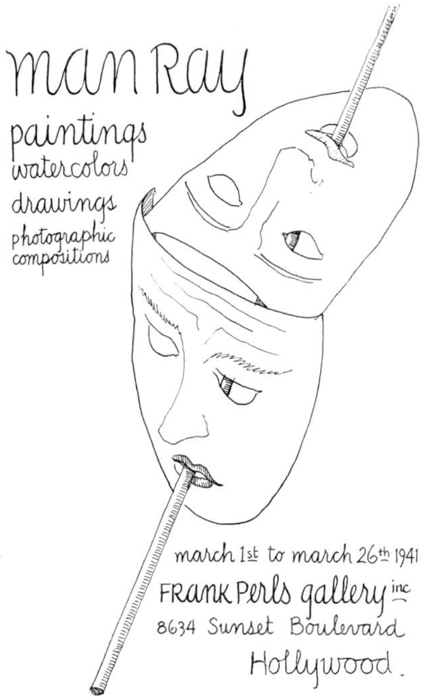

Fig. 53. Cover of Perls Gallery exhibition catalogue, 1941. Collection of Teruo Ishihara, Kyoto

Exiles in California: From the late 1920s through the 1940s, many refugees fleeing European fascism choose Southern California for their exile. Filmmakers, writers, musicians, scientists, and academics are drawn to Los Angeles by the climate, the Hollywood dream of self reinvention, and the hope of gainful employment. Among others, Theodor Adorno, Bertolt Brecht, Luis Buñuel, Dalí, Max Horkheimer, Fritz Lang, Thomas Mann, Richard Neutra, Jean Renoir, and Igor Stravinsky temporarily transform Los Angeles into a capital of world culture.

Man Ray is commercially unsuccessful, but museums are beginning to recognize his historical importance. During his early years in California he will have exhibitions at the M. H. de Young Museum in San Francisco (1941), the Santa Barbara Museum of Art (1943), Mills College Art Gallery (1943), and the Pasadena Art Institute (1944).

"i feel as if i had been exiled from our era, this is tahiti in the form of a big city. . . . since everything is so artificial, they even have an exaggerated feeling for nature, which becomes alienated. . . . they tell you that all the greenery is wrested from the desert by irrigation systems. scratch the surface a little and desert shows through: stop paying the water bills and everything stops blooming." —Bertolt Brecht's journal entry on living in California

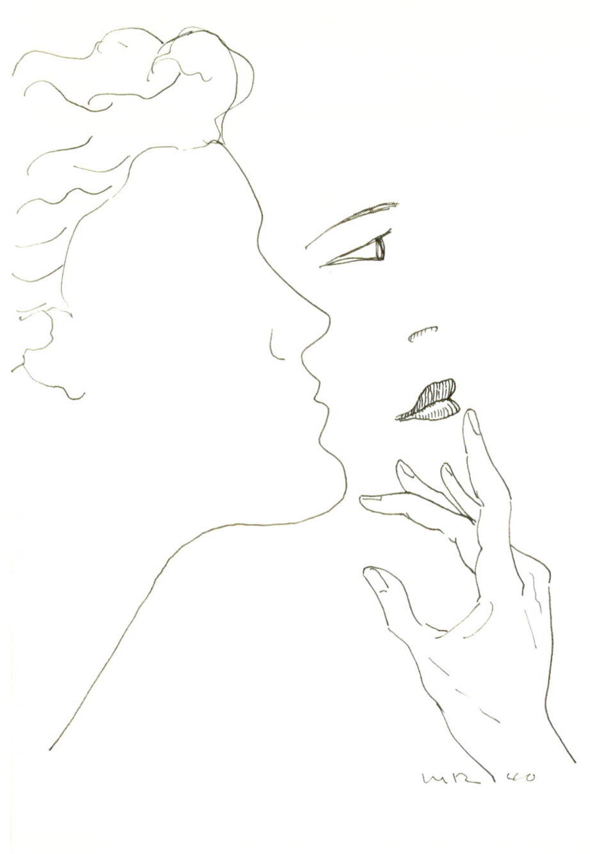

Fig. 54. *Faceless*, 1940. Ink on paper, 18 × 12 in. (45.7 × 30.4 cm). Collection of Marilyn and Larry Fields

Julien Levy arrives in California with his traveling gallery and rents a space on Sunset Boulevard in Hollywood. Other dealers who try to cultivate modern art patronage in Los Angeles include Frederick Kann (Circle Gallery), Paul Kantor (Kantor Gallery), Frank Perls (Perls Gallery), and Barbara Cecil's American Contemporary Gallery.

1942

1942

"California is a beautiful prison. I like being here but I cannot forget my previous life and long for the day when I can return to New York and eventually to France." —Man Ray, letter to his sister Elsie

The Pierre Matisse Gallery exhibition *Artists in Exile* in New York includes work by Eugene Berman, Breton, Chagall, Ernst, Léger, Jacques Lipchitz, Masson, Matta, Piet Mondrian, Amédée Ozenfant, Yves Tanguy, and Pavel Tchelitchev. James Thrall Soby pronounces the "death of Paris" in the catalogue preface; the center of the art world has shifted to New York. Man Ray and Duchamp are conspicuously absent from the exhibition.

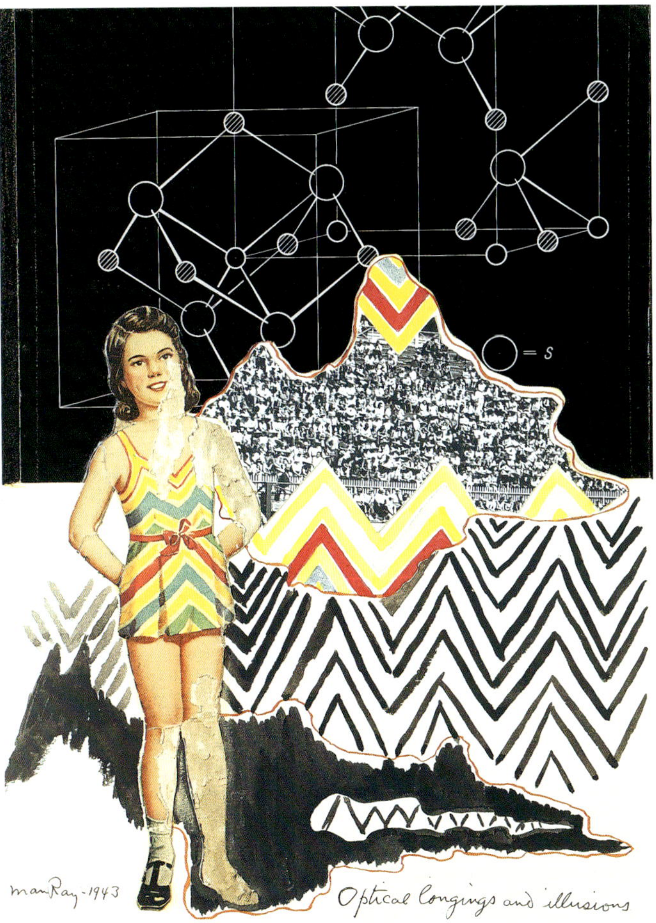

"One day while I was out driving, I discovered the enormous two-mile-long Los Angeles garbage dump, with everything from orange peels to grand pianos to whole houses. Smoke from the fires rose here and there; and at the bottom of the pit, on a small piece of land raised slightly from the piles of garbage, stood a couple of tiny houses inhabited by real people. . . . Man Ray and I wanted to make a film about it, but we couldn't raise the money." —Luis Buñuel, early 1940s

Breton and Duchamp organize the *First Papers of Surrealism* exhibition in New York, alluding to the European movement's path toward U.S. naturalization and citizenship. Peggy Guggenheim's Art of This Century gallery opens with an exhibition combining Surrealist and abstract art. Man Ray is included in neither exhibition.

1943

Man Ray's two-part essay "Photography Is Not Art" is published in *View* in April and October with ten of what he considers his best photographs. He writes: "The success with which the Artist is able to conceal the source of his inspiration, is the measure of his originality." Also in October, a how-to piece by Man Ray is published in *Minicam Photography*, a magazine for amateur practitioners.

1944

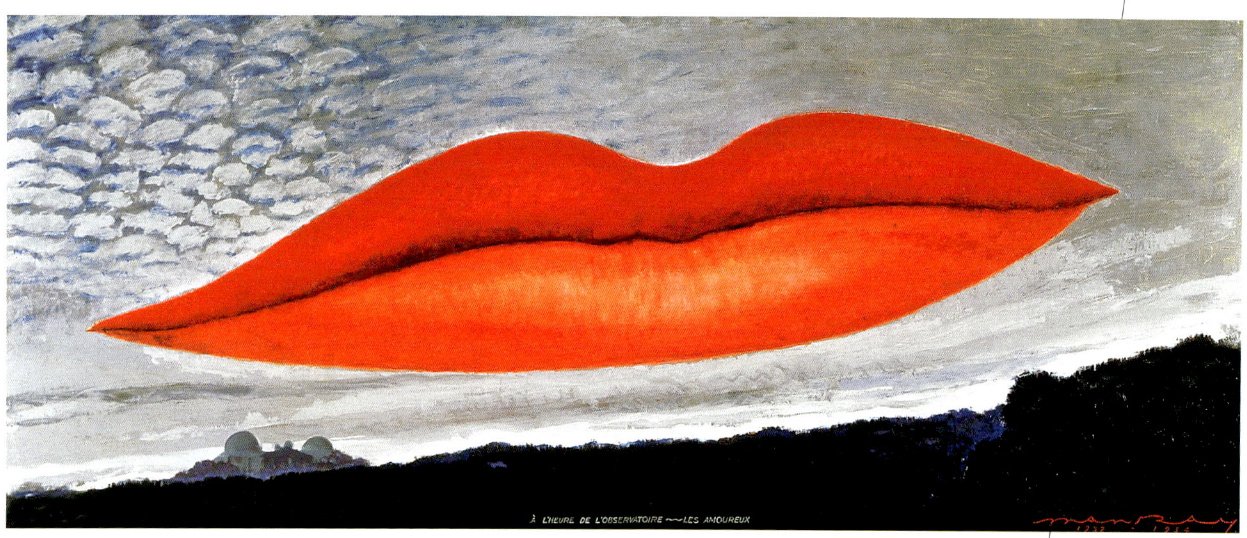

Fig. 56. *A l'heure d'observatoire—les amoureux*, 1934. Oil on canvas, 39⅜ × 99 in. (100 × 250.4 cm). Private collection

Man Ray recovers his painting *A l'heure d'observatoire—les amoureux* (*Observatory Time—The Lovers*; 1934), which has been rescued from Nazi-occupied France by Mary Reynolds, carried over the Pyrenees into Spain, then transported to the artist in Los Angeles.

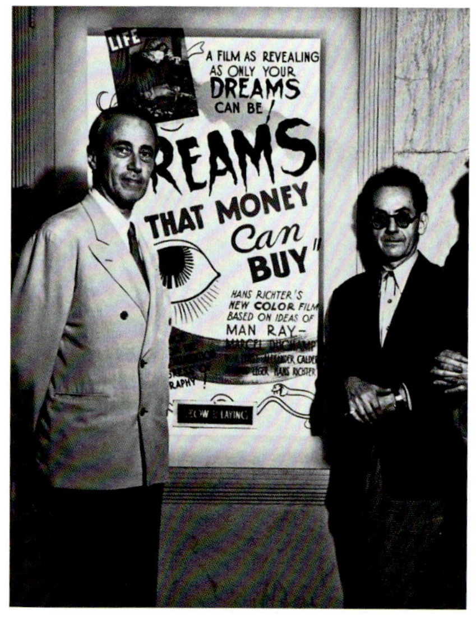

Fig. 57. Hans Richter and Man Ray with the poster for *Dreams That Money Can Buy*, 1947. Philadelphia Museum of Art, The Lynne and Harold Honickman Gift of the Julien Levy Collection

Man Ray's text "Ruth, Roses, and Revolvers," appearing in *View*, describes the incomprehension of a public that looks only at "prosaic details of value, country of origin, motto," without deeper consideration. In 1947, Hans Richter will adapt the short narrative, as well as scenarios by Alexander Calder, Duchamp, Ernst, Léger, and himself, in his film *Dreams That Money Can Buy*. It is Man Ray's sole involvement with filmmaking while in Hollywood.

1945

1946

Man Ray and Juliet Browner marry in a joint ceremony with Max Ernst and Dorothea Tanning at Walter and Louise Arensberg's home in Hollywood.

1946

Man Ray's *Objects of My Affection* at Julien Levy Gallery includes objects, paintings, drawings, and rayographs. The show is not particularly well received. "New York was just as backward as California as far as I was concerned," Man Ray later recalls. "Perhaps more so since it knew me as the photographer, had forgotten that I was one of the pioneer Surrealist painters. . . . It is really unfortunate to be a pioneer; it pays off to be the last, not the first."

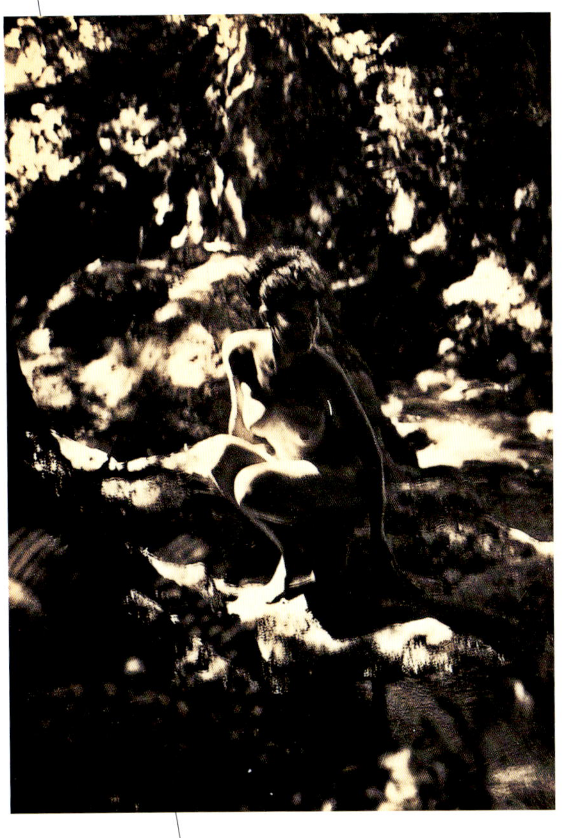

The exhibition *Pioneers of Modern Art* opens at the Whitney Museum of American Art in New York. The catalogue describes Man Ray as the "principal American member of the Dada movement and later of the original Surrealist group."

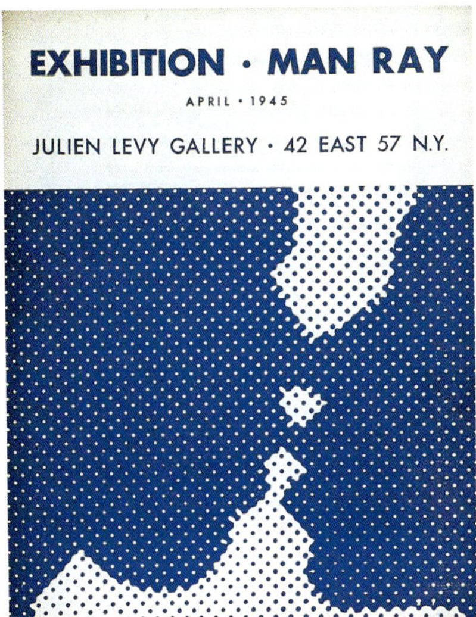

Fig. 58. Cover of *Man Ray: Objects of My Affection* exhibition brochure, Julien Levy Gallery, 1945. Artwork by Marcel Duchamp. Philadelphia Museum of Art, The Lynne and Harold Honickman Gift of the Julien Levy Collection

The San Francisco Museum of Art initiates the *Art in Cinema* series, one of the first comprehensive retrospectives of experimental filmmaking in the United States and Europe. Man Ray's films *Emak-Bakia*, *L'étoile de mer*, and *Les mystères du Château de Dé* are screened during its first season.

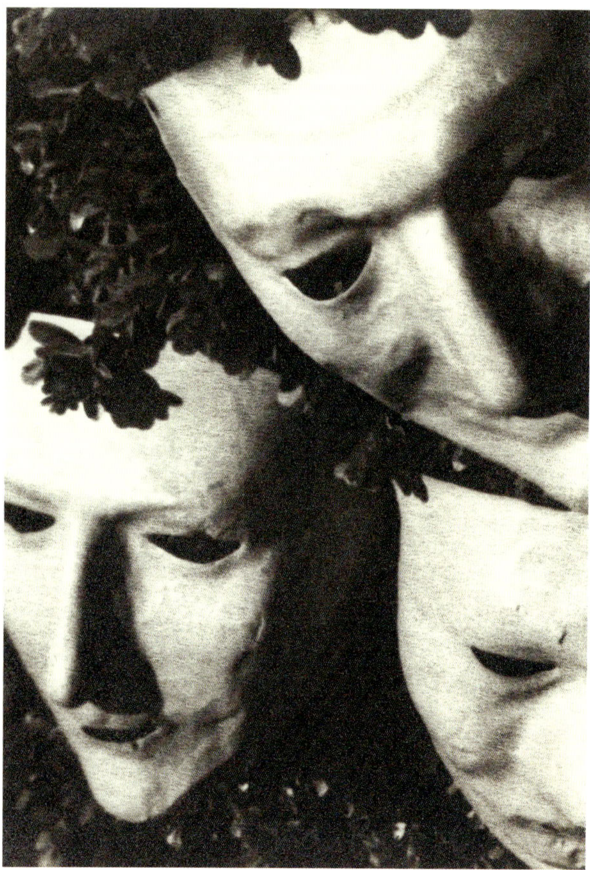

Fig. 60. *Masks*, 1946. Gelatin silver print, 6¹¹/₁₆ × 4¹¹/₁₆ in. (17 × 11.9 cm). The J. Paul Getty Museum, Los Angeles

The exhibition *To Be Continued Unnoticed* at Copley Galleries in Beverly Hills displays "Equations for Shakespeare, Non-Abstractions, Paintings Repatriated from Paris." For the opening the sidewalk in front of the gallery is converted into a Parisian-style café. The guest list includes Brecht, Buñuel, Ernst, Hans Hofmann, Aldous Huxley, Thomas Mann, Harpo Marx, Matta, Henry Miller, Isamu Noguchi, Jean Renoir, Edward G. Robinson, Stravinsky, Tanning, and Josef von Sternberg. No sales are made.

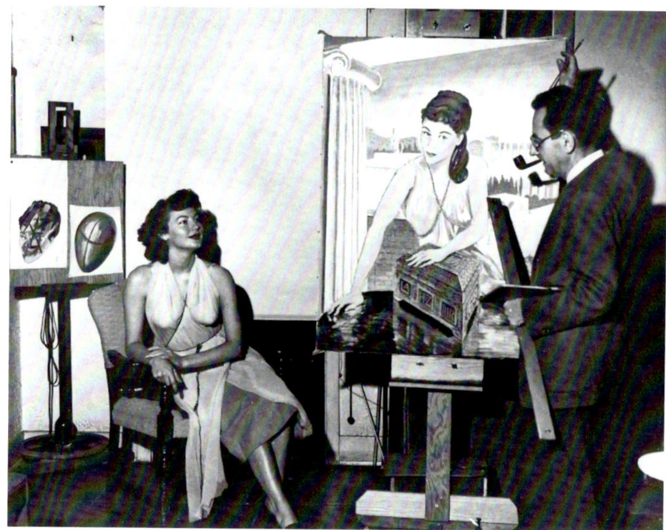

Fig. 61. Man Ray painting a portrait of Ava Gardner to be used in Albert Lewin's 1950 film *Pandora and the Flying Dutchman*. Man Ray Trust

1949

1950

1951

Man Ray and Juliet
Man Ray depart New
York on the *De Grasse,*
bound for France.

In a questionnaire that Duchamp conceives for the catalogue
of the Société Anonyme, now housed at the Yale University
Art Gallery, Man Ray lists his personal creed as: "To paint as
much as possible unlike other painters, above all, to paint
unlike myself—so that each succeeding work, or series of
works, shall be entirely different from preceding works."

"Cubism aims to destroy by design
disorder. Futurism aims to destroy
by a machine myth. Dadaism aims
to destroy by ridicule. Expressionism aims to destroy by aping the
primitive and the insane. . . .
Abstraction aims to destroy by
denial of reason. . . . Abstraction, or
non-objectivity . . . was spawned as
a communist product [that] has
brought down this curse upon us;
who has let into our homeland the
hordes of germ carrying art ver-
min."—Congressman George A.
Dondero, speech to the U.S. House
of Representatives

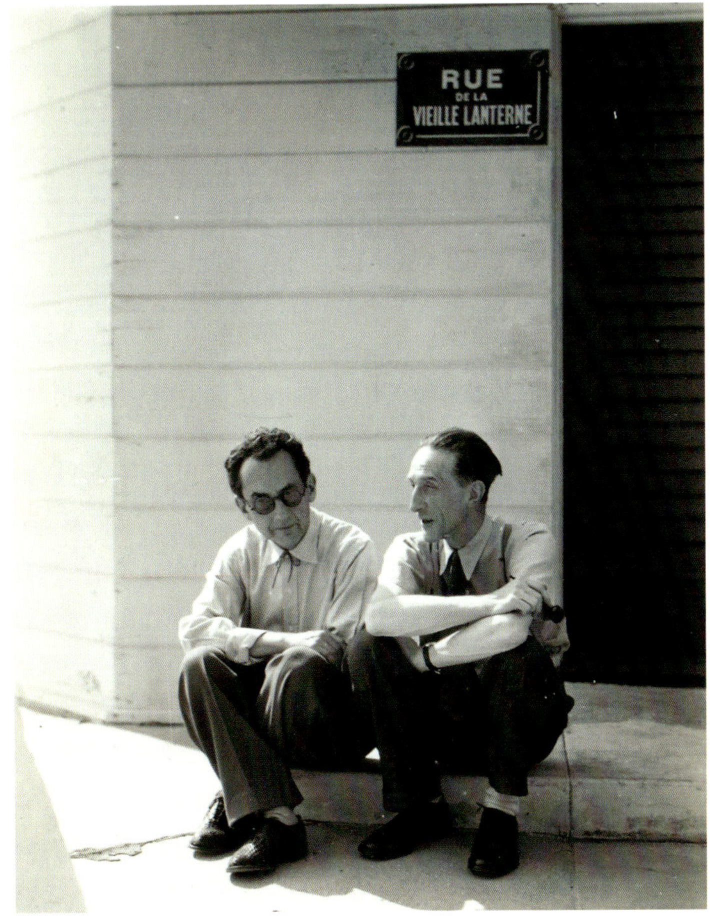

Fig. 62. *Man Ray and Marcel Duchamp seated
on a curb, Hollywood, 1949.* Gelatin silver
print, 3¾ × 2⅞ in. (9.5 × 7.3 cm). Francis M.
Naumann Fine Art, New York

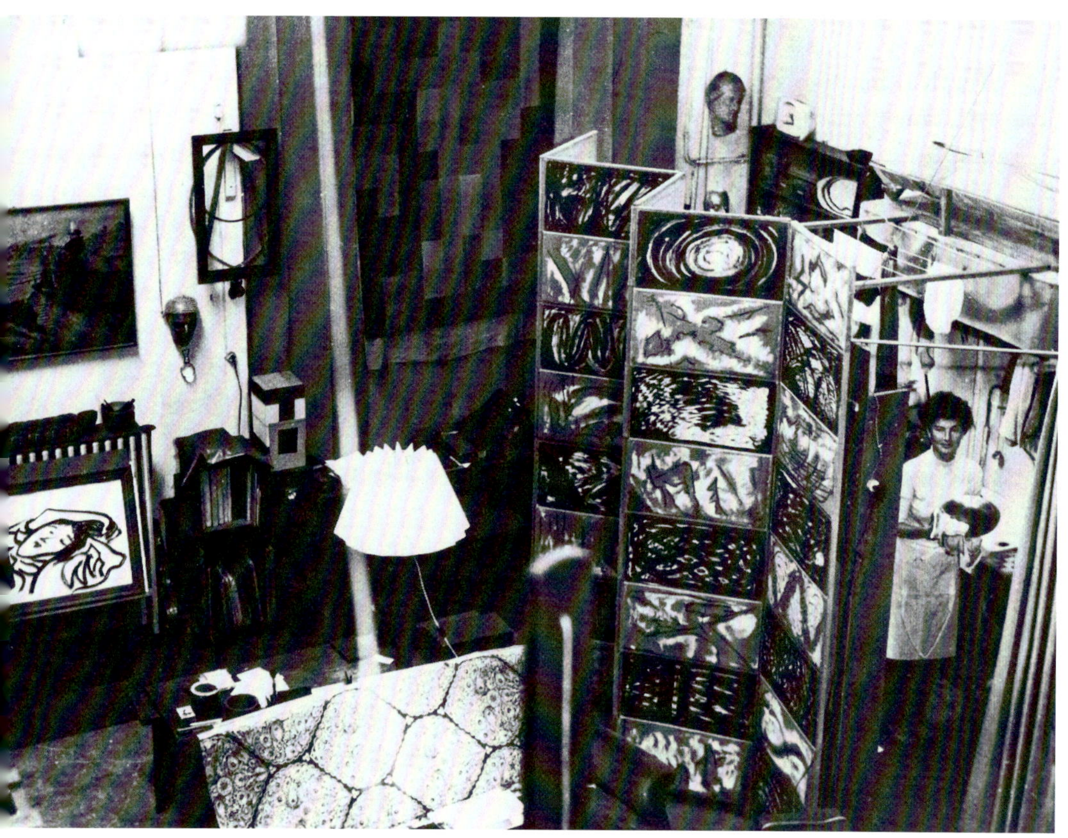

Fig. 63. Juliet in the rue Férou studio, c. 1955. The kitchen is separated by Man Ray's folding screen *The Twenty Days and Nights of Juliet* (1952)

Dada 1916–1923 opens at Sidney Janis Gallery in New York, inspiring a new generation of American artists to consider Dada. In the exhibition catalogue, Tzara writes: "Dada tried to destroy, not so much art, as the idea one had of art, breaking down its rigid borders, lowering its imaginary heights—subjecting them to a dependence on man, to his power—humbling art, significantly making it take its place and subordinating its value to pure movement which is also the movement of life."

1955

Walter Benjamin's *Schriften* (*Writings*), edited by Theodor Adorno, is published. It includes Benjamin's 1935 essay "The Work of Art in the Age of Mechanical Reproduction," which theorizes the nature of art in an era of reproducibility. Throughout his career, Man Ray creates multiple variants of his work, and beginning in the 1950s will authorize editions of his objects. He later explains in "Originals Graphics Multiples": "An original is a creation motivated by desire. Any reproduction of an original is motivated by necessity. . . . To create is divine, to reproduce is human."

1956

Max Ray dies in the Jewish Home for the Aged in Philadelphia; Elsie dies suddenly the following year. Man Ray attends neither funeral.

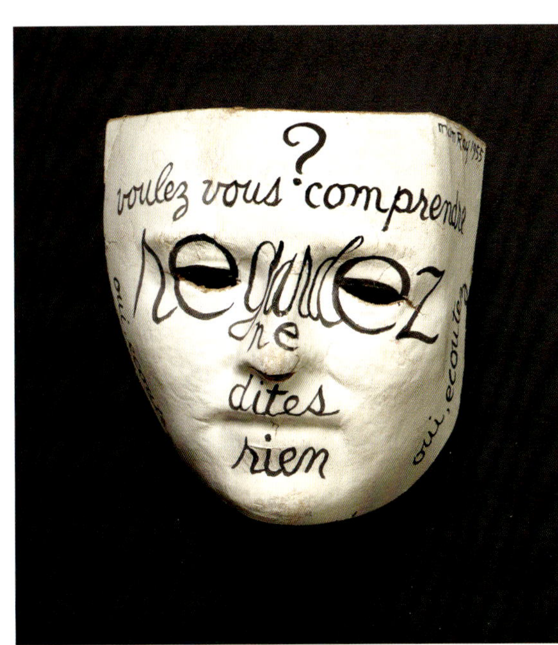

"Show NO photographs. Eliminate all Rayographs. I want to keep the two activities separate, otherwise there is a confusion if not downright devaluation of the paintings."
—Man Ray, giving directions for an upcoming exhibition in a letter to his niece Florence

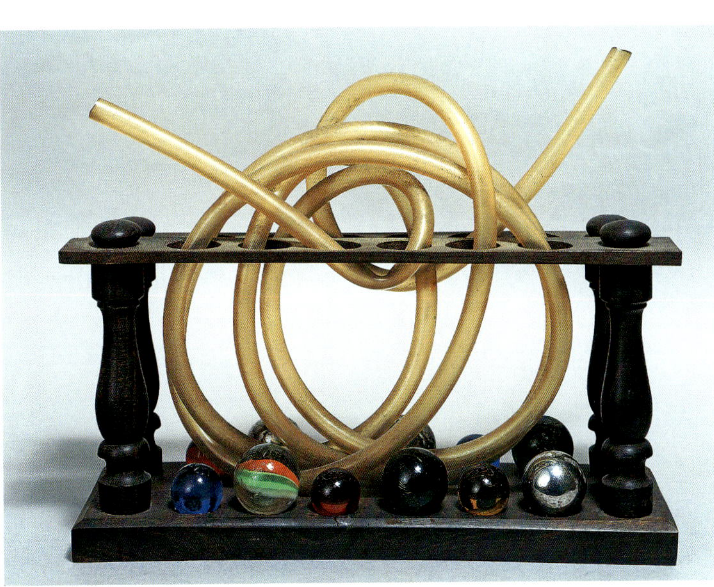

Fig. 64. *Smoking Device*, 1959/1970. Pipe rack, plastic tubing, and colored marbles, 7¼ × 8¹¹⁄₁₆ × 3¹⁄₁₆ in. (18.4 × 22.1 × 7.8 cm). Collection of Timothy Baum, New York

Exposition inteRnatiOnale du Surréalisme (EROS) (International Surrealist exhibition), organized by Breton and Duchamp, opens at Galerie Daniel Cordier in Paris. The exhibition embraces a wide range of younger artists interested in Surrealism as a political movement, including Jasper Johns, Louise Nevelson, Robert Rauschenberg, Tanguy, and Breton's daughter, Aube Breton.

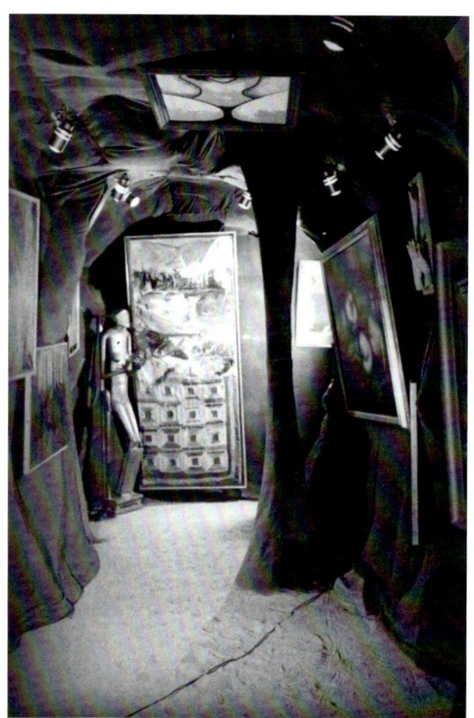

Fig. 66. Installation view of the EROS exhibition, 1959. Man Ray's painting *La Vierge* (1959) is visible on the ceiling, with Robert Rauschenberg's *Bed* (1955) and a sculpture by Alberto Giacometti at the end of the hall

Andy Warhol's *Campbell's Soup Cans*, a key work of Pop Art, employs advertising and popular culture imagery to subvert the importance of invention and originality in art. In 1974, Warhol devotes a series of paintings and seriographs to Man Ray.

Man Ray's autobiography, *Self Portrait*, begun in the late 1940s, is published in the United States. Despite his editor's requests, the book contains few dates. "I have purposely avoided a too chronological, or simply logical order, always keeping in mind [the term] 'Self Portrait.'" The book's publication corresponds with the opening of exhibitions at Princeton University Art Museum and Cordier-Ekstrom Gallery in New York.

Man Ray's Influence: A younger generation of artists in the late 1950s and the 1960s are influenced by Dadaist ideas of art into life, and Surrealist revolutionary ambitions. Among them are Johns, Allan Kaprow, Yves Klein, and Rauschenberg, as well as artists who contribute to Nouveau Réalisme, performance art, Neo-Dada, Pop Art, and Fluxus. For these artists, Man Ray, who maintains a busy schedule of solo and group exhibitions throughout Europe and the United States, is the living presence of Paris's legendary bohemian twenties.

The first large retrospective of Man Ray's work opens at the Los Angeles County Museum of Art. In his *New York Times* review, "Man Ray, Wandering Knight," the critic Philip Leider writes: "Nothing, perhaps, tells so much of the pervasiveness of his Europeanization than the fact that he could remain in America for the entire decade of the birth, maturation, and flowering of the Abstract Expressionist movement without seeming to have any grasp of its significance."

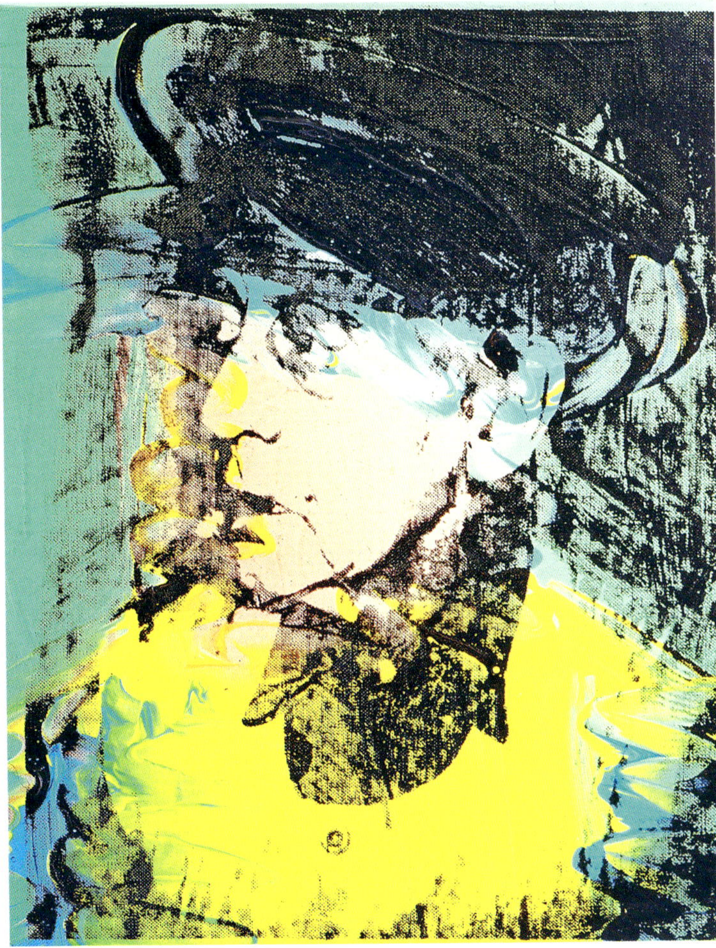

Fig. 67. Andy Warhol, *Man Ray,* 1974. Synthetic polymer paint and silk-screen ink on canvas. Andy Warhol Foundation for the Visual Arts

"I am trying to live in the present. I want to forget the past. As far as I am concerned, people seem to be too easily satisfied with dates, historical facts, so much so that they cannot get down to the actual ideas which these individuals of the past represent and stood for, fought for, as we did." —Man Ray

"Dadaism sought *to abolish art without realizing it,* and Surrealism sought *to realize art without abolishing it.* The critical position since worked out by the Situationists demonstrates that the abolition and the realization of art are inseparable aspects of a single transcendence of art." —Guy Debord, *The Society of the Spectacle*

Marcel Duchamp dies after spending an evening with the Man Rays, Robert Lebel, and Alexina ("Teeny"), his wife.

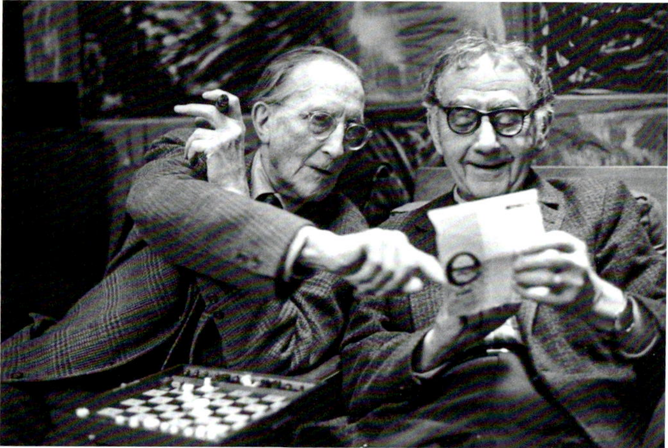

Fig. 68. Marcel Duchamp and Man Ray, at Man Ray's Paris home, 1968. Photograph by Henri Cartier-Bresson, Magnum Photos

Another niece, Helen, seeks out Man Ray at his Paris studio. "Promise me you'll never give any family history to the newspapers," he tells her.

A Man Ray retrospective is held at the Boymans–van Beuningen Museum in Rotterdam, and then travels to Paris and Denmark. Plans for it to travel to Philadelphia, the artist's hometown, are canceled due to a lack of funding.

The exhibition *Two Generations of Photographs: Man Ray and Naomi Savage* opens at the New Jersey State Museum, pairing the photographer with his protégée-niece. The accompanying catalogue offers no details on their familial relationship, and until the end of his life, Man Ray refuses to discuss his family background. "I am an enigma," he insists. "Answers, if they are to be had, will be found in my paintings and drawings. That is where my fears and anxieties are spelled out."

Fig. 69. Naomi Savage, *Man Ray,* 1963. Photographic print, 6⁵⁄₁₆ × 9⅞ in. (16 × 25 cm). Courtesy of the Naomi Savage papers on Man Ray, c. 1924–2005, Archives of American Art, Smithsonian Institution

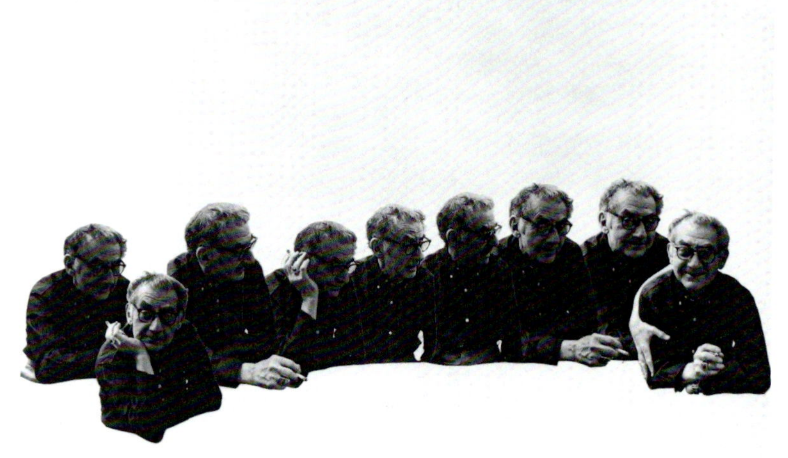

Man Ray is celebrated in an eighty-fifth-birthday exhibition, *Man Ray: Inventor, Painter, Poet* at the New York Cultural Center, organized by Roland Penrose.

Man Ray dies on November 18 at his rue Férou studio. He is buried in Montparnasse Cemetery, where the epitaph on his tombstone reads: "Unconcerned but not indifferent."

In the *New Yorker*, Harold Rosenberg refers to Man Ray as an "American vanguardist," grouping him with Stuart Davis, Charles Demuth, Marsden Hartley, and Joseph Stella.

Arturo Schwarz's monograph on the artist, *The Rigour of Imagination*, is published in 1977. For the first time, Man Ray's given name, Emmanuel Radnitzky, is made known to the public.

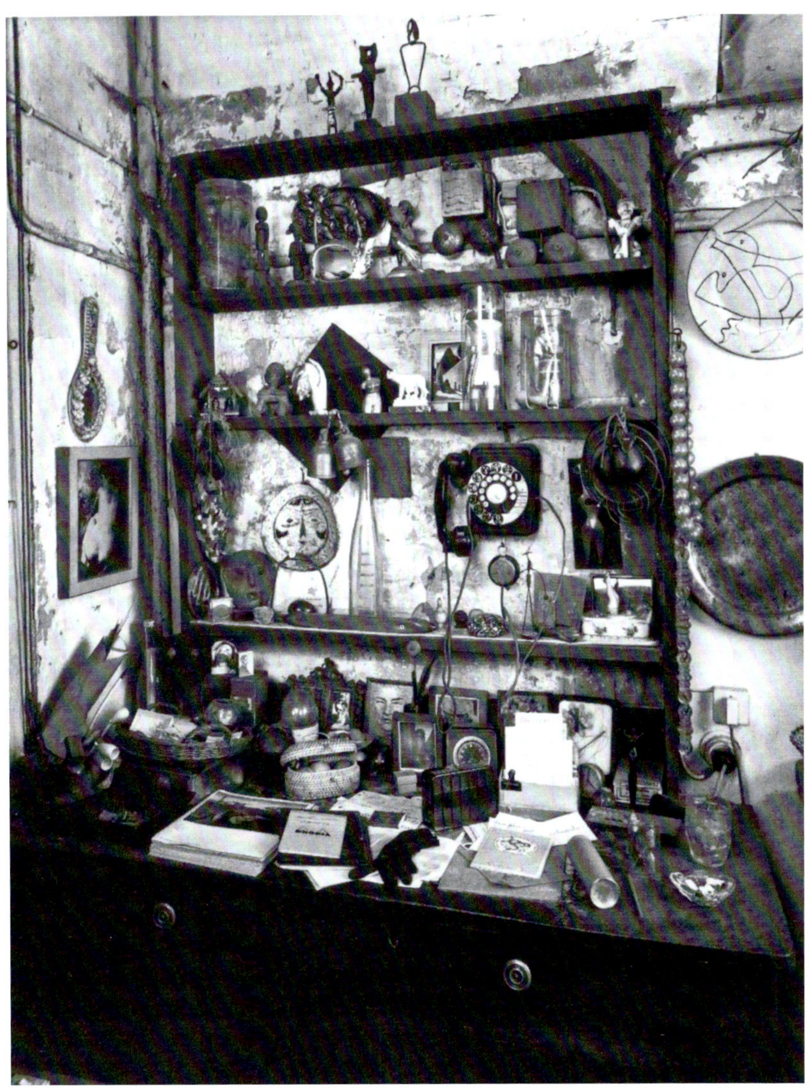

Fig. 70. A corner of the rue Férou studio in the 1980s. Man Ray called this collection of objects "The Cemetery."

notes

Alias Man Ray

Epigraph: Man Ray, "Ruth, Roses, and Revolvers," *View* (December 1944); repr. in Charles Henri Ford, ed., *View: Parade of the Avant-Garde, 1940–1947* (New York: Thunder's Mouth, 1991), 114.

1. Lewis Mumford, "The Art Galleries," *New Yorker*, September 29, 1934.

2. It was apparently Man Ray's brother, Sam (Samuel), who actually came up with the suggestion of changing the name Radnitzky to Ray. See Francis M. Naumann, *Conversion to Modernism: The Early Work of Man Ray* (New Brunswick, N.J.: Rutgers University Press, 2003), 230. I am indebted to this study for its many insights into the artist's formative years.

3. The avoidance of the Jewish question by critics and art historians, since Arturo Schwarz's first biographical effort in 1977, *Man Ray: The Rigour of Imagination* (New York: Rizzoli, 1977), was typical for the period. There was the occasional exception, such as Harold Rosenberg's often quoted remark, originally stated in 1966, the year of Man Ray's retrospective in Los Angeles: "The most serious theme in Jewish life is the problem of identity," and thus, "their art has been the closest expression of themselves as they are, including the fact that they are Jews, each in his individual degree." Rosenberg added the caveat that identity was by no means a problem monopolized by Jews. See his essay "Is There a Jewish Art?" in *Discovering the Present: Three Decades in Art, Culture, and Politics* (Chicago: University of Chicago Press, 1973), 230. The essay was adapted from a talk given at the Jewish Museum in New York in 1966, published in *Commentary* 42 (July 1966).

Only with the advent of identity-based critical methodologies of the last several decades have such complex subjects as Jewish identity, and gender and race, emerged. When Catherine M. Soussloff chaired a February 1996 College Art Association panel on Jewish identity, she said it was the "first time in the eighty-five-year history of the organization that Jewish identity had been the subject of a session." See her "Introducing Jewish Identity to Art History," in Soussloff, ed., *Jewish Identity in Modern Art History* (Berkeley: University of California Press, 1999), 1. While the question of "Jewish art" has been raised for some time, it has generally been concerned with the nineteenth-century emergence of Jewish artists in Europe, or with post–World War II art and symbolism. This critical focus has rarely addressed from a non–art historical vantage a figure such as Man Ray, a Jewish avant-garde artist of the early twentieth century whose oeuvre has been associated almost exclusively with the tenets and contexts of the Dada and Surrealist movements.

4. Milly Heyd has dealt incisively with Man Ray's suppression of his Jewish heritage, especially the fact that the artist hid his family's sweatshop experience out of shame, noting the significance of this phenomenon in relation to various other early twentieth-century first-generation American artists. She quotes Roland Penrose, Man Ray's longtime friend and the husband of Lee Miller, "No one has ever managed to elicit from him [Man Ray] the history of his family, which he affirms is long forgotten and better so, since it could only be a cause of embarrassment." My reading, which principally focuses on the ways in which Man Ray's conflicted need to assimilate is evidenced in the work, builds upon Heyd's assessment of the artist's hidden identity. See her "Man Ray/Emmanuel Radnitsky: Who Is Behind the Enigma of Isidore Ducasse?" in Matthew Baigell and Milly Heyd, eds., *Complex Identities: Jewish Consciousness and Modern Art* (New Brunswick, N.J.: Rutgers University Press, 2001), 115–41; above quotation originally in Roland Penrose, *Man Ray* (Boston: New York Graphic Society, 1975), 9.

Man Ray's decision to suppress his original last name has been sufficient evidence for some to claim that he was anti-Semitic; see George Mellyt, "Man Ray's Camera Obscura," *Interview*, October 1988. Such charges have been challenged by Francis M. Naumann; see his "Man Ray: An American Artist in Pursuit of Liberty," in Curtis L. Carter and Francis M. Naumann, *Man Ray in America*, exh. cat. (Milwaukee: Haggerty Museum of Art, Marquette University, 1989), 11–15.

5. The xenophobia that arose in response to Dada in Europe often took a virulent anti-Semitic slant—especially in the postwar French press, where the Dadaists were often portrayed as left-leaning outsiders, or foreigners, intimating Jews—has been addressed by Elmer Peterson, who cites numerous examples. See his "The Barbarians Breach the Walls—Dada's Press, Paris 1920," in Harriett Watts, ed., *Dada and the Press*, vol. 9 of *Crisis and the Arts: The History of Dada*, Stephen C. Foster, general ed. (Farmington Hills, Mich.: G. K. Hall, 2004), 227–43.

6. Barbara Kirshenblatt-Gimblett, "Introduction," in Barbara Kirshenblatt-Gimblett, ed., *Writing a Modern Jewish History: Essays in Honor of Salo W. Baron* (New York: The Jewish Museum; New Haven: Yale University Press, 2006), 3.

7. For a psychoanalytical reading of Man Ray and some of his works, see Aaron H. Esman, "What Is 'Applied' in 'Applied' Psychoanalysis?" *International Journal of Psychoanalysis* 79, part 4 (August 1998): 746–48.

8. Schwarz's comments are in his *Man Ray: The Rigour of Imagination*, 8. Man Ray's quotation ("I simply try to be as free as possible. . . .") appears in *To Be Continued Unnoticed: Some Papers by Man Ray* (Beverly Hills, Calif.: Copley Galleries, 1948), 4–5. Essentially, Schwarz surveys the artist's oeuvre through the filter of an art-historical and Jungian-based alchemical/archetypal symbolism. He accepts at face value Man Ray's admiration for the Comte de Lautréamont's *Les chants de Maldoror*, which, the artist claimed to Schwarz, revealed to him the "world I was looking for, a world of complete freedom"; see *Man Ray: The Rigour of Imagination*, 161.

9. Schwarz, *Man Ray: The Rigour of Imagination*, 8.

10. Ron Padgett, quoted in Neil Baldwin, *Man Ray: American Artist* (New York: Clarkson N. Potter, 1988), 330.

11. Jarvis Barlow and Man Ray, introductory comments, Pasadena Art Institute exhibition catalogue for *Retrospective*

Exhibition, 1913–1944: Paintings, Drawings, Watercolors, Photographs by Man Ray, September 1944, n.p.; quoted in Baldwin, *Man Ray: American Artist,* 250.

12. Man Ray reissued numerous vintage works in the 1960s and 1970s, unconcerned by notions of uniqueness, which he debunked, defying those who frowned on such policy. "Fortunately, upon demand, it was simple enough to reconstruct these objects despite the disapproval of those who valued only originals. Is a book or a bronze an original? I leave such considerations to well intentioned collectors and amateurs of the rare." Man Ray, "I Have Never Painted a Recent Picture," in Jules Langsner, ed., *Man Ray* (Los Angeles: Los Angeles County Museum of Art, 1966), 28. Rosalind Krauss addresses the question of Man Ray's work in relation to the notion of the original in her essay "Objects of My Affection," in *Man Ray: Objects of My Affection,* exh. cat. (New York: Zabriskie Gallery, 1985), n.p.

13. Man Ray, "Originals Graphic Multiples," in Man Ray, *Objets de mon affection* (Paris: Philippe Sers Editeur, 1983), 158. After his metronome, *Object to Be Destroyed* (1923), was dutifully wrecked by student anarchists at a gallery show in Paris in 1957, Man Ray reproduced the work in an edition with the new name *Indestructible Object* and began to launch numerous other editions of his objects.

14. Francis Naumann makes the correspondence, as well, in *Conversion to Modernism,* 9.

15. Esman, "What Is 'Applied' in 'Applied' Psychoanalysis?" 748. Esman continues, "Man Ray did . . . exchange letters with his parents and siblings, and his niece Naomi became in his later years a treasured student, colleague and confidante. Nonetheless, one can reasonably understand his expatriation, his reinvention of himself, his almost compulsive need to transform the lives of others and the material world in which he lived, as unconscious gestures of revenge and as statements of omnipotent autonomy."

16. The recent spate of Dadaist revisionism has tended to subsume Man Ray further within the general casts of the movement, looking at his work as one vector among the numerous figures who made up international Dadaism, or it has continued to align the artist with certain collaborators, notably Marcel Duchamp and Francis Picabia, whose aegis and weight magnify common threads among the artists' work. The two principal exhibitions of late are *Dada: Zurich, Berlin, Hannover, Cologne, New York, Paris* (2006), organized by the Musée national d'art moderne, Centre Georges Pompidou, Paris, and the National Gallery of Art, Washington, D.C., in collaboration with the Museum of Modern Art in New York, which focused on the movement's international aspects, examining it city by city; and *Duchamp, Man Ray, Picabia* (2008), organized by Tate Modern, London.

17. For "senilities" comment, see Hugo Ball, "Dada Fragments" (1916–17), in Lawrence S. Rainey, *Modernism: An Anthology* (Malden, Mass.: Blackwell, 2005), 478; for Cabaret Voltaire quotation, see Robert Motherwell, ed., *The Dada Painters and Poets: An Anthology,* 2d ed. (Cambridge, Mass.: Harvard University Press, 1981), xxv.

18. For a thorough account of the influence of the anarchist movement on the artist, see Francis M. Naumann, "Man Ray and the Ferrer Center: Art and Anarchy in the Pre-Dada Period," *Dada/Surrealism,* no. 14 (1985): 10–20; repr. in Rudolf E. Kuenzli, ed., *New York Dada* (New York: Willis, Locker and Owens, 1986). Also see Alan Antliff, "Man Ray's Path to Dada," in Antliff, *Anarchist Modernism: Art, Politics, and the First American Avant-Garde* (Chicago: University of Chicago Press, 2001), 73–94.

During this pivotal year of 1912, the young artist befriended Ferrer Center colleagues Samuel Halpert, Max Weber, and Adolf Wolff; and toward the end of the year, visited an artists' colony in Ridgefield, New Jersey, where he shared a modest cottage with Halpert. It is there, within a community of writers and painters, that Man Ray experimented with various modes of representation—from the mimetic to the nonmimetic—as he determined, in the autumn of 1913, to no longer paint from nature but from a more conceptual vantage. His work at the colony had heretofore consisted primarily of landscapes, still lifes, and some figures; the shift toward a more internally conceived model involved a conception of the art object as autonomous, not as illusory representation. See Man Ray, *Self Portrait,* 54.

19. Baldwin, *Man Ray: American Artist,* 74. For additional general consideration of the artist's single-minded evasion of fixed identity, within either a group or a specific aesthetic strategy, see Dickran Tashjian, "Man Ray on the Margins," in Tashjian, *A Boatload of Madmen: Surrealism and the American Avant-Garde, 1920–1950* (New York: Thames & Hudson, 1995), 91–110.

20. Philip Leider, "Man Ray, Wandering Knight," *New York Times,* November 6, 1966 (emphasis added); subsequent quotations are from this article, as indicated in text. Man Ray's insistence that there be no photography (apart from some rayographs) in his multimedia exhibition may have skewed a critical perspective, given the degree to which the artist's acclaim rested on photography.

21. Man Ray had expressed such ideas some twenty years before, anticipating questions regarding chauvinism and influence: "From time to time some artist or critic takes it upon himself in order to bolster the art he wishes to sell, to insist on the nationality of that art—free from the influences of other countries. . . . It is inconceivable that in the domain of art there should still be question of the limitation of influences." Man Ray, unpublished notes, "Hollywood Album," 1940–48, n.p., Man Ray Letters and Album 1922–76, boxes 3–4, Getty Research Institute, Los Angeles.

22. I thank Larry List for informing me of this cherished chess piece of both artists.

23. Although the statement was initially made in reference to his objects, its meaning has been ascribed more broadly to his work in general. See William Seitz, *The Art of Assemblage* (New York: Museum of Modern Art, 1961), 48. Among Man Ray's unpublished notes is a piece titled "Objects" about his fascination with par-

ticular kinds of object. He writes: "I am tired of being surrounded by objects I can smile at, be indulgent with—objects which amuse me and arouse in me a sense of tolerance and superiority. I want objects that disturb, mystify, and intimidate me, whose function I cannot divine, objects which I hope will never function for my comfort or my understanding. To become like certain objects, an *obstruction, useless, cumbersome,* yet *indispensable,* finally the cause of disintegration and *tragedy* (but not disillusionment), while continuing to exist after all the more *mobile* forms of matter and passion have spent themselves." Man Ray, "Hollywood Album."

24. *New York,* February 2, 1970, 57. Others felt similarly, among them Ron Padgett, who had been commissioned to review the Los Angeles retrospective and, despite his enthusiasm for Man Ray's work, noted its lack of chronology and its nondevelopmental principle. He concluded that the artist "paid the price of no apotheosis." The *New York* critic and Padgett are quoted in Baldwin, *Man Ray: American Artist,* 348, 331.

25. In his best nonconformist manner, Man Ray made a habit of confounding the critics of his day. His lack of a signature style was cited by William Rubin, chairman of the Department of Painting and Sculpture at the Museum of Modern Art, who reviewed the artist's 1963 mini-retrospective of paintings and objects (which deliberately excluded his photographs) at the Cordier-Ekstrom Gallery. Rubin, echoing sentiments that Man Ray had heard from others for nearly half a century, could respond favorably only to the artist's early work, acknowledging his achievements of the post-Armory and New York Dada period; he found fault with Man Ray's "stylistic meandering" and said that the artist had never exceeded the quality of works of the earlier period, when he "became the master of his talents." See Rubin, "Man Ray," *Art International,* June 1963.

26. While the subject of Man Ray's adopted name has been variously discussed, the obvious implications of assimilation, and its bearing on the evolution of the artist's work, have been

largely diluted or suppressed. Only after the closing decades of the twentieth century addressed identity politics as a lacuna in art-historical methodology have we seen early twentieth-century Jewish artists considered in terms of their assimilation or lack thereof. See Ken Silver and Romy Golan, *The Circle of Montparnasse: Jewish Artists in Paris, 1905–1945,* exh. cat. (New York: Universe and The Jewish Museum, 1985); Romy Golan, *Modernity and Nostalgia: Art and Politics in France Between the Wars* (New Haven: Yale University Press, 1995); and my essay "Modigliani Against the Grain," in Mason Klein, ed., *Modigliani: Beyond the Myth* (New York: The Jewish Museum; New Haven: Yale University Press, 2004), 1–23.

27. According to an interview with the artist's sister Do (Dora) Ray Goodbread and Florence Blumenthal, her daughter, Do protested the name because it sounded "too Irish," and preferred "Radin"; the only family member not to legally adopt the new surname was father Max. See Baldwin, *Man Ray: American Artist,* 16–17.

28. Such similarities as those between Duchamp's *Juggler of Gravity* and Man Ray's balancing *Rope Dancer,* or just formalist iconography between the two works, as in the upper and lower registers (and upper gendered female); significant shadows; rectilinear shapes, which roughly correspond to Duchamp's upper-register "Draft Pistons" or "Nets"; connecting umbilical cords, as seen in Duchamp's tendril-like "Capillary Tubes," have been pointed out by scholars, notably Linda Henderson, "Reflections of and/or on Marcel Duchamp's *Large Glass,*" in Francis Naumann with Beth Venn, *Making Mischief: Dada Invades New York* (New York: Whitney Museum of American Art and Harry N. Abrams), 237; and Naumann, *Conversion to Modernism,* 160. Man Ray's significant preoccupation with shadows goes back to his high school days. Duchamp's notes on *The Large Glass,* written during the three years before he came to New York in 1915, were first published in a facsimile edition by him, *La mariée mise à nu par ses célibataires, même* (Paris, 1934), and were reprinted with an English translation by Arturo Schwarz in *Marcel Duchamp: Notes and Pro-*

jects for the Large Glass (New York: Harry N. Abrams, 1969).

29. John Weichsel, "New Art and Man Ray," *East and West* 1, no. 8 (November 1915). See Naumann, *Conversion to Modernism,* 243 n. 29. After the article appeared, Man Ray wrote to Weichsel expressing his appreciation, and stating that "it was helpful in sensing my place in art-movements." See ibid., 231. Six of Man Ray's paintings shown at the Daniel Gallery were sold to the Chicago-based collector Arthur J. Eddy.

30. This was *The Rope Dancer*'s title when the painting was first exhibited, at the First Annual Exhibition of the Society of Independent Artists, in 1917, best known for the scandal that arose around the withdrawal of Duchamp's *Fountain.* Man Ray published Evreinof's play in the journal *TNT* in 1919.

31. Man Ray, *Self Portrait* (Boston: Little, Brown, 1963), 66–67.

32. Anne Umland, Adrian Sudhalter, and Scott Gerson, eds., *Dada in the Collection of the Museum of Modern Art* (New York: Museum of Modern Art, 2008), 209–13.

33. Naumann cites the historical invocation of the subject as one usually tied to "man's struggle for existence" but does not otherwise elaborate on its possible meanings in relation to the artist. See Naumann, *Conversion to Modernism,* 158.

34. Such was the painting's visual impact, Man Ray said, that "some of the painters whose works hung nearby were dissatisfied with the hanging—my painting made theirs look dull and insignificant—it was a publicity stunt, they argued"; see his *Self Portrait,* 71.

35. In Neil Baldwin's biography, Man Ray is referred to as having a "love-hate" relationship with New York, being intimidated because of his modest height, which was better suited to the architecture and lower skyline of Paris; see Baldwin, *Man Ray: American Artist,* 231.

36. Man Ray knew American painters, such as Max Weber, who had returned from Paris having been influenced by

Analytical Cubism, but it was the titanic influence of the Armory Show of 1913 that struck such a profound chord. In addition to Braque's painting, Man Ray saw Picasso's 1910 *Woman with Mustard Pot* (he had seen Picasso's work at Stieglitz's 291 gallery in 1909); Robert Delaunay's *Window on the City, No. 4* (1910–11); and Picabia's *Dances at the Spring* (1912), among others. As Merry Foresta has observed, although one may identify the Cubist style, it is the overriding imprint of the name and identity of Man Ray that one sees: "The painting's tiny dimensions belie its role as a personal icon. . . . His painted heraldry springs from deeper motives. It is not so much an attempt to practice cubism as an attempt to take possession of it. To speak of the picture's content, we must mention Man Ray; to refer to its style, again, Man Ray"; see her "Introduction," in Foresta, *Perpetual Motif*, 12.

37. Man Ray met Lacroix in the summer of 1913, soon after she and the poet and sculptor Adolf Wolff, an anarchist friend of Man Ray's whom he had met at the Ferrer Center the year before, moved from Belgium to New York. Wolff and Lacroix, in true bohemian fashion, had not married; they had a child, Esther, who was seven years old when Lacroix left Wolff and was invited, along with Esther, to move in with Man Ray in his cottage in Ridgefield.

38. "Man Ray, the tailor's son, had trouble keeping his restless hands still"; see Baldwin, *Man Ray: American Artist*, 92.

39. Man Ray describes the careful preparation for this portrait in *Self Portrait*, 19–20. The uncertain authorship of the photograph is discussed by Naumann in *Conversion to Modernism*, 238 n. 3. A Sotheby's auction catalogue lists the work as a self-portrait, perhaps because it was in Man Ray's possession, but it is neither stamped nor signed; see *Man Ray: Paintings, Objects, Photographs: Property from the Estate of Juliet Man Ray, the Man Ray Trust and the Family of Juliet Man Ray*, cat. for Sotheby's estate sale, London, March 22–23, 1995. In the frontispiece of Naumann's *Conversion to Modernism*, the photograph is dated c. 1915. I suspect an earlier date,

c. 1912, since in *Self Portrait* (19–20) the artist recalls the episode with Stieglitz when he was still living in Brooklyn with his family.

40. Man Ray's birth certificate reads "Michael Radnitzky"; his family may have considered "Michael," the anglicized version of "Emmanuel," a more suitable name for their American-born son. See Naumann, *Conversion to Modernism*, 235 n. 7.

Unlike his older brother, Sam would remain mired within the family fold, bound by a sense of obligation that he felt his brother had abandoned in distancing himself from his family; throughout his life, Sam never ceased to resent this, as he articulated in a story he wrote, "Man Proposes." Papers of Helen Ray Faden, present whereabouts unknown. After settling into his new digs in Ridgefield, Man Ray wrote his brother: "My dear Sam, I feel so much at cross purposes, both wishing to return and to remain here awhile yet. It isn't exactly concern for the future, it is the happy-go-lucky existence without any goal." Man Ray, letter to Samuel Ray, n.d.; quoted in Baldwin, *Man Ray: American Artist*, 31.

41. Man Ray, "Hollywood Album."

42. Man Ray, *Self Portrait*, 19.

43. Man Ray, "Hollywood Album."

44. Man Ray, *Self Portrait*, 223.

45. Baldwin, *Man Ray: American Artist*, 182.

46. Man Ray, *Self Portrait*, 225–26.

47. Schwarz's comment about the "first proto-Dada assemblage" is in his *Man Ray: The Rigour of Imagination*, 37. For the artist's remarks about his painting *Self-Portrait*, see Man Ray, *Self Portrait*, 71. Merry Foresta points out that Man Ray begins to represent himself symbolically, as in *Self-Portrait*, where he uses his handprint as a signature, and in the photograph of the eggbeater, *Man*; see Foresta, "Introduction," *Perpetual Motif*, 24.

48. Quotations are from Man Ray's statement for the catalogue of *Forum Exhibition of Modern American Painters* held at the Anderson Galleries in New York, March 13–25, 1916.

49. Interview with Arnold Crane, January 1970, Archives of American Art, Smithsonian Institution; also quoted in Baldwin, *Man Ray: American Artist*, 9.

50. Man Ray's passion for art was tolerated by his parents as long as it remained a secondary pursuit, peripheral to a more serious vocation. To them and to his relatives, an interest in painting was an understandable exponent of a career in architecture, for which he had already begun training and which seemed poised to become reality when he received an architecture scholarship to New York University. As family lore has it, though, the young Man Ray made it clear at his high school graduation that his future would be defined by creativity and passion and not by a willingness to conform to others' expectations. Garbed in a red shirt, while all the other boys in his class wore white shirts with their gray pants, he proudly received a leather-bound edition of Walt Whitman's *Leaves of Grass*, his award for finishing with top honors in English; see Baldwin, *Man Ray: American Artist*, 7, 9.

51. Ibid., 16. Since Man Ray and his brother, Sam, did not change their last name until the following year, the artist may well have signed the tapestry later, investing his quilt with the formal attributes of painting.

52. To invoke Jacques Lacan's words: "Mimicry reveals something in so far as it is distinct from what might be called an *itself* that is behind. The effect of mimicry is camouflage. . . . It is not a question of harmonizing with the background, but against a mottled background, of becoming mottled—exactly like the technique of camouflage practised in human warfare." *The Four Fundamental Concepts of Psychoanalysis*, trans. Alan Sheridan (London: Hogarth, 1977), 99.

53. Various publication dates have been given for *A Book of Divers Writings*; Naumann, *Conversion to Modernism*, January 1915; Schwarz, *Man Ray: The Rigour of Imagination*, April 1915; Baldwin, in *Man Ray: American Artist*, summer of 1914 (production), and February 1915 (publication).

54. Quoted in Alfred Kreymborg, "Man

Ray and Adon La Croix, Economists," *New York Morning Telegraph*, March 14, 1915, 7; see Naumann, *Conversion to Modernism*, 111, and page 172 of this volume.

55. One of two magazines published during the period in which Man Ray lived in Ridgefield; the other, *Others*, was a poetry magazine overseen by Alfred Kreymborg, poet, critic, musician, and chess player.

56. Another explanatory note, "We are *not* neutral," appeared beneath the periodical's title, countering President Woodrow Wilson's plea for the American people to remain neutral.

57. As a portrait photographer, Man Ray demonstrated an uncanny nimbleness in capturing his sitters, privately within themselves, seemingly alone, undisturbed. He obviously found that a lack of intrusiveness came naturally to him. His own presence is neutralized, hidden, if only to allow his subjects, from cultural icons to self-anointed important businessmen, to feel unself-conscious.

58. Man Ray, "Impressions of 291," *Camera Work* 47 (dated July 1914, published January 1915): 61. While Stieglitz was clearly an early mentor figure, and Man Ray's tribute to him heartfelt, I suspect his capitalization of the letter M in the repeated word "Man" was done more than simply "to imply the deification of his subject"; see Naumann, *Conversion to Modernism*, 30.

59. In response to the Rodin drawings, Man Ray said, "There was no anatomy in [them], they were an expression of self-assurance, of freedom, total freedom. I thought, this is the freedom I want." Schwarz, *Man Ray: The Rigour of Imagination*, 16.

60. See Susan W. Churchill, "Making Space for 'Others': A History of a Modernist Little Magazine," *Journal of Modern Literature* 22, no. 1 (Autumn 1998): 76–77. Churchill discusses the new poetry and *Others* in such terms, arguing that "the Modernist preoccupation with space indicates an engagement with predominant social issues of the time—gender and sexuality"; see her "Making Space for 'Others,'" 49.

61. These black trees would appear in one of his wife's poems, "Trees," for which Man Ray drew the title in a kind of hieroglyphic script. Other poems that appear in *Adonism* feature emotionally charged spatial metaphors—for example, "Spring": "In these dull tentative days when every little plant timidly pokes her head out of the ground and quickly withdraws again if one observes her—impatiently my desire reaches toward the full-blown summer, the love-steeped confident summer when nothing is denied and nothing withheld."

62. Lacroix's poem "Intimacy" and Man Ray's "Three Dimensions" appear in *Others* 1, no. 6 (Summer 1915): 107–8.

63. Naumann contrasts "Three Dimensions" to Lacroix's "Intimacy," claiming that Man Ray's poem "avoids such emotionally charged subject matter and, instead, presents a carefully constructed, rhythmic verse, describing a view of houses seen in the dead of night"; see *Conversion to Modernism*, 133.

64. In his openness to modernist literary and visual ideas, Man Ray was fulfilling his own interest in writing, which would remain an abiding interest for him and allow him to transfer the political, anarchistic ideals of freedom to a level of social interaction. He believed that his new community "might develop into something more than merely an artists' colony . . . [and] could become an advanced cultural center embracing all the arts." Man Ray, *Self Portrait*, 33.

65. As Duchamp noted to Pierre Cabanne, when he considered changing his identity in 1920, he initially alighted on the idea of choosing a Jewish name, but "didn't find a Jewish name that I especially liked, or that tempted me, and suddenly I had an idea: why not change sex?" Pierre Cabanne, *Dialogues with Marcel Duchamp*, trans. Ron Padgett (New York: Viking, 1974), 64. What Duchamp achieved, in conjuring the name Rrose Sélavy (a pun on *eros c'est la vie*—eros is life), was to have it both ways—to change gender and acquire a Jewish name—at once, since "Sélavy" includes within it one of the most common Jewish names,

Levy. See Rosalind Krauss, *Bachelors* (Cambridge, Mass.: MIT Press, 1999), 42.

66. Man Ray, *Self Portrait*, 69. The photograph of Duchamp is reproduced in *Conspiratorial Laughter—A Friendship: Man Ray and Duchamp* (New York: Zabriskie Gallery, 1995).

67. Man Ray, *Self Portrait*, 59.

68. Man Ray could easily have seen a reference to the publication, as it was advertised in Tzara's magazine *Dada* (nos. 4–5, May 1919).

69. Baldwin, *Man Ray: American Artist*, 38.

70. For the quotation, and a thorough reading of *Les chants*, see Barbara Lynne Teter-Goodale, "Textual/Sexual Inscription and the Extension of Boundaries in *Les chants de Maldoror*," Ph.d. diss., University of Pennsylvania, 1998. Man Ray's dual preoccupation with the literary and the visual, especially at Ridgefield, culminates in a sense in his aerographic technique. His lettering and hand-printing in works like *A Book of Divers Writings* were a passion, and "lettering" reemerges throughout his life, as in *Alphabet for Adults* (1948), which beyond its unbound portfolio of ink drawings was, like *Les mains libres* and most of Man Ray's other series, printed as a limited-edition book.

71. For the "juxtaposition" quotation, see Man Ray, "Tous les films que j'ai réalisés," *Études cinématographiques*, nos. 38–39 (Spring 1965): 43–46; quoted in Schwarz, *Man Ray: The Rigour of Imagination*, 161. Man Ray's comments on objects can be found in ibid., 158.

72. Man Ray inexhaustibly conjured new ways to undermine the notion of an original, lasting identity. He would photograph and then dispose of his "objects of affection," which he much later often re-created; convert one medium into another, reconceiving photographed objects as paintings, or vice versa; and produce three-dimensional punning objects, whose homophonic double or triple meaning—such as that of the 1958 *Pain peint (Blue Bred)* (blue/bread/well-bred/blue/blood)—would not only highlight the indeterminacy of identity but also, in its first version (two loaves

displayed on old grocery scales), upset the balance of meaning.

73. Maria Morris Hambourg, "Photography Between the Wars: Selections from the Ford Motor Company Collection," *Metropolitan Museum of Art Bulletin*, n.s. 45, no. 4 (Spring 1988): 6.

74. Man Ray made a replica in 1967 for the Museum of Modern Art exhibition *Dada, Surrealism, and Their Heritage* (1968); another replica was made in 1969 for the Moderna Museet in Stockholm; the maquette, now in the collection of the Israel Museum, Jerusalem, was made for the edition that Arturo Schwarz and Man Ray produced in 1971; and a final replica was made in 1972 to accommodate several retrospectives worldwide and was in the collection of Lucien Treillard. On some examples of the 1971 edition Man Ray placed a plaque reading: "Do Not Disturb." I thank Adina Kamien for assistance with this research.

75. Man Ray's "crave America" remark was in his letter to Ferdinand Howald, August 18, 1921. Papers of Ferdinand Howald, University Libraries, Ohio State University, Columbus. In addition to printing Tzara's response in its entirety, this first and only issue of *New York Dada* featured a cover designed by Duchamp with Man Ray's photograph of Rrose Sélavy; a photograph by Alfred Stieglitz; poetry by the artist Marsden Hartley; and illustrations depicting the Baroness Elsa von Freytag-Loringhoven, the star of Man Ray and Duchamp's film *Elsa, Baroness von Freytag-Loringhoven, Shaves Her Pubic Hair*. Tzara's *Dadaglobe* journal remained unpublished, a victim of Parisian Dada's internecine feuding.

76. Man Ray, letter to Tristan Tzara, June 18, 1921. Bibliothèque Littéraire Jacques Doucet, Paris.

77. Merry Foresta makes a similar point in Foresta, *Perpetual Motif*, 24.

78. For Mark Twain's reception and gradual fame on the Continent, see Archibald Henderson, "The International Fame of Mark Twain," *North American Review* (1910), in Frederick Anderson, ed., *Mark Twain* (London: Routledge, 1997), 302–12.

79. Man Ray's brand of linguistic humor was generally more representative of American vernacular than a more subtle variety. See Robert Pincus-Witten, "Man Ray: The Homophonic Pun and American Vernacular," *Artforum* 13, no. 8 (April 1975): 54–59.

80. See Krauss, "Objects of My Affection," n.p.

81. In 1925, Aragon defined the "marvelous": "Le merveilleux, c'est la contradiction qui apparaît dans le reel"; see "Idées," *La révolution surréaliste* 1 (April 1925): 30. In the last line of *Nadja*, Breton says: "La beauté sera convulsive ou ne sera pas" (Beauty will be convulsive, or it will not be); see André Breton, *Nadja*, trans. Richard Howard (New York: Grove, 1960), 160.

82. In an August 18, 1921, letter to his patron, Ferdinand Howald, Man Ray writes, "I am an infant here! Have I found the secret of eternal youth?" Papers of Ferdinand Howald, University Libraries, Ohio State University, Columbus. In letters to Howald and his brother, Sam, in July 1921, Man Ray refers to feeling like a "new-born baby." See Ferdinand Howald Correspondence, Archives of American Art, Smithsonian Institution (July 1921); quoted in Baldwin, *Man Ray: American Artist*, 82, 391. Such rebirth only underscored the artist's need to obliterate his past; but in Man Ray, one sees, too, a perfect candidate for what Hugo Ball defined in 1916–17 as an artistic model for the new Dada, writing of "childhood" and a "new world [with] everything childlike and symbolical in opposition to the senilities of the world of grown-ups." Ball, "Dada Fragments," 478.

83. Man Ray, letter to Ferdinand Howald, dated February 3, 1921, though actually from 1922, since Man Ray was still in New York throughout 1921. Papers of Ferdinand Howald, University Libraries, Ohio State University, Columbus.

84. Jean Cocteau, "Lettre ouverte à Man Ray, photograph américain," *Les Feuilles libres*, no. 26 (April–May 1922): n.p. In addition to making rayographs, the artist began his commercial photographic work after meeting Poiret in 1922, through Francis Picabia's first wife,

Gabrielle. Poiret, Man Ray notes in *Self Portrait*, encouraged him to experiment and elevate fashion photography: "He would speak to the mannequins, impress upon them that this work was not the ordinary showing of gowns, but portraiture as well, giving more human qualities to the picture"; see *Self Portrait*, 122.

85. Cocteau mentions Man Ray's photographic project with Barbette in "Le numéro Barbette," *Nouvelle revue française* (July 1926); repr. as *Le numéro Barbette* (Paris: Jacques Damase, 1980), 5–41. For more on Barbette and the attendant questions of gender, see Amy Lyford, "'Le Numéro Barbette': Photography and the Politics of Embodiment in Interwar Paris," in Whitney Chadwick and Tirza True Latimer, eds., *Modern Woman Revisited: Paris Between the Wars* (New Brunswick, N.J.: Rutgers University Press, 2003), 223–36.

86. The twenty-year-old Manya Louria was married to Melach Radnitzky the day she arrived in New York from Russia. But, according to Baldwin, "their marriage was not consummated that night." After Manya resisted her newly betrothed's advances, he slept on the floor. The next day she left to stay with one of her older sisters, Hannah, who also lived in New York, but returned to Melach after several weeks; see Baldwin, *Man Ray: American Artist*, 3; from anecdotal information supplied by Man Ray's sister Do Ray Goodbread and niece Florence Blumenthal.

In the end, the immigrant tale of Man Ray's parents is erased in *Self Portrait*, with no mention of their origins. Man Ray alters the otherwise known facts of his parents' meeting in America, exaggerating the length of time they separated from several weeks to a year, for example, and portraying them as having reunited by chance, when in fact his mother was staying with her sister.

87. The whereabouts of the original family photograph are unknown; the portrait is reproduced in its entirety in Baldwin, *Man Ray: American Artist*, opposite p. 1. Heyd also interprets the crop of the photograph as an "oedipal fantasy" in her "Man Ray/Emmanuel Radnitsky: Who Is Behind the Enigma of Isidore Ducasse?" in Matthew

Baigell and Milly Heyd, eds., *Complex Identities: Jewish Consciousness and Modern Art*, 119.

88. For more on object relations and self-psychology, in the context of narcissism or grandiosity, see Heinz Kohut, *The Restoration of the Self* (New York: International Universities Press, 1977), and Otto F. Kernberg, *Aggressivity, Narcissism, and Self-Destructiveness in the Psychotherapeutic Relationship* (New Haven: Yale University Press, 2004).

89. Baldwin, *Man Ray: American Artist*, 168.

90. The initial version of this work was *The Object to Be Destroyed* (1923). The other iterations were: *Object of Destruction* (1932), *Lost Object* (1945), *Indestructible Object* (1958), and *Perpetual Motif* (1972). Janine Mileaf examines *Object to Be Destroyed* in terms of its embodiment of the artist's psychosexual needs in "Beyond You and Me: Man Ray's *Object to be Destroyed*," *Art Journal* 63, no. 1 (Spring 2004): 4–23. One is tempted to wonder whether, at least unconsciously, Man Ray, as part of his tendency to merge with love objects, was conflating "eye" and "I."

91. Annoyed by the sense that people were eager to see more of his new production, rather than earlier work, the artist titled the accompanying text for his Los Angeles County Museum of Art exhibition "I Have Never Painted a Recent Picture."

92. Nearly all the principal Parisian Dadaists, it seemed, contributed texts to the catalogue, which informed: "It is no longer known where Man Ray was born. After a career as a coal merchant, millionaire several times over and chairman of a chewing-gum trust, he has decided to accept the invitation of the Dadaists to show his latest canvases in Paris." See Schwarz, *Man Ray: The Rigour of Imagination*, 56.

93. Alain Jouffroy, *La vie réinventée: L'explosion des années 20 à Paris* (Paris: Robert Laffont, 1982), 108 (trans. in Baldwin, *Man Ray: American Artist*, 125); Morris Gordon, "Man Ray, the Fiery Elf," *Infinity* 11, no. 9 (November 1962): 27–29 (quoted in Baldwin, *Man Ray: American Artist*, 312).

94. Man Ray, letter to Seymour Lawrence, November 26, 1962; Man Ray, letters to Seymour Lawrence, n.d.

(c. May–June 1961). Quoted in Baldwin, *Man Ray: American Artist*, 312–14.

95. Man Ray, "All the Films That I Have Made," in Arturo Schwarz, ed., *Man Ray: Sixty Years of Liberties* (Paris: Eric Losfeld; Milan: Galleria Schwarz, 1971), 44, 46.

96. See Naumann, *Conversion to Modernism*, 235 n. 3; and Man Ray, *Self Portrait*, 4.

97. W. R. Hearst, "The Appeal of Cuba," *New York Journal*, October 11, 1895, 4.

98. The popularity of *Hogan's Alley* and other comic strips at the turn of the century raised the level of the medium's artistic quality to include complex, simultaneous narratives. Highly populated imagery, with overlapping figures sharing an indeterminate space, and other effects may have influenced some of Man Ray's early work, such as his illustrations for the journal *Mother Earth*, the cover of *International*, and more significantly, early watercolors like *Metropolis* (1913).

99. Man Ray, "Hollywood Album."

100. Man Ray, *Self Portrait*, 6–7.

101. Ibid., 10, 31.

102. Baldwin, *Man Ray: American Artist*, 4. Baldwin's biography refers incorrectly to "Dick Carter" instead of "Nick Carter."

103. The date 1896 appears in Baldwin's *Man Ray: American Artist*. One can assume that Man Ray's younger brother, Sam, was sick at the time. His younger sister, Elka, or Elsie, was born in 1897.

104. Baldwin, *Man Ray: American Artist*, 3. Additional anecdotal information about Man Ray's parents provided by Do Ray Goodbread and Florence Blumenthal comes from interviews that Neil Baldwin conducted in 1984.

105. Man Ray, *Self Portrait*, 254. For a discussion of Man Ray's technique, see Alain Sayag, "Beyond Mirroring the Object," in Emmanuelle de L'Ecotais and Alain Sayag, eds., *Man Ray: Photography and Its Double* (Paris: Musée national d'art moderne, Centre Georges Pompidou; London: Gingko, 1998), 230–33, esp. 233 n. 13.

106. Jindřich Štyrský, "Picture," *Disk*, no. 1 (1923); trans. in Stephen Bann, ed.,

The Tradition of Constructivism (New York: Viking, 1974), 97–102; quoted in Maria Morris Hambourg with Christopher Phillips, *The New Vision: Photography Between the Wars* (New York: Metropolitan Museum of Art, 1989), 78.

107. Christopher Phillips, "Resurrecting Vision: The New Photography in Europe Between the Wars," in Hambourg with Phillips, *New Vision*, 77–78. Dada and Surrealism promulgated an entirely different critique of industrial and technological progress, contrasting this view of "machine romanticism" and its integration into society.

108. Man Ray, *Self Portrait*, 291–92.

109. After "burning" in the f-holes, Man Ray presumably exposed the photographic paper with the negative of Kiki. The work's title, *Le violon d'Ingres* (Ingres's violin), refers to the French artist's other avocation—playing the violin—an activity that was eclipsed by his career as a painter. During the nineteenth century, the words *violon d'Ingres* became an idiomatic expression denoting "hobby." This meaning may well have resonated with Man Ray as he began to focus increasingly on his new medium in Paris in the early 1920s.

110. "The transformation of revolutionaries into classicists, by way of the art of Ingres, was in fact taking place in ateliers all over Paris." See Kenneth E. Silver, *Esprit de Corps: The Art of the Parisian Avant-Garde and the First World War, 1914–1925* (Princeton, N.J.: Princeton University Press, 1989), 249. For further discussion of *Le violon d'Ingres* within the broader context of desire and de Sade, see Kirsten Hoving Powell, "*Le violon d'Ingres*: Man Ray's Variations on Ingres, Deformation, Desire and de Sade," *Art History* 23, no. 5 (December 2000): 772–99. For another enlightening, critical account of Man Ray's work of this period, see David Bate, *Photography and Surrealism: Sexuality, Colonialism, and Social Dissent* (London: I. B. Tauris, 2004), esp. chaps. 4 and 5.

111. Baldwin, *Man Ray: American Artist*, 21. For Breton's reference to Ingres, see "Liquidation," *Littérature*, March 1921, 4.

112. Although the figure in *Anatomies* has

never been definitively identified as Lee Miller, she is the likely subject, given its date and the nature of the series he made with Miller.

113. The former appeared in issue 2 of the journal *Le Surréalisme au service de la révolution*, October 1930, and the latter in issue 5, May 1933. Man Ray's own involvement with the Marquis de Sade can be traced to various sources, among them Paul Éluard, who was becoming a trusted friend. He had glorified Sade as *"fantastique"* and a "revolutionary" in *Le révolution surréaliste*, no. 8 (December 1, 1926). More important, Maurice Heine, Man Ray's neighbor in Montparnasse, had been gathering remnants of Sade's manuscripts for more than fifteen years. Man Ray, interview with Pierre Bourgeade, in *Bonsoir, Man Ray* (Paris: Pierre Belfond, 1972), 74–75. For more on Man Ray and Surrealism's enthusiasm for Sade, and the attendant implications, see Bate, *Photography and Surrealism*, chap. 5.

114. The complex questions of the inherent misogyny of Surrealism have been adequately addressed by others; see, for example, Mary Ann Caws, Rudolf Kuenzli, and Gwen Raaberg, eds., *Surrealism and Women* (Cambridge, Mass.: MIT Press, 1991).

115. Théophile Silvestre, *Histoire des artists vivants, français et étrangers: Études d'après nature* (Paris: E. Blanchard, 1856), 23; repr. as *Les artistes français*, vol. 2 (Paris: C. Crès, 1926); quoted in Powell, "Le violon d'Ingres," 772.

116. Louis Aragon, *Paris Peasant* (London: Pan, 1980), 217. The original book, *Paysan de Paris*, was published in 1926.

117. Bate situates this conflict with Freudian psychoanalytic terms, explained by Jean LaPlance and Jean-Bertrand Pontalis. "Freud argued: 'Any psycho-analytic attempt to elucidate the question of conflict in depth must inevitably open on to what is the nuclear conflict for the human subject—the Oedipus complex . . . as a dialectical and primal conjunction of desire and prohibition.'" See Jean LaPlance and Jean-Bertrand Pontalis, *The Language of Psycho-analysis* (London: Karnac, 1988),

362; quoted in Bate, *Photography and Surrealism*, 136.

118. In *Space Writing (Self-Portrait)* (1935) Man Ray wrote his name with light, another gesture of self-inscription that was characteristic throughout his career. I am indebted to Ellen Carey, associate professor of photography at the University of Hartford, for mentioning the mirror image of Man Ray's name in this photograph.

119. See Anthony Penrose, *The Lives of Lee Miller* (New York: Holt, Rinehart and Winston, 1985), 30; and Mario Amaya, "My Man Ray: Interview with Lee Miller," in *Art in America* 63, no. 3 (May–June 1975): 57.

120. Man Ray, "The Rayograph," preface to *12 Rayographs/1921–1928*, exh. cat. (Stuttgart: Schubert and Kapitzki, 1963).

121. *Dreams That Money Can Buy* includes seven episodes allied within a scenario about a man who sells dreams to skeptical customers: Max Ernst's *Desire*, Fernand Léger's *The Girl with the Prefabricated Heart*, Man Ray's *Ruth, Roses, and Revolvers* (with music by Darius Milhaud), Marcel Duchamp's *Discs*, Alexander Calder's *Circus* and *Ballet*, and Richter's own *Narcissus*.

122. Program notes for *Dreams That Money Can Buy*, 1947, Collection of Philadelphia Museum of Art, n.p.; quoted in Baldwin, *Man Ray: American Artist*, 250.

123. The double entendre of "script" is but another form of defense.

124. Man Ray, *Self Portrait*, 297.

125. Man Ray, "Hollywood Album."

126. See Merry Foresta, "Exile in Paradise: Man Ray in Hollywood, 1940–51," in her *Perpetual Motif*, 284.

127. Man Ray, unpublished notes, "Hollywood Album" ("Art and Science"), 1940–48, n.p., Man Ray Letters and Album 1922–76, box 3, Getty Research Institute, Los Angeles.

128. "Axiom: Because the pyramid . . ." appears in Man Ray, unpublished notes, "Hollywood Album."

129. Other art historians, such as Sandra S. Phillips, note how the artist's works of

the middle to late 1930s show a "charged sensitivity to shadow"; see her "Themes and Variations: Man Ray's Photography in the Twenties and Thirties," in Foresta, *Perpetual Motif*, 223.

130. Schwarz, *Man Ray: The Rigour of Imagination*, 72.

131. Man Ray, "A Note on the Shakespearean Equations," in *To Be Continued Unnoticed: Some Papers by Man Ray*.

132. When Max Ernst had taken him, in the mid-1930s, to see the mathematical models on display at the Institut Henri Poincaré in Paris, the original experience was mystifying to Man Ray. His photographic series of the models was published in the art journal *Cahiers d'Art* in 1936. As he would recall in a 1961 interview: "I didn't understand a thing, but the shapes were so unusual, as revolutionary as anything that is being done today in painting or in sculpture." This was what the artist was now trying to evoke, but really he was attempting to extrapolate the "symbolical relation between the subject and the [Shakespearean] title," privileging the ideational over the visual. The 1961 interview with Man Ray was shown in the film *Montparnasse Revisited: A Life in the Day of Man Ray* (1991), written and presented by Edwin Mullins, and edited and directed by Matthew Reinders; the second quotation is from Man Ray, *Self Portrait*, 369.

133. A varying degree of finish characterizes the artist's late work. In paintings such as *Little Basket with Pears* and *Plane and Bananas* (both 1948) and large paintings like *Image à deux faces* (1959) Man Ray seems to be appropriating the popular imagery of advertising and cinema, but in the traditional Surrealist manner of so many of his colleagues. One may see in such work a proto-Pop sensibility, which would develop into his series *Natural Painting*, made by squirting paint from a tube directly onto a board, and sandwiching another on top, which Man Ray or his wife, Juliet, would sit on to produce an instant multiple. Cynicism toward a revived painterly abstraction, as expressed in "A Note on the Shakespearean Equations," coupled with an ever more acute need to mythologize

himself, to prop himself up as an autonomous agent of innovation and adaptability, mark Man Ray's late career.

134. Man Ray, unpublished notes, "Hollywood Album."

135. Ibid.

136. Man Ray, *Self Portrait*, 356.

137. The interview, dated as 1983, is
quoted in Sotheby's estate sale catalogue
*Man Ray: Paintings, Objects, Photographs:
Property from the Estate of Juliet Man Ray, the
Man Ray Trust and the Family of Juliet Man
Ray*, 152.

138. Man Ray, *Self Portrait*, 357.

Lost in Translation

Epigraphs: Charles Baudelaire, "The
Salon of 1859," quoted in *Beaumont Newhall:
Essays and Images* (New York: Museum of
Modern Art, 1980), 113; "Interview with
Man Ray," in Jean-Hubert Martin et al.,
Objets de mon affection (Paris: Philippe Sers,
1983), 36.

1. John Russell, "The Whole Man Ray at
the Cultural Center," *New York Times*, June
20, 1974, 20; cited in Neil Baldwin, *Man
Ray: American Artist* (New York: Clarkson
N. Potter, 1988), 353–54.

2. Robert Melville, "Man Ray in London,"
Arts Magazine 33 (June 1959): 45–47.

3. Georges Ribemont-Dessaignes, untitled article in *Les feuilles libres*, May–June
1925; cited in Baldwin, *Man Ray: American
Artist*, 127.

4. Lewis Mumford, "The Art Gallery:
Critics and Cameras," *New Yorker*, September 29, 1934, 34–35.

5. Man Ray, *Self Portrait* (Boston: Little,
Brown, 1963), 98.

6. Arturo Schwarz, *New York Dada: Duchamp,
Man Ray, Picabia*, exh. cat. (Munich:
Städtische Galerie im Lenbachhous,
1974), 97, 95; cited in *Man Ray: Photographs
and Objects*, exh. cat. (Birmingham, Ala.:
Birmingham Museum of Art, 1980), 29.

7. Willard Huntington Wright, "Modern
Art: The New Spirit in America," *International Studio* 60 (November–February
1916–17): lxiv.

8. Man Ray's many and various Paris
associations and activities are detailed
by Billy Klüver and Julie Martin in "Man
Ray Paris," in Merry Foresta, ed., *Perpetual
Motif: The Art of Man Ray* (New York: Abbeville, 1988), 89–136.

9. Ibid., 93.

10. Tristan Tzara, "Pensée sur l'art," in
Exposition Dada Man Ray, exh. pamphlet
(Paris: Librairie Six, 1921), in the collection of the Bibliothèque Nationale, Paris.
The catalogue was a three-page pamphlet
comprising a checklist, a fictitious biography, a map of the gallery, and statements by the Dada group

11. Man Ray, *Self Portrait*, 115. Besides his
1916 painting *The Rope Dancer Accompanies
Herself with Her Shadows*, *Cadeau* is the only
artwork reproduced in the first edition
of his autobiography.

12. Ibid.

13. Tzara, Tristan, "Photographie en
revers," preface for *Les Champs délicieux*
(Paris: Société Generale d'Imprimerie,
1922), n.p. This limited-edition publication contained twelve rayographs by
Man Ray.

14. Jean Cocteau, "Lettre ouverte à Man
Ray, photograph américain," *Les Feuilles
libres* 26 (April–May 1922).

15. Man Ray, *Self Portrait*, 145.

16. "A New Method of Realizing the
Artistic Possibilities of Photography,"
Vanity Fair, November 1922.

17. A wide range of experts were invited
to respond in the December 1922 issue of
MSS to the question, "Can a photograph
have the significance of art?" Those invited
included Thomas Hart Benton, Charles
Chaplin, Carl Sandburg, and Charles
Sheeler. Though there were some who
wrote from Europe, Man Ray was not
invited.

18. Marius De Zayas wrote to Alfred
Stieglitz directly with his response. In
the letter he elaborates on what he terms
"Man Ray's false success." De Zayas to
Stieglitz, August 3, 1922, in "Can a Photo-
graph Have the Significance of Art?" 18.

19. The autumn 1924 issue of *Little Review*

published rayographs, drawings, and
watercolors, and photographs of "objects
to be destroyed." Jane Heap's description
of the rayographs was "chemical paintings." Baldwin, *Man Ray: American Artist*,
124.

20. Gilbert Seldes, review of *Emak Bakia*,
New Republic, March 1927; cited in Baldwin, *Man Ray: American Artist*, 135.

21. Jean Gallotti, "La Photographie est-
elle un Art?" *L'Art vivant*, 1928; quoted in
Arturo Schwarz, *Man Ray: The Rigour of the
Imagination* (New York: Rizzoli, 1977), 228.

22. The photograph, however, carried no
title when it appeared on the first page
of the first issue of *La révolution surréaliste*.

23. The caption for a 1924 rayograph
published in the June 1927 issue of *Transition* reads: "Man Ray is an American who
has lived in Paris several years, doing
painting, sculpture, and photography.
Within the past year, he has evolved an
abstract moving picture which may be
an important development in cinemato-
graphic art."

24. *Photographs by Man Ray 1920 Paris 1934*
(1934; reprint, New York: Dover, 1979).

25. *La Photographie n'est pas l'art*, preface by
André Breton (Paris: GLM, 1937).

26. André Breton, *Surrealism and Painting*,
trans. Simon Watson Taylor (New York:
Harper and Row, 1972), 32.

27. Man Ray, "Photography Is Not Art,"
View, no. 1, ser. 3 (April 1943): 23; no. 2,
ser. 3 (October 1943): 77–78, 97.

28. Man Ray, "Sur le réalisme photo-
graphique," *Cahiers d'art* 5–6 (1933):
120–21.

29. Man Ray, "A Note on the Shake-
spearean Equations," in *To Be Continued
Unnoticed* (Beverly Hills, Calif.: Copley
Galleries, 1948).

30. Harold Rosenberg, "American Drawing and the Academy of the Erased De
Kooning," *New Yorker*, March 22, 1976,
106–10; reprinted in Rosenberg, *Art and
Other Serious Matters* (Chicago: University
of Chicago Press, 1985), 239–48.

Man Ray's Culture Industry

1. "Days and Nights of Juliet: Juliet Man Ray Interviewed by George M. Goodwin," Oral History Program, University of California, Los Angeles, 1984, unrevised transcript, 12–13. The interview took place in Beverly Hills on July 27, 1981; the descriptions of Juliet Man Ray's distress during the interview are by Goodwin.

2. Milly Heyd, "Man Ray/Emmanuel Radnitsky: Who Is Behind *The Enigma of Isidore Ducasse*," in Matthew Baigell and Milly Heyd, eds., *Complex Identities: Jewish Consciousness and Modern Art* (New Brunswick, N.J.: Rutgers University Press, 2001), 115–41.

3. See Jennifer Mundy, ed., *Duchamp, Man Ray, Picabia*, exh. cat. (London: Tate, 2008). One exception to the silence around this trio's differing class origins would be the brief essay by Michel Sanouillet, "Duchamp and Man Ray: Exchanging Glances," in Emmanuelle de l'Ecotais and Alain Sayag, eds., *Man Ray: Photography and Its Double* (Corte Madera, Calif.: Gingko, 1998), 211–17.

4. The repression of this issue within Man Ray studies as well as studies of Dada and Surrealism remains extraordinary in its totality. Two exceptions might be named: It is my memory that as a teacher, Benjamin H. D. Buchloh always approached Man Ray's photography from the vantage point of its prediction of later techniques of domination and control within consumer culture. And in a brief review, the author of *Art Incorporated*, the photographer and critic Julian Stallabrass, outlines a counterreading of Man Ray's photographs around the issue of commodification. See Stallabrass, "Man Ray, London, Serpentine Gallery," *Burlington Magazine* 137 (April 1995): 261–62.

5. See Max Horkheimer and Theodor W. Adorno, "The Culture Industry: Enlightenment as Mass Deception," in Horkheimer and Adorno, *Dialectic of Enlightenment* (1944; New York: Continuum, 1994).

6. "Marcel, no more painting; go get a job." See Marcel Duchamp interviewed by James Johnson Sweeney, "Regions which are not ruled by time and space . . ." *The Writings of Marcel Duchamp* (New York: Da Capo, 1989), 133. It was Thierry de Duve who first put this note to use in an interpretation of the readymades in his *Pictorial Nominalism* (Minneapolis: University of Minnesota Press, 1991).

7. Molly Nesbit, "The Language of Industry," in Thierry de Duve, ed., *The Definitively Unfinished Marcel Duchamp* (Cambridge, Mass.: MIT Press, 1991).

8. While most commentaries stress the effect of the *Large Glass* on Man Ray's work, Michael Taylor proposes the two *Chocolate Grinder* paintings as talismanic for the New York Dada group. They were both exhibited at the Carroll Galleries in New York in March–April 1915, and were thereafter hung on the walls of the apartment of the Arensbergs. *Chocolate Grinder No. 2* was also reproduced on the cover of the second issue of the *Blind Man* in 1917. See Michael Taylor, "New York," in Leah Dickerman, ed., *Dada: Zurich, Berlin, Hannover, Cologne, New York, Paris*, exh. cat. (Washington, D.C.: National Gallery of Art, 2005), 281.

9. This is a pattern—Man Ray doing work for his artist friends, or for the galleries and movements with which he was involved—that would be repeated throughout the artist's adult life. For the details of Man Ray's employment, see Neil Baldwin, *Man Ray: American Artist* (New York: Da Capo, 1988), 1–49, and Man Ray, *Self Portrait* (Boston: Little, Brown, 1963), 11–35.

10. European writers on Man Ray would long associate his American identity with the forms of work and labor that Man Ray performed within the field of art, not unlike Duchamp's celebration of America for its "plumbing and its bridges." For example: "Architect, draftsman, painter, photographer, filmmaker, sculptor, writer, cabinet maker, creator of metal objects, he has had many other callings as well. Since he is of American origin—born in Philadelphia in 1890—he has been said to possess the diversified manual dexterity of the pioneers. . . . He designed abstract chessmen, jewelry, lighting fixtures, chairs, and other furniture whose very original appearance did not detract from their practical qualities." L. Fritz Gruber, *Man Ray's Celebrity Portraits* (1963; New York: Dover, 1995), vi.

11. Francis M. Naumann, *Conversion to Modernism: The Early Work of Man Ray* (New Brunswick, N.J.: Rutgers University Press, 2003), 5.

12. Baldwin, *Man Ray: American Artist*, 40.

13. "I can't draw hands," Man Ray was quoted as saying early in his artistic career (Baldwin, *Man Ray: American Artist*, 9). This statement would be inverted in a way in the wake of the artist's Surrealist years: "J'ai souvent rêvé de mains" ("I have often dreamed of hands"), Man Ray stated in his conversations with Pierre Bourgeade, in *Bonsoir Man Ray* (1972; Paris: Belfond, 1990), 131. One could analyze the trope of the hand throughout Man Ray's artistic production as a topic unto itself, both a displaced reference to manual labor, the work of the hand, and an ambivalent logo for the artist himself, a bilingual pun opening onto the artist's identity (*main*, or hand in French, sounding the same as "Man").

14. Naumann, *Conversion to Modernism*, 127.

15. Ibid., 137. The original citations are A.v.C., "Man Ray's Paint Problems," *American Art News* 54, no. 6 (November 13, 1915): 5, and Francis J. Ziegler, "Widely Different Phases of Modern Art," *Philadelphia Record*, 1915, clipping preserved in Willard Huntington Wright Papers, Princeton University.

16. Baldwin, *Man Ray: American Artist*, 31, 60.

17. Helen Molesworth, "Work Avoidance: The Everyday Life of Marcel Duchamp's Readymades," *Art Journal* 57, no. 4 (Winter 1998): 51–61. Also important to my thinking on this topic has been Molesworth's exhibition project *Work Ethic* (Baltimore: Baltimore Museum of Art, 2003).

18. See Jessica Stockholder and Joe Scanlan, "Art and Labor: Some Introductory Ideas," and Hirsch Perlman, "A Wastrel's Progress and the Worm's Retreat," *Art Journal* 64, no. 4 (Winter 2005): 50–51, 64–69.

19. Baldwin, *Man Ray: American Artist*, 61. To Arturo Schwarz, Man Ray recalled,

"They were furious. They thought I was a bad electrician." See Schwarz, *Man Ray: The Rigour of Imagination* (New York: Rizzoli, 1977), 136.

20. "Sublation" is a term to which I will return. Used to translate Hegel's German term *Aufhebung,* sublation characterizes the activity of the dialectic, where a quality is transformed only by being negated and yet preserved in a higher synthesis. Sublation encompasses all three of these dynamics—negation, preservation, and transformation—at once.

21. *Exposition Dada Man Ray* (Paris: Librairie Six, December 3–21, 1921), n.p.

22. Elizabeth Hutton Turner also points out that the Paris Dada catalogue's description of Man Ray as a "coal merchant" seems to describe the artist in the persona of his first and major patron of the moment, Ferdinand Howald, a retired coal merchant from Ohio. See Turner, "Transatlantic," in Merry Foresta, ed., *Perpetual Motif: The Art of Man Ray* (New York: Abbeville, 1988), 141.

23. Michael Taylor describes Man Ray and Duchamp, in their collaboration on the issue of *New York Dada,* as working "like a pair of advertising executives," in Taylor, "New York," 296. In a passage devoted to the pseudonym chosen by the photographer Claude Cahun, Rosalind Krauss has explored Duchamp's taking on of a Jewish identity with his alias Rrose Sélavy; see *Bachelors* (Cambridge, Mass.: MIT Press, 1999), 37–50. Although Man Ray was involved in all of the early presentations of Rrose Sélavy, the laying down of his actual Jewish name in the form of his own alias must be posed in distinction to Duchamp's gambit.

24. Man Ray's cinematic activities have been documented in Jean-Michel Bouhours and Patrick de Haas, *Man Ray, directeur du mauvais movies* (Paris: Éditions du Centre Pompidou, 1997).

25. Rosalind Krauss, "Corpus Delicti," in Krauss, Jane Livingston, and Dawn Ades, *L'amour fou: Photography and Surrealism,* exh. cat. (Washington, D.C.: Corcoran Gallery of Art; New York: Abbeville, 1985).

26. Man Ray would never relinquish these parallels, comparing throughout his life not only collage but the entire activity of painting to the work and tools of the barber. Thus, in 1949 he states: "When the spirit moves me, I use a stick with some hairs on it. I become a painter. My barber and the violinist above me also use sticks with hairs on them. We have much in common. We are also different. They try to do their work as well as possible. I simply try to be as free as possible." Man Ray, "To Be Continued Unnoticed," reprinted in Arturo Schwarz, *Man Ray: Sixty Years of Liberties* (Paris: Eric Losfeld, 1971), 52. And in 1969: "The painter holds his brush as a barber holds his shaving brush, the violinist his bow, the soldier his gun—that's how they hold their organs when they want to pee or make love." Man Ray, "The Unsaleable," reprinted in Schwarz, *Man Ray: Sixty Years of Liberties,* 62.

27. See Baldwin, *Man Ray: American Artist,* 107: "The public Kiki came under Man Ray's stylizing spell. He took her many steps beyond the primitive charcoal eyebrow-pencil she used for makeup as a teenager. They followed the same ritual every night before going out. After her obligatory hour-long bath, he designed Kiki's face and painted it on with his own hand. First Man Ray shaved her eyebrows completely, and then he applied others in their place, varying the color, thickness, and angle according to his mood. Her heavy eyelids, next, might be done in copper one day and royal blue another, or else in silver and jade."

28. Rosalind Krauss, "Notes on the Index," *The Originality of the Avant-Garde and Other Modernist Myths* (Cambridge, Mass.: MIT Press, 1986).

29. Man Ray had started out describing the camera as another "tool" within his production, an adjunct of the world of labor and work, like a "typewriter," as he once put it, or an "old shoe." See Baldwin, *Man Ray: American Artist,* 77, 102.

30. Susan Laxton describes the rayograph as "unproductive" in her essay "*Flou:* Rayographs and the Dada Automatic," *October* 127 (Winter 2009): 25–48.

31. "A New Method of Realizing the Artistic Possibilities of Photography," *Vanity Fair* 19 (November 1922): 50.

32. Adorno and Horkheimer express this meeting of opposites: "Culture is a paradoxical commodity. So completely is it subject to the law of exchange that it is no longer exchanged; it is so blindly consumed in use that it can no longer be used. Therefore it amalgamates with advertising." Horkheimer and Adorno, *Dialectic of Enlightenment,* 161.

33. Walter Benjamin, "Little History of Photography" (1931), in *Selected Writings, Volume 2, 1927–1934* (Cambridge, Mass.: Harvard University Press, 1999), 518.

34. Ibid., 518–19.

35. L. Fritz Gruber stresses this aspect of Man Ray's technique: "He was one of the first to reproduce perspective faithfully, with a long focal distance, enlarging the negative, which was necessarily small in this case. Up to that time, only large-format cameras and contact printing had been used. A portrait in the enlarger? Something to make honest technicians shudder. Very early on, Man Ray decided that sharpness of image is not the essential goal, but that it is more important to give the portrait its profound meaning. Between the time when those modifications were unavoidable and the time when they became intentional, Man Ray worked with a long focal distance. Its noble distance, its silent reserve when faced with a strong personality, were revealed to him." Gruber, *Man Ray's Celebrity Portraits,* vii.

36. See Rosalind Krauss, "The Object Caught by the Heel," in Francis M. Naumann with Beth Venn, *Making Mischief: Dada Invades New York,* exh. cat. (New York: Whitney Museum of American Art, 1996).

37. Stallabrass, "Man Ray, London, Serpentine Gallery," 261.

38. Man Ray, "L'aurore des objets," *Minotaure* 10 (Winter 1937): 41–44. The literal translation would be the "aurora" or the "dawn" of objects, but this is linked conceptually to the notion of the aura I have been exploring. See Hal Foster, "Auratic Traces," in Foster, *Compulsive Beauty* (Cambridge, Mass.: MIT Press, 1993).

39. I have sketched the Surrealist model of sculpture as prop in my essay "Rachel

Harrison: Mind the Gap," *Parkett* 82 (2008): 143–55.

40. The use of the de Chirico as a backdrop recalls Pictorialist studio practices and portraits, as if Man Ray's Surrealist portrait of Breton was meant explicitly as a transformation of this photographic formation.

41. Evidently, as my references to disease are meant to imply, Man Ray's painting understands public space as both dysfunctional and inherently pathological. I am using the term "public" as Rosalind Krauss once did in the context of her critical support of minimalism and post-minimalism; see Krauss, "Sense and Sensibility," *Artforum* 12, no. 3 (November 1973): 43–53. On Dada and the fraught nature of its relation to the public, see Leah Dickerman, "Dada's Solipsism," *Documents* 19 (Fall 2000): 16–19. The shadows cast by the readymade elements of *Self-Portrait* back onto the surface of the work in Man Ray's photographic document of it also relate to the later image of Breton positioned before de Chirico's *Enigma of a Day.* The key text on this aspect of Surrealist aesthetics, and on the changed relation of surrealism to the issue of the index, is Denis Hollier, "Surrealist Precipitates," *October* 69 (Summer 1994): 111–32.

42. On Man Ray's fashion photography, see Merry Foresta and Willis Hartshorn, *Man Ray in Fashion* (New York: International Center of Photography, 1990), and John Esten, *Man Ray: Bazaar Years* (New York: Rizzoli, 1988). Used by 1936 in his fashion photographs, the corporeal part-object of *Observatory Time—The Lovers* also functioned in other ways for the culture and fashion industry. It was hung like a "logo" of the Surrealist movement upon the opening of the Museum of Modern Art's 1936 exhibition *Fantastic Art, Dada, Surrealism,* and the sensation surrounding it caused Man Ray's image to be requested by cosmetics executive Helena Rubinstein. Man Ray gave the work to Rubinstein in the belief that she was going to purchase it, but she only borrowed the painting for a short while, to use as an advertising display in the window of her New York salon on Fifty-Seventh Street to sell lipstick.

43. The book was published by Man Ray at the same moment as Duchamp published the *Green Box,* his notes for his own metaphorical "self-portrait," the *Large Glass.* The two projects of 1934 should be seen in dialogue.

44. See Man Ray, *Self Portrait,* 324, and Merry Foresta, "Exile in Paradise: Man Ray in Hollywood, 1940–1951," in Foresta, ed., *Perpetual Motif,* 274.

45. It is of course no coincidence that Adorno formulates his notion of the culture industry in relation to his own exile in Los Angeles during these same years. Man Ray's Los Angeles address, 1245 Vine Street in Hollywood, sits just down the block today from the Pickford Center of the Academy of Motion Picture Arts and Sciences.

46. Dickran Tashjian, "A Clock That Forgets to Run Down: Man Ray in Hollywood, 1940–1951," in *Man Ray: Paris, LA* (Santa Monica: Smart Art, 1996), 46.

47. In *Self Portrait,* in the language of a postwar revision of his earlier career, Man Ray writes: "It always irritated me when someone, looking at my work, immediately conceived the idea of applying it to his particular interests. It happened often, especially with advertisers and editors of fashion magazines or with interior decorators" (166). He would also state, in 1966: "When asked to show his latest work—as if he were a fashion designer creating a new style for the season, to be set aside the following year for the newer style, also to be forgotten—when asked to show his latest work, the painter is overcome by a feeling of futility as if all his previous work has been discarded." Man Ray, "I Have Never Painted a Recent Picture," in Schwarz, *Man Ray: Sixty Years of Liberties,* 58.

48. Tashjian, "A Clock That Forgets to Run Down," 82, 83.

49. On the "White Ball" given by the Count and Countess Pecci-Blunt (the latter a niece of Pope Leo XIII), where all the guests had to wear white, with white plaster masks and wigs designed by Jean Cocteau and Christian Bérard, see Baldwin, *Man Ray: American Artist,* 165–66, and Man Ray, *Self Portrait,* 168–71.

50. Correspondence between Richter and Man Ray, March 9, 1948, Getty Research Institute, Special Collections; cited in Tashjian, "A Clock That Forgets to Run Down," 99.

51. Man Ray suggests this possibility to Bourgeade in *Bonsoir Man Ray,* 42–44. In the pamphlet produced for *Dreams That Money Can Buy,* half of a similar portrait image Man Ray made of himself with a full beard and a beret gets laid upon half of a portrait image of Richter, connecting this project in another way to *Self-Portrait with Half Beard;* for a facsimile reproduction, see Bouhours and de Haas, *Man Ray, directeur du mauvais movies,* 130–31.

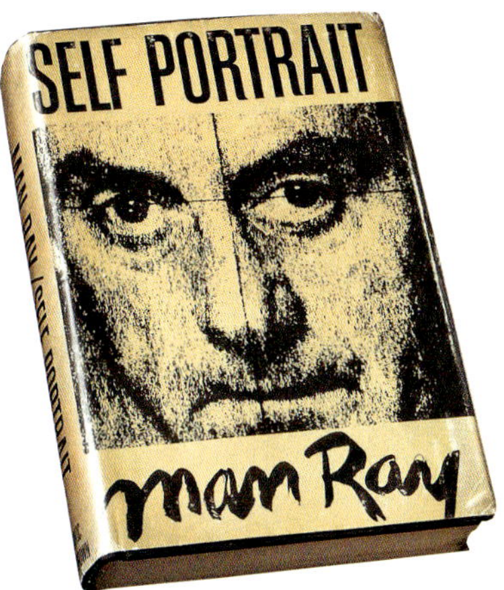

bibliography

By Man Ray

The Bum. Ridgefield, N.J.: Printed by the artist, ca. 1913.

Adonism. Ridgefield, N.J.: Printed by the artist and Adon Lacroix, 1914.

A Book of Divers Writings. With Adon Lacroix. Ridgefield, N.J.: Printed by the artist, 1915. Reprinted, Milan: Luciano Anselmino, 1976.

"Impressions of 291" (July 1914). *Camera Work* 47 (January 1915): 61.

Ridgefield Gazook. Ridgefield, N.J.: Printed by the artist, 1915. Reprinted in *Dada americano.* Ed. Arturo Schwarz. Milan: Mazzotta, 1970.

A Primer of the New Art of Two Dimensions. New York: Printed by the artist, 1916.

Visual Words, Sounds Seen, Thoughts Felt, Feelings Thought. Poems by Adon Lacroix (1916); layout by Man Ray. New York: Printed by the artist, 1917.

TNT. Edited with Henri S. Reynolds and Adolf Wolff. New York: Printed by the artist, 1919.

New York Dada. Edited by Marcel Duchamp and Man Ray. New York: Privately printed, 1921.

Letters and Hollywood Album, 1922–76, Getty Research Institute, Research Library, accession no. 930027.

Revolving Doors. Paris: Éditions Surréalistes, 1926. Reprinted in *Dada americano.* Ed. Arturo Schwarz. Milan: Mazzotta, 1970.

Photographs by Man Ray 1920 Paris 1934. Hartford, Conn.: James Thrall Soby, 1934.

La photographie n'est pas l'art. Paris: GLM, 1937.

"Photography Is Not Art." *View,* series 3, no. 1 (April 1943): 23.

"Photography Is Not Art, Part II." *View,* series 3, no. 3 (October 1943): 77–78, 98.

"Ruth, Roses, and Revolvers." *View,* series 4, no. 4 (December 1944). Reprinted in *View: Parade of the Avant-Garde, 1940–47.* Ed. Charles Henri Ford. New York: Thunder's Mouth, 1991.

To Be Continued Unnoticed: Some Papers by Man Ray. Beverly Hills, Calif.: Copley Galleries, 1948.

"The Rayograph." In *12 Rayographs/1921–1928.* Exh. cat. Stuttgart: Schubert and Kapitzki, 1963.

Self Portrait. Boston: Little, Brown, 1963.

Oggetti d'affezione. Turin: Einaudi, 1970.

On Man Ray

Amaya, Mario. "My Man Ray: Interview with Lee Miller Penrose." *Art in America* 63, no. 3 (May–June 1975): 54–61.

Amaya, Mario, and Roland Penrose. *Man Ray: Inventor/Painter/Poet.* Exh. cat. New York: New York Cultural Center, 1974.

Baldwin, Neil. *Man Ray: American Artist.* New York: Clarkson N. Potter, 1988.

Baum, Timothy. *Man Ray's Paris Portraits: 1921–1939.* Washington, D.C.: Middendorf Gallery, 1989.

Bouhours, Jean-Michel, and Patrick de Haas. *Man Ray: Directeur du mauvais movies.* Paris: Centre Georges Pompidou, 1997.

Bourgeade, Pierre. *Bonsoir, Man Ray.* Paris: Pierre Belfond, 1972.

Carter, Curtis L., and Francis M. Naumann. *Man Ray in America.* Milwaukee: Haggerty Museum of Art, Marquette University, 1989.

Ceuleers, Jan, ed. *Man Ray, 1890–1976.* Antwerp: Ronny Van de Velde; Ghent:

Ludion; Paris: Albin Michel; and New York: Harry N. Abrams, 1995.

Cocteau, Jean. "Experiments in Abstract Form, Made Without a Camera Lens, by Man Ray the American Painter." *Vanity Fair,* November 1922, 50.

Coleman, A. D. "Introduction." *Man Ray: Photographs, 1920–1934.* New York: East River, 1975.

Conspiratorial Laughter: A Friendship, Man Ray and Duchamp. Exh. cat. New York: Zabriskie Gallery, 1995.

Duchamp, Marcel. "Man Ray." In *Collection of the Société Anonyme: Museum of Modern Art 1920.* Ed. George Heard Hamilton. New Haven: Yale University Art Gallery, 1950.

Esten, John, Merry Foresta, and Willis Hartshorn. *Man Ray in Fashion.* New York: International Center of Photography, 1990.

Foresta, Merry A. *Man Ray.* New York: Pantheon; Paris: Centre National de la Photographie, 1989.

———, ed. *Perpetual Motif: The Art of Man Ray.* New York: Abbeville, 1988.

Greenidge, Delano. *Man Ray, Paris Photographs 1920–34.* New York: Delano Greenidge Editions, 2000.

Grossman, Wendy. "Only the Shadow Knows: Warhol's Art of Self-Invention and the Legacy of Man Ray." In *Reframing Andy Warhol: Constructing American Myths, Heroes, and Cultural Icons,* exh. cat. College Park: Art Gallery, University of Maryland, 1998.

Hill, Paul, and Thomas Cooper. "Man Ray." In *Dialogue with Photography: Interviews,* 9–20. New York: Farrar, Straus & Giroux, 1979.

Kovács, Steven. "Man Ray as Filmmaker." *Artforum* 11, no. 3 (November 1972): 77–82.

———. "Man Ray as Filmmaker: Part II." *Artforum* 11, no. 4 (December 1972): 62–66.

Langsner, Jules. *Man Ray.* Exh. cat. Los Angeles: Los Angeles County Museum of Art, 1966.

L'Ecotais, Emmanuelle de. *Man Ray: Rayographies.* Paris: L. Scheer, 2002.

L'Ecotais, Emmanuelle de, and Alain Sayag, eds. *Man Ray: Photography and Its Double.* Paris: Centre Georges Pompidou; London: Gingko, 1998.

L'Ecotais, Emmanuelle de, Katherine Ware, and André Breton. *Man Ray, 1890–1976.* Ed. Manfred Heiting. Cologne: Taschen, 2000.

Lottman, Herbert R. *Man Ray's Montparnasse.* New York: Harry N. Abrams, 2001.

Man Ray. Exh. cat. London: Hanover Gallery, 1969.

Man Ray: A Selection of Paintings. Exh. cat. New York: Cordier-Ekstrom, 1970.

Man Ray: Objects of My Affection. Exh. cat. New York: Zabriskie Gallery, 1985.

Martin, Jean-Hubert, et al. *Objets de mon affection.* Paris: Philippe Sers, 1983.

McCabe, Susan. "'Delight in Dislocation': Stein, Chaplin, and Man Ray." In *Cinematic Modernism: Modernist Poetry and Film,* 56–92. Cambridge, England: Cambridge University Press, 2005.

Mellyt, George. "Man Ray's Camera Obscura." *Interview,* October 1988.

Melville, Robert. "Man Ray in London." *Arts Magazine* 33 (June 1959): 45–47.

Miller, Lee. "I Worked with Man Ray." *Lilliput,* October 1941.

Molerings, Herbert. *Man Ray and L. Fritz Gruber: Years of Friendship, 1956–1976.* Göttingen, Germany: Steidl; London: Thames & Hudson, 2008.

Naumann, Francis M. *Conversion to Modernism: The Early Works of Man Ray.* New Brunswick, N.J.: Rutgers University Press, 2003.

Naumann, Francis M. *Man Ray: The New York Years, 1913–1921.* Exh. cat. New York: Zabriskie Gallery, 1988.

Palazzoli, Daniela, and Gilbert Perlein. *Man Ray: Rétrospective, 1912–1976.* Exh. cat. Nice: Musée d'Art Moderne et d'Art Contemporain, 1997.

Penrose, Roland. *Man Ray.* New York: Thames & Hudson, 1989.

Perl, Jed. *Man Ray.* New York: Aperture, 1997.

Powell, Kirsten Hoving. "*Le Violon d'Ingres:* Man Ray's Variations on Ingres, Deformation, Desire and de Sade." *Art History* 23, no. 5 (December 2005): 772–99.

Ribemont-Dessaignes, Georges. *Man Ray/G. Ribemont-Dessaignes.* Paris: Gallimard, 1929. (The original edition of this book erroneously gives a publication date of 1924.)

Rubin, William. "Man Ray." *Art International,* June 1963.

Schaffner, Ingrid. *The Essential Man Ray.* New York: Wonderland and Harry N. Abrams, 2002.

Schwarz, Arturo. *Man Ray: The Rigour of Imagination.* New York: Rizzoli, 1977.

———, ed. *Man Ray: Sixty Years of Liberties.* Exh. cat. Paris: Eric Losfeld; Milan: Galleria Schwarz, 1971.

Setford, David F. *Man Ray's Man Rays.* Exh. cat. West Palm Beach, Fla.: Norton Museum of Art, 1994.

Shrock, Peggy Elaine. "Man Ray's *Le Cadeau:* The Unnatural Woman and the De-Sexing of Modern Man." *Woman's Art Journal* 17, no. 2 (Autumn–Winter 1996–97): 26–29.

Tashjian, Dickran, Tom Patchett, and Robert Berman. *Man Ray: Paris—LA.* Santa Monica, Calif.: Smart Art, 1996.

Vanci-Perahim, Marina, ed. *Man Ray.* Trans. Willard Wood. New York: Cameo/Harry N. Abrams, 1998.

Weichsel, John. "New Art and Man Ray." *East and West* 1, no. 8 (November 1915): 242–43.

Dada

Ades, Dawn. *The Dada Reader: A Critical Anthology.* Chicago: University of Chicago Press, 2006.

Barr, Alfred H., Jr., ed. *Fantastic Art, Dada, Surrealism.* Exh. cat. New York: Museum of Modern Art, 1937.

Béhar, Henri, and Catherine Dufour, eds. *Dada: Circuit total.* Lausanne, Switzerland: L'Âge d'Homme, 2005.

Belz, Carl. "Man Ray and New York Dada." *Art Journal* 23, no. 3 (Spring 1964): 207–13.

Dachy, Marc. *Archives Dada/Chronique.* Paris: Hazan, 2005.

———. *Dada: The Revolt of Art.* Trans. Liz Nash. New York: Harry N. Abrams, 2006.

———. *The Dada Movement, 1915–1923.* Trans. Michael Taylor. New York: Rizzoli, 1990.

Dickerman, Leah, ed. *Dada: Zurich, Berlin, Hannover, Cologne, New York, Paris.* Washington, D.C.: National Gallery of Art and Distributed Art Publishers, 2005.

———, ed. *October: Dada, A Special Issue* 105 (Summer 2003).

Dickerman, Leah, and Matthew S. Witovsky, eds. *The Dada Seminars.* Washington, D.C.: Center for Advanced Study in the Visual Arts, National Gallery of Art, and Distributed Art Publishers, 2005.

Elderfield, John, ed. *Flight out of Time: A Dada Diary by Hugo Ball.* Trans. Ann Raimes. Berkeley: University of California Press, 1996.

Foster, Stephen C., ed. *Dada: The Coordinates of Cultural Politics.* New York: G. K. Hall, 1996.

Foster, Stephen C., Rudolf E. Kuenzli, and Mary Ann Caws. *Dada Spectrum: The Dialectics of Revolt.* Madison, Wisc.: Coda, 1979.

Gale, Matthew. *Dada and Surrealism.* London: Phaidon, 1997.

Gammel, Irene. *Baroness Elsa: Gender, Dada, and Modernity; A Cultural Biography.* Cambridge, Mass.: MIT Press, 2002.

Gaughan, Martin Ignatius, and Stephen C. Foster, eds. *Dada New York: New World for Old.* New Haven: Yale University Press, 2003.

Hopkins, David. *Dada and Surrealism: A Very Short Introduction.* Oxford: Oxford University Press, 2004.

———. "Men Before the Mirror: Duchamp, Man Ray, and Masculinity."

Art History 21, no. 3 (Summer 1998): 303–23.

Huelsenbeck, Richard, ed. *Dada Almanach.* Berlin: Erich Reiss, 1920.

Huelsenbeck, Richard, Hugo Ball, Walter Serneret, et al. *Blago Bung, Blago Bung, Bosso Fataka! First Texts of German Dada.* Trans. Malcolm Green. London: Atlas, 1995.

Jones, Amelia. "Equivocal Masculinity: New York Dada in the Context of World War I." *Art History* 25, no. 2 (April 2002): 162–205.

———. *Postmodernism and the En-Gendering of Marcel Duchamp.* Cambridge, England: Cambridge University Press, 1994.

Jones, Dafydd, ed. *Dada Culture: Critical Texts on the Avant-Garde.* Amsterdam: Rodopi, 2006.

Krauss, Rosalind. *Bachelors.* Cambridge, Mass.: MIT Press, 2000.

Kuenzli, Rudolf E. *Dada.* London: Phaidon, 2006.

———, ed. *Dada and Surrealist Film.* Cambridge, Mass.: MIT Press, 1996.

———, ed. *New York Dada.* New York: Willis Locker & Owens, 1986.

Le Bon, Laurent, ed. *Dada.* Paris: Centre Georges Pompidou, 2005.

Motherwell, Robert, ed. *The Dada Painters and Poets: An Anthology.* 2nd ed. Cambridge, Mass.: Belknap Press of Harvard University Press, 1981.

Mundy, Jennifer, ed. *Duchamp, Man Ray, Picabia.* Exh. cat. London: Tate, 2008.

Naumann, Francis M. *New York Dada, 1915–1923.* New York: Harry N. Abrams, 1994.

Naumann, Francis M., with Beth Venn. *Making Mischief: Dada Invades New York.* New York: Whitney Museum of American Art, 1996.

Pegrum, Mark A. *Challenging Modernity: Dada Between Modern and Postmodern.* New York: Berghahn, 2000.

Richter, Hans. *Dada, Art and Anti-Art.* Oxford: Oxford University Press, 1978.

Ring, Nancy J. "New York Dada and the Crisis of Masculinity: Man Ray, Francis Picabia, and Marcel Duchamp in the United States, 1913–1921." Ph.D. diss., Northwestern University, 1991.

Sawelson-Gorse, Naomi, ed. *Women in Dada: Essays on Sex, Gender, and Identity.* Cambridge, Mass.: MIT Press, 1998.

Schwarz, Arturo. *New York Dada: Duchamp, Man Ray, Picabia.* Munich: Prestel, 1973.

Sheppard, Richard. *Modernism—Dada—Postmodernism.* Evanston, Ill.: Northwestern University Press, 2000.

Tashjian, Dickran. *Skyscraper Primitives: Dada and the American Avant-Garde, 1910–1925.* Middletown, Conn.: Wesleyan University Press, 1975.

Umland, Ann, Adrian Sudhalter, and Scott Gerson, eds. *Dada in the Collection of the Museum of Modern Art.* New York: Museum of Modern Art, 2008.

Waldberg, Patrick. *Dada: La fonction de refus.* Paris: Éditions de La Différence, 1999.

Watts, Harriet, ed. *Dada and the Press.* Vol. 9 of *Crisis and the Arts: The History of Dada.* General editor, Stephen C. Foster. Farmington Hills, Mich.: G. K. Hall, 2004.

Surrealism

Adamowicz, Elza. "The Surrealist (Self-) Portrait: Convulsive Identities." In *Surrealism: Surrealist Visuality.* Ed. Silvano Levy. Keele, England: Keele University Press, 1996.

Ades, Dawn, Simon Baker, and Fiona Bradley. *Undercover Surrealism: Georges Bataille and Documents.* London: Hayward Gallery, 2006.

Batchelor, David, Briony Fer, and Paul Wood. *Realism, Rationalism, and Surrealism: Art Between the Wars.* New Haven: Yale University Press, 1993.

Bate, David. *Photography and Surrealism: Sexuality, Colonialism, and Social Dissent.* London: I. B. Tauris, 2004.

Benjamin, Walter. "Surrealism: The Last Snapshot of European Intelligentsia." In *One-Way Street and Other Writings.* Trans. Edmund Jephcott and Kingsley Shorter. London: Verso, 1992.

Billeter, Erika, and José Pierre, eds. *La femme et le Surréalisme.* Lausanne, Switzerland: Musée Cantonal des Beaux-Arts Lausanne, 1987.

Caws, Mary Ann. *The Surrealist Look: An Erotics of Encounter.* Cambridge, Mass.: MIT Press, 1999.

Caws, Mary Ann, Rudolf E. Kuenzli, and Gwen Raaberg, eds. *Surrealism and Women.* Cambridge, Mass.: MIT Press, 1991.

Chadwick, Whitney, ed. *Mirror Images: Women, Surrealism, and Self-Representation.* Cambridge, Mass.: MIT Press, 1998.

———. *Women Artists and the Surrealist Movement.* Boston: Little, Brown, 1985.

Cohen, Margaret. *Profane Illumination: Walter Benjamin and the Paris of Surrealist Revolution.* Berkeley: University of California Press, 1995.

Foster, Hal. *Compulsive Beauty.* Cambridge, Mass.: MIT Press, 1995.

Gallagher, Jean. *World Wars Through a Female Gaze.* Carbondale: Southern Illinois University Press, 1998.

Gronberg, Tag. "Beware Beautiful Women: The 1920s Shopwindow Mannequin and a Physiognomy of Effacement." *Art History* 20, no. 3 (September 1997): 375–96.

Hammond, Paul. *The Shadow and Its Shadow: Surrealist Writings on the Cinema.* San Francisco: City Lights, 2000.

Hubert, Renée Riese. *Magnifying Mirrors: Women, Surrealism, and Partnership.* Lincoln: University of Nebraska Press, 1994.

Hulten, Pontus. *The Surrealists Look at Art: Éluard, Aragon, Soupault, Breton, Tzara.* Venice, Calif.: Lapis, 1990.

Kovács, Steven. *From Enchantment to Rage: The Story of Surrealist Cinema.* London: Associate, 1980.

Krauss, Rosalind. *The Optical Unconscious.* Cambridge, Mass.: MIT Press, 1993.

————. *The Originality of the Avant-Garde and Other Modernist Myths.* Cambridge, Mass.: MIT Press, 1986.

Krauss, Rosalind, Jane Livingston, and Dawn Ades. *L'Amour Fou: Photography and Surrealism.* Exh. cat. Washington, D.C.: Corcoran Gallery; New York: Abbeville, 1985.

Lévy, Sophie, ed. *A Transatlantic Avant-Garde: American Artists in Paris, 1918–1939.* Berkeley: University of California Press, 2003.

Lyford, Amy. *Surrealist Masculinities: Gender Anxiety and the Aesthetics of Post–World War I Reconstruction in France.* Berkeley: University of California Press, 2007.

Malt, Johanna. *Obscure Objects of Desire: Surrealism, Fetishism, and Politics.* Oxford: Oxford University Press, 2004.

Montagu, Jemima. "André Breton and Man Ray: The Marvelous and the Everyday." In *The Surrealists: Revolutionaries in Art and Writing, 1919–35.* London: Tate, 2002.

Mundy, Jennifer. *Surrealism: Desire Unbound.* Princeton, N.J.: Princeton University Press, 2001.

Pierre, José. *Investigating Sex: Surrealist Discussions, 1928–1932.* Trans. Malcolm Imrie. London: Verso, 1992.

Sawin, Martica. *Surrealism in Exile and the Beginning of the New York School.* Cambridge, Mass.: MIT Press, 1995.

Spitteri, Raymond, and Donald LaCross, eds. *Surrealism, Politics, and Culture.* Aldershot, England: Ashgate, 2003.

Stich, Sidra. *Anxious Visions: Surrealist Art.* Exh. cat. Berkeley: University Art Gallery, University of California at Berkeley; New York: Abbeville, 1990.

Suleiman, Susan Rubin. *Subversive Intent: Gender, Politics, and the Avant-Garde.* Cambridge, Mass.: Harvard University Press, 1990.

Tashjian, Dickran. *A Boatload of Madmen: Surrealism and the American Avant-Garde, 1920–1950.* New York: Thames & Hudson, 1995.

Weisberger, Edward, ed. *Surrealism, Two Private Eyes: The Nesuhi Ertegun and Daniel Filipacchi Collections.* Exh. cat. New York: Solomon R. Guggenheim Museum and Harry N. Abrams, 1999.

Modernism

Anderson, Margaret C. *My Thirty Years' War: The Autobiography: Beginnings and Battles to 1930.* New York: Horizon, 1970. (Reprint of 1930 edition.)

Antliff, Allan. *Anarchist Modernism: Art, Politics, and the First American Avant-Garde.* Chicago: University of Chicago Press, 2001.

Antliff, Mark. "The Jew as Anti-Artist: George Sorel, Anti-Semitism, and the Aesthetics of Class Consciousness." *Oxford Art Journal* 20, no. 1 (1997): 50–67.

Aron, Robert. "Films of Revolt." In *French Film Theory and Criticism: A History/Anthology, 1907–1939,* 432–36. Ed. Richard Abel. Princeton, N.J.: Princeton University Press, 1988.

Austin, John Langshaw. "Performative Utterances." In *Philosophical Papers,* 233–52. Ed. J. O. Urmson and Geoffrey James Warnock. Oxford: Oxford University Press, 1979.

Avrich, Paul. *The Modern School Movement: Anarchism and Education in the United States.* Princeton, N.J.: Princeton University Press, 2005.

Baigell, Matthew, and Milly Heyd, eds. *Complex Identities: Jewish Consciousness and Modern Art.* New Brunswick, N.J.: Rutgers University Press, 2001.

Barron, Stephanie, Sabine Eckmann, and Matthew Affron. *Exiles + Emigrés: The Flight of European Artists from Hitler.* Exh. cat. Los Angeles: Los Angeles County Museum of Art, 1997.

Bataille, Georges. *Eroticism: Death and Sensuality.* Trans. Mary Dalwood. San Francisco: City Lights, 1986.

Benstock, Sharon. *Women of the Left Bank: Paris, 1900–1940.* Austin: University of Texas Press, 1986.

Birnbaum, Paula J. "'Femmes Artistes Modernes': Women, Art, and Modern Identity in Interwar France." Ph.D. diss., Bryn Mawr College, 1996.

Blessing, Jennifer, ed. *Speaking with Hands: Photographs from the Buhl Collection.* New York: Solomon R. Guggenheim Museum, 2004.

Breton, André. *Nadja.* Paris: Gallimard, 1963.

Brilliant, Richard. *Portraiture.* London: Reaktion; Cambridge, Mass.: Harvard University Press, 1991.

Bürger, Peter. *Theory of the Avant-Garde.* Trans. Michael Shaw. Minneapolis: University of Minnesota Press, 1984.

Burgin, Victor, ed. *Thinking Photography.* Basingstoke, England: Macmillan, 1982.

Carlin, John, et al. *Masters of American Comics.* New Haven: Yale University Press, 2005.

Carroll, David. *French Literary Fascism: Nationalism, Anti-Semitism, and the Ideology of Culture.* Princeton, N.J.: Princeton University Press, 1995.

Caws, Mary Ann. *The Poetry of Dada and Surrealism: Aragon, Breton, Tzara, Éluard, and Desnos.* Princeton, N.J.: Princeton University Press, 1970.

Chadwick, Whitney, and Tirza True Latimer. *The Modern Woman Revisited: Paris Between the Wars.* New Brunswick, N.J.: Rutgers University Press, 2003.

Churchill, Suzanne. *The Little Magazine* Others *and the Renovation of Modern American Poetry.* Aldershot, England: Ashgate, 2006.

Corn, Wanda M. *The Great American Thing: Modern Art and National Identity, 1915–1935.* Berkeley: University of California Press, 1999.

de Zayas, Marius. *How, When, and Why Modern Art Came to New York.* Ed. Francis M. Naumann. Cambridge, Mass.: MIT Press, 1996.

Esman, Aaron H. "What Is 'Applied' in 'Applied' Psychoanalysis?" *International Journal of Psychoanalysis* 79, part 4 (August 1988): 746–48.

Golan, Romy. *Modernity and Nostalgia: Art and Politics in France Between the Wars.* New Haven: Yale University Press, 1995.

Greenberg, Clement. *Art and Culture: Critical Essays.* Boston: Beacon, 1961.

Gross, Jennifer R., ed. *Société Anonyme: Modernism for America.* New Haven: Yale University Press, 2006.

Hambourg, Maria Morris, with Christopher Phillips. *The New Vision: Photography Between the World Wars.* Exh. cat. New York: Metropolitan Museum of Art, 1989.

Haworth-Booth, Mark. *The Art of Lee Miller.* New Haven: Yale University Press, 2007.

Hoffmann, Frederick J., Charles Allen, and Carolyn F. Ulrich. *The Little Magazine: A History and Bibliography.* Princeton, N.J.: Princeton University Press, 1946.

Jones, Amelia. *Irrational Modernism: A Neurasthenic History of New York Dada.* Cambridge, Mass.: MIT Press, 2005.

Jones, Caroline A. "The Sex of the Machine, Mechanomorphic Art, New Women, and Francis Picabia's Neurasthenic Cure." In *Picturing Science, Producing Art,* 145–80. Ed. Caroline A. Jones and Peter Louis Galison. New York: Routledge, 1998.

Kernberg, Otto F. *Aggressivity, Narcissism, and Self-Destructiveness in the Psychotherapeutic Relationship.* New Haven: Yale University Press, 2004.

Klein, Mason. *Modigliani: Beyond the Myth.* Exh. cat. New York: The Jewish Museum; New Haven: Yale University Press, 2004.

Kohut, Heinz. *The Restoration of the Self.* New York: International Universities Press, 1977.

Kreymborg, Alfred. *Troubadour: An Autobiography.* New York: Sagamore, 1957.

Lacan, Jacques. *The Four Fundamental Concepts of Psychoanalysis.* Trans. Alan Sheridan. London: Hogarth, 1977.

Lautréamont, Isidore [Ducasse] de. *Maldoror & the Complete Works of the Comte de Lautréamont.* Trans. Alexis Lykiard. Berkeley, Calif.: Exact Change, 1994.

Marek, Jayne E. *Women Editing Modernism: "Little" Magazines and Literary History.*

Lexington: University Press of Kentucky, 1995.

McGee, Daniel T. "Dada Da Da: Sounding the Jew in Modernism." *ELH* 65 (2001): 501–27.

Penrose, Anthony. *The Lives of Lee Miller.* New York: Holt, Rinehart and Winston, 1995.

Péret, Benjamin. *Oeuvres complètes.* 7 vols. Paris: Association des Amis de Benjamin Péret and Librairie Corti, 1995.

Rainey, Lawrence S. *Modernism: An Anthology.* Malden, Mass.: Blackwell, 2005.

Rosenberg, Harold. *Discovering the Present: Three Decades in Art, Culture, and Politics.* Chicago: University of Chicago Press, 1973.

Sachar, Howard Morley. *A History of the Jews in America.* New York: Alfred A. Knopf, 1992.

Schwarz, Arturo. *Marcel Duchamp: Notes and Projects for the Large Glass.* New York: Harry N. Abrams, 1969.

Seigel, Jerrold E. *The Private Worlds of Marcel Duchamp: Desire, Liberation, and the Self in Modern Culture.* Berkeley: University of California Press, 1995.

Selz, Peter. "The Impact from Abroad: Foreign Guests and Visitors." In *On the Edge of America: California Modernist Art, 1900–1950,* 97–120. Ed. Paul Karlstrom. Berkeley: University of California Press, 1996.

Seitz, William. *The Art of Assemblage.* Exh. cat. New York: Museum of Modern Art, 1961.

Silberstein, Laurence Jay, ed. *Mapping Jewish Identities.* New York: New York University Press, 2000.

Silver, Kenneth E. *Esprit de Corps: The Art of the Parisian Avant-Garde and the First World War, 1914–1925.* Princeton, N.J.: Princeton University Press, 1989.

Silver, Kenneth E., and Romy Golan. *The Circle of Montparnasse: Jewish Artists in Paris, 1905–1945.* New York: Universe, 1985.

Sochen, June. *The New Woman: Feminism in Greenwich Village, 1910–1920.* New York: Quadrangle, 1972.

Sousslouff, Catherine M. *Jewish Identity in Modern Art History.* Berkeley: University of California Press, 1999.

Soyer, Daniel. *Jewish Immigrant Associations and American Identity in New York, 1880–1939.* Detroit: Wayne State University Press, 2001.

Stein, Gertrude. *The Autobiography of Alice B. Toklas.* New York: Vintage, 1990.

Stein, Gertrude, and Amy Feinstein. "The Modern Jew Who Has Given Up the Faith of His Fathers Can Reasonably and Consistently Believe in Isolation." *PMLA* 116, no. 2 (March 2001): 416–28.

Teter-Goodale, Barbara Lynne. "Textual/Sexual Inscription and the Extension of Boundaries in *Les chants de Maldoror.*" Ph.D. diss., University of Pennsylvania, 1998.

Watson, Steven. *Strange Bedfellows: The First American Avant-Garde.* New York: Abbeville, 1991.

Wiser, William. *The Twilight Years: Paris in the 1930s.* New York: Carroll & Graf, 2000.

Young, Dean. "Man Ray's [— — —— — ————]." In *Dark Horses: Poets on Overlooked Poems; An Anthology,* 149–51. Ed. Joy Katz and Kevin Prufer. Urbana: University of Illinois Press, 2007.

Contributors

George Baker is associate professor of art history at the University of California, Los Angeles. He is an editor of the journal *October* and its publishing imprint October Books, and he writes as a critic for *Artforum*. His books include *The Artwork Caught by the Tail: Francis Picabia and Dada in Paris* (2007), *Gerard Byrne: Books, Magazines, and Newspapers* (2003), and *James Coleman: Drei Filmarbeiten* (2002).

Lauren Schell Dickens is the Neubauer Family Foundation Curatorial Assistant at The Jewish Museum, for which she recently organized *The Danube Exodus: The Rippling Currents of the River.*

Merry A. Foresta, founding director and senior curator of the Smithsonian Photography Initiative, joined the Smithsonian Institution in 1977. She has organized more than fifty exhibitions at the Smithsonian, including *Perpetual Motif: The Art of Man Ray*. Her most recent book is *At First Sight: Photography and the Smithsonian* (2003).

Mason Klein is curator of fine arts at The Jewish Museum, where he organized *Modigliani: Beyond the Myth* and has worked on other exhibitions, including *Berlin Metropolis: Jews and the New Culture, 1890–1918* and *Voice, Image, Gesture: Selections from The Jewish Museum's Collection, 1945–2000*. He has contributed to *Artforum, Frieze, Arts Magazine,* and *World Art* and written curatorial essays for the Wexner Center for the Arts, Philadelphia Museum of Art, American Folk Art Museum, and other institutions.

Index

Page numbers in *italics* refer to illustrations.

illustration Credits

Boldface numerals refer to page numbers.

All works by Man Ray © 2009
Man Ray Trust/Artists Rights Society
(ARS), NY/ADAGP, Paris

ABBREVIATIONS

AR: Art Resource, New York

BMA: The Baltimore Museum of Art

BRB: Beinecke Rare Book and Manuscript Library, Yale University, New Haven, Connecticut

CGP: CNAC/MNAM/Dist. Réunion des Musées Nationaux/Art Resource, New York/Musée national d'art moderne, Centre Georges Pompidou, Paris, France

CMA: Columbus Museum of Art, Ohio

FMN: Francis M. Naumann Fine Art, New York

HM: High Museum of Art, Atlanta

HMAH: Heckscher Museum of Art, Huntington, New York

IDFA: Isidore Ducasse Fine Arts

JPG: The J. Paul Getty Museum, Los Angeles

MM: Collection of Marion Meyer, Paris

MoMA: Digital Image © The Museum of Modern Art/Licensed by SCALA/Art Resource, N.Y.

NB: Neil Baldwin

OSU: The Ohio State University Cartoon Library and Museum, Columbus

PMA: Philadelphia Museum of Art

PC: © Man Ray Estate/The Penrose Collection. All rights reserved

RG: Photograph by Richard Goodbody

RMJ: Rosalind and Melvin Jacobs Collection

TB: Collection of Timothy Baum, New York

TFA: Tokyo Fuji Art Museum

WMAA: Whitney Museum of American Art, New York

Front cover: MoMA
Frontispiece: JPG
Copyright page: TB/RG
Donor page: Collection of Mr. and Mrs. George L. Lindemann, Florida
Foreword: Fisher Collection, San Rafael, California
Back cover: Courtesy of Timothy Baum, New York/RG

Klein Essay: 2 Smithsonian American Art Museum, Washington, D.C./AR. 3 RMJ. 4 PC/National Galleries of Scotland (left), MM (right). 5 CGP. 6 FMN. 7 CGP. 8 Allen Memorial Art Museum, Oberlin College, Ohio. 9 National Gallery of Art, Washington, D.C. 10 MoMA. 11 Collection of Scott and Beth Ullem/Photograph by Jamie Stukenberg. 12 Bibliothèque littéraire Jacques Doucet, Paris (top), The Jewish Museum, New York/RG (bottom). 14 Bibliothèque littéraire Jacques Doucet, Paris. 15 RG. 16 HM. 17 Courtesy of Timothy Baum, New York (top), TB (bottom). 19 MoMA. 21 The Menil Collection, Houston/Photograph by Hickey-Robertson, Houston. 22–23 OSU. 24 Museum of Fine Arts, Houston. 25 TFA. 26 CGP/Photography by Adam Rzepka. 27 TB/RG. 28 The Kantor Collection, Beverly Hills, California/© 2009 Estate of Pablo Picasso/Artists Rights Society (ARS), New York. 29 JPG. 30 CMA. 32 Albright-Knox Art Gallery, Buffalo. 34 CGP. 35 MoMA. 36 Courtesy of Francis M. Naumann (top left), WMAA/Photograph by Geoffrey Clements, New York (top right). 37 PMA. 38 CGP. 39 PMA (top left), Betsy Miller Collection, New York (top right), PMA (bottom). 40 PMA. 41 From Merry A. Foresta, ed., *Perpetual Motif: The Art of Man Ray* (New York: Abbeville, 1988), 15. 45 BRB. 47 San Francisco Museum of Modern Art. 48 Collection of Sarah and Gary Wolkowitz/RG. 50 TFA (top), © The Israel Museum, Jerusalem, photograph by Avshalom Avital (bottom). 51 Sylvio Perlstein Collection, Antwerp. 52–53 TB. 54 The Metropolitan Museum of Art, New York (top), IDFA (bottom). 56 Fondazione Marguerite Arp, Locarno. 57 Courtesy of Timothy Baum, New York/RG (left), Collection of Karen Amiel Baum, New York/RG (right). 58 TFA. 59 Fondazione Marguerite Arp, Locarno (bottom). 63 MoMA. 64 Galerie 1900–2000, Paris. 65 FMN. 66 NB/RG. 68 Collection of Karen Amiel Baum, New York. 69 The Menil Collection, Houston (top), HMAH (bottom). 70 Montclair Art Museum, New Jersey. 71 NB/RG (top), PC (bottom). 72 MoMA. 73 PC. 78 Courtesy of Timothy Baum, New York/RG. 83 BMA. 84 MoMA. 85 JPG. 86 RMJ.

88 MM/RG. **89** MoMA (left), PC (right). **90** © The Israel Museum, Jerusalem, photograph by Avshalom Avital. **91** The Menil Collection, Houston/Photograph by Janet Woodward. **92** Bowdoin College Museum of Art, Brunswick, Maine (top), Richard and Ellen Sandor Family Collection, Chicago (bottom). **93** TB/RG. **95** IDFA. **96** WMAA/Photograph by Sheldan C. Collins. **98** PMA/Photograph by Graydon Wood (top), Richard and Ellen Sandor Collection, Chicago (bottom). **99** Sylvio Perlstein Collection, Antwerp. **100** The Getty Research Institute, Los Angeles (top), New Orleans Museum of Art (bottom left), TB (bottom right). **101** Kunsthaus Bielefeld. **102** Hirshhorn Museum and Sculpture Garden, Smithsonian Institution. **103** JPG. **104** Collection of Peter and Renate Nahum at The Leicester Galleries, London. **105** CGP.

Foresta Essay: **109** Collection Goldberg/d'Afflitto, New York. **110** IDFA (top), HM. **111** Kunsthaus Zürich. **112** The Bluff Collection LP. **113** PMA/Photograph by Graydon Wood. **114** BMA. **116** Richard and Ronnie Grosbard Collection/RG. **117** Collection of André Baum, New York (top), BMA (bottom). **119** Private collection of Thomas and Janine Koerfer-Weill. **120** PC. **121** Rare Books Division, The New York Public Library, Astor, Lenox and Tilden Foundations. **122** RMJ/Photograph by Bill Orcutt. **123** CGP. **124** PC. **126** Collection of Mr. and Mrs. George L. Lindemann, Florida. **127** Collection of Joan and Michael Salke, Naples, Florida.

Baker Essay: **130** JPG (top), Kunsthaus Zürich (bottom). **131** Collection of Joel and Paula Friedland (top), TFA (bottom). **137** BMA. **138** MM. **139** CGP. **140** Collection of Steven M. Sumberg, c/o Edwynn Houk Gallery, New York. **141** MoMA (top left, top right), Private collection of Thomas and Janine Koerfer-Weill (bottom). **142** WMAA. **143** Bruce Silverstein Gallery, New York (bottom). **144** PMA. **145** Collection of Gérard Lévy, Paris. **146–47** HMAH. **148–49** TB/RG. **150** HM. **152** HM (top), Richard and Ronnie Grosbard Collection/

RG (bottom). **155** IDFA. **156** Museum of Fine Arts, Houston. **161** Naomi Savage Estate.

Cultural Timeline: **163** Courtesy of Michigan State University Museum (left), NB/RG (right). **164** Collection of Morris Trichon. **165** From Barbara Haskell, *The American Century: Art and Culture, 1900–1950* (New York: Norton, 1999), 91/RG. **166** FMN (left), BRB (right). **167** Collection of Constance and Albert Wang. **168** Collection of Mr. and Mrs. Edward A. Fuller/Photograph by William C. Cabrera, Splashworks. **169** Tamiment Library, New York University/© 2009 Delaware Art Museum/Artists Rights Society (ARS), New York (right), Widener Library, Harvard University, Cambridge, Massachusetts (middle, left). **170** NB/RG (left), Widener Library, Harvard University, Cambridge, Massachusetts (top), CMA (right). **171** PMA (top), The Phillips Collection, Washington D.C. (bottom). **172** General Research Division, New York Public Library, Astor, Lenox and Tilden Foundations. **173** NB/RG. **174** Collection of Teruo Ishihara, Kyoto. **175** The Metropolitan Museum of Art, New York. **176** PMA. **177** HIP/AR/Ann Ronan Picture Library, London (right). **178** Kunsthaus Zürich (right), PMA (top), WMAA (right). **179** Solomon R. Guggenheim Museum, New York (left), Private collection of Cornelia and Meredith Long (middle), MoMA (right). **180** BRB. **181** Spencer Collection, Humanities and Social Services Library, New York Public Library/© 2009 Artists Rights Society (ARS), New York/ADAGP, Paris/Succession Marcel Duchamp. **182** From Leah Dickerman, ed., *Dada: Zurich, Berlin, Hannover, Cologne, New York, Paris* (Washington, D.C.: National Gallery of Art and Distributed Art Publishers, 2005), 368/RG (left), From *Man Ray: Paintings, Objects, Photographs,* cat. for Sotheby's estate sale, London, March 22–23, 1995, 138 (right). **183** Golda Meir Library, University of Wisconsin. **184** NB/RG (top), Harvard Theatre Collection, Harvard University Library, Cambridge, Massachusetts (bottom). **185** The Bluff Collection LP. **186** From Man Ray, *Self Portrait* (Boston:

Little, Brown, 1988), 211/RG (top), Courtesy of Forum Gallery, New York and Los Angeles (bottom left) BMA (bottom right). **187** New Orleans Museum of Art (top), John Jay Library, Brown University (bottom left), CMA (bottom right). **188** FMN. **190** Bildarchiv Preussischer Kulturbesitz/Art Resource, New York/Kunstbibliothek, Staatliche Museen zu Berlin. **191** The Metropolitan Museum of Art, New York. **192** Houghton Library, Harvard University, Cambridge, Massachusetts (left). **193** MoMA. **194** Collection of Mark Kelman, New York. **195** TB/RG. **196** NB/RG. **197** Collection of Teruo Ishihara, Kyoto. **198** Collection of Marilyn and Larry Fields/Photograph by Jamie Stukenberg. **199** Collection of Timothy Baum and Karen Amiel Baum, New York. **200** Banque d'Images, ADAGP/Art Resource, New York (top), PMA/Photograph by Andrea Nuñez (bottom). **201** PMA/© 2009 Artists Rights Society (ARS), New York/ADAGP, Paris/Succession Marcel Duchamp (left), IDFA (right). **202** JPG (left), Man Ray Trust (left). **203** FMN. **204** From Man Ray, *Self Portrait* (Boston: Little, Brown, 1988), 309/RG. **205** TB (left), San Francisco Museum of Modern Art (right). **206** From Jennifer Mundy, *Surrealism: Desire Unbound* (Princeton, N.J.: Princeton University Press, 2001), 283/RG. **207** The Andy Warhol Foundation, Inc./AR. **208** Magnum Photos (top), Archives of American Art, Smithsonian Institution (bottom). **209** From Man Ray, *Self Portrait* (Boston: Little, Brown, 1988), 316/RG.